TEACHING MATHEMATICS TO THE LEARNING DISABLED

Nancy S. Bley
Park Century School

Carol A. Thornton
Illinois State University

AN ASPEN PUBLICATION®
Aspen Systems Corporation
Rockville, Maryland
London
1981

Library of Congress Cataloging in Publication Data

Bley, Nancy S.
Teaching mathematics to the learning disabled.

Includes index.
1. Mathematics—Study and teaching (Elementary)
2. Learning disabilities.   I. Thornton, Carol A.
II. Title.
QA135.5.B56   371.9'044   81-3569
ISBN 0-89443-357-1   AACR2

371. 9044
B61t
1/9273
Sept. 1981

Library of Congress Catalog Card Number: 81-3569
ISBN: 0-89443-357-1

Printed in the United States of America

1 2 3 4 5

To our husbands, Michael and Denis,
and to our children,
Chris,
Stephanie, and Jennifer,
for their patient understanding
and support
throughout this project.

Table of Contents

About the Authors

Preface

Teaching Mathematics to the Learning Disabled is written in the belief that, though they may learn "differently," most learning disabled students *can* master important mathematical concepts and skills. This belief has evolved out of our own personal experiences with learning disabled students. Approaches and techniques that we have found most successful are interwoven in the suggestions given throughout the text.

After a brief overview of learning disabilities and the effect they have on learning elementary and junior high or middle school mathematics, Chapter 1 focuses on ten general techniques that can aid classroom planning and instruction for the learning disabled. The remaining eight chapters deal with specific areas of school mathematics instruction.

Rather than treat comprehensively all topics in the school mathematics curriculum, emphasis is on those topics that commonly cause learning disabled students the most difficulty. Background information at the beginning of each section typically summarizes standard approaches to the topic and points out particular problems learning disabled students may have with the concept or skill. Then usually, in follow-up, a sequence of suggested activities and exercises is given. It is assumed that teachers are familiar with standard approaches for handling the topics. The intent of the sequences is to highlight instructional alternatives for meeting special needs and to give instances where special visual, auditory, or kinesthetic support is appropriate.

Color coding, for example, is among the visual cueing techniques that are consistently employed. In general, it might be suggested that students be checked for intact color vision and, if there is any difficulty, similar techniques like bold print or underscoring might be used instead. Cueing used during early instruction on a topic is, of course, gradually withdrawn as students become more confident and able to work independently. And that indeed is the goal: to help students learn to compensate for any disability and to deal effectively with mathematics both in academic and common daily situations. Any inspiration we are able to share for accomplishing this goal comes primarily from the students with whom we have worked and from whom we ourselves have learned.

Nancy S. Bley
Carol A. Thornton

July 1981

Chapter 1

Planning Instruction for Special Needs

A learning disabled child is unable to learn the way most children do. For this reason, there is characteristically a discrepancy between the child's learning potential and performance in mathematics. Recent legislation, notably the Education for All Handicapped Children Act of 1975, has spurred growing concern to remedy this situation. How does one plan mathematics instruction so that teachers can teach in a way the children will learn?

The problem is compounded when learning disabled students are mainstreamed or taught in resource rooms along with children having uniquely different learning styles, abilities, and interests. The mathematics teacher must somehow deal with the diverse learning needs of each student. In some instances, the established curricular goals set by the school district seem unrealistic for certain individuals. How does one adequately teach the expected content and still help those with legitimate learning difficulties? This book suggests some answers. Its focus is the learning disabled child; its purpose is to support practical, manageable, and effective ways of helping that child to learn and implement elementary and junior high school mathematics. It is hoped that the ideas presented will be useful to both regular class and special education teachers who meet learning disabled students in their mathematics classes.

Probably the single biggest obstacle to learning that these children have is their inability to perform independently. They cannot do so for any number of reasons:

- They are unable to use logical thinking without specific training.

- They have visual perception difficulties that preclude seeing accurately what is presented to them.

- They have poor retention.

- Auditorially, they misperceive words or parts of words.

1

Some learning disabled students have good study skills and are highly motivated. They are willing to learn and try to stay "on task." Typically, this willingness decreases with age as other problems, like those mentioned above, continually frustrate learning attempts. Students then begin to misbehave, withdraw, or simply not attend.

In regular mathematics classes, attempts to handle the different learning styles through learning center modules are sometimes thwarted. The teacher may be able to spend some time working individually with a child, but overall the setting demands independent work skills. These cannot be assumed. They must be specifically taught and then monitored.

An additional hindrance is the need to use textual materials written for regular class students. Most commercial texts are visually confusing. Often, children cannot copy and space out the work as intended. Lessons frequently are not sequenced to provide adequate transition between topics, and there is usually not enough review of important concepts and skills. For learning disabled students who cannot transfer concepts from the concrete to the abstract without teacher assistance, the use of manipulatives may be meaningless.

There are ways of circumventing these difficulties so that these students can learn in a way that is appropriate for them. The following pages will share techniques and ideas for altering the standard mathematics program where necessary to meet the individual needs of learning disabled students. The remainder of the chapter is devoted to

- providing the reader with an overview of learning disabilities as they relate to mathematics, and

- suggesting general techniques that can aid classroom instruction and planning for the learning disabled.

The remainder of the book will illustrate, for selected topics, how these specialized techniques can be used within sequences of instruction. A major purpose is to provide ideas for arranging instruction so that teachers *can* teach and children *will* learn. It is hoped that the book will thus act as a springboard for teachers in developing their own ideas for teaching learning disabled children.

LEARNING DISABILITIES AND HOW THEY AFFECT MATHEMATICS PERFORMANCE

Most mathematics teachers are familiar with at least some of the following situations:

- A homework assignment that is "wrong" because sloppy copying led to misreading or nonalignment of digits.

- The child who consistently receives high scores on quizzes of isolated basic facts, yet misses these same facts while doing larger computations or solving word problems.

- The child who never seems to pay attention when there are oral quizzes or explanations and cannot answer questions in class.

- The older elementary student who "refuses" to learn the basic facts.

- Children who add when they should multiply or skip steps in division problems.

The list is endless. Each teacher could probably pinpoint at least one child who matches each of the above descriptions.

Such situations can be very frustrating for both teacher and student. While they may represent only a small percentage of the class, the nature and magnitude of the problems may be large enough to affect presentation of material.

Each situation could possibly involve a learning disabled child. Since learning disabled children typically have average or above average intelligence, teachers may mistakenly think they are not trying, lazy, or just not paying attention. Because they are frequently misunderstood, learning disabled students may have mixed feelings about themselves. They do not look different. In many instances they can participate competitively with peers in class activities. This may be due to the nature of the activity or to compensatory techniques they have developed. They work just as hard as others do, "take notes," and do the homework. But they still cannot achieve in mathematics. They still fail tests. Often learning disabled children do not study with others for fear they will feel dumb. They also feel they are missing out on a lot of fun.

There are many variations on this type of child. Enrolled in a resource room, they feel "marked." Even in mainstreamed situations they feel left out.

Understanding a child's disability sometimes helps teachers plan instruction to minimize frustrations and social pressure due to the handicap. Toward this end, the following paragraphs review common learning disabilities that influence success in mathematics. The major disabilities have been divided into several general topics, under the overall headings of visual and auditory perception problems; spatial and temporal disabilities; and motor, memory, integrative, and behavioral deficits. Table 1-1 summarizes discussion on these topics. Comments on the implications of Piaget's developmental theory for teaching students with learning disabilities conclude the section.

Table 1-1 Examples of Learning Disabilities Affecting Performance in Mathematics

	Visual Deficit	Auditory Deficit
Perceptual Figure-ground	-may not finish all problems on page -frequently loses place -difficulty seeing subtraction within a division problem -difficulty reading multidigit number (see closure)	-trouble hearing pattern in counting -difficulty attending in the classroom
Discrimination	-difficulty differentiating coins -difficulty differentiating between or writing numbers (3 for 8; 2 for 5) -cannot discriminate between operation symbols -cannot discriminate between size of hands on clock -difficulty associating operation sign with problem (see abstract reasoning)	-cannot distinguish between 30 and 13 (see receptive language) -difficulty with decimal numbers
Reversal	-reverses digits in a number (may also be a sequential memory problem) -difficulty with regrouping	
Spatial	-trouble writing on lined paper -difficulty with concept of before/after, so trouble telling time -trouble noticing size differences in shapes -trouble with fraction concept due to inability to note equal-sized parts -difficulty writing decimals -difficulty aligning numbers -difficulty with ordinal numbers -difficulty writing fractional numbers (may also be reversal)	-difficulty following directions using ordinal numbers
Memory Short-term	-trouble retaining newly presented material -difficulty copying problems from the board (may be spatial)	-difficulty with oral drills -difficulty with dictated assignments

	Visual Deficit	Auditory Deficit
Long-term	-inability to retain basic facts or processes over a long period -difficulty solving multioperation computation	
Sequential	-difficulty telling time -difficulty following through a multiplication problem -difficulty following through long division problems -difficulty solving column addition problems -difficulty solving multistep word problems	-cannot retain story problem that is dictated
Integrative Closure	-difficulty visualizing groups -difficulty reading multidigit number (see figure-ground) -difficulty with missing addends and missing factors -inability to draw conclusions, therefore trouble noticing and continuing patterns -difficulty with word problems -trouble continuing counting pattern from within a sequence	-difficulty counting on from within a sequence
Expressive language	-rapid oral drills very difficult	-difficulty counting on -difficulty explaining why a problem is solved as it is
Receptive language	-difficulty relating word to meaning (may be spatial) -difficulty with words that have multiple meanings	-difficulty relating word to meaning -difficulty writing numbers from dictation
Abstract reasoning	-inability to solve word problems -inability to compare size of numbers, using symbols -cannot understand patterning in counting -difficulty with decimal concept	

Visual and Auditory Perception Problems

Figure-Ground Difficulties

Children with visual figure-ground difficulties may exhibit a variety of symptoms. These are the children who frequently lose their place on the page, do not finish all their work, or do not appear to concentrate when copying problems from the book. They mix up parts of problems and often copy wrong symbols. Because most books have many problems on a page, learning disabled students may not differentiate between the problem number and the problem itself and may include neighboring digits in the computation. As a result, their work appears carelessly done.

The worksheet shown in Figure 1-1 illustrates some of these difficulties. The computation in the first problem is almost accurate but includes the problem number in the final step. Problem 2 is started correctly. The answer to 12 subtract 6 is 6, but the answer is placed under problem 3. Since 7 subtract 1 is also 6, the student proceeded with the computation, not realizing that an entire problem had been skipped. In problem 5, the child is still adding, possibly because of the similarity of numbers in problems 4 and 5. Problem 6 was begun but not finished, without awareness.

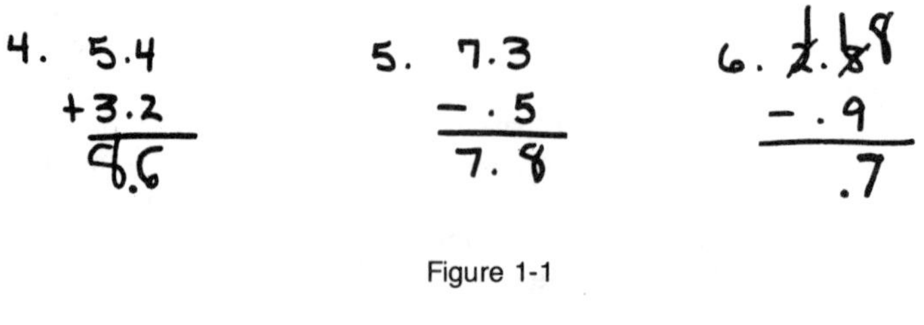

Figure 1-1

Figure-ground deficits also interfere with the solution of multioperation procedures, such as long division. Children may have a hard time sorting out the subtraction problem within the division computation. In the problem of Figure 1-2, the child recognized subtraction was required but used the wrong numbers. Subtracting 6 from 6 left ''0,'' and the child then continued to solve to the end. On other occasions, children might locate the right numbers but forget what they are to

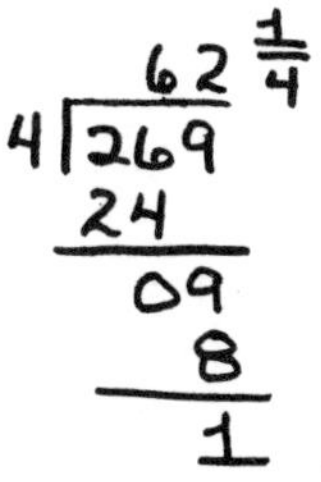

$$62\tfrac{1}{4}$$
$$4\overline{)269}$$
$$\underline{24}$$
$$09$$
$$\underline{8}$$
$$1$$

Figure 1-2

do with them. Rather than viewing a multidigit number as a whole, children with figure-ground difficulties tend to focus on individual digits. They do not spontaneously group the digits. In the example of Figure 1-3, despite firm place-value understanding for three-digit numbers, the child may be unsure whether to say "sixty-one two" or "six hundred twelve." Often, if the teacher verbalizes alternatives for the number, these same children can associate correctly.

Children with auditory figure-ground deficits may have trouble attending in class. They cannot sort out extraneous stimuli, such as the sound of chalk, from the teacher's explanation. They may seem to be daydreaming or disruptive, when in fact they are trying to attend but simply cannot listen and learn simultaneously.

Auditory figure-ground difficulties can also interfere with a student's ability to hear counting patterns. Although place-value ideas form the basis of our number system, most young children learn to count by tuning in on repetitive patterns they hear. Even five- and six-year olds learn to count by fives and tens, although they have no idea of place value. Learning to skip count does not come so easily to learning disabled children. They are often unable to discover the pattern without a much stronger oral emphasis than is generally used. They cannot localize the repetitive part of the pattern and repeat it.

Figure 1-3

Problems of Discrimination

Visual discrimination errors may cause students to misread numbers. Very young children are often not ready developmentally to discriminate one number from another. They tend to write numbers backwards, especially 2, 3, or 5. Often they do not even notice the reversal. This difficulty is generally outgrown by the age of about seven. Children with learning disabilities, however, may exhibit the problem beyond the normal developmental stage. Because they do not perceive the numbers correctly, the task of writing numbers, copying problems from the board, or spontaneously writing them from dictation can be extremely difficult. By the time a number is written, they will have lost their place or be so far behind in copying that the teacher may be ready to erase the board.

Telling time or recognizing coins can also be very difficult for children who cannot discriminate size differences. The ability to recognize and differentiate between coins requires that a child notice discrete differences in size. Some children may recognize size differences in general but be unable to apply this skill to a practical situation. They may perform slower than classmates because of the perceptual deficit. Telling time, for example, takes longer because they must consciously look for the smaller hand on the clock, a perceptually difficult task.

As children encounter more and more symbols, perceptual problems become prominent. Figure 1-4 illustrates several perceptually related errors made by children who in fact knew how to handle the computation involved.

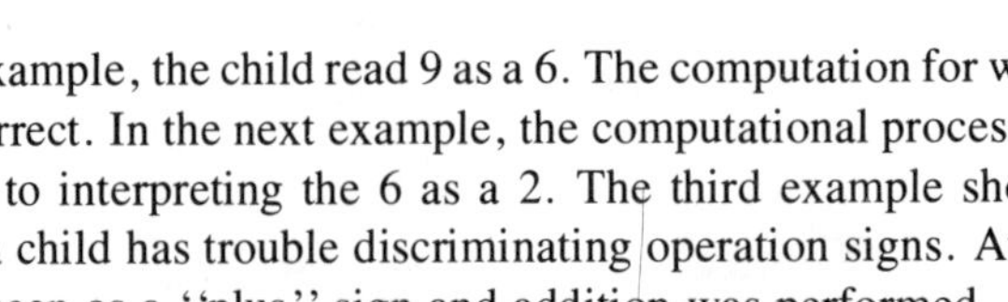

$$
\begin{array}{cc}
9 \\
+7 \\
\hline
13
\end{array}
\qquad
\begin{array}{cc}
\overset{1}{4}6 \\
\times\ 7 \\
\hline
294
\end{array}
\qquad
\begin{array}{cc}
\overset{1}{6}4 \\
+\ 8 \\
\hline
492
\end{array}
$$

Figure 1-4

In the first example, the child read 9 as a 6. The computation for what was seen, however, is correct. In the next example, the computational process is right. The errors are due to interpreting the 6 as a 2. The third example shows what can happen when a child has trouble discriminating operation signs. At first the sign was correctly seen as a "plus" sign and addition was performed. At the second step of the problem, however, the child perceived the sign as one for multiplication and proceeded to use that operation.

An example of an auditory discrimination problem is the inability to hear numbers correctly. This can affect a child's ability to count. Often children miss endings of words and thus a counting pattern such as the following may develop: ". . . 9, 10, 11, 12, 30, 40, 50, 60, 70, 80, 90, 20." The subtle aspect of this problem is that children, if asked to count aloud, may in fact *say the numbers correctly*. But internally they misperceive what they hear themselves say. Depending on the severity of the problem, they may or may not be able to correct the pattern if the symbols for 13 through 20 are placed before them.

Reversals

Another common perceptual difficulty is that resulting in reversals. Children with reversal tendencies not only make mirror images of individual digits as noted in the section on discrimination. They may also reverse the digits of a two-digit number when reading or writing. This problem naturally leads to errors in computation. Children may, for example, carry the wrong number when it is necessary to regroup. The most common reversals are in the teens: 21 for 12, 31 for 13, 41 for 14, and so on. An example of how reversals can affect multiplication computation is illustrated in Figure 1-5.

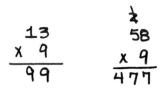

Figure 1-5

The child read 31 for 13 in the first problem and consequently multiplied the 1 by 9. In the subsequent step, the digit "1" was correctly located in the 10s place and was multiplied next. Again, 9 was recorded in the product.

In the second problem, the digits were reversed when they were written down, thus accounting for the 7 in the 1s place. The rest of the problem was computed accurately.

This last example illustrates the importance of teaching children, especially those with learning disabilities, first to write the number that is to be carried. More severe reversal and discrimination problems may require color coding or alternate methods of computing. Some of these approaches are discussed in Chapters 2 and 5.

Spatial and Temporal Disabilities

Spatial and temporal organization can greatly affect a child's performance in mathematics and its practical applications outside the classroom. Although children with temporal disabilities may be able to tell time by rote, their concept of time and therefore their general planning ability is often considerably impaired.

Other problems characterize the child with spatial disabilities. Difficulty locating position in space—knowing right from left or up from down—can make the task of number alignment almost insurmountable. Renaming in computation becomes even harder. Children with this handicap (1) need to understand *why* the number carried is placed above the ten's digit and (2) need visual and kinesthetic clues to help them locate and "feel" what "above" means.

Difficulties with spatial organization can prevent children from properly forming a number that they actually see accurately. They may reverse the position or invert it. Verbal cues such as "right" and "left" or "top" and "bottom" carry little meaning and are therefore no help in starting the number. Specific training involving motor activities, color coding, and continual integration with other skills is essential.

At the upper levels, spatial difficulties can interfere with the study of decimals, fractions, and word problems. Conceptual understandings may be strong and still difficulties arise. Locating where the decimal point belongs, determining the correct sequence of steps in a word problem, or properly placing the numbers in a fraction or mixed number can be extremely difficult for a child with these deficits.

Motor Deficits

For many children, the actual process of writing numbers may be so difficult that the ability to succeed in mathematics is greatly affected. Children with perceptual motor difficulties have trouble relating what they see to what they write. They cannot coordinate their eyes with the proper hand movements. As mathematical problems become longer and more involved, it becomes extremely difficult for these children to complete written assignments. So much time and energy are expended retrieving the necessary finger movements for number formation that they forget what they are doing.

Memory Deficits

Although memory difficulties can be classified under perceptual deficits, we have chosen to separate them for purposes of remediation and planning. Many children seem to understand what is presented in class and may even accurately complete classroom assignments. But these same students may not carry through on homework. Or they may appear "lost" when teachers continue a topic the next class day after only a short review. Initially, they may do quite well at the time of presentation. But, because there is only a limited review in the text, they quickly forget and appear never to have learned the material. These are the children who are often accused of not listening, of copying a friend's work or of doing careless work.

In other cases, teachers may be baffled because classwork and homework are good. Yet later these same students may be unable to use the material as a basis for learning a new concept or skill. And when it comes time for a unit test on the material, they do very poorly.

The difficulty in each of these examples may be due to specific short- or long-term memory problems that preclude the children's retaining material over a period of time. These children require training to provide them with ways of remembering. They also need a considerable amount of overlearning before they will retain a concept or skill.

Short-term visual memory deficits manifest themselves in several ways. For some children, the process of copying numbers from the board or textbook may be extremely difficult. The inability to retain visual images long enough to write them on paper causes slowness and errors. Unlike their peers who can hold an entire problem in their minds (e.g., 48 + 63), these children must keep checking to see what it is they are to write. The time involved in this process greatly impedes the amount of work that can be done. Even when worksheets are provided and it is unnecessary for students to copy the problems, they may still be unable to retain enough information to perform accurate and quick computations.

Auditory short-term memory deficits can often result in an inability to learn basic facts. When presented with oral drills, children may not be able to retain the isolated numbers long enough to give an answer. Visual memory deficits may prevent retrieval of the correct answer, even if the problem is written down for the child.

Visual and auditory short-term memory problems can also hamper a student's ability to solve word problems. Although children may have no difficulty reading or comprehending the material, they may be unable to retain information long enough to solve a problem. This may be especially true of problems involving two or more steps.

Although some children may be able to learn visually from textbooks, the pace may be too fast. Often there is not enough review and skill incorporation for the necessary overlearning to occur. As a result, they may understand the material when presented but be unable to retain it or use it as a building block for future learning.

There are many areas of mathematics that require considerable sequencing ability. Students with sequential memory deficits have an especially hard time in these areas. Most children, for example, learn to tell time by the age of seven or eight. But if there is trouble retaining a sequence, the task suddenly causes much more trouble. Think for a moment of the very basic steps involved in telling time:

- Which hand do I look at first?

- What number does that hand refer to?

- What number should I say first?

- What number does the other hand refer to?

- How do I count by fives?

Assuming there is no spatial or temporal difficulty, there are still a considerable number of steps to sequence properly in order to tell time. Children with memory-sequencing problems must be taught each step, to the point of overlearning, in order for each step to act as a transition to the next.

Sequential memory also affects the ability to count money, compute using the four basic operations, and to solve word problems. Auditorially, it affects a student's overall ability to process and understand what is taught to the class as a whole. For some children, only isolated segments of what is said will be retained.

Figure 1-6 shows the work of a student whose primary disability is one of memory, long-term and sequential. A close look will indicate that the child probably understands basic computation at the middle-grade level. But because the processes at this level become quite long and involved, there are great demands on the child's retention and sequencing abilities. This child is probably unaware that the problems are incomplete. Only so much could be held in the memory at one time.

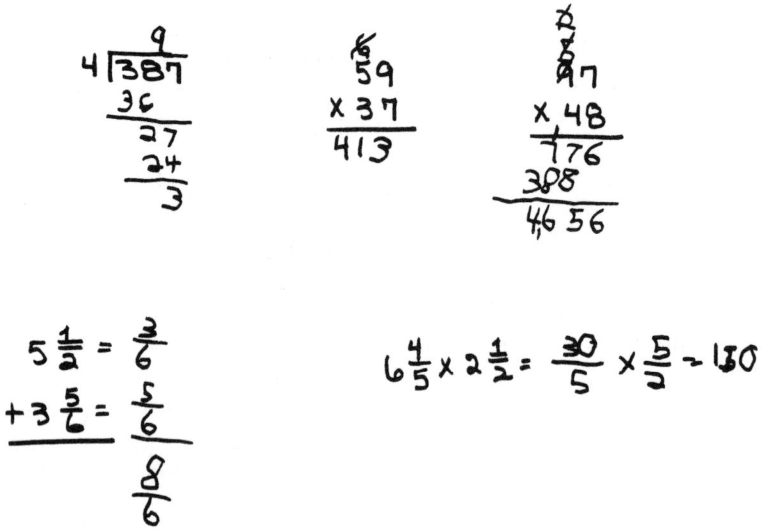

Figure 1-6

Integrative Deficits

Learning disabled children often have trouble integrating what they learn. There is some interference that prevents them from pulling information together to draw conclusions, to make associations, or simply to use building blocks of information to learn material adequately. Following are some examples of common integrative problems.

Closure Difficulties

Children with closure problems may have an especially difficult time reading multidigit numbers. They fail to group digits logically as they read the numbers. They may be able to count by rote or continue a sequence of four or five numbers; yet, given a single number and asked what comes next, they may not be able to elicit a response independently.

These are the same children who have trouble with classification tasks. Given a group of numbers that are similar in some way (e.g., the even numbers), they cannot identify that similarity. They also may be unable to pick out similar numbers from a larger group of numbers. Making comparisons and drawing the necessary conclusions involved in this task may be impossible. (It should be noted that, regardless of the disability involved, it is generally much harder for the learning disabled child to find similarities than to find differences.)

Counting on, a technique often taught early in the primary grades, can be very difficult for these students. Although they may have little trouble locating the starting point, eliciting the next number may be impossible. Counting on from within a sequence, especially when skip counting is involved, is extremely difficult. Considerable drill and training are usually required to internalize the technique.

Mathematics educators today debate the merits of teaching missing addends to young primary students. Retrieving the missing number involves many discrete tasks that must be tied together before the child is able to recall the answer. Step by step, the major tasks include

- number discrimination;

- determining the correct operation to solve the problem;

- mentally sorting out the correct response using visual imagery but without visual cues; and

- eliciting the correct answer, either verbally or in writing.

For learning disabled children with integrative deficits, carrying out the above steps may be very difficult. Even if they can easily perform the first two steps, the final two require skills in which they are often weakest. There is simply too much to be retained and associated for the child to sort out and express the answer.

Expressive Language Problems

Children with expressive language difficulties cannot verbalize clearly, if at all, what they so obviously understand. These are the children who have trouble with rapid oral drills. They may not participate in class because they cannot express in words what they are thinking. They tend to do better on written homework or in situations in which they are given visual cues and enough time to respond. They cannot produce on demand. Timed tests, whether oral or written, only make this disability more apparent, since the students cannot express answers rapidly.

A common way of having children show that they understand a concept is to have them explain or apply it, either verbally or manually. For children with expressive language problems, visual cues are necessary to help them retrieve the words and sequence the steps once recalled. Students often can more easily distinguish between right and wrong processes than they can explain them. When a mistake is made, they may recognize that something is not right but be unable to correct it spontaneously unless given alternatives.

Reading and writing decimals can be very hard for those with expressive language difficulties. By comparison, fractions are easier. When one writes "2/100" or says "two one hundredths," it is clear that a "2" and a "100" are included among the digits for the fraction. Decimals lack this cueing. Hearing "two one hundredths" does not so readily reveal the number of decimal digits in the number. Neither does looking at ".02" automatically cue the response "two one hundredths "

Receptive Language Difficulties

"What do you mean?" "Please repeat that." "Can I have a clue?" These questions, and many others, are frequently asked by children with receptive language deficits. These students have difficulty associating meaning with words. All of us on occasion hear common words, perhaps in context, and temporarily "blank out" on the meaning. Usually the lapse is only temporary, a second or two. This is similar to what regularly happens to learning disabled children. They hear a word, recognize it as a unit, but fail to grasp the meaning intended.

In mathematics, this disability manifests itself in the following ways:

- difficulty following directions
- difficulty understanding mathematical terms, especially those with multiple meanings, such as sum, times, difference, and so on
- difficulty solving a computational problem set up differently than originally presented

Children with receptive language deficits often appear to be very literal. However, they may not understand jokes that others do and generally find it hard to make sense of much of what they hear or read. They can repeat the exact words and often go through rote processes that are similar. But they cannot repeat the same process if there is the slightest variation in presentation.

Problems of Abstract Reasoning

One of the most difficult areas for children with learning problems, and for their mathematics teachers, is that of abstract reasoning. As a general rule, new mathematical topics can and should be presented concretely. There are many learning aids to assist children in seeing, feeling, and dramatizing new concepts and skills. When ideas are presented in this "hands-on" manner and discussed, a natural basis is established for the transfer of meaning to written symbols. Indeed, written symbols normally would be associated with the models illustrating the idea or process before being used alone.

Generally, when concrete aids are used, however, at least one of the following is required of the student:

- the ability to verbalize what has been learned or observed
- the ability to associate what is happening with symbolic representation
- the ability to understand, auditorially or receptively, what is being explained or shown

For children who have trouble making associations because of poor abstract reasoning, it is often impossible to perform any of the above. These children need the immediate and repeated association of numbers, operation signs, and other mathematical symbols that we substitute for words. This approach provides the needed repetition and visual associations for the child to begin to understand the concept.

For learning disabled children with a deficit in this area, the repetition and rote drill of a page helps them feel comfortable with the process or idea. Once this occurs, they can more easily begin to make associations that eventually will lend meaning to what they do. Through repeated drill and reassociation with concrete aids, the child develops

- the understanding of the specific concept,
- the ability to reason and associate in general, and
- a stepping stone for later reasoning.

As noted earlier, children with learning disabilities require a considerable amount of overlearning. Most textbooks provide drills, especially in the area of computation. However, for those students with reasoning deficits, these pages can also provide a hindrance. The repetition of the same process relieves the need to make any decisions. An entire page of addition with carrying does not help the child to learn when it is necessary to carry, only how to carry. If the goal is, in fact, learning when to carry, then it might be sufficient for the child to cross out all the problems that do not require carrying.

Behavioral Difficulties

Before concluding the overview of learning disabilities, it is important to note behavioral disabilities that can affect classroom performance and mathematics achievement. Following are the more common problems in this area.

Distractibility

Many learning disabled children are highly distracted either by external stimuli that most of us would ignore or by internal stimuli of which we are often not aware. These children find it difficult to stay on the task. They seem to be in constant motion and never to be paying attention. The slightest sound or sight distracts them and they lose their place. Sometimes they are unable to find it again or even know that they have lost it. It may appear they are purposely thinking about other things in order to avoid work. These are the children who are inordinately attentive to marks on a page or specks of dust. The sound of the chalk on the board may prevent them from listening to the teacher. In fact they cannot sustain attention for a long period of time. When they appear to short circuit, it is often necessary to let them change activities in order to regain their attention.

Perseveration

Perseveration is another disability that shows itself in many ways. Children may perform the same operation throughout a page because they do not notice that the signs have been changed. They may continue doing whatever was instructed in the first problem. Such behavior patterns are compulsive, not merely carelessness.

Figure 1-7 illustrates other ways perseveration can affect a child's computational work. In the first problem, for "17 − 9," the child continued counting backwards, unable to stop at 8. Similarly, in the second problem the count was extended further than necessary for "6 + 5." This child has no internalized means of stopping.

Once children have begun attending, which may be almost immediate, they may have an extremely difficult time changing activities unless they are reminded or physically drawn into doing so. Techniques such as handing children a clean sheet

$$
\begin{array}{r}
\overset{3}{\cancel{4}}\overset{17}{\cancel{7}} \\
-29 \\
\hline
17
\end{array}
\qquad
\begin{array}{r}
\overset{1}{46} \\
+35 \\
\hline
82
\end{array}
$$

Figure 1-7

of paper on which to write or asking them to move from their seats to the board may help in extreme cases. Perseverations should be stopped whenever they are noted. This change is necessary to avoid perseverating from one academic subject to another.

Problems of Disinhibition and Impulsivity

Children exhibiting disinhibition or impulsivity often have trouble making transitions from one topic to another during class sessions. Turning the page of a book to a new topic may divert their attention from the introduction being given by the teacher. They are very quick to answer questions but often give irrelevant responses. Estimating answers is extremely difficult for them since they tend to guess wildly. Their thoughts are often triggered by some word that they read or hear. They may not realize the association was made even though they talk as if they do. It is often necessary to change activities in order to refocus their attention.

Reading

Although they may not be behavior disorders, reading difficulties are included in this section because when they interfere with mathematics performance they can affect a child's behavior. Most schools use state-adopted mathematics textbooks. Generally, these texts involve a lot of reading that may put the learning disabled child at a severe disadvantage. Most of the books require a high degree of abstract reasoning and the ability to transfer and retain skills over time. They also require that the child have at least on-grade level reading. Many children with learning disabilities do not have on-grade level reading. They are capable of performing on grade level or above in math if there is not much reading required. The math area is made increasingly difficult by the dependency on reading.

PIAGET AND LEARNING DISABILITIES

Most mathematics teachers, and primary school teachers in particular, are aware of the implications of Piaget's developmental theory for mathematics learning. There are certain developmental stages through which children progress as they master mathematical concepts and skills. With learning disabled children who have difficulty making associations, however, it is often necessary to structure instruction in light of these stages as new and more abstract skills are learned. The purpose of the following paragraphs is to give the teacher an idea of how this type of instruction might be carried out with learning disabled children.

One-to-One and One-to-Many Correspondence

Most children begin developing the idea of one-to-one matching at the concrete level by the time they are five or six years old. Gradually, this skill develops to the point where the child is able to count and perform simple computational problems. This last step, though at a higher level cognitively, is a one-to-many correspondence. As children begin to internalize their thinking, specific instruction usually ceases. They are then generally able to extend the simpler one-to-one matching skill to computational situations requiring one-to-many matchings.

In terms of one-to-many matchings, the application to multiplication involving single or multidigit multipliers is readily apparent. Regardless of the method of presentation, children ultimately must use one-to-many matching to be sure they have finished the problem. In Figure 1-8, it would not be unusual for the teacher to remind students to multiply all parts of the number 58 by 9. Reviewing one-to-one and one-to-many matchings with learning disabled children before teaching multiplication will make the process a much simpler one.

Figure 1-8

Classification

Classification involves the ability to group objects or ideas by a common characteristic. The skill can involve any of the following abilities:

- spatial organization
- reasoning
- discrimination (visual or auditory)
- expressive language (verbal or manual)

As mathematics becomes more symbolic, the concrete presentation of classification is generally deemphasized. However, for children who are learning about equivalent fractions and decimals, a high degree of internalized classification is necessary. Suppose, for example, these children are presented with different sizes and shapes—each having one of four equal parts shaded. On the basis of this common characteristic, the children must be able to classify each shaded part as equivalent to one-fourth.

Children with learning disabilities may find this task extremely difficult even though they are developmentally ready. Students with a reasoning deficit may not be able to determine the similarity without specific tools to help them make a decision. These children might benefit from a flip chart like that in Figure 1-9. Each page would show a different fractional relationship. The child could match the concrete shapes with the pictorial representation and words. Children with figure-ground problems may not see the four equal parts because they cannot properly focus their attention. These children would be aided by writing a number in each section, beginning with the shaded one. They could then circle the number 1 in the shaded section in order to see more readily the 1-out-of-4 idea.

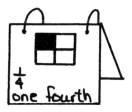 

Figure 1-9

Flexibility

Children exhibit flexibility of thought when they show they can deal with

- multiple meanings,
- different ways to express given sums or products, and
- horizontal and vertical formats for basic facts.

In general, flexibility is the ability to classify by more than one characteristic. It also involves the ability to use those characteristics in order to solve more advanced problems.

How does flexibility apply to mathematics beyond the more developmentally concrete stages? Figure 1-10 shows the work of an 11-year-old boy who failed to exhibit real flexibility of thought. When questioned whether he noticed the signs, his reply was, "Sure, but you always change the bottom number when they're written this way." This child had been taught to multiply mixed numbers horizontally and to add them vertically. Although he readily recognized that the second problem was multiplication, the vertical position confused him. In this case, it might be necessary to review briefly the horizontal and vertical multiplication of whole numbers and then relate this idea to fractions. Chapter 7 will offer further suggestions for handling problems of this nature.

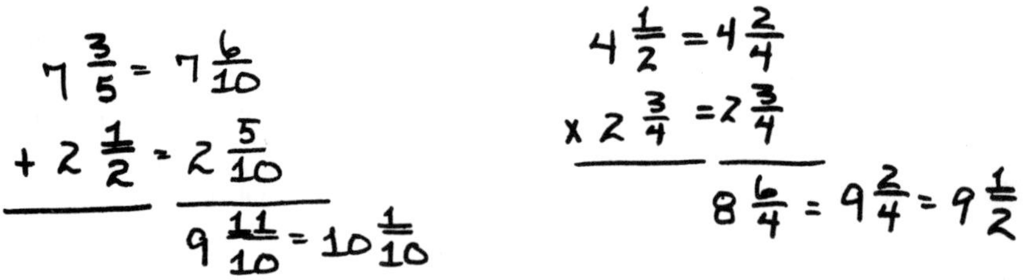

$$7 \tfrac{3}{5} = 7 \tfrac{6}{10}$$
$$+\, 2 \tfrac{1}{2} = 2 \tfrac{5}{10}$$
$$9 \tfrac{11}{10} = 10 \tfrac{1}{10}$$

$$4 \tfrac{1}{2} = 4 \tfrac{2}{4}$$
$$\times\, 2 \tfrac{3}{4} = 2 \tfrac{3}{4}$$
$$8 \tfrac{6}{4} = 9 \tfrac{2}{4} = 9 \tfrac{1}{2}$$

Figure 1-10

Seriation

Seriation involves discrimination skills as well as spatial or temporal organizational abilities. Many children with learning difficulties in mathematics have disabilities in these areas. To be able to organize numbers in some specific order requires that one understand the concepts of "more" and "less," "before" and "after," and ordinal counting. Children may be able to understand these concepts and to order numbers. However, applying the seriation skill to more advanced mathematical topics, such as solving multistep word problems or ordering decimals and fractions, may be extremely difficult. Children may, for example, be able to tell you what is done first, second, third, and so on, when presented with the specific steps. Yet when asked to organize these thoughts independently, they may be able to tell you only that several steps need to be included. Because of learning deficits, they may not have the means of ordering the steps without first being presented with a basic concrete model. One way of helping with multistep word problems is to highlight each step of the problem in a different color. The first step would be green. An accompanying worksheet would give the step numbers in matching colors.

Conservation

The ability to conserve implies the understanding that the basic value or amount does not change even though the shape or arrangement does. Some children are slow to conserve. Learning disabled children in particular tend to have a hard time applying the notion of conservation to more advanced mathematical topics.

The very early stages of conservation require that children recognize the invariance of quantity in spite of changes in shape. Similarly, the older child who is studying basic facts, using symbols only, needs to realize that 6×4 really equals 4×6. By the time children learn to use a calculator for higher level computations, they need a solid understanding of the equivalence of fractions and decimals. Conservation again emerges as the underlying basis for understanding this equivalence.

The preceding examples illustrate the importance of carefully tuning in on a child's thinking at every level of mathematics. From the Piagetion perspective, the examples serve to emphasize the developmental readiness required for mastering particular concepts and skills. It may be necessary for the learning disabled child to review very basic ideas, often at the concrete level, before pursuing more sophisticated topics. The provision of specific help, such as that suggested above, is critical in this process.

GENERAL TECHNIQUES FOR DEALING WITH LEARNING DISABILITIES IN THE MATHEMATICS CLASSROOM

J. is very attentive in class, seems to follow most presentations, and usually is able to answer whatever questions the teacher asks. However, his work is always sloppily done, answers to problems run into each other, and it is generally impossible for the teacher to match his work with either the assignment or his solutions.

A. regularly gets 100 percent on weekly basic fact tests but can never seem to give the right answers to facts when called upon to do so in class. She consistently makes many fact errors when solving written word problems. And though she obviously knows *how,* she is often unable to complete a page of computation accurately.

Then there is P. who never seems to complete his work, especially classroom assignments. When given time during class to copy the problems, he asks to get a drink, breaks a pencil, or otherwise wastes time. When he does manage to copy and finish an assignment, he makes many errors. His method of solving may be correct but his solutions are wrong.

The above situations represent only some of the problems a mathematics teacher might encounter. They serve to illustrate the demands placed on teachers to meet the needs of all students within the class. The children described, though seemingly covered by an umbrella of carelessness, could all be exhibiting learning disabilities with which they are inefficiently coping. An overriding goal of the mathematics teacher is to plan and implement instruction so that all in the class will benefit. What can be done to avoid spending an inordinate amount of time with one individual child to the exclusion of others in the class, or vice versa? The techniques described in the remainder of this section are written to help teachers in this regard.

Use Visuals and Manipulatives to Illustrate New and Important Ideas

Learning disabled children, like their peers in regular class mathematics, are basically concrete in their thinking. As a general rule, the use of simple or familiar objects to illustrate facts, ideas, and written symbols or processes will promote both understanding and retention.

Use Visual Cueing: Boxes, Circles, and Lines

Boxes

An earlier section showed how learning disabled children with figure-ground trouble may have difficulty finding the problems they are to do in standard textbooks. They cannot visually separate the problems from each other. A useful, inexpensive tool for handling this difficulty is a geometric shape template. The template can be used to box the problems in the book so that children can readily find them. Separating one problem from another prevents a child from seeing all the problems as one.

Circles

Another common difficulty for many children is separating the problem number from the problem itself. In more and more books, these numbers are colored to differentiate them from the problems. Even then, however, they may be spatially so close to the problem that many children cannot see the difference. In some texts, they are still printed in the same black type as the problems that are to be solved. Circling the problem number before solving has proved to be a very effective way of handling this difficulty.

More Circles and Boxes

Homework, especially from the text, can be a mammoth undertaking for a child with either fine-motor or figure-ground difficulties. It is not unusual, particularly at the intermediate and upper levels, for students to be assigned a page of 25 or 30 computational problems. Often these problems must be copied out of the book before solving. Many learning disabled children are so overwhelmed by the magnitude of the task that they do not do it at all. They are then accused of being lazy or irresponsible.

Think for a moment of what is involved in a seemingly easy review task of copying problems from a book. Children must be able to

- sort the problem number from the problem itself,

- remember what they are copying and what the numbers look like so that they do not have to trace them or continually look back at the page,

- space the problems on the page so that they can read the numbers and solve without mixing one problem with another,

- align the numbers properly while copying to avoid errors in subsequent computation.

This is the time to have the children circle the problem numbers or even cross them out. They can also be urged to box the problems immediately after copying. It may be necessary to help children use the shape template or a ruler to spatially organize their papers before beginning an assignment. Rather than lined paper, provide centimeter-square graph paper that can be boxed as shown in Figure 1-11.

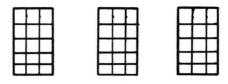

Figure 1-11

Just Boxes, No Lines

For some learning disabled children, the use of lined paper, even as an aid for number alignment, often leads to more confusion than it eliminates. The added visual stimulus of the lines makes it hard for the children to organize their work, especially if there are fine-motor deficits involved. They may have so much trouble staying on or within the lines and figuring out how to use them that their work will be even more illegible than ever. In these cases, insist that the children use unlined paper. Figures 1-12 through 1-15 give samples of sheets that can be kept in a file and drawn upon as needed for this purpose. Chapter 5 gives more specific suggestions for using pages of this type as an aid to computation.

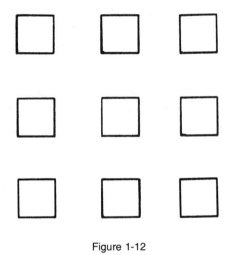

Figure 1-12

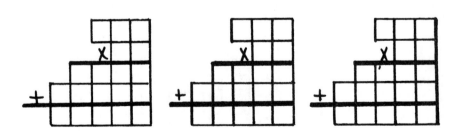

Figure 1-13

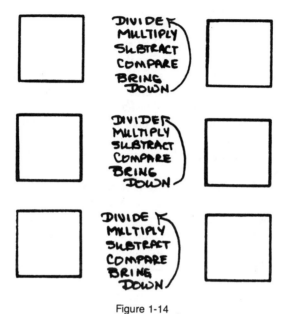

Figure 1-14

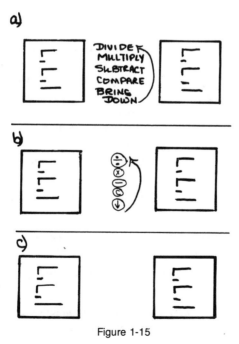

Figure 1-15

Planning Ahead: Boxes, Circles and Lines

Before school starts each year, solicit the help of a parent, aide, or other volunteer to prepare textbook pages and different kinds of spatially formated papers. The geometric-shaped template can be used to organize the pages spatially in the first chapters of the textbook. Problem numbers could also be circled. Important directions or examples could be underlined with bright colors or heavy lines. A file drawer containing special worksheet formats for children with spatial or perceptual difficulties could also be stocked at this time. Figures 1-11 to 1-15 present samples of pages that may be useful. Chapters 2 through 10 provide other ideas along this line.

Eventually, children should learn to perform some of these self-help skills themselves. Early in the year, it may be necessary to set aside 5 or 10 minutes each day for children with learning problems to learn to box, circle, or underline as needed. Alternatively, this may be as much a part of a specific assignment as the computation itself. These exercises are important, since they teach the children ways of dealing with their handicaps. Compensatory techniques, such as boxing or otherwise delineating the material, allow the children to keep up and be more a part of the mathematics class. These techniques also have obvious carryover to other subjects.

Assign Fewer Problems and Minimize or Eliminate Copying from the Textbook or Board

It is always important to remember the goal of any given mathematics lesson. Suppose the purpose is to review a computational skill. Then for students with severe spatial, motor, or perceptual deficits, teachers might have a better means of evaluating performance if other difficulties are minimized. This may mean employing techniques like those described above, or it might mean

- assigning only every fourth or fifth problem, rather than all the problems on a page, or

- providing worksheets so that children do not have to copy problems.

If the children are highly distractible, it may also be helpful to

- have them place an "x," a chip, or their fingers on the problem while computing so that they do not lose the place,

- create several standard formats for worksheets and provide construction paper masks that blot out all but one-fourth or one-third of the page at a time, or

- actually cut a worksheet into fourths or thirds and assign only one small section at a time.

Use Visual Cueing: Color Code

Color coding, although it can appear confusing to those of us without memory or perceptual difficulties, can be an effective way to teach many learning disabled children. It provides them with any or all of the following:

- a way of focusing attention

- a way of properly sequencing steps

- increased ability to recall information

- a way of identifying starting and stopping points

- a cue to the appropriate response

- increased ability to be independent

Generally, it is advisable to code the first step green and the last step red. Children can then be reminded of a traffic light and told to "go on green and stop on red." When using more than two colors, it is important to use colors that are easily distinguished from each other. Do not make Step 2 orange and Step 3 red. For those few students who are color blind, heavy lines can be used instead of colors.

If students have auditory memory or perceptual difficulties, an effort should be made to keep verbal directions and explanations short and to the point. Reinforce them with visual cues. In the case of children with reading or language interference, present concrete examples or board illustrations that they can look at while explanations are given. The use of color to focus, delineate, or cue in illustrations and other visuals will also make them useful to students with visual perception or memory problems. Teachers can use colored chalk or marking pens during teaching sessions for this purpose. Later, they can make special follow-up worksheets, using the same colors, available to individual students. Figures 1-16 and 1-17 present ideas for color-coded pages that can be kept on file and distributed as needed. Other ideas are included in subsequent chapters.

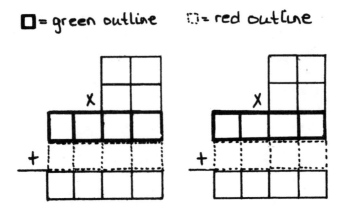

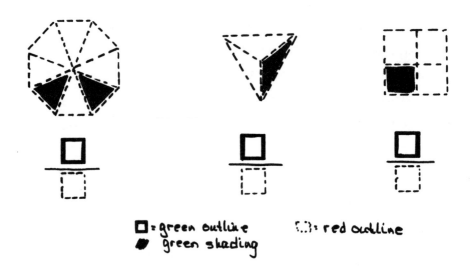

Figure 1-16

Figure 1-17

Colors can also be used when boxing, circling, or underlining sections of textbooks. For example, directions (''read these first'') might be underlined in green. This simple technique will prevent children from spending an inordinate amount of time searching for the directions or separating them from the problems.

Alter, Adjust, or Reinforce the Standard Text Presentation When This Meets a Special Need

Most textbooks provide a standard sequence to follow, but with some children the sequence may not be appropriate. For example, more and more texts are introducing decimals and decimal computation before fractional computation. For children with auditory discrimination, spatial organization, or abstract reasoning problems, a more careful review of basic fraction concepts and symbolism and simultaneous presentation of them may be necessary. Even in written form, fractions are more "concrete" than decimals. They more graphically trigger the visual image of what is represented. The suggested review provides a basis for helping children learn decimal notation by associating it with fractions.

Another technique can be drawn from the area of basic facts. If children have memory difficulties and are familiar only with certain basic facts, it is important to use these facts when presenting a new computational skill or topic to the class. This approach eliminates the need for children to draw on weaknesses while trying to learn something new. Controlling the presentation with known facts allows children to learn along with their peers. In the process, known facts are reinforced, an essential aspect of overlearning that is necessary for fact mastery.

A final technique deals with homework assignments. Instead of assigning all problems on a given page, draw from several pages. Selectively list the problems and the order in which they should be completed. An assignment might look like this:

- Page 235: Problems 3, 7, 8, 5 (these problems might be three of one kind and a fourth that is slightly different)
- Page 182: Problems 2 and 14
- Page 203: Problems 1 through 4, and 7
- Page 182: Problems 7 and 1

Insist that the children solve these in the order presented as a means of avoiding perseveration, of developing sequencing skills and improving reasoning. There is no reason why the entire class cannot be presented with an assignment of this sort. Note that it includes a review of previously learned material.

Allow Children to Finger Trace or Use Other Tactile Cues

In some cases, seeing or hearing is not enough. More total involvement is required. The standard procedure parallels that often used in reading: finger trace, say, then write. Sometimes children may be instructed to close their eyes while finger tracing a textured example. Specific suggestions for using this general technique are described in the chapters that follow. One technique, used for reversals, is finger tracing a textured numeral, then retracing the shape in midair or on paper before writing it.

Another technique can be used to reinforce retention of basic facts. Using the answer side of a flash card, children with visual memory problems might finger trace both problem and answer. Upon turning the card over, the children should try to give the answer immediately. If they forget, finger tracing the problem again often triggers the correct response.

Capitalize on Patterns and Other Associations to Promote Understanding or Retention

Many learning disabled children can be helped by instruction that is based on the use of patterns or relevant associations. One technique may be drawn from the area of basic facts. Often children can learn harder facts by associating them with easier, known ones. The "one more than" idea is powerful in this regard. "5 + 5 = 10, so 5 + 6 is one more (11)," or "12 − 6 = 6, so 13 − 6 is one more (7)." Three additional examples are illustrated in Figure 1-18. Other suggestions are detailed throughout the following chapters.

Use Auditory Cueing

Children with visual, perceptual, or memory disabilities generally require a high degree of auditory reinforcement. At times, for example, it may be helpful for children to close their eyes to block out distracting visual stimuli and just *listen*. They might read a basic problem and its answer into a tape recorder, then listen to the playback for reinforcement. Examples of this basic approach are presented throughout the following chapters.

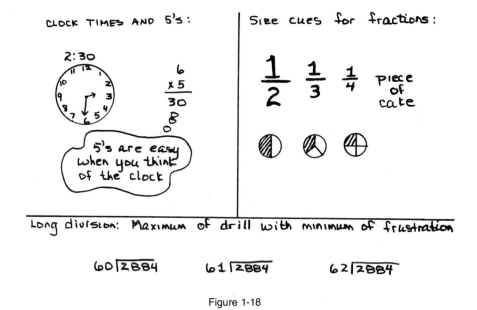

Figure 1-18

Make Sample Problems or Charts Available for Students Who Need Them

Technique 9

Number Charts

Many classrooms have wall charts stretching all the way around the room. The charts may show manuscript or cursive letters. Be sure to include a number chart as well, even at the upper levels. It will help students who are capable of proceeding mathematically but lack the visual memory or other capabilities to put the skills into practice. The chart will serve as an unobtrusive aid and will minimize the chance of students being teased by others in the class.

Charts for Special Topics

Figure 1-19 presents a chart that is very useful for children with receptive language deficits. The technique pictured in Figure 1-20 has proved helpful to many students with learning difficulties in mathematics. Charts like these are necessary references for children in need. Usually they are helpful to the rest of the class as well.

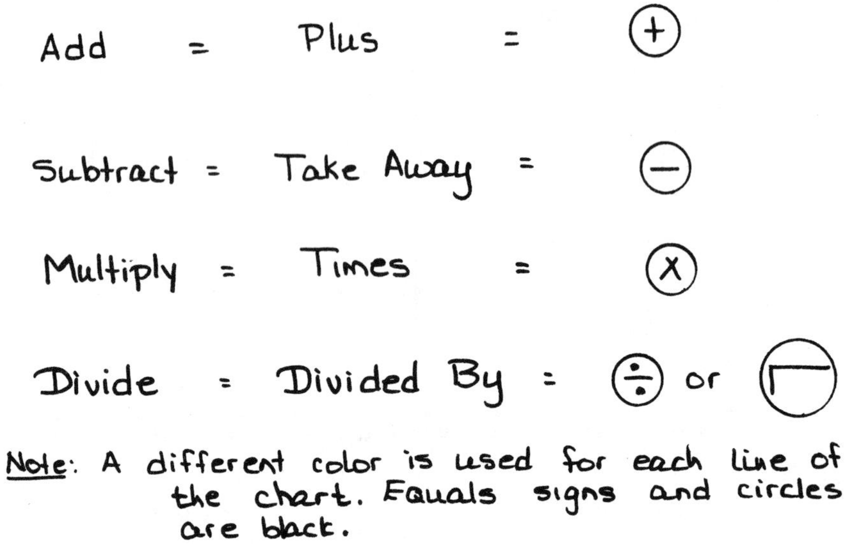

Add   =   Plus   = $\oplus$

Subtract = Take Away = $\ominus$

Multiply = Times = $\otimes$

Divide = Divided By = $\oslash$ or $\boxed{\overline{}}$

<u>Note</u>: A different color is used for each line of the chart. Equals signs and circles are black.

Figure 1-19

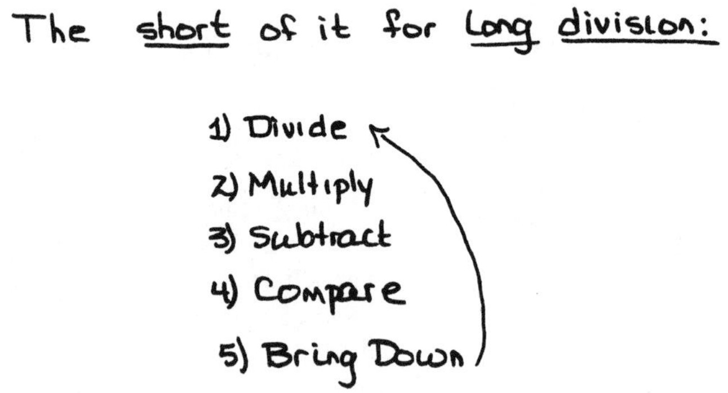

The <u>short</u> of it for <u>Long</u> division:

1) Divide
2) Multiply
3) Subtract
4) Compare
5) Bring Down

Figure 1-20

Other Examples

To help children who confuse or forget the sequence of a computation, techniques like those illustrated in Figure 1-21 might be employed:

- visual directional clues in a sample problem

- flip charts for a sample problem, with a separate page for each step

- a sample problem, completed step by step, at the top of a worksheet

Figure 1-21

Carefully Sequence Instruction in Small Steps, with Adequate Provision for Practice and Review

The sequencing of instruction is critical for students with learning disabilities. Extra developmental and practice time are necessary for both understanding and retaining concepts and processes. Breaking instruction into small, meaningful segments makes learning possible rather than "overwhelming" for these students. Specific suggestions in applying this technique are outlined for selected topics in each of the chapters that follow. Sometimes, learning packets with special practice pages can be prepared in advance to support the need for smaller increments and more review. A tape recorder can also be used to provide extra practice for those requiring auditory learning. A tape recorder is often helpful for those students with visually based difficulties who are strong auditorially.

There are many motivating games that can be used to reinforce the learning of each small step. Care must be taken, however, to help students transfer learning from games to paper and pencil work. Many learning disabled students cannot make this transfer. For example, some children can play basic-fact dice games very easily. They can recognize the groupings and may be able to give answers without counting. However, they may not be able to perform the exact computations on paper or mentally. They simply do not make the associations independently. For these children, it may be necessary to keep pages such as those illustrated in Figure 1-22 to aid the transition.

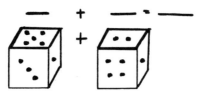

Figure 1-22

It is often possible to make assignments or plan activities that build perception, auditory association, visual memory, or other processing skills. Those students with perceptual difficulties, for example, might be assigned numbers or number sentences to copy, just as other children practice handwriting. If this task is perceptually too hard, keep strips with number sentences on them for the children to copy during their study or learning-center time. Alternatively, one can prerecord number sentences on tape for the children to write or match with problems.

DISCUSSION

This chapter has focused on several important aspects of the planning of mathematics instruction for students with specific learning disabilities. It first presented an overview of the major disabilities from the perspective of their effect on mathematics performance. Knowing and understanding a handicap is the first prerequisite for effectively dealing with it during instruction. Ten general techniques for meeting the needs of learning disabled students in the mathematics classroom were then discussed. More detailed applications of these techniques to selected mathematical topics appear in the chapters that follow.

No attempt will be made to deal with the content of the entire elementary school mathematics curriculum. It is assumed that teachers are familiar with standard sequences and approaches for presenting topics basic to that curriculum. Rather the emphasis is on selected topics that commonly cause learning disabled students much difficulty. For each of these topics, sequences of instruction that incorporate special techniques and adaptations necessary for meeting special needs will be outlined. Most of the suggestions can be carried out in regular classrooms as well as in resource, clinical, or self-contained settings. It is hoped that the sample sequences and the ideas they offer will set the stage for applying similar approaches to other related mathematical topics.

Chapter 2

The Early Number Program

Number and numeration topics play an important role in early grade instruction. In the beginning, children deal only with the numbers 1 to 10. They then study 2-, 3-, and higher-digit whole numbers. At each step, the focus is first on using objects to illustrate the numbers meaningfully. Then, when children can both read and write the associated numerals, number comparisons and sequencing tasks are introduced. Since number words are used in writing checks, these normally would be dealt with as soon as a child's reading skills are developed enough to handle them.

It is assumed that teachers and educators using this book are familiar with standard sequences and techniques for developing each topic cited above. From the perspective of the learning disabled child, however, standard approaches often fall short of reaching specific learning needs. This chapter focuses on eight areas within the early number program that typically are troublesome to many learning disabled students:

1. recognizing sight groups
2. writing numerals 0 to 10 (focus on reversals)
3. naming the number after a given number
4. counting on
5. writing two-digit numbers (focus on reversals)
6. counting and skip counting: two-digit numbers
7. reading and writing larger numbers
8. comparing larger numbers

A general section outlining ideas for using a hand calculator to help learning disabled students with number and numeration topics concludes the chapter.

For each of the eight major topics, typical disabilities contributing to the problem are identified, and a carefully tailored sequence of learning activities and exercises is suggested. Special techniques, such as finger tracing and visual or auditory cueing, are illustrated within the sequences. Most of the suggestions made can be carried out in regular as well as in resource or clinical settings.

Due to space limitations, some problems experienced by learning disabled students within the early number program could not be included. It is hoped that the ideas outlined in the eight sequences chosen for this chapter will serve as prototypes for handling other difficulties.

RECOGNIZING SIGHT GROUPS

Problem area: Counting from one each time rather than immediately recognizing the number for groups having four or less objects.

Typical disabilities affecting progress: Difficulties with visual discrimination, visual memory, closure, and expressive language.

Background: When students are first introduced to the numbers one to four, they are generally encouraged to move each object as it is counted. Tactual counting in this manner is necessary so that children do not skip objects in the count or count some objects twice. This counting procedure promotes the "one number, one object" idea, a component of meaningful or "rational counting." Rather than saying "one-two, three-four-five" as the count for two balls, children must slow their count to match the objects actually in front of them: "one, two" (see Figure 2-1).

Figure 2-1

By the time children can demonstrate their understanding of the numbers one to four by (1) bringing the correct number of objects upon request and (2) associating the proper numeral with each cluster of objects, they should be familiar enough with the small groupings to give the number immediately. It should no longer be necessary for them to count from one each time to tell the number in groups having four or less objects. This sight group recognition for smaller groups is the basis for more efficient counting of groups having five or more objects (see Figure 2-2). When children spot a familiar subgroup, they can count on from there to tell the number in a larger group. Many students, because of the disabilities identified above, find it difficult to name the number in small groups by sight. The following sequence suggests an approach for helping children who have this problem.

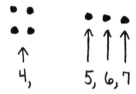

Figure 2-2

Suggested Sequence of Activities and Exercises

1. **Is this two?** (For individuals or small groups; adapt to large group instruction by using an overhead projector.) Place two small objects under each of five boxes on a table. Give each child a numeral "2" card showing two spots. One by one, lift each box so that children can have a quick peek before it is replaced. Ask: "Is this two?" Start as a group activity, then call on individuals to respond. Check by allowing the children, in turn, to place each object over a spot on their "2" card. Repeat, but vary the arrangement of objects under the boxes. Sometimes place only one object under a box. In some cases, it may be necessary, at first, to use one color for all "two" clusters. Gradually, however, this cue would be eliminated.

   - *Example:* Let green be the cueing color. At first use only green objects for the "two" clusters: two green sticks under one box, two green beads under another, and so on. As a next step, use objects of different colors for the "two" clusters, but place them inside a green loop, such as that drawn with crayon on paper. Gradually fade the loop out of the picture.

- *Follow-up activity:* Have children paste cloth scraps or construction paper pieces, by twos, on cards. "See how many different ways you can make two." Later use the cards, along with others, showing only one item, in an "Is This Two?" flash card activity.

- *Note:* With some children, especially those having expressive language deficits, it helps to associate the numeral 2 with the "two" clusters during early phases of the activity. The additional visual cueing provides students with a handle to help them elicit the appropriate response and promotes overlearning as well.

- *Example:* After students have pasted the cloth scraps, by twos, have them match each card with a green numeral 2. As the cards showing one item are added as distractors, the green "2" cards could still be used (see Figure 2-3). The color cue, then the numeral itself, would gradually be eliminated.

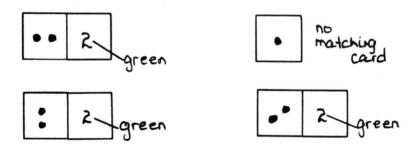

Figure 2-3

2. **Is this three?** Adapt the previous activity to sight group recognition for three. Place the three objects before introducing other distractors (one or two items). Use a different color (e.g black) if cueing is necessary.

3. **Say what you see.** Use flash cards made by the children in the follow-up activity above (cards showing two or three objects). Include others showing only one item. Flash the cards, asking students to tell how many they see. Use a thin underscore (e.g. green for two, black for three) only if necessary, and plan systematically to fade the prompt.

- *Note:* If possible, cover the cards with contact paper or acetate. Then, if underscoring is necessary for only some students, the cards can more easily be wiped clean and reused.

4. **Crayon up! crayon down!** Pass out worksheets like that shown in Figure 2-4, containing one, two, or three items in each box. Sheets should be kept face down on desks until a turn-over signal is given. Tell the children: "When I say 'crayon up,' I want you to turn the sheet over and circle all groups of three with a black crayon. I will give you a very short time, then I will say 'crayon down.' It's all right not to finish. Just find all the threes you can." Later, the children can count from one within each box to check.

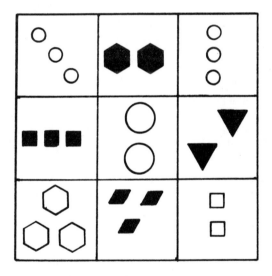

Figure 2-4

- *Variation:* Flash a "2" or "3" numeral card, and have the children circle the appropriate number of objects. Initially use colored numeral cards (e.g. a green "2"; a black "3"). Gradually eliminate the color cue.

5. **Adapt activities 2, 3, and 4 to sight group recognition for four.**

WRITING NUMERALS 0 to 10

Problem area: Number reversals (ε for 3, 6 for 9), disorientations (⌐), and other disfigurations.

Typical disabilities affecting progress: Difficulties with visual discrimination, spatial organization, and visual motor integration.

Background: Before children begin writing numerals, at least two prerequisites should be met:

1. Ability to count out the correct number of objects for each numeral being written.
2. For students with motor coordination difficulties, preliminary work at the gross motor level. In extreme cases this may include movement exercises, such as hopping, crawling, jumping, and ball catching.

Activities such as the following may also be used. Note the continued reference to the number of objects named.

- *Trace.* Draw large numerals on the chalkboard so that children can use a finger or wet sponge to trace over them. Guide each child's hand and give verbal cues to prompt correct formation if necessary. Example: "Down, around, the 6 curls up; the 6 sleeps sound." After making several 6s, have the child draw six balls to show "how many" the numeral stands for. Note: If a child is confusing two numerals, such as the 6 and 9, give verbal cues for only *one* of the pair. If the "curl around, sleep sound" cue is given for 6, then 9 is just the "other one." When cues are given for both numerals, children start confusing cues.

- *Finger play.* Have children form numerals in damp sand. If necessary, make patterns for them to trace over and use verbal cues, as above. It sometimes helps to have children close their eyes as you guide their formation of a numeral. "Feel the 6 go down, around. Now you make it" . . . first with eyes closed, then with eyes open. Have the children make six anthills (or other sand objects) to illustrate "6." Note: If a child has severe spatial organization problems, it is good to confine all writing activities to a horizontal plane, even at this early stage. The down stroke on the "4" made by a child sitting at a desk, for example, has a different orientation to the body than that made while standing. It may be necessary in cases such as this to teach an alternate pattern for writing a 4 and a 5—one which involves only the one stroke (see Figure 2-5). These patterns have also helped children with severe reversal tendencies. If children still have difficulty with reversals, the following basic sequence may help.

"One-stroke" patterns for 4 and 5

4 green

5 green

Figure 2-5

Suggested Sequence of Activities and Exercises

1. **Stencil in.** Provide stencils that children can use to write given numerals. Place a green dot on the stencil to indicate the starting place. In Figure 2-6 the loop is outlined in red. This helps distinguish the 6 from a 9. When necessary, have children finger trace before starting, and use verbal cues.

green

red

Figure 2-6

2. **Get the feel**
   - *Variation 1*—for children who confuse two numerals (e.g. 6 for 9), to help them discriminate one from the other. Have children use stencils to form both numerals. Use green dots for both numerals to show the starting place. Orally name both numerals, but for one

use additional color and verbal cueing, as above, to emphasize its shape. For this number have the child use objects to show "how many" are represented. Then tell the child to "close your eyes. I'll move your hand. Am I making a 6?" (If no, ask "Am I making a 9?") If the child is not ticklish, write one of the numerals on the child's back. "Tell me what I'm writing. . . . Yes, 6. Go to the chalk tray and pick out a picture card showing six things."

- *Note:* It often helps to have textured numerals in front of the children while you finger trace on their backs. Felt numbers are better than sandpaper because they are less abrasive. While you trace, have the children look at the numerals to help fix the association. When finished, have them trace over the numeral they think you made. If correct, and if they are able to write numerals, they can be requested *immediately* to do so on the chalkboard, on paper, or in sand.

- *Variation 2*—for children who make mirror images of given numerals (see Figure 2-7). Move the hand or write on the back so the child can "feel" the numeral being written. Then have the child form the numeral in the air (on the desk). This can be done *as* you write the numeral on the child's back.

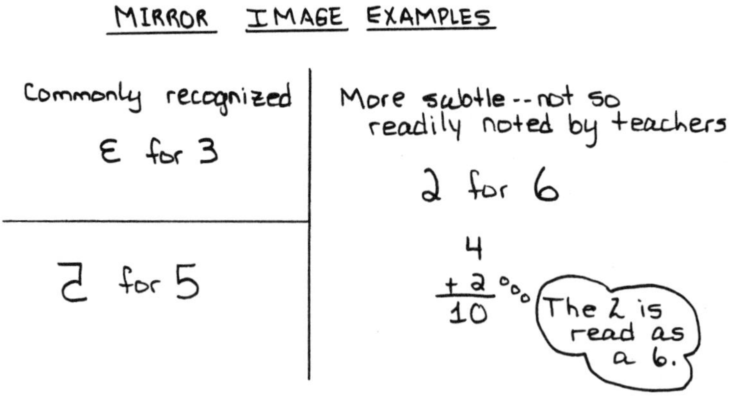

MIRROR   IMAGE EXAMPLES

Commonly recognized	More subtle -- not so readily noted by teachers
E for 3	∂ for 6
ᒼ for 5	$\begin{array}{r} 4 \\ +\,\partial \\ \hline 10 \end{array}$ (The ∂ is read as a 6.)

Figure 2-7

3. **Count and trace**
- *Variation 1*—for children who confuse two numerals, such as 6 for 9. Have children count and complete the numeral to show how many, as in Figure 2-8. If necessary, use a green dot to show the

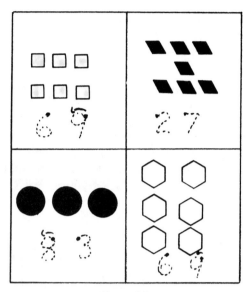

Figure 2-8

starting place, and have children trace the numeral before writing it. "Does it feel like the 6? Does it circle round to sleep sound?" Use red outlining on the loop, as above, if this helps.

- *Variation 2*—for children who make mirror images of given numerals. Children count and write a row of the numeral showing "how many." Use color coding to start the numeral. In Figure 2-9, the top curve is green. Solid, then dotted lines are used. Children may need to finger trace a few numerals before using pencil. Prompt with verbal cues when necessary.

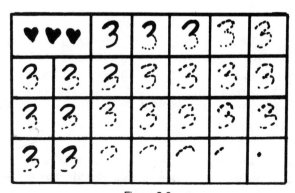

Figure 2-9

- *Note:* We prefer *not* to bring incorrect mirror images into the picture. In our experience, emphasizing correct models has more quickly remedied the problem.

- *Follow up worksheet* (Figure 2-10): It is typical for children to revert to former reversal patterns. The problem, though correctable, does take time to resolve. Worksheets like this, requiring only occasional independent writing of a numeral, provide self-correction when children forget the correct writing movement. As children trace over given samples, teachers might ask: "Do you feel you do it the same way when you write it?"

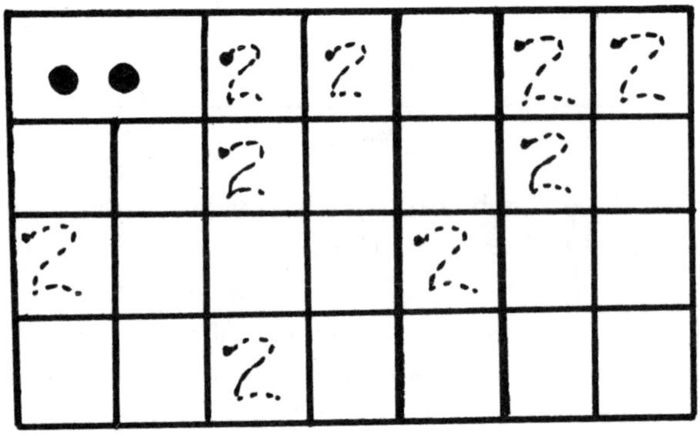

Figure 2-10

- *Optional follow-up:* For children who have been introduced to addition (or other operations and related basic facts), it may be necessary to help transfer the numeral recognition skill to problem situations. Figure 2-11 suggests a way of doing this. Children would be asked to complete the numeral, to give the correct answer and to cross out the wrong one.

- *Note:* Children can also be helped to transfer number recognition to printed numerals. Have them find and circle given numerals which appear in newspaper ads.

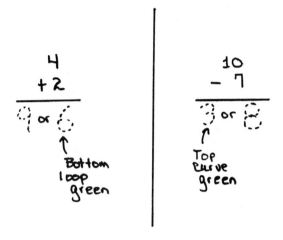

Figure 2-11

4. **You do.** Children now begin, independently, to write the "problem" numeral(s) on paper. A green dot can again be used to show where to start (Figure 2-12a). Children should count the objects, trace the solid numeral, and use it as a pattern for writing other numerals in that row. If necessary, a yellow highlighter can be used when dotted lines no longer appear to guide correct formation. Eventually, numeral patterns are given only at the top of a worksheet (Figure 2-12b). In these examples, color outlining of the "6" loop would be used if needed, but this would be eliminated gradually.

   • *Optional follow up:* Simple number combinations that involve the specific numerals being worked on would again be given. This time, however, the dotted numerals of Figure 2-11 would not be shown. Figure 2-13 illustrates a way of making the activity self-checking. Write problems on the bottom part of a sheet of construction paper, as shown. Cover this part with contact so that children can use a washable marker or grease pencil to write the answers. Children can then fold the top part down over the problems and compare answers with those given.

   • *Note:* Activities and exercises similar to those in the preceding sequence can be used to help children having other writing problems; that is, disorientation or disfiguration of numerals. Have model numbers available to which children can refer.

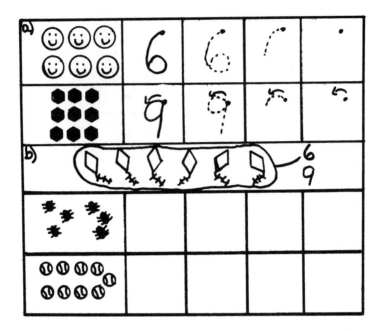

Figure 2-12

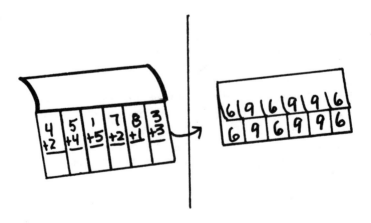

Figure 2-13

NAMING THE NUMBER AFTER A GIVEN NUMBER

Problem area: Counting from 1 each time rather than immediately naming the number that comes after another in the counting sequence.

Typical disabilities affecting progress: Difficulties with visual or auditory association, visual or auditory memory, closure.

Background: Some children with the disabilities identified above *can* match objects one to one and tell you: "The side with extras has more, so 5 is more than 4" (Figure 2-14). They may also realize that when a number means more, it comes after the other when you count. A related difficult task is to jump in, as it were, in the middle of a counting sequence and immediately say or write the number just after that given. Familiarity with the counting sequence does not "naturally" instill this skill, particularly for children with the specific learning disabilities cited. As a prerequisite for counting on, the skill is well worth developing. When children can give the number just after another, it is easier to continue that sequence to find answers to simple addition sums or to check change received from a small purchase (Figure 2-15). The developmental work outlined below sets the stage for the Section 4 "count on" activities.

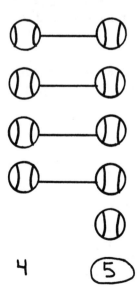

Figure 2-14

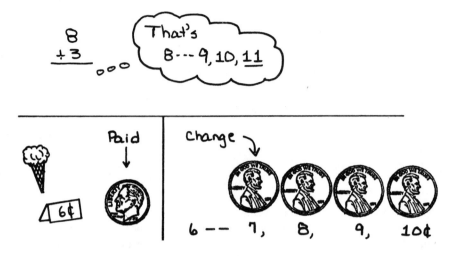

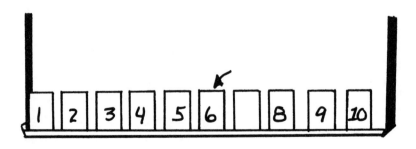

Figure 2-15

Suggested Sequence of Activities and Exercises

1. **Turn over.** Line large numeral cards along the chalk tray. Let children see you turn one card over (e.g. the "7" card in Figure 2-16). "Read this card, Amy." (6) "What comes after 6?" (7) Turn the card over to check.

   - *Note 1:* It might help some children to say a number, finger trace and say the number after, then close their eyes while the card is turned over.

Figure 2-16

- *Note 2:* For at least the first few times, it is helpful to count from 1, stopping (in this case) with 7. Emphasize that "we say 6, then 7."

- *Follow-up Activity 1:* As above, but let the children use their own centimeter ruler to check the number sequence. This is something they can keep at their desks and refer to easily.

- *Follow-up Activity 2:* As above, but encourage the children to study the ruler or card sequence so that they remember "in their heads" where the numbers are. Then have them close their eyes while you turn over a numeral card.

2. **Walk on!** Use a large walk-on numberline. Have children close their eyes. Decide on a number and cover all numbers after that (a roll of shelf paper does nicely, see Figure 2-17). Then, when the children open their eyes and examine the numberline, call on someone to tell you quickly the number after the last one showing. Remove the paper to check. A good followthrough is to have the child stand on one number (e.g., 6) and show that just one more step takes you to the number after (7).

   - *Note:* It may be again helpful to count from 1, emphasizing the last two numbers of this counting sequence.

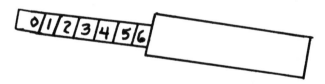

Figure 2-17

3. **Peek!** Suggest that the children study their own rulers so that they remember where the numbers are. Then, using a large scale ruler or numberline, decide on a number and cover all numbers to the right of that one with an arrow card (Figure 2-18). "What's the arrow pointing to, Bob?" (6) "What comes after 6?" (7) Have the child guess, if nothing else, then peek to check. If necessary, count from 1 to emphasize the last two numbers in the counting sequence. Note that:

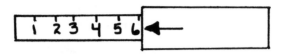

Figure 2-18

- This is an activity that can be repeated frequently throughout the day, even as children enter or leave the room for lunch, recess, or another class.

- For special cases, it may prove reinforcing to have children say and *then write* the number pair being focused on (in these examples, 6 and 7). An alternative is to have the children finger trace the number pair on their own rulers.

The above sequence can be adapted to: (1) counting on from a given number until signaled to stop, or (2) naming the number *before* another. Counting backwards to give the number before, indeed the very concept of *before,* is typically harder for children than naming the number after. Techniques similar to those used in this sequence, combined with the action of walking backwards on a floor model numberline, have helped.

COUNTING ON

Problem area: Failure to apply skills like sight group recognition of smaller groups or the ability to name the number after, to help

- tell the number in larger groups of objects,

- find simple addition sums, and

- check change returned from small purchases (only pennies involved in the change received).

Typical disabilities affecting progress: Difficulties with visual or auditory association, closure, figure ground.

Background: In Section 1 we mentioned the importance of counting on from sight groups to find the number in a larger group. Section 3 discussed briefly how this skill can be extended to help one check change from small purchases or to find simple addition sums. Counting on is a very efficient technique in each of these cases. There is no need to count from 1.

Several more sophisticated examples of the use of this skill can be cited:

- Example 1: Count on from a known double to find harder addition sums (Figure 2-19).

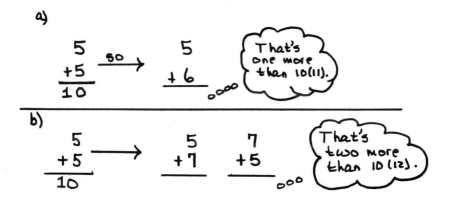

Figure 2-19

- Example 2: Count on from some other easy fact to find a harder sum (Figure 2-20).

a)
```
   3    so      4      One
  +7    ──→    +7      more
 ────          ──      than 10(11).
  10            °°°
```

b)
```
   8            8      That's
  +2           +5      3 more
 ────          ──      than 10(13).
  10        °°°°
```

Figure 2-20

Note: For each of these two examples, some children may find it easier simply to spot the greater addend and count on from there. Other learning disabled students feel it is faster and just as easy to count on from a known fact for addition sums like these. See Chapter 4 for more detailed suggestions for helping children learn basic facts.

- Example 3: Count on from a given time to find another. This often requires the ability to count by 5s. For example: (1) ''It's 2:20. The brownies should bake 25 minutes.'' (2) ''It's 7:40. My TV show starts in 20 minutes.'' See Section 6 of this chapter for help in this regard. Chapter 3, devoted to time and money topics, elaborates further on suggestions for teaching these and related skills.

- Example 4: Count on from the cost of an item until the amount paid is reached (coins other than pennies involved in the change). Suggestions for this topic are further detailed in Chapter 3.

Certainly counting on has many useful applications. Rather than helping children build the skill, many textbooks (and hence, many teachers) frequently assume it. The sequence that follows suggests a way of tuning in on special needs in the development of counting on abilities.

Suggested Sequence of Activities and Exercises

Prerequisites
1. For counting larger groups of objects: sight-group recognition of smaller clusters (see Section 1).
2. The ability to name the number after that given (see Section 2).

Basic Sequence of Activities: Counting On from Sight Groups to Tell the Number in a Larger Group

1. **How many?** Show six objects, a cluster of four and two more (Figure 2-21a). Point to the four objects. "How many here?" (4) Have a child place a numeral card beneath the four items (Figure 2-21b). "How many in all?" Prompt if necessary: "4 here (pointing), 5, 6. Six in all." Count from 1 to check. Repeat with other objects for each new number studied (to 10). If necessary, use objects of one color to cue sight group recognition within the larger group.
2. **Clip!** Give the children a tagboard "6" card and eight or nine paper clips. Ask them to find the edges on the card that have been covered with tape. "That's for your paper clips. You won't need all the clips, just six. Put them anywhere on the taped edges." As a followup, have the children, in turn, show how they made "6" with their clips.

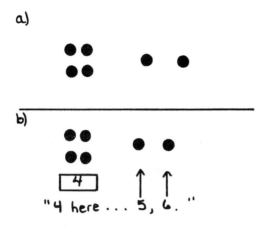

Figure 2-21

Encourage them to count on from a known sight group rather than from 1. Jan (Figure 2-22) might say: "I have 2—3, 4, 5, 6 on my card." Jan might also have counted on from 4. *Note:* It may be necessary to make sight group cards available to aid children with visual memory or figure-ground difficulties.

Figure 2-22

3. **Draw 'n' toss.** Use navy or lima beans. Spread them on a newspaper and spraypaint one side a bright color. Have the children draw a numeral card, choose that many beans, and toss them into a designated playing area. Have them count aloud to "prove" the beans and numeral card match. Encourage them to spot a sight group and count on from there (Figure 2-23).

Figure 2-23

Extending the Basic Sequence: Counting On to Find Simple Addition Sums

Note: If the children experienced any difficulty counting on in the preceding activities, refer to the activity suggestions of Section 3. Play "turn over," but this time turn over two to four cards so that children can count on from a given number. In the "walk on" and "peek" activities, have the children count on from the last number shown until you give a signal to stop.

1. **2 more.** This is to prepare children to count on in addition problems having 2 as an addend (e.g. 6 + 2, 2 + 5, 7 + 2). Emphasis is on the auditory patterning involved. Use the ruler and arrow card from the "peek" activity. Point the arrow to a numeral (3 to 9) and have the children tell you the number 2 more. Demonstrate the auditory pattern that makes this easy. For example:

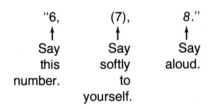

Repeat with other numbers.

- *Note 1:* Some children with auditory deficits or perseveration tendencies may have difficulty saying the middle number softly. These children might be taught to tap the table or point to the 7 on the numberline while speaking softly.

- *Note 2:* As advance preparation for adding facts like 5 + 7 (2 more than a double), some teachers may want to extend this activity to include telling 2 more than a given teen number.

2. **3 more.** As above, but ask the children to tell the number 3 more than that to which you point. Demonstrate the following auditory pattern:

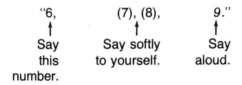

3. Mix requests to give the number 2 or 3 more than that to which you point. The counting on should be done mentally, *not* on fingers. Experience suggests this can be done.

4. **Come again.** Prepare two card decks:

- Deck 1: 24 cards, four of each numeral, 4 through 9.

- Deck 2: 24 cards, twelve "2" cards, twelve "3" cards. In turn, the children draw a card from Deck 1 and say "Come again." This time they draw from Deck 2. A "2" draw means they quickly tell the number 2 more than that first drawn. A "3" draw means: quickly tell the number 3 more. Students keep both cards if they answer quickly. (It should be obvious when children are counting on rather than counting from 1.) Students can use the ruler sequence to check themselves.

  Note: Children successful with Activities 1 through 4 above should be able to count on for simple addition facts, as suggested in Chapter 4.

Extending the Basic Sequence: Counting On to Check Change from Small Purchases Involving Only Pennies

Cashier. Use real objects or paste catalog pictures to cards. Attach a price tag to each. In turn, the children count on aloud to check the change given them by the cashier (teacher or able student). Set the amount to be paid (e.g. 10¢, 15¢, 20¢) so that the change each time involves only pennies. Refer to the Figure 2-15 example.

TWO-DIGIT NUMBERS: FOCUS ON REVERSALS

Section 5

Problem area: Writing 23 for 32; 41 for 14, and so on.

Typical disabilities affecting progress: Difficulties with visual memory, visual discrimination, visual or auditory sequential memory.

Background: Four basic steps to instruction normally ensure a child's successful understanding and use of two-digit numbers (Rathmell & Payne, 1975, pp. 138-154):

1. Children group objects such as popsicle sticks or chips by tens and then *tell* the number of tens and number of ones left over.
2. Children count orally by tens and use objects to show the count: ''2 tens, twenty; 6 tens, sixty,'' and so on. When multiples of ten are established, extra ones are included: ''2 tens and 3: twenty-three.'' Because of naming irregularities, teens are dealt with last.
3. Children group objects by tens and *write* to describe the grouping. The tens-ones labels, used in early stages, are gradually eliminated (Figure 2-24). Note: In Chapter 1 we discussed how reading can interfere with success in mathematics. Figure 2-24b illustrates a format for children who are afraid of reading or who have real deficits in this area.
4. Children use objects (tens and ones) in early stages to help compare and sequence numbers.

When these steps are followed, most children understand the tens-ones placement of digits within numbers. Sometimes the teens provoke reversals, even among children exhibiting no particular reversal tendency. The reminder that, ''Teens are different; remember, we have to watch them,'' often corrects the problem in these cases. With children showing consistent reversal tendencies in

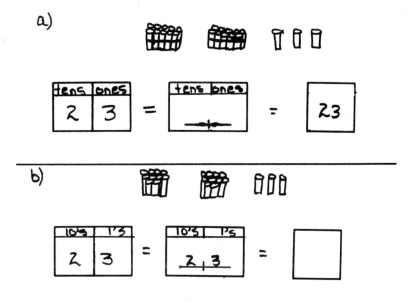

Figure 2-24

writing two-digit numerals, however, more specialized programming, such as that outlined below, is necessary. Note: For children making mirror image digits (e.g. Ɛ 9 for 39), refer to the suggestions of Section 4.

Suggested Sequence of Activities and Exercises

1. **Tens and ones.** Used colored chips or graph paper pieces (see Figure 2-25a). Give the child 2 tens and 4 ones. "How many stacks of 10?" (2) Have child place a green textured numeral beneath the 2 ten-stacks. "How many ones?" (4) Position these to the right of the ten-stacks, and have the child place a red numeral beneath the 4 ones (Figure 2-25b). "Two tens and 4, that's twenty-four. Finger trace the 24 so you get the feel of it. Start with tens." The child should say the number aloud as it is traced.

   - *Follow-up Discussion:* "Think of a stoplight. Suppose you want to walk across the street. When can you start?" (When the light is green.) "Yes, green means start. Red means stop. Look at the numerals we used. When you read or write numbers like this (point), you *start* with tens, the green one, and *stop* with ones."

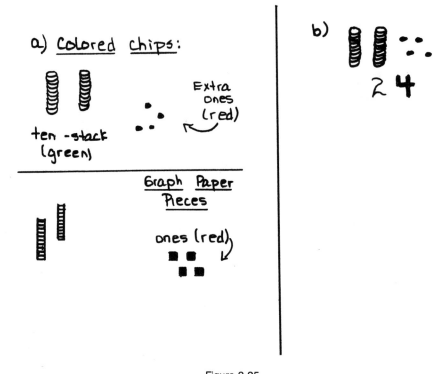

Figure 2-25

- *Note:* If the child has any difficulty relating 2 tens to twenty, 4 tens to forty, and so on, take time out to reinforce this relationship. Use ten-stacks to dramatize the counting by tens. Capitalize on any phonetic similarities (e.g. *six* tens, *six*ty; *five* tens, *fif*ty). Repeat the activity with other numbers. Omit teens until later, when naming irregularities can again be pointed out.

2. **Start with tens**

- Give the child 2 tens and 4 ones as in the preceding activity. "Let's write how many chips you have. Where do we start?" (Tens—2 tens.) "Write the '2' in green." "How many ones?" (4) "Write it in red (Figure 2-26a). What number did we write?" (Twenty-four.) "Finger trace the number as you say it. . . . Now close your eyes and picture it while I say it. . . . Open your eyes. Is this what you saw?" (Refer again to Figure 2-26a.) Note: Prompt the child as necessary throughout this dialog.

Color coding is used for
a) and b) below:

ten's digits → green
one's digits → red

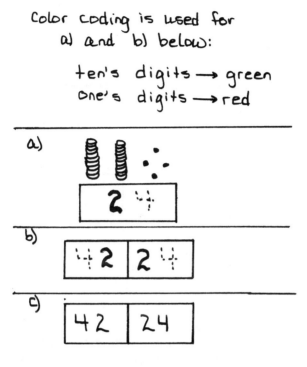

Figure 2-26

- Show the child Figure 2-26b. "Which of these say 24?" (Last one.) "How do you know?" (It starts with 2 tens.) Have the child finger trace, as above.

- Show the child Figure 2-26c. "This time there's no color. Can you remember which says twenty-four?" (First one.) "How do you know?" (It starts with 2 tens.)

Repeat with other two-digit numbers. A worksheet like that of Figure 2-27 can be used in conjunction with the activity. Boxes can be filled in during discussion with the child. Note that:

- It may be sufficient merely to underline the tens digit in green, the ones digit in red.

- The separation of tens-ones columns into individual boxes has been avoided. When this is done, some students, for closure reasons, do not see "24." They see a 2 and a 4. In our experience, these same students accept and profit from the color distinctions.

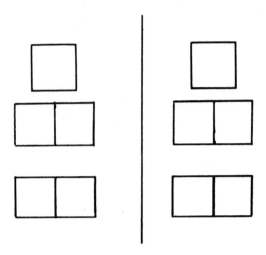

Figure 2-27

Follow-up Worksheets: Worksheets similar to that of Figure 2-28 are fairly common in commercial workbooks. It may sometimes be necessary, particularly for children with sequential memory deficits, to color code these pages. In Figure 2-28a, for example, one could underscore the tens groups in green and the ones groups in red.

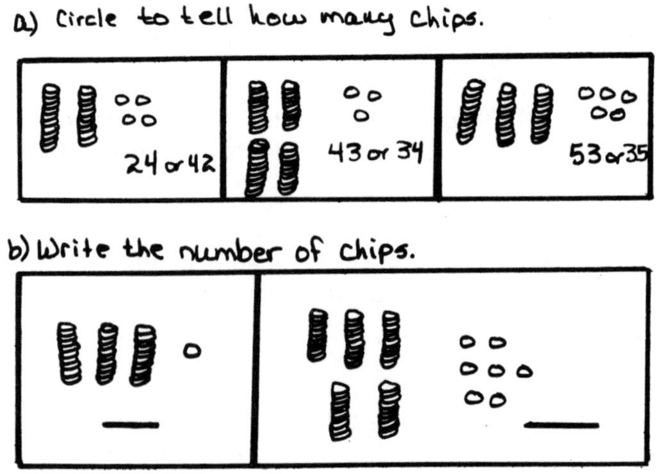

a) Circle to tell how many chips.

ⅼⅼ ₀₀ ₀₀ 24 or 42	ⅼⅼ ₀₀ ₀ 43 or 34	ⅼⅼⅼ ₀₀₀ ₀₀ 53 or 35

b) Write the number of chips.

Figure 2-28

Similarly, in Figure 2-28b, the response line could be highlighted in green (tens place) and red (ones place). The first problem on a page could be marked as in Figure 2-29, serving as an example for completing the remainder of the page. No color coding would be used, except in the example. Rather than altering individual worksheets, some teachers may prefer to make cards available, similar to those of Figure 2-30, to which children can refer while doing these types of pages. The cards would show materials commonly used by children and displayed on their worksheets.

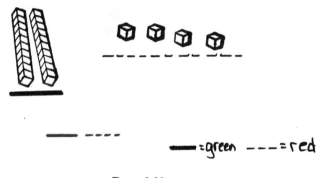

Figure 2-29

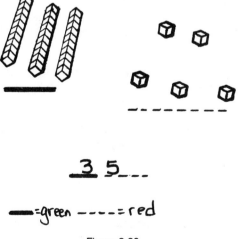

Figure 2-30

3. **Write and show.** Pre-recorded cassette tapes are excellent for this type of activity. Script suggestions are shown in the following quotes: "I'll say a number. You write it. Remember to start with tens. Here's the first number: twenty-four." (Tape off while the child writes.) "Now use tens and ones to show twenty-four." (Tape off while the child selects the ten-stacks and ones needed.) "You should have two tens and four ones, twenty-four. Check it out. Turn to page A of the answer book" (see Figure 2-31).

Figure 2-31

- *Note 1:* Providing paper with predrawn boxes for children's responses will help avoid random placement of numbers.

- *Note 2:* If a child is highly distractible, setting up a definite workspace helps. Use a plain sheet of paper, a plastic mat, or even a piece of smooth plastic tablecloth for this purpose. Use the workspace to focus the child's attention. "Use tens and ones to show me twenty-four in your workspace. . . . Good! Now clear your workspace."

- *Variation:* Provide a worksheet correlated to the tape. Have the child circle the correct numeral: 24 or 42. For the first part of the tape, the tens digit could be color coded.

4. **Dot to dot.** Provide a prerecorded tape that dictates two-digit numbers, with a pause between each. (If necessary, the tape can be turned off between numbers.) Correlate a dot-to-dot pattern with the tape, so that a picture is formed if the child connects dots between each number dictated. The tape could begin with the reminder to "start with tens." If necessary, the tens place of each two-digit numeral on the dot-to-dot sheet can be written or underlined in green.

5. **Secret message** (optional). Ask the child to number a paper one through nine. Now dictate a two-digit number to be written beside each. Example:

1. 32	4. 28	7. 81
2. 64	5. 73	8. 35
3. 45	6. 54	9. 93

Tell the child the two-digit numbers are page numbers in a book. Instruct the child to use the book to find the penciled letter written beside each page number. "Look up number 1 (page 32). Do you see an 'A?' Write 'A' in the number 1 box on your worksheet." (Figure 2-32) "Do the same for the others. See if you can answer the riddle. Remember to start with tens when looking for pages."

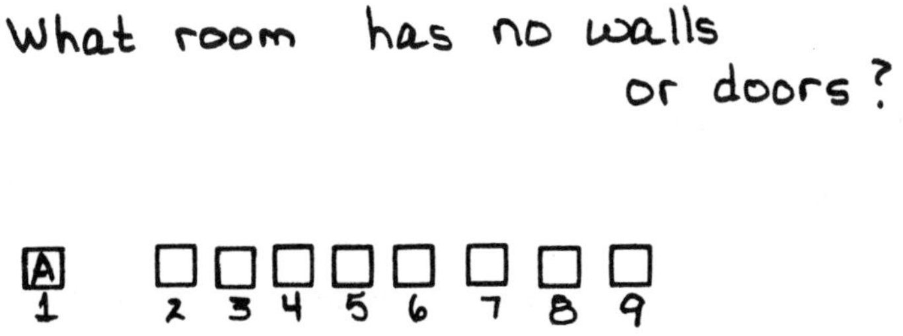

What room has no walls
                              or doors?

Figure 2-32

- *Note 1:* This has proved a very motivating activity for students with auditory memory problems. It is an activity that can be constructed quickly. Use a riddle book from a public library to help.

- *Note 2:* Children with spatial or severe visual perception difficulties may have trouble doing worksheets of this nature. The numbers 1 to 9 may "run together" with others written from dictation. It may be necessary to provide prenumbered sheets for the numbers 1 to 9 (numbers written in a distinctly different color than that to be used by the child during dictation). If lined paper is used, skip a line between numbers. Or provide centimeter strips (Figure 2-33) and have the children write a dictated number in alternate squares. For severe cases it may be necessary to omit worksheets of this type.

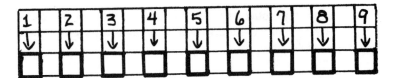

Figure 2-33

6. **Here and there.** Here are several other suggestions for giving a child the opportunity to practice writing two-digit numbers correctly.

- Provide short lists of two-digit numbers to be copied.

- Have the child count and write down the number of books in a bookcase, the number of straws left in a box, and so on.

- Have the child mentally add doubles, such as 24 + 24, where no renaming is involved, and then write the sum. Note: This task may be too difficult for children with visual or auditory memory problems.

- Have the child compare two two-digit numbers and write the larger or smaller. The children could use ten-stacks and ones to picture each if necessary. Or the tens digit of each could be color coded green as a reminder to "start here to compare."

- Have the child sequence three two-digit numbers, low to high, then use a centimeter ruler, numberline, or page numbering of a book to check the written ordering (numbers that mean *more* come after the others).

7. **Terrible teens!** Naming irregularities of the teens should be pointed out to students:

> 2 tens and 4: "twenty-four" (24);
>
> 4 tens and 6: "forty-six" (46);

But ⟶ 1 ten and 7: "seventeen" (17).

One still starts with tens to write teens. It is just that the verbal naming pattern does not hold. One must listen carefully to determine whether the ending is "teen" or "ty." (11 and 12 are in categories all their own.) Children can be helped to focus on the ending by worksheets like those of Figure 2-34. The "teen" and "ty" endings are written in red. Note: The "6teen, 6ty" technique is effective even with nonreaders. The difference in configuration makes it easy to "read" the two forms.

Which is it?

6 teen ⟍ ⟍ 16 6 ty ・	9 teen ・ 90 9 ty ・
thir teen ・ 30 thirty ・	fifteen ・ 15 fifty ・
7 teen ・ 17 7 ty ・	8 teen ・ 18 8 ty ・

Figure 2-34

COUNTING AND SKIP COUNTING: TWO-DIGIT NUMBERS

Problem area: Not understanding the patterning for counting, even though basic numeration concepts are well established.

Typical disabilities affecting progress: Difficulties with abstract reasoning, closure, visual or auditory association, and expressive language.

Background: It is often assumed that a child with adequate numeration understanding for two-digit numbers can use these numbers to count. This is not always the case. Some children, such as those with disabilities listed above, may be able to use objects (tens and ones) to illustrate given written numerals. Upon hearing a two-digit number, they may also be able to write it and use objects to picture it. Yet these same children may be unable to extend correctly a counting sequence of two-digit numbers. And quite often they fail at even simple skip counting, such as counting by 5s or 10s.

Children such as these characteristically lag behind peers who rote count with two-digit numbers even before they formally study them. In all likelihood, they do not yet possess skip counting skills that are very useful for early multiplication and daily situations involving time or money. Suppose brownies should bake 25 minutes. These children may have difficulty counting on from the present time (by 5s) to determine when the brownies should be taken from the oven. Likewise, they may be unable to count by 5s or 10s to tell the value of given coins or to check change received.

These children have difficulty making associations and recognizing patterns that ordinarily make counting and skip counting a reasonably simple task. For such cases, special instruction, such as that outlined below, is required. Rather than basing activity immediately on number, the sequence first involves the child in *patterning*. As the root of the problem, this is the appropriate starting place. At first, the child is given simple shapes and visual/auditory cues to help in recognizing and extending a pattern. Then, when the child is successful with number sequences (easily distinguishable numerals), color-coded counting charts are used.

Suggested Sequence of Activities and Exercises

1. **Finish the pattern.** Use wood or construction paper circles and squares (circles one color, squares another). Lay out a simple repeating pattern with the blocks. On two slips of paper, trace (same color as actual shapes) the dotted outlines of the next two blocks in the pattern (see Figure 2-35). Have the child name the shapes, in order, so that the "square, square, circle, circle" auditory pattern is heard. Then ask the child to find the missing blocks and finish the pattern. When all blocks are in place, have the child "read" the pattern (name all the shapes displayed, in order). Then ask the child to use blocks to copy the completed pattern. Follow-up: Repeat with other patterns, gradually omitting the dotted cue.

2. **Draw it in.** As above, but draw the repeating shape patterns on worksheets. At first, use two different colors and include the dotted outlines. Ask the child to "read" and complete each pattern. Then ask that the entire pattern again be read aloud. Provide space (and templates, if necessary), so that the child can copy the completed pattern. Gradually use harder patterns, fade the color cueing, and omit the dotted outlines. See if the child can add the next two or three shapes to the pattern without extra prompts. Experience suggests this is possible when pattern difficulty is gradually incremented along with gradual fading of prompts.

Figure 2-35

3. **What's next?** Follow the same "read, complete, read again, copy" format of the two preceding activities, but this time use numerals that can be readily distinguished (e.g. Figure 2-36). Similar cueing techniques can also be used if necessary.

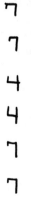

Figure 2-36

4. **An easy one.** Show the child Figure 2-37. "This is an easy one. Tell me what's alike in the numbers." (All end in 0.) "Read the numbers" (to hear the auditory pattern). "What comes next?" (70) "How do you know?" (7 comes after 6.) Have the child finish the sequence and read it aloud. "Look at the numbers so you can remember them in your head. . . . Now close your eyes and tell me the numbers." Prompt as necessary throughout this dialogue. Repeat parts of the dialogue as necessary. Note: If more patterning work is needed, adapt Activity 7 below to provide the needed practice.

$$1\,0$$
$$2\,0$$
$$3\,0$$
$$4\,0$$
$$5\,0$$
$$6\,0$$

Figure 2-37

5. **Count on:** Provide dimes the child can use for counting by 10s. If necessary, use a counting chart as in Figure 2-38, on which the child lays the dimes while counting. (If a child's money concepts are too weak for this activity, refer to the Chapter 3 suggestions.) Eventually the child should be able to count by 10s independently of the chart. Variation (to prepare for counting money amounts and checking change received): Lay four dimes (40¢) on the counting chart and have the child count on by 10s from 40¢. Repeat, but vary the number of dimes initially laid on the chart.

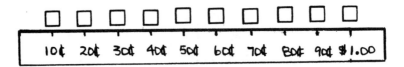

Figure 2-38

6. **To 100.** (Prerequisite: The child can count orally to 10. It is also assumed that the numeration instruction summarized in Section 4 of this chapter has been carried out.)

   Show the color-coded counting chart of Figure 2-39 (tens digits green). This chart is sequenced vertically rather than horizontally as is commonly the case. Experience has shown that the vertical presentation makes it easier for children to see the patterning of the number sequence.

0	10	20	30	40	50	60	70	80	90	100
1	11	21	31	41	51	61	71	81	91	
2	12	22	32	42	52	62	72	82		
3	13	23	33	43	53	63				
4	14	24	34	44						
5	15	25	35							
6	16									
7	17									
8	18									
9	19									

Figure 2-39

Have the child count by 10s *across* the columns. Now mask out all but the first column (0-9), and have the child read it aloud. Then slide the mask so that the first two columns show. Discuss how the second column is like the first. (The ones column in both is the standard counting sequence. This can be related to the idea of one more as described earlier.) Have the child note the pattern that all numbers in the second column begin with 1. "This is the teen column." Count from 1 with the child, emphasizing the "teen" endings of the last numbers read.

Slide the mask again to reveal the third column. "This is the 20s column." Have the child read the numbers in the column. "What numbers come next?" Write as the child orally continues the counting sequence to 29, prompting as necessary. For this, as for other columns of the chart, the child can be shown how the standard counting sequence of the ones digits will help. Later retrace the tens digits with green, recounting aloud with the child to emphasize the "20" part of each number named. Have the child finger trace the first digits during an independent recount, if this helps. Let the child, eyes closed, count the "20s" aloud. Then choose a number in a preceding column and count on from there—first using the chart, then looking away. Stress the "19-20" column shift.

Repeat for other columns during this or follow-up sessions. Make the chart available to the child for reference. Use it as long as needed during review sessions in which the child either orally counts or writes the numbers in sequence.

- *Follow-up Activity 1:* Reinforce the tens transition with repeated oral work. First the teacher says a few patterns emphasizing the switch. Then the student completes patterns started by the teacher. Example:

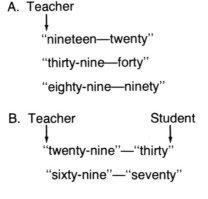

- *Follow-up Activity 2:* When the auditory pattern for sequential counting is established, use objects (tens and ones) to dramatize and reinforce the meaning of the oral count. Example: Lay out 2 tens and 1. "I will add sticks, one at a time. Count aloud so we can keep track of the number of sticks that are on the table each time" (see Figure 2-40). Repeat, varying the number of tens and ones initially placed on the table. It may now also be necessary to redevelop concepts and skills for comparing and ordering two-digit numbers. Suggestions from Sections 3 and 5 of this chapter can be adapted to this purpose.

Figure 2-40

7. **By 5s.** Use a worksheet similar to that of Figure 2-41 to lay the groundwork for the patterning involved in skip counting by 5s. Following the sequence of patterns on the worksheet, first review the easier patterns with shapes, then turn to numbers used when counting by 5s.

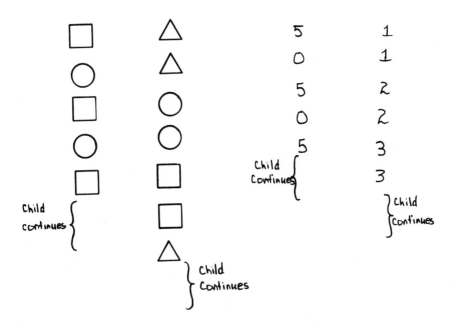

Figure 2-41

Next show Figure 2-42 (tens digits coded green). Ask the child to read the column, then to describe any patterns seen (numbers end in 5 or 0; in the tens place there are two 1s, then two 2s). In order for some children to see these patterns, they may need to cover first the ones column and then the tens column with a card.

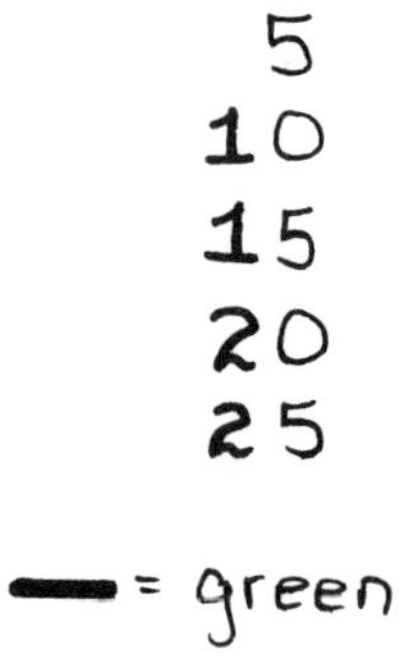

$$5$$
$$10$$
$$15$$
$$20$$
$$25$$

— = green

Figure 2-42

"What two numbers would come next?" Write as the child says them: 30, 35. Prompt if necessary. Discuss why these two numbers were chosen. Then have the child say all the numbers aloud, continuing the count as far as possible (to 100). Write as the child gives the extended count. Underscore the tens digits green if this helps to cue additional entries in the sequence. Then see if the child can repeat the counting pattern without looking at the chart. Make the chart available to the child for future reference, and continue to use it as needed during review sessions.

8. **Nickel countdown.** Adapt the "count on" activity above to counting by 5s with nickels. Note that the idea of counting by 5s and 10s can be extended to include (1) counting on from clock times, or (2) using nickels and dimes first to count by 5s then switching to counting by 10s (and vice versa). The latter skill is often needed for counting money amounts or checking change received.

Note: The "peek" activity of Section 3 as well as dot-to-dot patterns can be used to reinforce most of the activities of this section.

READING AND WRITING LARGER NUMBERS

Problem area: Difficulty reading or writing three- and higher-digit numbers.

Typical disabilities affecting progress: Difficulties with visual perception (figure-ground, visual discrimination), visual association, closure, abstract reasoning, and auditory processing.

Background: Many factors influence a child's success in reading and writing larger numbers. The opportunity to group objects by 10s and to further cluster the groups into 100s or even 1000s is helpful to all students (Figure 2-43a). Besides establishing place-value understandings for hundreds and thousands, experiences such as these help children develop a *feel* for larger numbers. Graph paper pieces (Figure 2-43b) can also be used to illustrate three- and four-digit numbers.

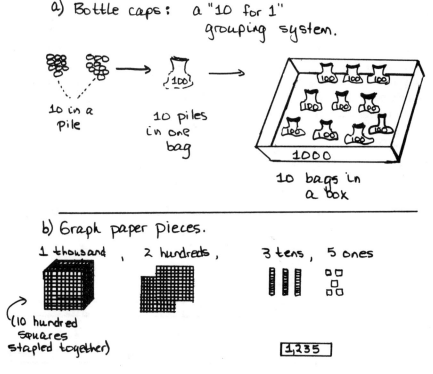

Figure 2-43

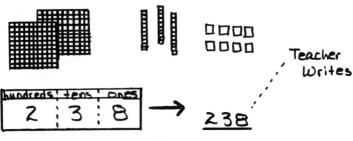

Figure 2-44

It is important that early numeration instruction use materials to illustrate numbers in some physical, hands-on manner. Then common problems, such as writing ''20038'' for ''two hundred thirty-eight'' or reading ''415'' as ''forty-one, five'' have a basis for treatment.

To remedy the first problem a teacher might, for example, ask a child to gather 2 hundreds, 3 tens, and 8 singles from a box of graph paper pieces. After recording the number of each kind of piece (Figure 2-44), the teacher might write the number in standard form and ''model'' the way it *should* be read. Teacher and child can then switch roles. After taking graph paper pieces and recording the number of each kind, the child could write the number in standard form and read it to the teacher. As a follow up, the teacher and student can take turns drawing a three-digit number card, reading it, and asking the other to show it with graph paper pieces (Figure 2-45). Stamps for hundreds, tens, and ones, available from many school supply companies, can also be used for this purpose. They should be among the mathematics materials of every elementary school classroom.

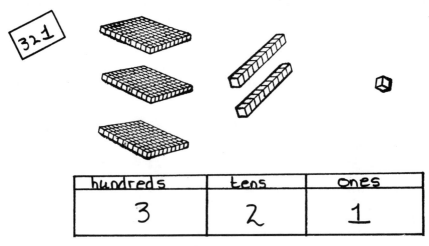

Figure 2-45

Activities such as those described above have proved quite effective. They provide a visual frame of reference that helps the children to read and write three-digit numbers when materials are no longer used. The modeling by the teacher, correctly writing and saying the number represented by the pieces, is a vital part of the sequence. Correct teacher modeling is also necessary to prevent children from reading "238" as "two hundred *and* thirty-eight." The "and" is properly reserved for the decimal point, as in $2.38 (two dollars *and* 38 cents) or 4.2 (four *and* two tenths). Only in special cases would children be allowed to use "and." Some students may need to use it as a pause for remembering how to group digits for reading a number. Using "and" in this manner is a crutch that can and should be discarded when it is no longer needed. This situation parallels that of using "uh" or pausing to keep from stuttering.

For students who read "415" as "forty-one, five," underlining the hundreds digit sometimes helps. Examples:

$$\underline{4}15 \longrightarrow \text{"4 hundred 15"}$$
$$\underline{2}23 \longrightarrow \text{"2 hundred 23"}$$

Teachers might point out that the only new part is the first digit. Students already know how to read the rest. Provide a card for the child to move along, as in syllabicating, while reading the number. Illustrating each three-digit number with graph paper pieces, as above, also helps.

As students begin to work with four-digit numbers, more specialized techniques are sometimes necessary for those having the learning disabilities identified above. These techniques are outlined in the suggestions that follow.

Suggested Sequence of Activities and Exercises: Reading and Writing Four-Digit Numbers

Prerequisites

1. Ability to read and write three-digit numbers. This includes a firm grasp of place-value ideas for three-digit numbers, including the understanding that "when you hear hundreds, the number has three digits. Sometimes a zero is needed to show no tens or ones, as in 403 and 620."

2. Prior work modeling four-digit numbers with graph paper pieces (refer to Figure 2-43b).

Basic Sequence of Activities

1. **Look!** As a first step, present number pairs visually to the children (Figure 2-46). The thousands digit is green; others are red. Explain that one comma in a number is read "thousand." The only new part comes before the comma. "You already know how to read the rest." Have children finger trace the part that is the same within the pair, then read both numbers. Note:

   • Use no "0s" in the hundreds place at this time.

   • Do not use colored digits with children having closure difficulties. To do so activates their tendency to treat multidigit numbers as a series of disjoint, unrelated digits.

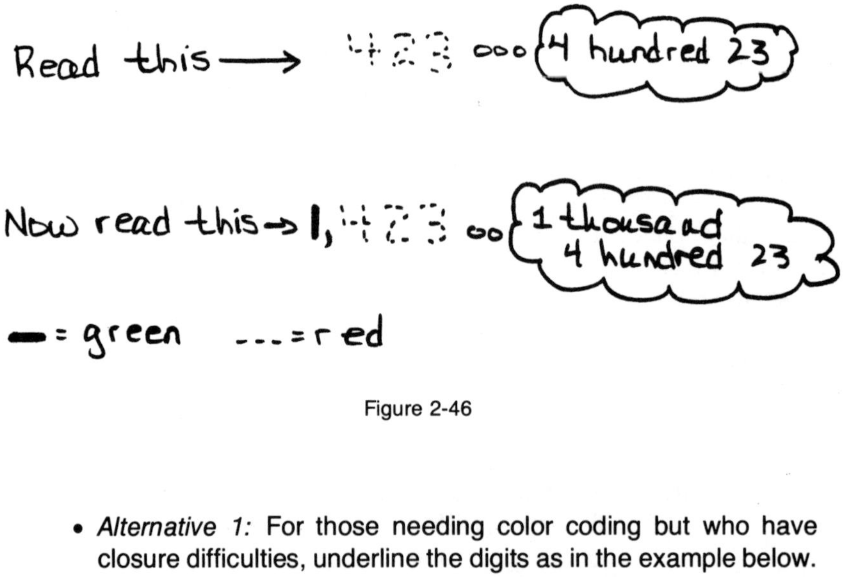

Read this ⟶   423 ooo (4 hundred 23)

Now read this ⟶ 1, 423 oo (1 thousand 4 hundred 23)

━ = green   --- = red

Figure 2-46

   • *Alternative 1:* For those needing color coding but who have closure difficulties, underline the digits as in the example below. Generally this can be used anytime and, except in severe cases, it works as effectively as color-coded digits. Example:

     Read this: 423

     Now read this: 1,423

   • *Alternative 2:* Use no colors at all. Have the child use a card as when learning to syllabicate (Figure 2-47).

Given
number:

1,423 → 1,☐ → 1,423 ☐ "

Figure 2-47

2. **Word match.** If the children can read number words, written practice exercises like those of Figure 2-48 can be given. The skill being reinforced is one that is used in check-writing. The exercise also prepares for the dictation of Activity 4 below. The number of thousands is written in green to match the green underscore of the thousands place. The three-digit part, both underscoring and words, is in red. The words *thousand* and *comma* are the same color, so that the children learn to associate the two. Later, when the children need to learn to place the comma themselves, the format can be modified as in the second example of Figure 2-48.

Example 1:

three thousand two hundred twenty-six —,------.
                        ↑
                       red

Example 2:

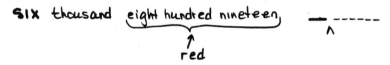

six thousand eight hundred nineteen, _ _____
                     ↑   ∧
                    red

Figure 2-48

3. **Find it.** Children match color-coded words (as in Figure 2-48) to noncolor-coded numbers. Follow-up: Same type of match exercises, but without colors.
4. **Hear and find.** Dictate four-digit numbers and have the children circle each from a given group of numbers. Include three-digit distractors on the sheet as well. At first, use color coding as above.

5. **Zero holds the place.** Dictate "seventy-three" and ask children to write the number on the dotted lines (Figure 2-49a). Discuss why the digits are placed in the last two spots. (No hundreds.) Explain that in a four-digit number, "0" is used to show no hundreds (Figure 2-49b). Present color-coded number pairs for children to read (the thousands digit green; others red). This time focus on four-digit numbers having "0" in the hundreds place.

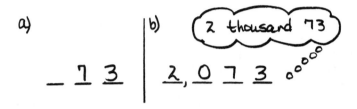

Figure 2-49

6. **Adapt** Activity 4 above to focus on four-digit numbers having "0" in the hundreds place. Include some numbers with no zeroes as well. When the exercise is complete, have the children read aloud the four-digit numbers they circled.

7. **Tape it to me.** Dictate four-digit numbers and have the children write them. Alternatively, have the children play a prerecorded tape that dictates the numbers. Responses can be checked against a key.

Extending the Basic Sequence: Reading and Writing Five- and Higher-Digit Numbers

Ideas from the above sequence can be adapted to help students read and write larger numbers. A card chart such as that illustrated in Figure 2-50 is also useful. Within each period, the child reads the familiar one-, two-, or three-digit number—*then* adds the "family" name (i.e. the name of the period). Except for students with closure difficulties, a green-black-red color coding of digits within each period can be used to emphasize this idea. The chart can later be extended and used for reading decimals.

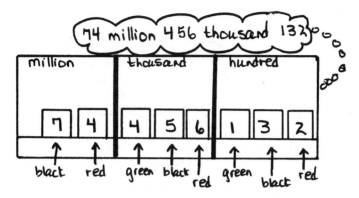

The vertical lines cue a student to give the name of the period.

Figure 2-50

COMPARING LARGER NUMBERS

Section 8

Problem area: Inability to compare multidigit numbers using greater than (>) and less than (<) symbols.

Typical disabilities affecting progress: Difficulties with abstract reasoning, visual discrimination, visual association, spatial organization, and visual memory.

Background: Several basic approaches for comparing numbers greater than 10 appear in elementary school mathematics textbooks. At first, children may be asked to represent the numbers with grouping aids and to match one-to-one as in Figure 2-51. The focus is on starting big, with the tens (hundreds) to compare. Many children with the disabilities identified above can understand comparison illustrated in this manner. Difficulties arise when materials are no longer used or the children are expected to use the less than and greater than symbols to express the comparison. Many of the students confuse the symbols or fail to associate any meaning with them. Some reverse the symbols when writing them. Others forget "which means which." Numberline models (e.g. Figure 2-52) sometimes help, unless a child has difficulty with the concepts *before* and *after*.

a)

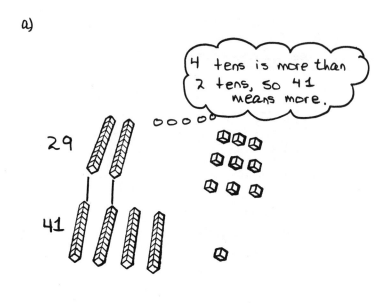

b)

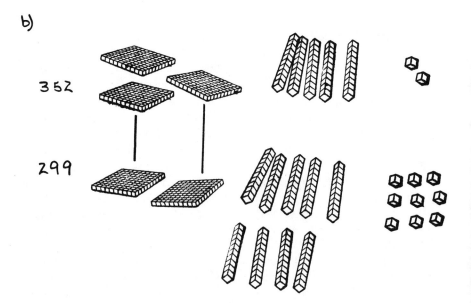

Figure 2-51

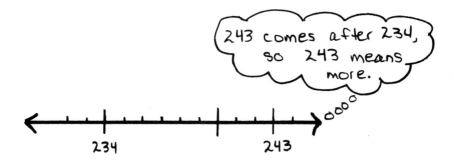

Figure 2-52

If the children study algebra in high school, an attempt must be made to help them to use correctly the symbols for number comparison. Otherwise one can forget the symbols and focus only on the basic idea: "Which means more?" As a daily living skill, this concept is a critical one. It enters into comparison shopping—determining whether one has enough money to buy what is needed—and a myriad of other common situations. The important point of the following sequence, then, is to help students to compare larger numbers even when materials are no longer used. The use of symbols is secondary and in some individual cases would be omitted.

Suggested Sequence of Activities and Exercises

Prerequisites

1. A strong grasp of place-value understanding for the numbers involved.
2. Prior work with grouping aids, as in Figure 2-49, for comparing two- and three-digit numbers.
3. Ability to use more/less to compare one-digit numbers.
4. Understanding the concepts of before and after.

Basic Sequence

1. **"Come after" means more.** Present two two- or three-digit numbers with *different* first digits as in Figure 2-53. Have the children use materials to represent each number (Figure 2-53b). Underscore the first digit of each number green and discuss how you always "start big" to compare. Be sure children understand that 32 means more than 24 (more tens). "Yes, 32 means more. It comes after 24 when you count." Repeat with other numbers.

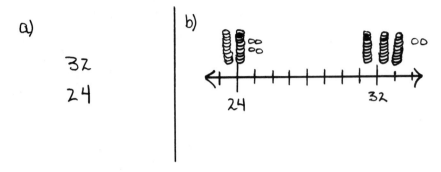

Figure 2-53

2. **Another look.** To reinforce the "more than" idea and to review the vocabulary "less." Use two two- or three-digit numbers as in Activity 1.

- Pose the situation where _____ and _____ (use names of people the children know) are reading the same book. Write two page numbers to indicate how far each has read. Have the children find these page numbers in a book. Who has read more pages? Underscore the first digit of the numbers to emphasize that you "start big" to compare. Using the example of Figure 2-54, you might have the children note how the number for more pages, 341, comes after 215: "215 pages is less by comparison." Place markers at each page, close the book, and have the children *feel* that 215 pages is less. Repeat with the other page numbers.

- If the children are strong in money concepts and skills, compare money amounts from catalogs. Use play money to represent each price. Discuss which of two given prices means more or less. Emphasize, using color underscores, that you "start big" to compare.

Figure 2-54

3. **Match and check.** Choose the one approach from Activities 1 and 2 above which seems to be effective with the individual or group. Use two- or three-digit numbers as in Activity 1.

- Write two numbers. Have the children copy them onto a worksheet illustration where they "belong." For example, the child is given 118 and 231. The child then writes the numbers into a book to show which means more and which means less, as in Figure 2-55. Discuss how 231 means more pages.

Figure 2-55

- Have each child cut out the worksheet illustrations and glue them on cards (Figure 2-56). Write just the two numbers (in random order) on the front of the cards. Underscore the first digits if necessary. The children should then use the deck by (1) studying the numbers on the front; (2) closing their eyes to imagine what the numbers would look like if pictured; (3) writing the number that means more and the number that means less; and (4) turning the card over to check, that is, comparing the shaded number with what they wrote.

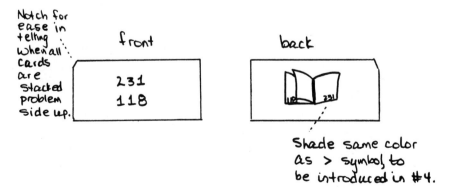

Figure 2-56

4. **Alligator Al.** Use auditory and tactile cues to help students attach meaning to the comparison symbols. For example, make an alligator hand puppet with the mouth clearly outlined. Use two different colors and textures, as illustrated in Figure 2-57a. Carry through the storyline that Alligator Al is always hungry and always reaches for the greatest number. Make a poster or file-card miniature of Al's two views available to students. Provide sandpaper and felt symbols for them to place between numbers as you show them how to position and read the symbols (Figure 2-57b). Use two two- or three-digit numbers with different first digits. Invite the children to finger trace the symbol while reading the comparison. For some number pairs, ask the children to retell Alligator Al's story (he always reaches for the greatest number). It is sometimes necessary to have children verbalize an association if they are to grasp and retain it.

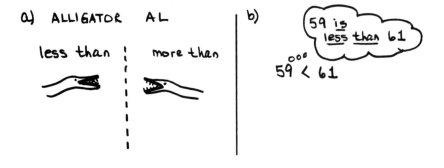

Figure 2-57

- *Follow up:* Prepare cards like those of Figure 2-58. Underscore the first digits of each number if necessary. Have the children copy the numbers and place or write the symbol that shows the comparison. They can then turn the card over to check. For students with visual perception, association, or memory difficulties, it may be necessary to provide a prerecorded tape, keyed alphabetically to the card labels. After the children quietly read each comparison, they can use the tape along with the back side of the card to check. In all cases, the hand puppet or poster/file card replication should be made available for reference.

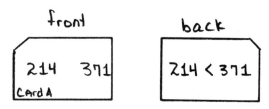

Figure 2-58

5. More comparisons

- Dictate two numbers, a two- and a three-digit number, for children to write on the dotted lines (Figure 2-59). Discuss why the two-digit number is placed on the last two lines (no hundreds). Write a dotted "0" in the hundreds place, if necessary, to help students with the comparison. Referring to Figure 2-59, you might note: "You always start big to compare. Here, "big" means hundreds. *1* hundred is more than *no* hundreds, so 132 is more than 53." Repeat with other numbers. Use worksheet exercises to reinforce. At this point, the children could simply circle to indicate which number means more (less). Note: Justifying digit placement and aligning digits one on top of the other, as in Figure 2-59, emphasizes the greater than/less than comparison.

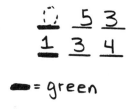

Figure 2-59

- Adapt the above activity to focus on two two- or three-digit numbers having first digits *alike* (e.g. 46, 49; 258, 262). "You always start big to compare. If the digits are alike, you compare the next two" (Figure 2-60).

- Use symbols to compare the numbers presented in the above activities. Adapt ideas from "Alligator Al" above.

- Provide mixed-review exercises that require students to use symbols for comparing all types of two- and three-digit numbers.

$$
\begin{array}{c}
2\ 5\ 8 \\
\infty\infty\ |\ \ |\ \ |\ \infty\infty \\
2\ 6\ 3
\end{array}
$$

The Same.

6 is greater than 5, so 262 means more.

Figure 2-60

USING A HAND CALCULATOR

Section 9

Exercises using a hand calculator can be designed to serve two purposes:

1. to reinforce basic number and numeration skills
2. to build visual and auditory memory skills

Since some learning disabled students have difficulty merely locating the numbers on a calculator, teachers will want to check for the following prerequisites before requiring its use:

- Prerequisite 1: the students can discriminate among the numerals on the calculator.

- Prerequisite 2: the students have sufficient eye-hand coordination to punch the correct key.

When these prerequisites are in hand, exercises such as the following can be carried out with the students.

- Example 1 (visual memory): Provide a list of numbers for the children to enter. For multidigit numbers, encourage them to look at, then punch, the *entire number* (or at least as many digits as they can).

- Example 2 (visual memory): Provide a list of number pairs. The children enter the greatest (least) of each pair, then check against a key.

- Example 3 (auditory memory): Dictate a number (or use a prerecorded tape for this purpose). Have the children punch in the number, then compare it with a key. Children with severe problems could be allowed to write the number before entering it in early phases of the activity.

- Example 4 (auditory memory): Dictate a number (or use a prerecorded tape for this purpose). Have the children enter the number after that given, then check with a key.

Reference

Rathmell, E., and Payne, J. Number and numeration. In J. Payne (Ed.), *Mathematics Learning in Early Childhood*. Reston, Virginia: National Council of Teachers of Mathematics, Inc., 1975.

Chapter 3

Money and Time

Even before they enter school, many children can discriminate among a penny, a nickel, and a dime. They may not always associate the right coin with the right name, but they usually will use one of the three names when referring to a coin. Most preschoolers also develop some sense of time and many even learn to tell time by the hour. They know dinner is at 6:00, when the ''little hand is on the six.''

If it's on the five, it's not dinner time.

Basic concepts and skills for money and time are formally introduced, reinforced, and expanded during the primary school years. Most mathematics programs relate early number work to the development of money and time skills. Usually by the end of first grade, children can tell time to the half hour, and most can recognize the difference between the five coins by name and value. Many can find the value of coin groups to 25 cents and make change for amounts up to 10 cents.

As children's base of experience and training broadens, most develop a feel for time that helps them know how long they have to complete an activity or wait for another to begin. Most children also develop a general sense of how much money is needed for particular items (''lots'' or ''a little''), what change is, and how long it will take to save money for something they want or need.

As children learn to handle larger amounts of money and to tell time more accurately, the vocabulary involved places greater demands on both receptive and expressive language skills. Children must now begin to deal with familiar words in new contexts. Expressions like ''ten minutes *ago*,'' ''*in* a half hour,'' ''*later*,'' and ''making *change*'' all include words that may be part of their vocabularies but are now presented in a different way. If children use one of these expressions, it must be more than a mere parroting of what others say. When a child says, ''I'll be there in 10 minutes,'' it must be said with real understanding.

As students progress through school, the demands to use time and money efficiently increase. By the time children reach the middle grades, they are expected to read time to the nearest minute and deal with larger money amounts. Older students in middle school or junior high are expected to count out money amounts and make change without relying on paper and pencil calculations. They also must learn to write checks and handle bank accounts—daily living skills of practical importance.

Children's success in mastering concepts and skills like these for money and time can be greatly hindered by learning disabilities they may have. Many of the tasks outlined in the preceding paragraphs require good visual and auditory memory, discrimination, and sequencing skills. To count money, for example, students must be able to discriminate between size differences and accurately retrieve from memory the correct name or value to match the size. To tell time from a standard clock, they must discriminate the size of the hands, retain part of a sequence while discriminating, and then associate each hand with the correct digit and its meaning. As children begin to use money and time on a daily basis, a high degree of visual and auditory memory, as well as visual and spatial discrimination, is involved.

This chapter addresses some of the more common problems learning disabled students face in the mastery of money and time skills. The first part of the chapter focuses on money. An introductory section suggests materials to keep in the classroom for use in teaching money. The remaining sections present ways of approaching the following five topics with learning disabled students:

1. coin discrimination
2. counting money amounts to $1.00 (using a quarter, rather than coin substitutes for the quarter, for amounts over $.25)
3. counting money amounts to $1.00 (using coin substitutes for the quarter for amounts over $.25)
4. paying for items and making change (for amounts to $1.00)
5. writing money amounts greater than $1.00.

The last part of the chapter deals with teaching time to learning disabled students. After an introductory section on classroom materials helpful for this purpose, ways of handling the following topics are explored:

- reading clock times
- reading *and* writing clock times
- naming the correct hour

- understanding the many ways to tell a time

- understanding and using temporal expressions

For each topic section, a basic sequence of activities and exercises is presented. Where necessary, alternate approaches for meeting the needs of particular disabilities are noted.

CLASSROOM MATERIALS FOR TEACHING MONEY

Concrete aids and real-life applications help children build and develop confidence with new concepts and skills. This principle is particularly important when teaching children how to handle money. The following materials are useful for this purpose.

- real money

- coin and paper money stamps

- several ink pads and bottles of colored ink

- laminated coin lines

- play money, including color coded coins

- dice games and other money activities

- practice pages (filed away, ready for use)

- empty food cans (labels on, lids cut out from the bottom) or other items for a play store

Real money should be used whenever possible, particularly in early activities. Keep a bag of change (locked when not in use). Experience has shown that even very young children can learn to handle money with care and not lose it. After all: "Money has *value*. We use it to buy what we need and want. People work hard to *earn* money. The coins in the bag belong to the teacher who has worked hard to get them, but who is loaning them out so we can learn about money." These are very basic concepts that are part of "money sense" for young learners.

As work progresses, real money should continue to be used whenever possible. At times, however, this is just not practical, and money substitutes must be introduced. When this is done, it is essential that the play money and pictures resemble real money as closely as possible. Learning disabled students, like many of their peers, find it difficult enough to relate money substitutes to real money.

Coin stamps, heads and tails, and paper money stamps are extremely useful money substitutes and can be purchased commercially from many school supply companies. Ink pads will be needed for the money stamps, but keep several on hand for use with different colors of ink. Color-coded coins can be very useful, especially when teaching or reinforcing coin discrimination.

Figure 3-1 is an example of a color-coded coin line that is easy to make, using either stamps and colored inks or colored paper. It can be laminated, covered with contact paper, or kept in a plastic holder. The following sections give details for using the coin line. Because of the color coding, it is particularly useful with children weak in visual figure-ground, discrimination, or other visual perception skills.

Although it takes time, play money can be made from the paper money and coin stamps. If this is done, teachers may want to color the pennies brown and the silver coins gray to make them more nearly resemble real coins. In addition, for children with visual perception or memory problems, color-coded coins can be made. Use the coin stamps and the same colors as for the coin line, only this time cut the shapes out. Children can use these when playing games, playing store, or for otherwise counting out money amounts. The use of these coins will serve to eliminate the interference of the learning deficit while building up overlearning.

There are many dice and other money games that can be played to reinforce money skills. A master copy of several types of coin die is provided in Figure 3-2. Ideas for using the dice are included in the sections that follow.

Throughout the chapter, various worksheet ideas will be illustrated that can be made up and kept on file. These are useful for homework, learning centers, and extra reinforcement of specific skills.

COIN DISCRIMINATION

Problem area: Inability to discriminate coins by name and value.

Typical disabilities affecting progress: Difficulty with visual disrimination, receptive and expressive language, figure-ground, and auditory memory.

Background: Very young children, preschool to about age six, often have a hard time discriminating fine differences in size. They readily see gross differences such as that between the size of a dinner plate and a quarter. But they may not be developmentally ready to do much more than to order coins by size with the aid of finger tracing or matching one on top of the other.

Yet, with continual exposure, most primary grade children gradually learn to distinguish the coins. They begin to look more closely at coins, to study them and

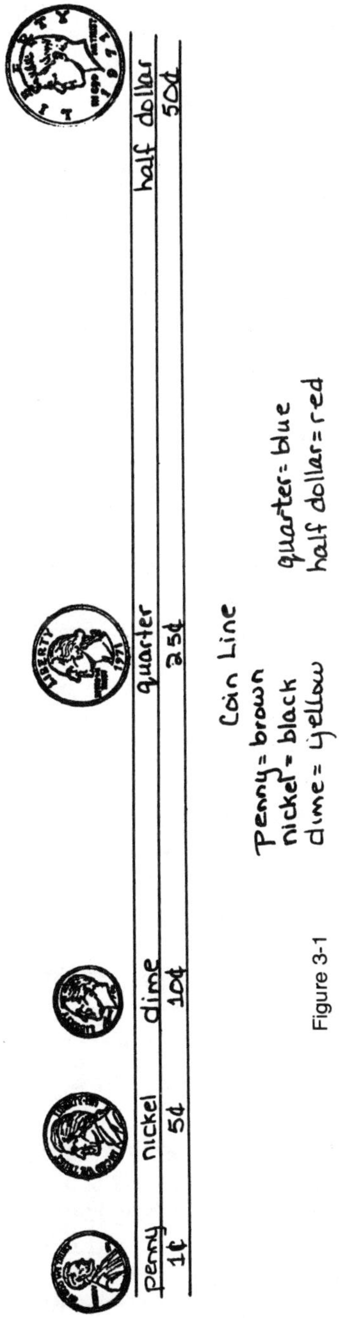
penny
1¢
nickel
5¢
dime
10¢
quarter
25¢
half dollar
50¢
Coin Line
penny = brown
nickel = black
dime = yellow
quarter = blue
half dollar = red

Figure 3-1

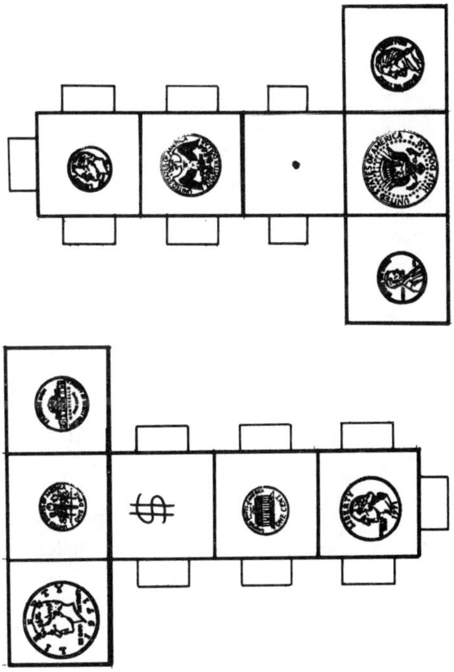
$

Figure 3-2

feel them. Their understanding of bigger and smaller may still be weak; they may have no "handle" to grasp when trying to determine the correct name. It often is meaningless or even confusing to say, "The bigger one is a nickel." What does bigger mean? How can it be bigger if the dime is worth ten cents and the nickel is worth five cents? Does bigger mean size or value? Through repeated experience, careful instruction, and developmental growth, however, the children learn to associate the correct name with the coin. By the time they are six or seven, most children can accurately match the coin with its name, and often with its value.

For children with disabilities like those listed above, however, the discrete differences and sequencing involved in discriminating coins preclude much chance of automatically making these associations. "Give me the nickel, Peter." A thoughtful analysis highlights the requirements and sequences involved in responding to this request:

- Receptively, the child must at least understand the meaning of the word "nickel."

- The child must be able to see that the coins are in fact different sizes.

- The child must be able to (1) revisualize a nickel or (2) tactually feel the difference between the nickel and the other coins.

- Once the image has been recalled, the child must be able to retain it long enough to associate it with the correct coin.

For most children, the above steps probably take about one or two seconds, once the process has been mastered. For the learning disabled child, the effort to comply with the request may end in total frustration, wild guesses, or refusal to answer. More specialized instruction, such as that outlined below, is needed. A general approach is presented that can be adapted to the school level at which a child is working. If one is dealing remedially with an older child, for example, then all five coins would be introduced, one at a time, in the manner suggested. In introducing the coins to younger children, however, greater care would be taken to correlate the work with the early number program. The quarter, for example, would be introduced only *after* children can meaningfully read and write two-digit numbers.

Suggested Sequence of Activities and Exercises

1. **Penny first.** The penny should be introduced first because it is more readily distinguished by its color. Show the children all five coins, but focus only on the penny. Let them pick it up and feel it. If they do not already know, tell them its name (penny). Discuss likes and differences between it and other coins in the pile. Emphasize color, size, pictures on the coin, and whether the edge is rough or smooth.

2. **Coin line.** Have the children place the penny on top of the penny pictured on the coin line. Get them to note how the size and color of the two coins are the same. Some children have difficulty relating a real coin to its picture, thus the need for care in early lessons to relate the two. If possible, allow the children to use a penny coin stamp on brown construction paper to make their own penny pictures.
3. **Penny line-up.** Give each child an envelope of coins (pennies and other silver coins). Have the children sort out all the pennies and place them under the penny of the coin line. Personal coin lines may be given to each child for this purpose.
4. **Penny match.** Give each child about 15 pennies. Use real coins if possible. If the group is so large that this is impractical, use the penny stamp on brown construction paper to make play coins for this purpose. Provide activity sheets like that of Figure 3-3 and instruct the children to cover each penny on the page with the one given them. "The penny pictures on the activity sheet are not colored, but they have the same picture and are the same size as the pennies you have. Can you find all of them?" If the page is covered correctly, the shape that is formed by the pennies should be the letter "P." Discuss how one makes the "P" sound when naming the penny.

   • *Variation :* For those children who learn kinesthetically, give tracing paper along with the activity sheet of Figure 3-3. Children should place (or tape) the tracing paper over the sheet. Then, using a penny or a stencil the shape and size of a penny, they can trace over each penny on the sheet. When finished, the shape formed by the tracing should be the letter "P."

5. **One penny is worth 1¢.** Discuss how money has value, since we use it to buy what we need and want. Introduce the cent sign. Explain that a number with a cent sign (¢) means that the number stands for an amount of money. The value of a penny is 1¢. Write on the board: 1 penny = 1¢. (Use "1 penny ⟶ 1¢" if children do not understand the equal sign.) Give each student about 10 pennies. Pose questions and carry out activities like the following:

   • Have everyone put four pennies in a pile in front of him. "How many cents do you have there?" . . . "Put 2¢ in a pile in front of you. How many pennies do you have?"

   • "Suppose I wanted to trade with you. If I gave you three pennies, how many cents would you give me so we'd have a fair trade?"

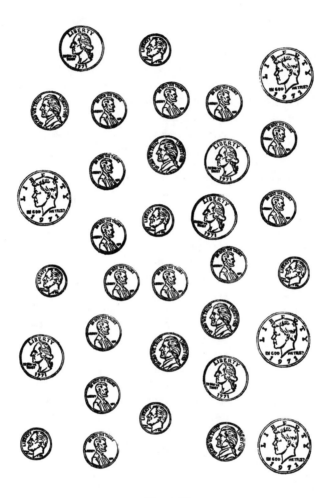

Figure 3-3

- "If you give me 5¢ and I give you four pennies back, is that a fair trade?"

- "Suppose you are at a store and want to buy this gum. Look at the price tag (5¢). How many pennies do you need to pay the cashier?"

Continue until children recognize and understand the meaning of cent in relation to pennies.

6. **What coin next?** Use activities similar to those above for presenting other coins. The normal introduction of the coins, in order, is: penny, nickel, dime, quarter, half dollar. If a child has difficulty with discrimination or size perception, a better sequence would be penny, *quarter,* nickel, dime, half dollar. In our experience, this has proved easier because of the greater difference in size between the penny and quarter. Even when size perception is no problem, we tend to deviate from the standard sequence. After the penny and nickel, we introduce the quarter. Not only is its value bigger, but its size as well.

7. **Size it up.** As the coins are introduced, provide reinforcement pages, like that of Figure 3-4, which are color coded to match the coin line. The purpose of these pages is to help the children respond to size differences in the coins. Such pages also emphasize the value of each coin. Initially children match the colored paper coins with the circles. Then these coins are replaced with real coins. Gradually the color cues are eliminated entirely. Children can be asked to name the coins they have placed on the sheet.

Cover the circles with the right coin.

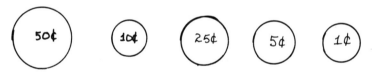

50¢   10¢   25¢   5¢   1¢

Coin outlines and values match
colors on Coin Line (Figure 3-1)

Figure 3-4

8. **Bingo.** For those children with language deficits, a bingo game is a useful and fun way to build up a weakness while using a possible strength, that of visual perception. The calling cards, the markers, the pictures on the bingo cards, or the space beneath each picture on the cards can be color coded to match the coin line colors if necessary. The space below each coin picture in Figure 3-5 is where a child would place the correct word or value when it is called. The calling cards (Figure 3-6) have the name of the coin on one side and both the coin and the name on the other. The coin picture clue helps the student to know what to call the coin. The winner is the child who covers a row in any direction—down, across, or diagonally.

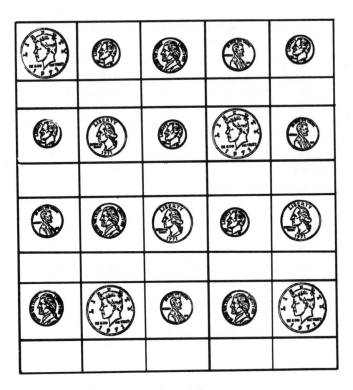

Figure 3-5

Calling Card: Side 1

Calling Card: Side 2

Figure 3-6

- *Variation:* Instead of writing the names of coins on the calling cards, write coin values. Children then cover the coin that matches the value called. For example, if 10¢ is called, children would place a 10¢ marker beneath a picture of a dime.

COUNTING MONEY AMOUNTS TO ONE DOLLAR USING QUARTERS

Problem area: Inability to find the value of a group of coins in which quarters rather than quarter coin substitutes are used.

Typical disabilities affecting progress: Difficulty with expressive language; sequential memory; visual perception, particularly figure ground; and closure.

Background: Once coin recognition and basic values of coins have been established, most children begin to learn to find the values of groups of coins. Early work starts with values to 10 cents and gradually extends to the counting of money amounts to one dollar. At the same time they are finding the values of various coin groups, children must start realizing the difference between quantity and value. There may be fewer coins than the actual cent value. It also is helpful at this point if children learn to recognize the value of some coin groups by sight. While it is not necessary, for example, that children immediately relate to two nickels as "10¢," the ability to do so does make the handling of money easier and more efficient. As children encounter larger groups of coins, they then can count on from the value of a small, known group within the larger collection of coins. A child's ability to do so often hinges upon being able to apply skip counting by 2s, 5s, or 10s to money situations and to *count on* by 2s, 5s, or 10s from various starting points. Learning disabled children having the difficulties identified above may be unable to use their skip-counting skills in this way. They may not recognize what pattern to use or when to switch from one pattern to another. The activities below give ideas for helping children cope with these problems. The following prerequisites are assumed:

- The children can recognize a number pattern as one which involves skip counting by 2s, 5s, or 10s.

- When dealing with numbers alone apart from money, the children can *continue* a skip-counting pattern that has been started.

- The children have been introduced to "switch" skip counting (e.g. they can start counting by 5s, then continue counting by 10s, or vice versa). An example of a written pattern finding exercise that reinforces this skill is illustrated in Figure 3-7.

- The children can recognize the following substitutions: two nickels for a dime, five pennies for a nickel, two quarters for a half dollar, three quarters for seventy-five cents, and four quarters for one dollar. Automatic recognition of these coin equivalents is desirable. An example showing how to use

25   30 35 __ __ __ 60   70 __ __

20   30 40 __ __ __ 75 80 85 __ __

Sample number sequence to reinforce switch
skip counting

Figure 3-7

tailed coins on a money line to reinforce the relation of coin equivalents is shown in Figure 3-8. Laid end to end, it takes *two* nickels to equal (the length of) the dime. Coin ''tails'' are made from masking tape, attached to the coin, then folded lengthwise in half. Tails can be colored to match the colors of the coins on the coin line.

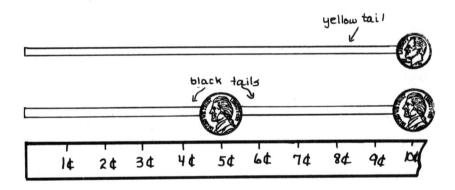

yellow tail

black tails

| 1¢ | 2¢ | 3¢ | 4¢ | 5¢ | 6¢ | 7¢ | 8¢ | 9¢ | 10¢ |

Figure 3-8

Suggested Sequence of Activities and Exercises

1. **Count it out.** Keep dittos such as that illustrated in Figure 3-9. Each line should be a different color. Use colored dittos or give the child four crayons, each clearly different in color from the others but including a green and a red. The child underlines each row of words with a different color but begins with the green and ends with the red. Next, give the children a shape stencil like that shown in Figure 3-10. The four shapes should be outlined to match, respectively, the colors of the four rows of Figure 3-9. Given a group of coins, the children place them inside the shapes in an appropriate se-

I have ＿＿.
Now I have ＿＿.
Now I have ＿＿.
Now I have ＿＿.

I have ＿＿.
Now I have ＿＿.
Now I have ＿＿.
Now I have ＿＿.

Figure 3-9

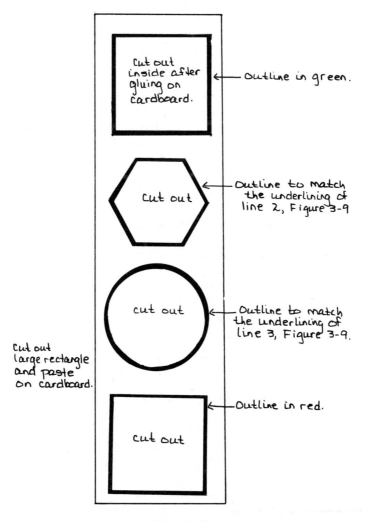

Figure 3-10

quence—greatest valued coins first, pennies last. This step will initially require teacher assistance. After grouping the coins, the child fills in the blanks on the sheet. As each blank is filled, the child should be instructed to read the entire sentence aloud before filling in the next blank. For children with closure difficulties who have trouble finding starting points and continuing patterns, the colors provide the needed cues. For those who have trouble expressing thoughts or retaining a sequence, verbalizing the words "I have. . . ." helps focus attention and initiate the thought process. The colors will help maintain the sequence.

2. **"Switch" skip counting.** Finding the value of coin groups can be difficult because of the "switch" skip counting involved. Due to integrative processing deficits or perseveration, the student may be unable to switch from one counting pattern to another as is often required when using money. Consider the coin group of Figure 3-11. One possible way to organize the counting is shown in Figure 3-12. Of course there are others. The important point is that there are three counting patterns involved: fives, tens and ones. To help develop the needed counting skills, keep charts such as that of Figure 3-13. Insert the charts into plastic holders and give the children grease pencils to use with the holder. Have them put a large X in any two squares in each row. Instruct them to write into the empty box the money value obtained after counting the coins to the left *and* above the empty space. If fine motor coordination is a problem, eliminate the writing (your goal is to develop switch counting, not writing). Have the children place chips, with the correct value written on them, in the empty spaces. When the card is filled in, the children can use an answer key to grade it, or the teacher or another student can check it. Children then can read the entire sequence aloud. Examples (refer to figure 3-13):

Row 1: 25-27¢.
Row 2: 10-15-25¢

- *Follow-up:* Counting money basically requires good auditory processing and visual, auditory, and sequential memory. Writing values down as one counts is a technique to aid learning, but eventually one has to be able to add coin values mentally. With this in mind, the next step in the activity above would be to have the children cover two squares in each row as before. Instead of writing the total value obtained, however, the children should count the entire sequence aloud to the teacher or a friend, or into a tape recorder.

Figure 3-11

Figure 3-12

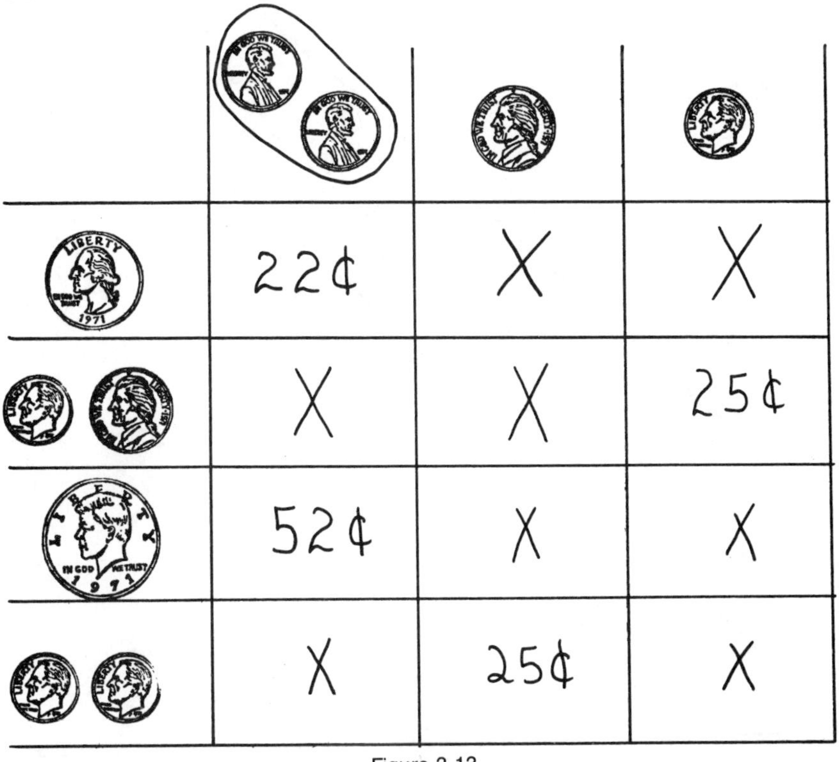

	22¢	X	X
	X	X	25¢
	52¢	X	X
	X	25¢	X

Figure 3-13

3. **Money line** (alternate approach). Another approach for helping students count to find the value of a group of coins is to use tailed coins on a money line. In Figure 3-14a, for example, the child is given one quarter, one nickel, two dimes, and one penny to count. Tailed coins for each of these coins are chosen and laid end to end on the money line, greatest valued coins first (Figure 3-14b). Figure 3-15 illustrates the use of the money line by building or reinforcing skills for "switch" skip counting. The children can practice with the tailed coins or refer to them as necessary until they master the technique using real coins.

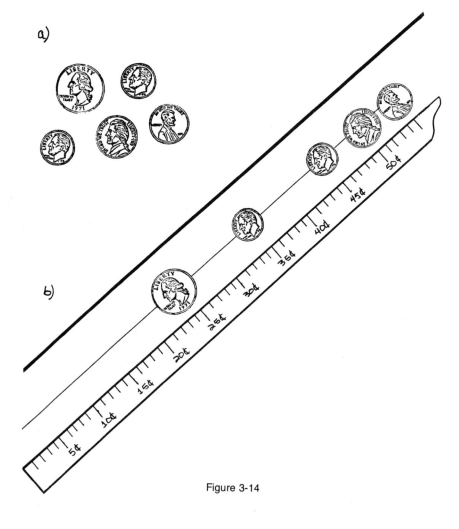

Figure 3-14

Figure 3-15

COUNTING MONEY AMOUNTS TO ONE DOLLAR USING QUARTER COIN SUBSTITUTES

MONEY
Section
4

Problem area: Difficulty finding the value of a group of coins in which a cluster of coins equivalent to the quarter rather than a quarter itself is used.

Typical disabilities affecting progress: Difficulty with integrative processing and closure.

Background: Using different combinations of coins, there are many ways to make amounts like 76¢ or 63¢. Children must learn to recognize various equivalent coin combinations, and this is usually harder for larger amounts, 50¢ to one dollar. The group of coins in Figure 3-16 is representative of a coin substitution that is frequently used. Most children, after a fair amount of experience counting coins, automatically recognize the two dimes and one nickel as being worth twenty-five cents. The learning disabled child may well recognize this, too. Unfortunately, there may not be an automatic transfer in thought to "a quarter— therefore the value of this group is fifty cents, because two quarters make fifty cents."

Figure 3-16

One approach to the problem would be to teach children to try grouping the coins differently and finding another counting pattern. They could, for example, begin with the single coin that is worth the most money. However, for most older children, it is more expedient to recognize the substitution and be able to use it. The following activities can be used to help develop this skill.

Suggested Activities and Exercises

1. **The odd pieces.** Younger children enjoy puzzles. Those shown in Figure 3-17 can be cut out, pasted on 3 × 5 index cards and used for individual activities in a learning center. Note the circling to cue

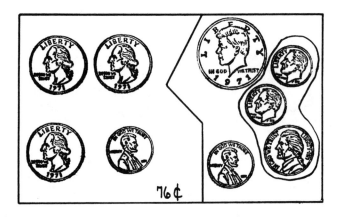

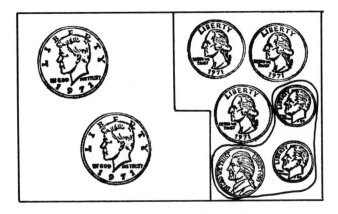

Figure 3-17

recognition of the three coins as one unit, equivalent in value to a quarter. Include one or two distractors in the puzzle set, like that shown in Figure 3-18, to force thinking. Children could be challenged to find the odd pieces (the distractors).

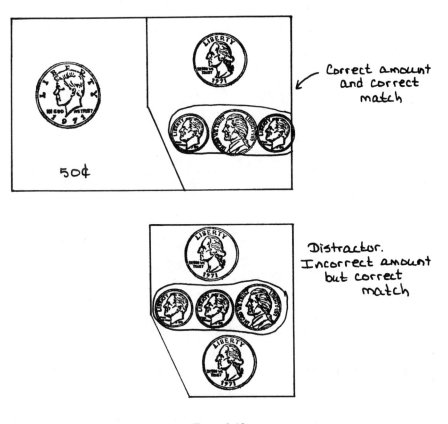

Correct amount
and correct
match

Distractor.
Incorrect amount
but correct
match

Figure 3-18

2. **Bingo.** Bingo cards, similar to those in Figure 3-5, can be made. The calling cards would have coins pictured on them like those on the right of the Figure 3-17 puzzle pieces. The game is played as a regular Bingo game.
3. **Fill in.** For older children, keep dittos such as those in Figure 3-19. Figure 3-19a is especially helpful for students with expressive language deficits. Gradually the transition can be made to pages like that of Figure 3-19b.

a)

50¢ = ___ dimes ___ nickels and ___ quarter

75¢ = ___ quarters ___ dimes and ___ nickels

75¢ = ___ half dollar ___ dimes and ___ nickel

___ ___ ___ ___ ___ ___ ___ ___ ___ ___ ___

b)

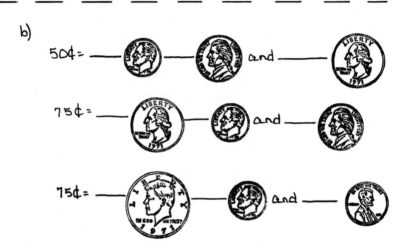

Figure 3-19

PAYING FOR ITEMS AND MAKING CHANGE FOR AMOUNTS TO ONE DOLLAR

Problem areas: Difficulty in selecting, from a larger collection of coins, money needed to pay for an item; difficulty making change for values to one dollar.

Typical disabilities affecting progress: Difficulty with auditory sequencing, integrative processing, closure, sequential memory, visual figure-ground.

Background: Being able to count and tell the value of a group of coins is a prerequisite to a more challenging skill: being able to select, from a larger collection, those coins needed to make a given amount. This latter skill is typically needed in day-to-day situations, when one examines the coins in a purse or pocket to see if there is enough to pay for an item. Some learning disabled students cannot transfer the first skill to its application in the second. Children with figure-ground difficulties often have problems finding the coins they want because they cannot sort them out from the group. Other children may be easily frustrated because the simplest (most familiar) way of making a given amount is not possible with the coins they have. The first set of activities below suggests ways of handling these problems.

The other activities of this section focus on another important skill—that of checking change received. Modern cash registers subtract the cost from the amount given a clerk, telling how much change should be given in return. The most efficient way to check in this situation is to *count up* from the cost until the amount paid is reached. This, of course, is the usual procedure used by cashiers for giving change if their registers do not internally subtract and display the amount to be given back.

Learning to count out one's change in this way is perhaps the most difficult money skill to master. Children must realize that the *exact* amount of money needed to pay for an item is not always available. Sometimes one has to pay *more* than an item is worth, and then receive change in return. To actually determine the amount of money to be given (or received) as change, a new counting process is required. When counting to find the value of a group of coins, children often start with the single coin of *greatest* value. It is now necessary to retain the purchase price in memory and count on from this cost using *smaller* valued coins first. Other coins are then added until the amount paid is reached. Children with sequential memory problems usually find this very difficult. Other children having the disabilities identified above may fail to recognize the different skip-counting patterns involved or be unable to produce them automatically. The second set of activities below has proved helpful in dealing with these problems.

Suggested Activities and Exercises

Paying for an Item

1. **You find.** Some students with figure-ground difficulties cannot find, from a larger collection, the coins they need to pay for an item. For these students, keep laminated cards and priced items such as those of Figure 3-20. The cards show the coins available to a child to pay for an item. The child draws a card and takes (from a bank of extra coins) all the coins pictured on the card. If necessary, allow the child to place coins on top of those pictured until the card is full. These coins are then placed in a separate pile. Next show the child a picture of an item to be purchased, such as the bat in the first

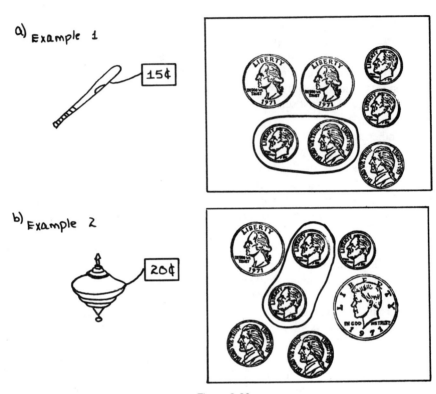

a) Example 1

15¢

b) Example 2

20¢

Figure 3-20

example of Figure 3-20. With a grease pencil draw a circle around the coins on the child's card that are needed to pay for that item. "You need a dime and a nickel." (Figure 3-20a) Instruct the child to select coins from the pile to cover those circled on the card. Repeat, using different cards or different items for the purchase. The children themselves gradually are able to circle and tell the needed coins. As they become more proficient, the circling can be eliminated and the children can merely cover the proper cards. In our experience, this approach leads to independent recognition of needed coins.

2. **Pay.** Set up a "store" in the classroom and give each child a purse or envelope of coins. (Alternatively, a container of coins could be placed on the cashier's counter for all the children to use.) At first, as students pay for items, accept any coins they give to pay for an item (as long as the amount given is correct). For example, a child may choose to use two nickels rather than a dime. By observing a child's pattern of selection, the teacher can gradually suggest better

choices, in a manner that is logical to that student. One might provide enough coins so that a child can pay for a given item in at least two ways. If the child uses the *fewest possible coins* to pay for an item, a compliment is in order. If a combination is given that involves more coins than is necessary, point out that there is a better way. "Yes, you have a dime and five pennies to equal 15¢. That is good, but did you notice that you can use one nickel in place of these five pennies?" Or, "You used six coins. Can you pay using only two coins?"

- *Follow-up:* Use worksheets such as that illustrated in Figure 3-21. If necessary, use the coin line color to outline the circles on the page. Gradually this prompt would be eliminated.

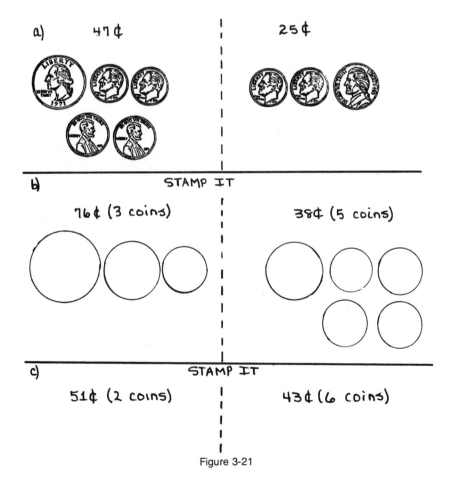

Figure 3-21

3. **Use what you have.** Point out that sometimes you do not have the proper coins to pay the way you would like. For example, one might want to buy ice cream that costs 25¢. If a person does not have a quarter, then two dimes and a nickel, or five nickels, or even twenty-five pennies would do. Give the student several coins and ask for an amount of money that cannot be made in the "usual way" with the coins given. For example, give five nickels and ask for 20¢. As children become more proficient, give a quarter, five nickels, and four pennies for this task to force selection from a larger group of coins.

- *Follow-up:* Use worksheets like that of Figure 3-22. For the example shown, the children can circle or place real coins on those pictured to show 20¢. If necessary, one could use coin line colors to outline the coins needed in the first few exercises.

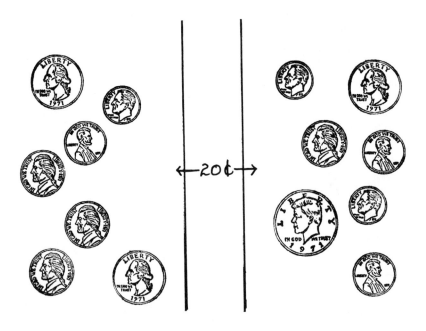

Figure 3-22

Making Change for Amounts Paid up to One Dollar

1. **Count up.** Use tailed coins on a money line, as in Figure 3-23, to introduce the idea of counting up to get from one number (the cost) to another (the amount paid). This approach concretizes the process of counting up and aids visual memory. A set of price tag cards, like that shown, is also needed. Children draw a card and place it on the line as illustrated to indicate where one starts the count. Tailed coins are then used to dramatize the counting on to 25¢. Children should be encouraged to use *as few coins as possible*—four pennies and one nickel rather than nine pennies in this example.

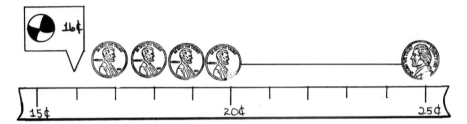

Figure 3-23

2. **Go and stop.** Students with auditory sequencing or memory deficits usually find it easier to turn at this point to worksheets such as that illustrated in Figure 3-24. The first example is for younger children with a lower reading vocabulary. The second is its parallel for older students. The children fill in the first four blanks. Then, as they *count up* from the cost, they check each coin as if they were actually picking it up. They next count and record the change—in this example, 9¢.

   To cue meaning, the words "go on" ("begin at") could be written in green and "stop at" in red. For those in need of extra cueing, the word "cost" ("price") could also be coded green, the words "you give" ("amount given") could be coded red. Answer lines would be colored to match the words. Gradually all colors would be eliminated as the vocabulary meanings and the counting process itself become internalized. The amount of information to be personally recorded by students is also gradually lessened as they become more proficient in counting. Recording the numbers to "go on" and "stop at" are first to be dropped. As short-term memory or counting skills improve, the price and the amount given might also be eliminated.

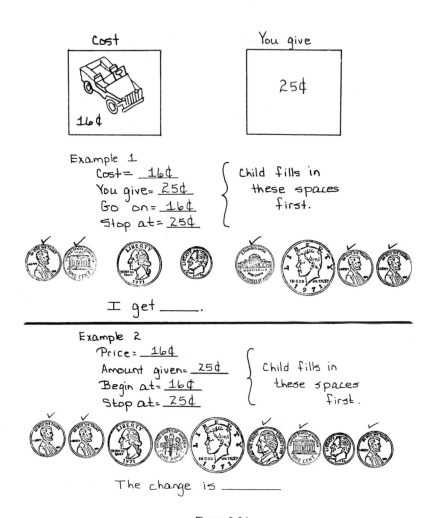

Figure 3-24

3. **Real coins now.** As above, but provide real coins rather than stamped pictures of coins. At first, it may be helpful to keep a worksheet showing the coin stamps as reference. If children tend to perseverate, do not be too quick to eliminate the writing while using real coins. It serves to break the counting and hence decreases the perseveration.

   • *Note:* Children with integrative processing deficits may have difficulty recognizing whether or not they have the correct coins to pay exactly or to make the needed change. They may try to force the issue, as in Figure 3-25. In this example, the value of the dimes became meaningless and they were treated as pennies. To help, have the children first fill in the charts of activity 2 above. Then have them compare the coins they checked with the coins they have. In the example of Figure 3-25, the first coin needed is a penny so the child cannot give the needed change.

Price = __16¢__
Amount given = __25¢__

{ Coins child has
to choose
from

"16¢ .... 17¢ 18¢ — 19¢ — 20¢ — 25¢

The change is __9¢__.

Figure 3-25

WRITING MONEY AMOUNTS GREATER THAN ONE DOLLAR

MONEY
Section
6

Problem area: Reversal tendencies or other difficulties in writing money amounts using the dollar sign and decimal point.

Typical disabilities affecting progress: Difficulty with spatial organization; visual perception.

Background: Children who are unable to organize their space either due to visual or perceptual deficits or spatial disorganization may have considerable difficulty writing down money values. For example, since one says, *"Three dollars* and sixteen cents,"* children often tend to reverse the position of the value and the dollar sign (see Figure 3-26). Or they may not associate all the words with symbols. Specifically, they may not "see" the dollar sign and decimal point when reading or writing the numbers. The activities outlined below are directed toward helping students with these problems.

Three dollars and sixteen cents = 3$.16

Figure 3-26

Suggested Sequence of Activities and Exercises

1. **Dollar sign.** For those who have reversal tendencies, it often helps
   to approach the problem in small steps. If children learn well through
   kinesthetic involvement, have them finger trace felt numerals and
   symbols, *dollar value first, then the sign.* Then have them rewrite
   the pattern traced—*dollar value first, then the sign.* Although this is
   an unusual order, it provides a more immediate association between words and symbols. Each time a word is said, something is
   written. The more traditional way requires the student to write one
   symbol ($) while saying or thinking an unrelated symbol (e.g. 4).
   Figure 3-27 shows a sample page that might be used as a follow-up
   to this exercise. First, in Step 1, the children finger trace examples

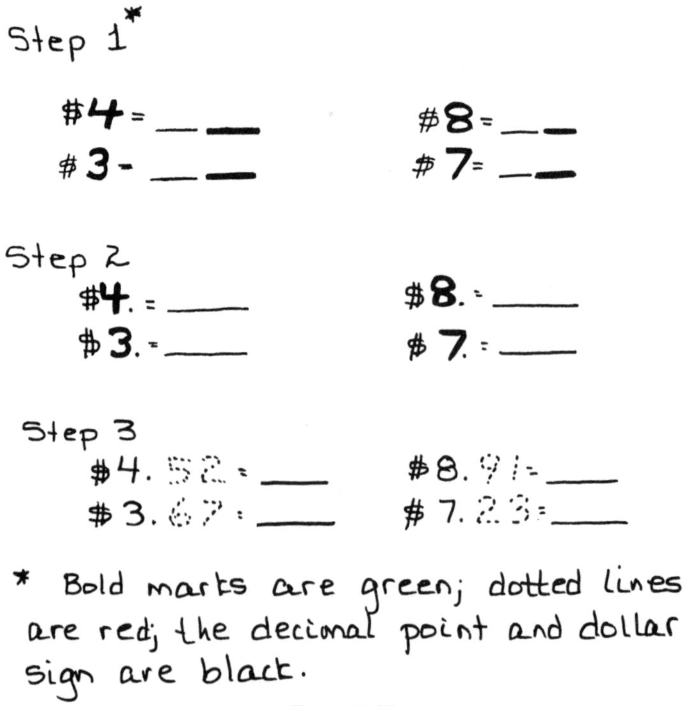

Step 1*

$4 = __ __ $8 = __ __
$3 - __ __ $7 = __ __

Step 2
$4. = __ $8. = __
$3. = __ $7. = __

Step 3
$4. 52 = __ $8. 91 = __
$3. 67 = __ $7. 23 = __

* Bold marks are green; dotted lines
are red; the decimal point and dollar
sign are black.

Figure 3-27

and write four dollars ($4) as described above. In Step 2 the decimal point is introduced and associated with the word "and." The last step is to include the number of cents. All three steps provide room (after the "equals" sign on the worksheet) for children to write the money amount independently.

2. **Greatest value.** This is a practice activity for two or three to play. Provide the following five dice:

   - Die 1: "$" written on each of the six sides
   - Die 2: "." written on each of the six sides
   - Die 3: 0, 1, 2, 3, 4, 5
   - Die 4: 0, 5, 6, 7, 8, 9
   - Die 5: 3, 4, 5, 6, 7, 8

   Also provide a five-space chart for the dice (see Figure 3-28a) and a "greatest-value" record sheet for each player (Figure 3-28b). In turn, the children throw the dice and arrange them in the five spaces of the chart to show the greatest dollar value possible. If the amount is written and read (aloud) correctly, it is entered on the player's record sheet for that round. The player with the greatest total after four rounds wins.

   - *Note 1:* Using grease pencils or washable markers on the laminated record sheet makes for easy reuse by players.
   Note 2: If the column addition is too hard for the students at this time, use a tally system: one tally for dollar values $3.00 or less, two tallies for dollar values between $3.00 and $6.00, and three tallies for dollar values of $6.00 or greater.

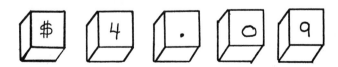

Figure 3-28a

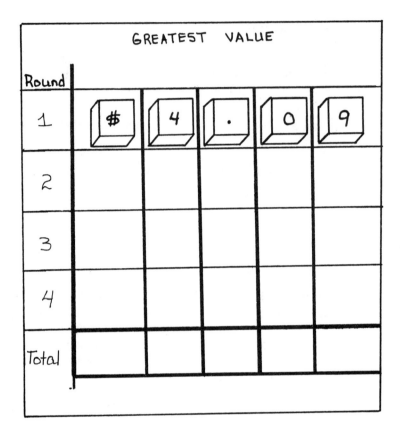

Figure 3-28b

3. **Follow-up.** For additional drill, keep pages on file like that of Figure 3-29. Children read, then write the given dollar value. If reading is a problem, a cassette tape for the left part of the page can be prepared for the children to use while completing the page. The color coding, important in early work, can gradually be eliminated.

   • *Note 1:* For some students, it may be preferable to have them write the dollar value first, *then* the sign, as explained in Activity 1, above.
   Note 2: Being able to read and write number words is important for checkwriting, thus worth the practice focused upon in this exercise.

1) <u>Four</u> <u>dollars</u> <u>and</u> <u>sixteen</u> cents = $\_\_ \_\_ \_ \_$
  ↑   ↑   ↑   ↑   ↗ ↑ ↑ ↖
Color #2   green   color #3   red   green #2 #3 red

2) <u>Seven</u> <u>dollars</u> <u>and</u> <u>twenty five</u> cents = $\_\_ \_\_ \_ \_$
   ↑   ↑   ↑   ↑   ↗ ↑ ↑ ↖
 Color #2   green   color #3   red   green #2 #3 red

Figure 3-29

CLASSROOM MATERIALS FOR TEACHING TIME

Most classrooms have a wall clock and perhaps a toy clock for the children to use. However, except for workbook pages, there may be little else in the room that is realistically related to teaching time. There are, however, several items that teachers can make available to students that would greatly aid them in acquiring time concepts and skills:

- a small clock, about four inches in diameter

- a geared clock with a knob on the back to move the hands (the hands should be clearly different in size)

- clock stamps and ink pads (one red, one green)

The small clock will be useful for those children with visual discrimination or other perceptual problems. These students may have difficulty with the wall clock simply because it is too far away for them to make any clear discriminations. Figure 3-30 gives an example of the size and face of the smaller clock. The size of the hands is clearly different and the minute intervals are spaced far enough apart for the child to point with a finger or a pencil. The student can use this type of clock to ''feel'' the time. This kinesthetic approach is often necessary for children with visual perception or spatial difficulties.

Since it is impractical to teach time only on a real clock, a geared clock provides the next best aid. Children can see how the hands move at different rates. They can actually ''feel'' the slowness of the hour hand movement in contrast to that of the minute hand.

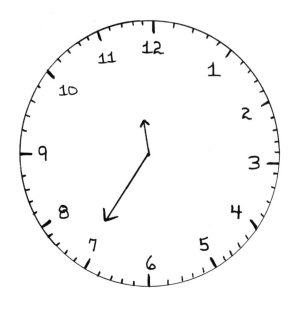

Figure 3-30

As digital clocks are so common, it is essential that children learn to read them. Most mathematics curriculums now include them within their chapters on time. Once children can read the numbers on a digital clock, they can be helped to make associations with the standard clock. One can actually place a digital clock next to a standard clock as an aid for "reading" its time.

At this point it may be appropriate to give a word of caution regarding digital clocks. As convenient and useful as they are for teaching children to tell time, they do not help develop a *sense of time*. It is questionable, at best, whether this sense can be taught at all. The movement of time is mysterious enough, and digital clocks only reinforce the magical occurrence. At least with a standard clock, there is some concrete way for children to begin to get a feel for how long an activity will last. One can, for example, use the overlay and shading technique of Figure 3-31 to illustrate the time allotted to an activity. On a digital clock this would be impossible.

To help with this and other aspects of telling time, there are clock stamps available commercially that should be standard materials for every classroom. They can easily be used by both teacher and student. When drawing in the hands, one should be careful to distinguish clearly between the lengths of the minute and the hour hands. Figure 3-32 illustrates the type of clock stamp we have found most useful.

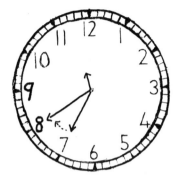

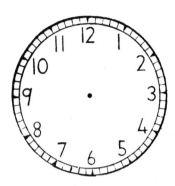

Figure 3-32

Plastic overlay put over clock
with the amount of twelfths
colored in to show time.

Figure 3-31

The sections that follow suggest ways of using each of these materials to help learning disabled students develop important time concepts and skills. In addition, several workpages are illustrated that can be kept on file and pulled for reinforcement, homework, and other independent work.

READING CLOCK TIMES

TIME
Section
2

Problem area: Difficulty associating the correct hand on a standard clock with the spoken or written word.

Typical disabilities affecting progress: Difficulty with visual discrimination, visual sequential memory, short-term memory, visual memory, expressive language.

Background: As mentioned earlier, many children develop some comprehension of time before they enter school. It is not uncommon for young children to be up earlier on school days than on weekends. Once the routine of going to school has been established, their internal clock begins to plan accordingly. They do not automatically begin dressing for school on Saturday. They may not know why they do not have to, but there is a sense that something is different.

Gradually parents' words begin to have meaning, and on school days children understand that at 8:00 it's time to leave. They may not actually tell time, but if a parent says, "In five minutes it will be eight o'clock," the child understands. Later the clock becomes more meaningful and the child thinks, ''The little hand is on the 8. It must be time to go to school.''

In the primary grades, intuitive understandings such as these are formally developed. While there are several sequences that can be used, one of the more common for teaching a child to read time from a standard clock is the following sequence:

- time by the hour (e.g. 2:00)

- time by the half hour (e.g. 2:30)

- time by the quarter hour (e.g. 2:15 or 2:45)

- time by five-minute intervals (e.g. 2:25 or 2:40)

- time by minute intervals (e.g. 2:26 or 2:41)

For most children the above sequence works well. When teaching time on the hour, many teachers simplify the clock as in Figure 3-33a. Using a clock with only an hour hand makes it possible for most children to ''tell time'' as soon as they can read the numerals 1 to 12. The child can relate this one-handed clock to a spinner and ''read time'' by telling the number the hand is closest to. When children can tell time to the nearest hour in this way, then teachers can point out the hour hand on a *two-handed clock*. The next step is to practice telling time on this type of clock by focusing on the hour hand as in Figure 3-33b. If necessary in early work with the two-handed clock, children could be instructed to cover the minute hand.

When children can read and write two-digit numbers, the spinner idea can be reintroduced for reading minutes (Figure 3-33c). Now the child tells time more precisely by reading the ''hour'' then the ''minute'' spinner. Gradually the association between the minutes and the twelve clock digits can be made. Additional experiences with a geared clock can help the children to see that as the hour hand moves from one hour to the next, the minute hand travels all the way around the clock.

Children with good visual perception and long-term memories quickly learn to associate what one says for given configurations of the hands. For example, ''The little hand is just past the 3 and the big hand is on the 2—that's 3:10.''

The normal approach, critical for students with memory difficulties, is to learn to count by fives and relate this to reading the minute spinner. This approach provides a logical framework for reading minutes and aids recall when memory fails. When the half and quarter hour times (e.g. 2:15, 2:30, 2:45) are emphasized first, then most children can learn to count on from these points for rapid telling of other times. Suppose it is 2:40. Then it is quicker to count on by fives from 2:*30* than to count, ''5, 10, 15, 20, 25, 30, 35, *40*—it's 2:40.'' Children also must learn to count on from five-minute times to give time to the nearest minute.

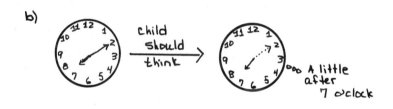

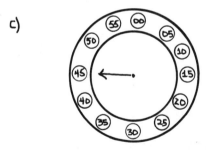

Figure 3-33

Learning handicapped children, particularly those with the disabilities listed above, may have difficulty with even this simple approach to telling time. One common difficulty is in correctly locating where the hands are pointing. Another is correctly associating each hand with what one should say in order to read the time indicated by those hands. For example, some learning disabled students *can* skip count by fives, yet fail, even after repeated use of the skip-counting technique, to make the necessary association. The following activities have proved successful in handling these special difficulties. Since the goal is for children to read the hour first, then minutes, green color coding is used for hour times and red coding for minutes.

Suggested Activities and Exercises

1. **Hour hand first.** On a large tagboard circle, glue or draw smaller circles at each of the twelve clock positions, as in Figure 3-34a. Make a deck of 52 "cards," all circles, similar to those shown in Figure 3-34b. The circles should be the same size as those drawn in the clock positions of the larger circle. Place the numerals 1 through 12 (four of each numeral) in the same relative position on the smaller circles as they would appear on a standard clock. Write the numeral 13 on the remaining four circles. The numerals and the small arrow simulating the hour hand should be green. The child "deals," placing one card from the deck face down on each of the twelve clock positions of the large circle. A 13th card is placed in the

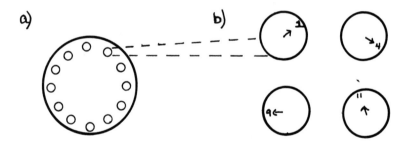

Figure 3-34

center. This procedure continues until all 52 cards have been placed on the board (Figure 3-35). The child turns over the first card of the center pile and places it, face up, under the pile on the board that corresponds to the clock position shown (see Figure 3-36). The top card of that pile is then turned over and play continues as before. Every time "13" is turned over, it is placed face up under the four cards in the center. The child wins the game if all the cards are placed face up in the proper position on the board before the four cards with "13" are uncovered. Variation: As above, but the child *says* the hour time whenever a card is properly placed.

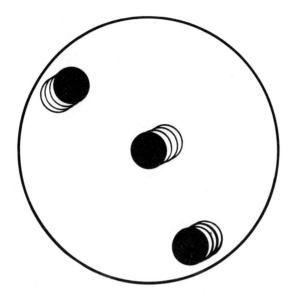

Figure 3-35

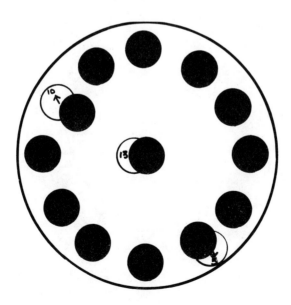

Figure 3-36

2. **Now minutes.** A game similar to that of Exercise 1 above can be played to reinforce the skip-counting pattern of the minute hand. This time, make 52 cards beginning with 00 and stopping at 60 (the 60 is for the center pile). Be sure the hand pointing to the numeral is noticeably longer and red, as shown in Figure 3-37. Use the large circle of Exercise 1, but place a rim around the outside containing twelve circles for the five-minute times (see Figure 3-38).

Figure 3-37

Figure 3-38

3. **Both hands.** Play the following bingo-type game with the students. Make a set of calling cards picturing times on standard clocks. Use green for the hour hand and red for the minute hand of each clock. Provide 4 × 4 inch gameboards for students with times written at the bottom of each square, as shown in Figure 3-39. Give each child 16 "clock" chips that fit into the space above each time written on the gameboard (see Figure 3-40). These can be made by placing gummed labels on ordinary gameboard chips and drawing a clock face on the label. Do not color code the hands on the clock chips. To play, a caller (child or teacher) holds up a color-coded clock. Players decide whether the time shown by that clock is on their gameboard. If so, they place a clock chip showing that same time on the gameboard just above the written time. The winner is the first person to complete a row in any direction.

- *Note:* If the gameboards are covered with acetate or clear contact paper, then color coding can be used when needed and wiped off. Hour digit(s) would be green, minute digits red.

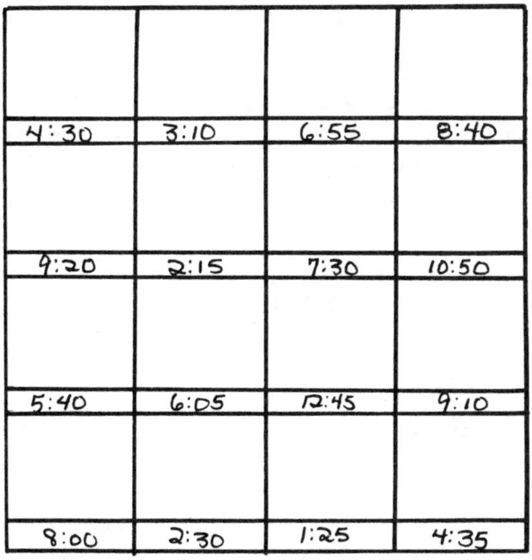

4:30	3:10	6:55	8:40
9:20	2:15	7:30	10:50
5:40	6:05	12:45	9:10
8:00	2:30	1:25	4:35

Figure 3-39

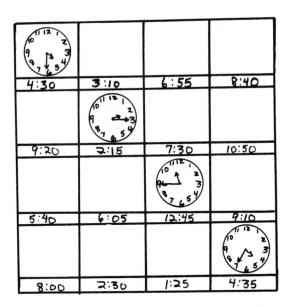

4:30	3:10	6:55	8:40
9:20	2:15	7:30	10:50
5:40	6:05	12:45	9:10
8:00	2:30	1:25	4:35

Figure 3-40

- *Variation 1:* Alter the activity by placing clock faces on the game-board and color-coded numbers on the calling cards. Game chips would also contain the written clock times. If necessary, these can also be color coded.

- *Variation 2:* Place clock chips upside down on the board, to match the clock times shown. As a card is held up, the players decide whether they have that time on their board. If so, the chip is turned over. The first player to complete correctly a row in any direction wins.

READING AND WRITING CLOCK TIMES

TIME
Section
3

Problem area: Difficulty telling time on a real clock.

Typical disabilities affecting progress: Difficulty with spatial organization, visual perception, visual sequential memory, short-term memory, expressive language.

Background: Many learning disabled children need a considerable amount of paper-and-pencil work before they can use a real clock to tell time. The paper-and-pencil activities provide

- overlearning,

- less interference due to visual perception deficits because of the proximity of the paper, and

- kinesthetic involvement for those children who need it (they can run their fingers or pencils along the paper and feel where the hand is).

The following ideas can be used to accomplish these goals.

Suggested Activities and Exercises

1. **Color coded dittos.** Several types of dittos can be filed for ready use. In Figure 3-41 the numerals 1 through 12 are green and 00 through 55 are red. The boxes below the clock are also coded, the first green and the second red. The use of boxes rather than lines during early practice sessions also strengthens the relationship between digital and standard clocks, a relationship that must be consciously reinforced for some children. One approach is to have the students themselves draw a simple version of a digital clock in the classroom and then use that picture as a model for the worksheet boxes.

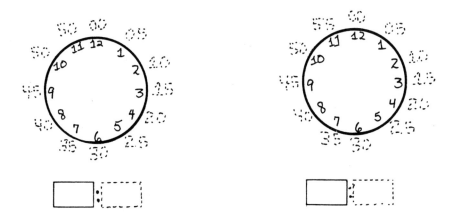

Figure 3-41

2. **Fade the cue.** Figure 3-42 illustrates one way of gradually fading the color cue. The red numbers have been replaced with red dots. The next step would be to eliminate the colors on the hands of the clock. For some children, especially those with more severe visual perception difficulties, you might eliminate the colors in the boxes

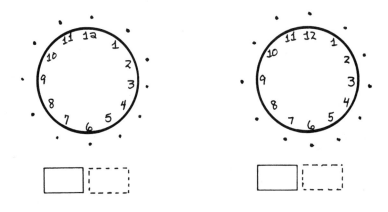

Figure 3-42

first and then those on the hands. An alternative would be to keep pages on file, such as those shown in Figure 3-43, on which there is a color coded example at the top. In Figure 3-43a, the remainder of the clocks have only green and red lines for answers. Make the green line noticeably shorter than the red line. Then provide auditory cueing by asking the child which hand on the clock looks most like the short green line. "Which hand do you 'go' on ?"

3. **Card to help.** For those still needing color reinforcement, especially as they make the transition to the real clock, keep a tagboard clock in the room. Cover it with acetate or contact so that it can be color coded when this is needed. If the color cueing is necessary, the child can use a green and red marker or grease pencil to write over the numbers. If this proves too hard motorically, the teacher should do it. The child can then use this card to help associate the hands and the sequence for reading clock times.

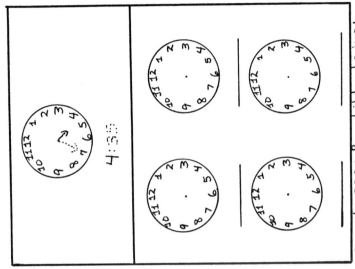

Sample page for child who just needs a reminder, but is strong in skip counting by 5's. Nothing is color coded except example at the top. (Hour hand and "4" are green; dotted figures are red.)

Sample page for child who still needs colors but is beginning to make a transition. Bold hands and hour digits are green; dotted figures are red.

Figure 3-43

4. **Strips.** As children make the transition to a real clock, they may still need to write down what they see before they are able to express it. This is especially true for

- students with memory problems that prevent them from retaining the entire sequence, and

- students with expressive difficulties who have trouble learning if their flow of thought is interrupted.

The writing is an intermediate step that allows them to take one part of the sequence at a time until overlearning has occurred. Keep strips such as those shown in Figure 3-44. The children can work in pairs to complete these strips. Using the geared clock, one child sets the time shown on one of the clocks in Figure 3-44a. The other writes the time down on paper, as in Figure 3-44b. If necessary, clocks on the strips can be color coded to aid students in expressing times correctly—hour first, *then* minutes. Make the hour hand green and the minute hand red, as suggested earlier.

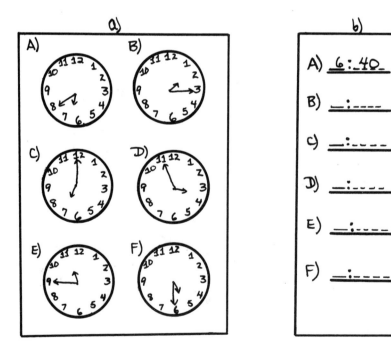

Figure 3-44

- *Note:* The worksheets illustrated in this section, especially those with color coding and numbers around the outside rim, make it possible to teach time even though the child may be weak on skip counting by fives. For many, it actually provides the way to over-learning.

NAMING THE CORRECT HOUR

Problem area: Difficulty knowing in which direction to look when the hour hand is between two numbers.

Typical disabilities affecting progress: Difficulty with spatial orientation, visual perception, and memory.

Background: Some children may clearly know what words and numbers to associate with each hand. They may have learned which hand to look at first. What they are still unclear on is which number to use when the hour hand is between two numbers. If their spatial abilities are weak, telling them to look at the number "in front of" or "before" may be meaningless. To tell them to look at the lower number is also confusing. What is the lower number? There is no numeral underneath the "1." What happens when the hour hand is between the "12" and the "1"? The following ideas should prove helpful in handling this problem.

Suggested Sequence of Activities and Exercises

1. **Point the way.** Make a small green arrow, as in Figure 3-45, which fits around the small desk clock. When the children are working with the clock, have them place the arrow at the top of the hour hand so that it curves around and points to the correct number. A small hook could also be used on the clock pages.

a)

b)

Figure 3-45

- *Variation:* If children have trouble manipulating the arrow, keep a clear plastic overlay that covers the clock face. Using a marker or grease pencil, draw an arrow on the face. The child can then place the plastic face over the real clock, rotating it until the arrow is in place.

2. **Reinforce.** When providing children with clock pages for practice, include the arrows on the page. Have the children run a pencil, or preferably a finger, over the line and say the number pointed to. In our experience, with continued kinesthetic reinforcement of this type, even younger children are soon able to draw their own lines well enough to determine which number to look to for the hour.

UNDERSTANDING THE MANY WAYS TO TELL A TIME

Problem area: Understanding expressions using "past," "after," "before," and "until."

Typical disabilities affecting progress: Difficulty with spatial organization, receptive language, and abstract reasoning.

Background: Any given time can be expressed in many different ways. For the child with abstract reasoning or receptive language deficits, this can prove very frustrating. When looking at the clock in Figure 3-46, for example, such a child is likely to hear it described in any of the following ways:

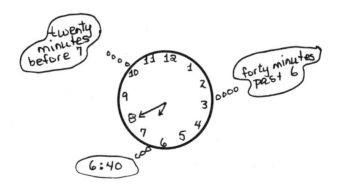

Figure 3-46

- six forty

- twenty minutes until seven

- forty minutes after six

- twenty minutes before seven

- forty minutes past six

With all the possible descriptions, the child is expected to associate the correct time with the words. But for the very young child or for the student with learning disabilities, it is often impossible to make these transfers. Even though the various ways for naming a time may not be formally taught, most young children gradually "catch on" to these expressions as they mature and repeatedly hear them in daily situations. Learning disabled students, however, because of the deficits identified above, may be unable to relate to all these expressions without special help.

Children who have trouble with multiple meanings or synonyms need to learn the different expressions one at a time. Initially, tell the time by using only the numbers themselves: "It is now 1:20 and it's time for math." Do not confuse the child by saying, "It's twenty past one," until you are sure the child understands the meaning of "past." It may be difficult to use only one format consistently, but it is essential that these children have a carefully structured program. When equivalent forms are introduced, it is generally easier to start with "after" and "before," since these concepts are taught in the basic number program. These terms can readily be incorporated into the time unit by using the circular number-line described below. After the children clearly understand the similarity between 5:20 and 20 minutes after 5, then "past" can be introduced. Similarly, when children can relate time expressions like 5:40 and 20 minutes before 6, then "until" would be introduced. The sequence outlined below can be adapted for this purpose.

Suggested Sequence of Activities and Exercises

Minutes After and Minutes Before

1. **Circular numberline.** Once children are able to tell time using numbers only, review the concept of *before* and *after* using a circular numberline (spinner, with the numbers written in sequence rather than in random order). Establish the idea that, on the circle (spinner), "after" still means the numbers get larger. Only now the direction changes. Instead of going forwards and backwards, we are going around. To help establish eye movement on the clock, present pages such as those shown in Figure 3-47.

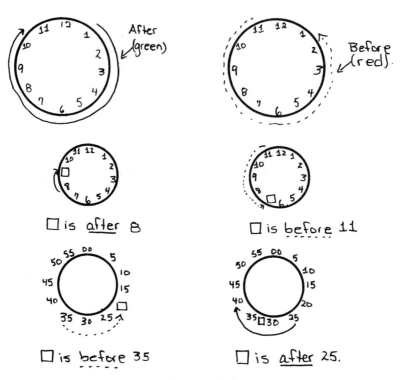

□ is _after_ 8   □ is _before_ 11

□ is _before_ 35   □ is _after_ 25.

Figure 3-47

2. **Geared clock.** Once the ideas of *before* and *after* are clear, begin relating these concepts to a clock. Use the geared clock and ask the children to turn the hands according to your instructions (see Figure 3-48). At this point, the single goal is to get the children to "feel" how hands move in different directions.

Teacher: It is 8:10.
Set a new time
that is after
8:10.

Figure 3-48

3. **Worksheets.** Practice pages of color-coded clocks, such as that in Figure 3-49, are often helpful. On these clocks, the numerals 1 through 5 are green and 7 through 11 are red. The child writes the time shown and then fills in the second blank below the clock.

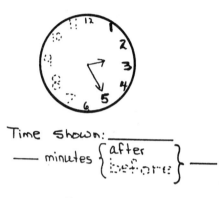

Figure 3-49

- *Note:* A prerequisite at this point is knowing which hand represents minutes and which represents hours. The children will then know what hand to look to for deciding the number of minutes "before" or "after" an hour. Children should also know, for any given hour, what the *next* hour will be. This skill is necessary for helping them determine the time before and after an hour. For example, 6:40 means 20 minutes before (the next hour) 7.

4. **Toward "overlearning."** For those requiring overlearning, provide several practice pages using only one concept (after *or* before). Very shortly, however, the pages should be mixed, using both before and after. Mixing the concepts will avoid perseveration and provide reasoning and problem solving.

5. **One step only.** As shown in Figure 3-50, the children first write the time and then write the equivalent expression using minutes before or minutes after. As they become more secure with this two-step process, begin to eliminate the first step. (Some children, especially those with a tendency to reverse, may not be able to eliminate for a while.) Figure 3-50 shows one possible sequence. In Figure 3-50a, the child need not decide whether the time is before or after the hour. The word is color coded to aid in the overlearning. When children become comfortable with these pages, follow up with worksheets using the format illustrated in Figure 3-50b.

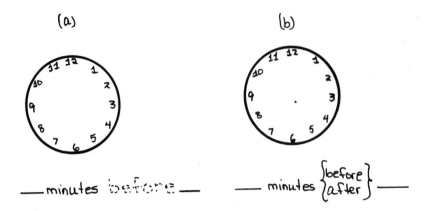

Figure 3-50

6. **Puzzle match.** For an independent activity, make puzzle cards like those shown in Figure 3-51. Whenever the word "before" is used, the clock is on the right. For the word "after," the clock is on the left.

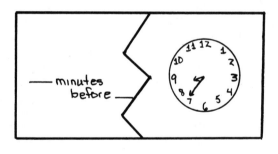

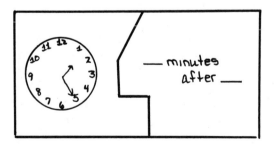

Figure 3-51

7. **Special help.** For those with receptive language deficits, pages like those of Figure 3-52 present a helpful way to build up comprehension. Initially allow the children to have a standard clock in front of them. Gradually eliminate the clock, since the use of the words "before" and "after" in time expressions requires comprehension even though there may be no clock visible. If reading is a problem, provide a tape to be used in conjunction with the page.

$$\underline{3\!:\!15} \; = \; \underline{15} \; \text{minutes} \left\{ \begin{matrix} \text{before} \\ \text{after} \end{matrix} \right\} \underline{3}$$

$$\underline{} \; = \; \underline{} \text{minutes} \left\{ \begin{matrix} \text{before} \\ \text{after} \end{matrix} \right\} \underline{}$$

$$\underline{} \; = \; \underline{} \text{minutes} \left\{ \begin{matrix} \text{before} \\ \text{after} \end{matrix} \right\} \underline{}$$

$$\underline{} \; = \; \underline{} \text{minutes} \left\{ \begin{matrix} \text{before} \\ \text{after} \end{matrix} \right\} \underline{}$$

$$\underline{} \; = \; \underline{} \text{minutes} \left\{ \begin{matrix} \text{before} \\ \text{after} \end{matrix} \right\} \underline{}$$

Figure 3-52

UNDERSTANDING AND USING TEMPORAL EXPRESSIONS

TIME Section 6

Problem area: Difficulty understanding and correctly using temporal expressions like "in ___ minutes," "___ minutes ago," "earlier" and "later," and so on.

Typical disabilities affecting progress: Difficulty with spatial organization, receptive or expressive language, and closure.

Background: For some learning disabled children, the process of telling time involves merely looking at the clock and saying some numbers. This serves the purpose of getting them where they have to be on time or knowing what time an activity is to begin. However, this skill alone does not enable them to predict or plan their time. Some children, particularly those with language or spatial deficits, do not understand temporal expressions like "in ten minutes" or "fifteen minutes ago," "earlier" or "later." They hear a familiar word, such as "in," but because it is used in an unfamiliar context they cannot meaningfully relate to it. Being able to read time from a clock and being able to interpret, predict, and plan, using one's ability to tell time, are clearly two different things. It is important that children develop this latter skill as well. The activities that follow address one aspect of developing a *sense of time* or an *awareness of time* beyond merely reading clock numbers. The goal is to help students learn and meaningfully use expressions such as "in _____ minutes," "_____minutes ago"; "earlier," and "later." The basic ideas presented can be adapted for helping learning disabled children understand and use other temporal expressions as well.

Suggested Sequence of Activities and Exercises

Prerequisites

Children should be able to handle successfully the following.

- Skip count by 5s to 55.
- Count on from within this counting sequence, with visual reinforcement.
- Understand the meanings of before and after for clock times.
- Understand which hand moves most rapidly and, ideally, associate it with minutes.
- Identify the minute hand on the clock and realize that one counts on from this hand (the *minute* hand, not the hour hand) to determine "in _____ minutes" or "_____ago."

Basic Sequence

1. **Move forward to see.** Set a time on a geared or a real clock. At first, use only "five-minute" times like 2:15, 2:25, or 2:40. Have the children tell or write the time. Then, while moving the hands of the clock, ask the question, "What time will it be in five minutes?" As you

say " . . . *in* five minutes," emphasize the word "in" and move the hands of the clock. The children then say or write the new time. Continue this procedure until the concept of "in" is firmly established. Do not have the hour change during the activity.

2. **Move back.** Use the same procedure as above to answer the question, "What time was it five minutes ago?" Initially, it is important to keep the two questions separate. Once the child readily feels the difference between the two words, then mix the questions. Children should practice moving the hands on the clock according to your instructions. At this point, you might not even require them to tell the time. Your major goal is to develop, kinesthetically, the *feeling* of the two expressions. Later, when the children cannot move the hands of a clock, the feeling will still be there. Many children actually move their fingers as if turning the clock. This helps them determine, visually, which direction to go on the clock when counting.

3. **Minute-hand card.** Give the child a "minute-hand" card with a hole in the center (Figure 3-53a) and a page of clocks showing various times. The hole in the card should match the dot where the two clock hands meet in the center. First, the child writes the time shown on a clock. Then the card is placed over the clock face so that the minute hand points to the next number, as in Figure 3-53b. The child says, "In five minutes it will be 6:45." As proficiency is gained, use intervals other than five minutes. Use the minute-hand card as long as it is needed. Direct the child to point it to the next numeral—that which indicates the next time for minutes. This will ensure counting on from the proper place. Variation: For those with good visual imagery, an alternative is to have the child use a finger and point to the next number.

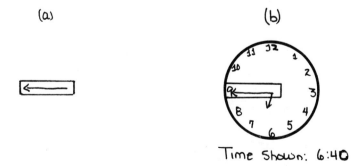

Time Shown: 6:40

Figure 3-53

4. **Follow-up.** Sample pages to reinforce this skill are shown in Figure 3-54a. As noted in the previous section, it is often necessary to have the children go through the two-step process at first. Initially, the pages would deal with only one concept. Very quickly move to pages that mix these ideas, as in Figure 3-54b.

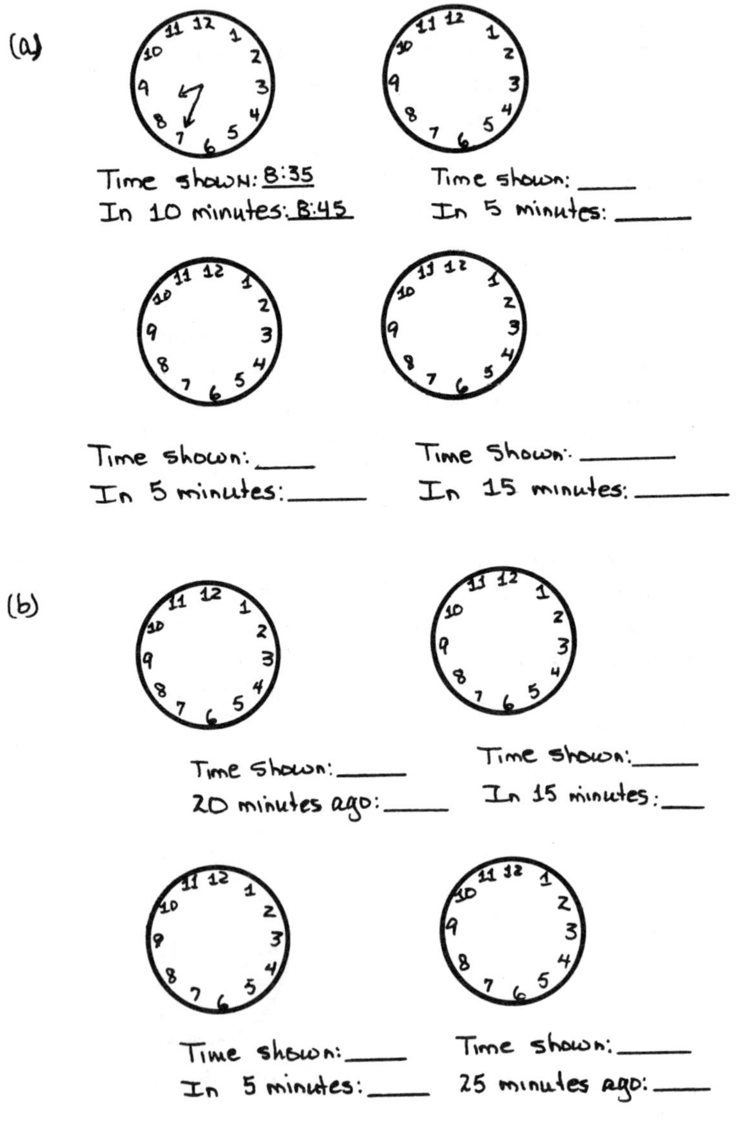

(a)

Time shown: 8:35
In 10 minutes: 8:45

Time shown: _____
In 5 minutes: _____

Time shown: _____
In 5 minutes: _____

Time shown: _____
In 15 minutes: _____

(b)

Time shown: _____
20 minutes ago: _____

Time shown: _____
In 15 minutes: _____

Time shown: _____
In 5 minutes: _____

Time shown: _____
25 minutes ago: _____

Figure 3-54

- *Note:* Some children may need help associating "in" and "ago" with "after" and "before." For those who do, write "in" using green and "ago" using red (refer back to Figure 3-47).

5. **One step only.** When the child no longer needs to write down the time, eliminate this first step. Show the child how to use a finger or the minute card to determine the stated time. For auditory cueing, it often helps to remind the student to "Think: It is now _____, so in 10 minutes it will be _____."

6. **Card game** (for two or three to play). A variation of the card game "Go Fish" can now be played. Make a deck of 20 cards with a clock face on each card (see Figure 3-55a). Make a second set of 20 cards with a temporal expression on each, as in Figure 3-55b. Each child is dealt five cards from Deck A. The remainder of the cards are placed face down in the center. Deck B is placed face down next to it. In turn, each child will draw a card from Deck B and think of a card in his hand. Suppose the child draws the expression "in 15 minutes." A request is made, to the person on the left, for a clock showing the time 3:35. If that person has the card, it is given to the caller who lays down the pair. The child places the expression card in a discard pile and the game moves on. If the child to the left does not have the requested clock, the caller draws from the fish pile until the clock is drawn or until five cards are drawn. The winner is the one with the most pairs at the end. If necessary, the discard pile is shuffled and reused.

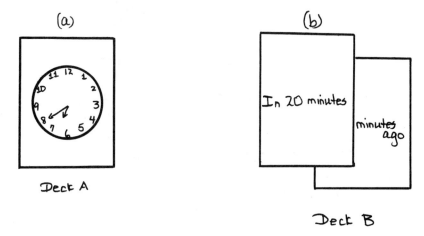

Figure 3-55

7. **Compare.** For those children needing more concrete associations for particular temporal expressions, keep a gameboard such as that shown in Figure 3-56. Also provide a deck of cards with clock faces on them. Each space on the board counts for five minutes. In turn, children draw two cards and place them, in the order drawn, at the bottom of the gameboard. Children verbally fill in the blank and choose the correct word (e.g. "earlier" or "later"). They move by fives to dramatize the difference between the two clock times. Since the cards drawn in Figure 3-56 have a difference of 15 minutes, the child moves backwards three spaces, counting by fives. The move is backwards because the second clock shows an earlier time. Note: It is best to keep all the clocks within a two-hour time span.

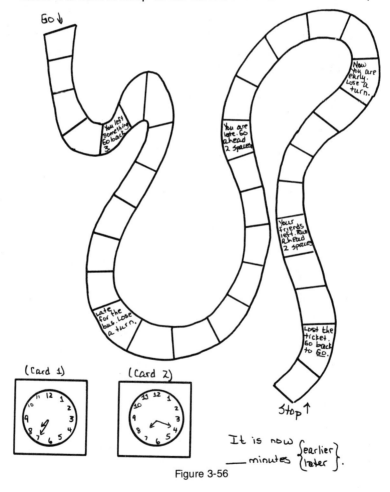

Figure 3-56

Chapter 4

The Four Operations: Basic Concepts, Basic Facts

Add, subtract, multiply, divide—that is much of what the elementary school mathematics program is all about. Children use these operations in paper-and-pencil computations, in estimating and problem solving, and in making calculator computations. Much of their success with these tasks depends on (1) adequate understanding of each operation, and (2) adequate mastery of the basic arithmetic facts. This chapter addresses the question of how to help learning disabled students who otherwise might fail in one or both of these areas. Specifically, the focus is on the following ten topics related to basic concepts or facts for each operation:

1. the four operations: building concepts
2. tracking for basic facts
3. addition facts: models and strategies
4. hiding activities for subtraction
5. teen minuends
6. comparison subtraction
7. multiplication facts: models, patterns, and strategies
8. families to help with subtraction and division
9. zero
10. using a hand calculator

Learning disabled students, like their peers, typically need much oral and manipulative work to build a strong conceptual background for each operation. Suggestions for using and extending textbook treatment in this regard are discussed in Section 1 below. The other sections of the chapter focus primarily on ideas for helping learning disabled students memorize the basic facts. Section 2 presents suggestions that may be applied to facts for all four operations. Sections 3 through 8 look separately at facts for each operation. Handling common difficulties with zero is discussed in Section 9. A final section outlines calculator ideas to help learning disabled students master basic concepts or facts for the four operations.

Sometimes students get ''bogged down'' in higher level computation because they do not know the basic facts or because they do not recognize simple, *known* facts in multidigit problems. Specific ideas for handling these difficulties are outlined in the first sections of Chapter 5. It may be of interest to study those suggestions along with those of this chapter as background for planning a program of fact study for students.

A general note regarding the importance of relating basic understandings and skills to common daily settings is in order at this point. Many learning disabled students need a structured program that emphasizes practical applications of the mathematics they are learning. They otherwise will not make the transfer and will fall short when it comes to using math where it counts—in day-to-day living. With respect to the four operations, activities like the following are helpful.

- Activity 1: Pose a situation, such as that involving money to purchase needed items, and ask the children to tell which of two given operations is appropriate. Example: ''Buy a pencil for 5¢ and a small eraser for 8¢. What is the cost?'' Select situations very familiar to the children. If possible, involve them in dramatizing the situations.

- Activity 2: Have the children circle *one* problem on a practice sheet of number facts. Ask them to describe a situation outside the classroom that might involve that number fact. Example: 2 + 5 = _____ is circled. The child might suggest: ''Two red flowers, five yellow outside our front door; seven in all.''

Other applications in the mathematics textbook might be highlighted and more carefully interwoven with the topics of this chapter. Selected ''word'' or ''story'' problems and measurement applications, such as finding perimeter and area, fit this category.

BUILDING CONCEPTS

Problem area: Inability to associate real meaning with written number sentences for addition, subtraction, multiplication, or division.

Typical disabilities affecting progress: Difficulty with abstract reasoning, visual or auditory association, receptive language.

Background: Diane looked at the problem 4 × 2 and quickly wrote 8. The teacher asked Diane to make a picture for 4 × 2. Diane didn't hesitate at all. She drew four dots beside the "4" and two dots beside the "2." It didn't bother Diane that she had drawn six dots but had written "8" to indicate the number in all. Conceptually, Diane is in trouble. Unless cued, she will not know when to multiply rather than add in a simple problem situation.

Diane's response is not atypical of other learning disabled students with reasoning or association problems. Children with expressive language difficulties may correctly select the one drawing from several that illustrates a basic fact, but, like Diane, they may be unable themselves to draw it on request. It is important that children "see" what we mean when we say add, subtract, multiply, or divide. Then they will be more likely to *use* the appropriate operation to solve problems in day-to-day settings. In many situations, it is also necessary that they be able to assign meaning to the written sign for each operation.

"Big ideas" must be understood. Addition means "put together." Subtraction has several interpretations (see Section 5 below). The simplest, and that used in beginning instruction, is "take away." (Some children, for emotional reasons, have difficulty with subtraction because of the idea of *take away*. Being sensitive to this possibility is important.)

Multiplication and division have to do with groups equal in number. To multiply we join or put together equal-sized groups, then tell how many in all. To divide we *share*. This is the simplest approach, now used with increasing frequency in beginning instruction. We start with a larger number of objects and give the same number to each of several persons. Children later learn both to tell the *number in each group* and the *number of groups* as the result of a division for particular situations (see Figure 4-1).

Figure 4-1

Most mathematics textbooks contain excellent suggestions for developing these "big ideas" with regular class students. The activities below highlight or supplement these suggestions for learning disabled students having reasoning or association difficulties.

Suggested Activities and Exercises

1. **Act it out.** Physically dramatize the "big idea" of an operation. Emphasize oral-manipulative work at first to help children learn what you mean when you say add, subtract, multiply or divide.

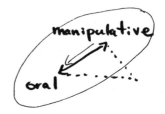

- *Example* (addition): "When we *add* we *put things together.* Here are three pieces of chalk. Take these two pieces and add them to the pile." (The child walks to the chalk tray to do so.)

- *Example* (division): "Eight cookies to share with two boys. *Divide.* Give *the same number* to each." (Physically act out this division.)

Emphasize oral-manipulative work to help children understand other vocabulary related to an operation.

- *Example* (multiplication): Give the children a box of chips and request they lay out rows of four. Comment about the groupings made. "How many fours? (Figure 4-2). . . . One four, two fours, three fours—*three times* you laid out a row of four."

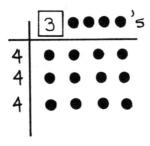

Figure 4-2

2. **Talk it out.** Get the children themselves to use the new terms throughout the activities. Hearing themselves often triggers the intended meaning or association.
3. **Tap it out.** If the children are strong auditorially, have them close their eyes and use sound or kinesthetic cues in association with new vocabulary.

   - *Example* (subtraction): The child looks at five felt hearts (velcro stapled to the backs and attached to a velcro strip as in Figure 4-3). The child then closes eyes. "Feel the hearts now. How many? (5) Open your eyes so we can subtract. *Take away* 2. Now how many?"

velcro
strip

Figure 4-3

   - *Example* (multiplication): The child closes eyes. Take the child's finger and tap it on the desk. "Let's tap out groups of four:

     (tap-tap-tap-tap) . . . . that's four—one four;

     (tap-tap-tap-tap) . . . . . . that's four again—two fours;

     (tap-tap-tap-tap) . . . . . that's four again—three fours.

     Three *times* we tapped out a group of four."

   As follow-up, have the child independently identify the number of times a group of four (or three, or two . . .) is tapped.
4. **Small steps.** Building concepts with learning disabled students, particularly those having the difficulties identified above, is often a *slow* process. It helps to keep the step size of the instruction *small*. The following multiplication exercises illustrate the point:

   - *Activity 1.* Use colored loops and chips as in Figure 4-4. Reinforcing follow-up worksheets should use the same color coding. Key questions to ask are: "How many groups?" "How many chips in each group?" "How many chips in all?"

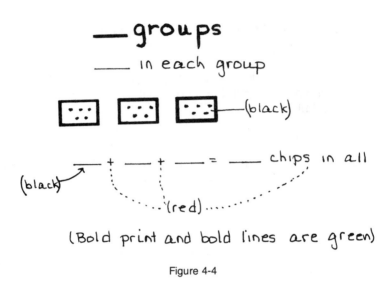

_____ groups

_____ in each group

_____ + _____ + _____ = _____ chips in all

(black)

····(red)····

(Bold print and bold lines are green)

Figure 4-4

- *Activity 2.* As above, with the modification suggested by Figure 4-5. Note that the color coding is consistent with that used previously. The children complete the example shown by filling in "3   5s = 15." Some children spontaneously draw five dots on the line instead of writing the digit 5. They say it makes more sense. (It does.)

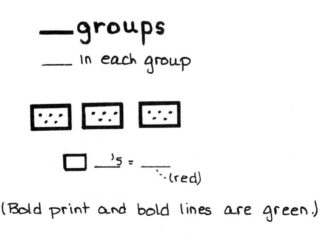

_____ groups

_____ in each group

☐ _____'s = _____

····(red)

(Bold print and bold lines are green.)

Figure 4-5

• *Activity 3.* Introduce the "times" sign (×). Use chips to form equal-sized groups as before. Have the children describe the grouping. In Figure 4-6 there are 4 threes. "Yes, four *times* we have a group of three. This '×' (point) is the multiplication sign. When we see it, we *say* 'times' and *think* 4 threes. 4 × 3, that's 12 in all." (The sign could be texturized or color coded. See Suggestions 5 and 6 below.) Follow-up worksheets using the format of Figure 4-6 would then be assigned with color coding as illustrated.

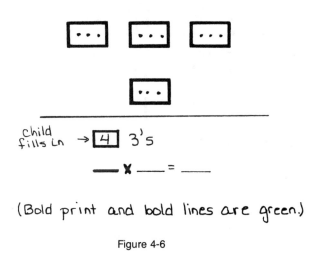

Figure 4-6

Note 1: Discussion at this point should bring out the fact that multiplication deals with equal-sized groups. "When we have equal-sized groups like this, and we need to know how many in all, we can multiply." Follow-up activities should present some situations in which equal-sized groups are *not* involved. This forces students to decide whether multiplication is indeed appropriate in the situation. The ability to make this decision affects success with "word problems."

Note 2: Care with new vocabulary is necessary. The sequence of examples above illustrated how one might informally use the term *times* in a multiplication context both before and during the presentation of the written multiplication sign. An activity sequence similar to that outlined, used remedially for Mark, led him to comment: "So that's what *times* is all about. I could get the multiply part, but I could never figure out that times."

- *Activity 4.* Additional reinforcement is usually necessary. Use colored chips and loops as in Figure 4-7. Purposely provide more chips than needed to force thinking. Have the children fill loops to picture 5 twos, 3 fours (or other groupings). For each, the corresponding multiplication sentence should then be written. Next, follow-up worksheets using the format of Figure 4-7 would be assigned, with color coding as illustrated.

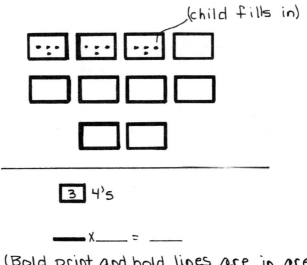

(Bold print and bold lines are in green.)

Figure 4-7

- *Activity 5.* Have the children complete worksheets like that of Figure 4-8. Color code the sign to match the box as in previous activities. This helps establish the relationship between "4   3s" and "4 × 3." For selected problems, the children could be asked to draw dots or use chips to show the number of *times* a group of a given size appears.

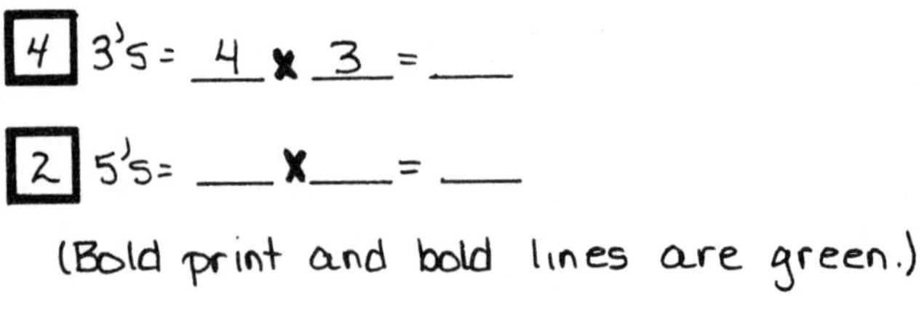

[4] 3's = 4 × 3 = ___

[2] 5's = ___ × ___ = ___

(Bold print and bold lines are green.)

Figure 4-8

5. **Symbol feel.** Texturize the new symbol for an operation. Have children finger trace as they read an expression containing the symbol. Guide the hand, if necessary, so that the writing movement is correct from the start. Next have the children *close their eyes,* finger trace, and say the name for the symbol. As a follow up, have the children trace out the symbol on a desk or in midair.

6. **Symbol look.** Color code each operation a distinctly different color and place it on a wall chart for ready reference. In the chart of Figure 4-9, for example, all terms and symbols relating to subtraction are green. Note that a diagram appears on the chart which illustrates the meaning of the symbol. Use the color coding for the operation symbol during board work and on worksheets as long as this seems helpful.

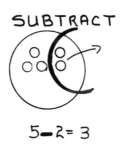

Figure 4-9

7. **Act it out.** Provide experiences where the children themselves use manipulatives to illustrate *written* work. One example is in Figure 4-9 above. Here is another: Given "3 + 2 = _____," the child counts

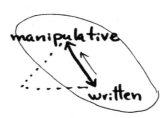

out three objects, then two more. The child then recounts to find the number in all. Later, as the children become more familiar with addition, encourage them to *count on* from the number in a small sight group rather than count from one each time.

8. **Across and up and down.** Because it follows the left-right reading motion, many teachers introduce the horizontal before the vertical format for simple number combinations. Eventually, the vertical format is needed as a prelude to computation. To help the children associate the two forms, it may be helpful to use the technique of Figure 4-10 where the double bar simulates the equal sign.

$$3 + 2 = 5 \qquad \begin{array}{r} 3 \\ + 2 \\ \hline\hline 5 \end{array}$$

Figure 4-10

9. **Turn arounds** (commutative property). Many learning disabled children need special help to recognize that 2 + 4 and 4 + 2 indeed give the same answer, that "when you know one you know the other, too." Glue chips to strips as in Figure 4-11a.

- Have the children write the expression illustrated by the strip (2 + 4).

- Use chips and a felt addition sign to lay out 4 + 2, as illustrated in Figure 4-11b. Have the children write the number sentence represented by this second configuration.

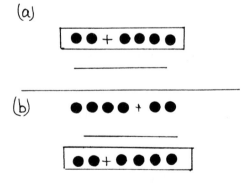

Figure 4-11

- "Are there as many chips in the first row as in the second?" Have the children match the loose chips and sign one-to-one with those on the strip. "Yes, there are just as many." The children should complete the number sentences to tell the number in all (4 + 2 and 2 + 4 = 6). Provide auditory reinforcement: "When you know one, you know the other, too."

- Adaptation (for multiplication): Use a similar approach. Provide cards such as that of Figure 4-12.

Figure 4-12

TRACKING FOR BASIC FACTS

Problem area: Difficulty memorizing the basic facts.

Typical disabilities affecting progress: Difficulties with visual, auditory, or long-term memory; visual or auditory discrimination, expressive language.

Background: Even for regular class students, school mathematics textbooks rarely include enough work on basic facts to promote real mastery. The problem is exaggerated for learning disabled children. Memory, discrimination, or expressive language deficits may interfere to make the learning of the facts very difficult. One way to promote the desired mastery for students with these disabilities is to employ the ''tracking'' technique described and illustrated in the sequence below.

Tracking basically involves presenting only a few carefully chosen facts at a time. Much as a hunter would track a deer in the woods, children track or look for a small set of facts that are mixed in with others. An example of a tracking exercise is presented in Figure 4-13. The technique forces children to focus on given facts. As a result, they tend to learn the facts faster and retain them longer.

Sometimes, as in the case of those with expressive language disabilities, children may know a fact but be unable to say or write answers immediately upon request. One way to accommodate this problem in the tracking exercises is to place, randomly, fact answers on a chart or paper. Then the children can either point to

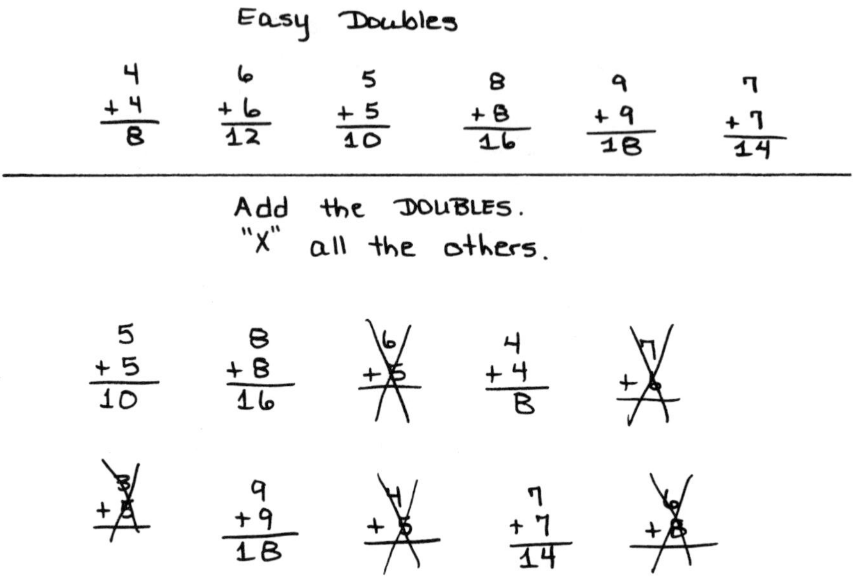

Easy Doubles

$$\begin{array}{cccccc}
4 & 6 & 5 & 8 & 9 & 7 \\
+4 & +6 & +5 & +8 & +9 & +7 \\
\hline
8 & 12 & 10 & 16 & 18 & 14
\end{array}$$

Add the DOUBLES.
"X" all the others.

$$\begin{array}{ccccc}
5 & 8 & 6 & 4 & 7 \\
+5 & +8 & +5 & +4 & + \\
\hline
10 & 16 & & 8 & \\
\end{array}$$

$$\begin{array}{ccccc}
3 & 9 & 4 & 7 & 9 \\
+ & +9 & +5 & +7 & +8 \\
\hline
 & 18 & & 14 & \\
\end{array}$$

Figure 4-13

an answer or simply refer to the list before writing or telling it. In the beginning, teachers may want to limit the number of problems given to the students. Gradually, this number can be increased, one problem each day.

Tracking is important in early fact work where the goal is getting children to memorize the facts. Since fact mastery implies giving *accurate* answers *quickly,* and being *consistent in performance* over time, follow-up practice exercises are also necessary. Activities such as those described near the end of the sequence below are useful for this purpose.

The tracking technique is not a cure-all. It is rather a general approach that has helped many of our students and can be applied to fact learning for all four operations.

Suggested Sequence of Activities and Exercises

1. **Pretest.** Determine each child's level of fact mastery. Timed written tests of themselves do not tell which specific facts are indeed mastered. Individual testing, either written or oral, is best. One can then circle on a matching sheet those facts for which correct answers are given without hesitation. Or, if flash cards are used, two piles can be formed: "mastered" and "not mastered."

2. **Cluster.** Group facts into clusters for easier learning. For addition facts having sums to 10, for example, facts might be clustered by the size of the sum (e.g. sums of 5: 0 + 5, 1 + 4, 2 + 3, . . . 5 + 1; sums of 6: 0 + 6, 1 + 5, . . . 6 + 0, and so on). Ideas presented in Sections 3 through 9 below may provide a more appropriate basis for clustering other facts. For example, addition doubles, such as 5 + 5, 3 + 3, and 6 + 6, might be clustered. Subtraction facts having 10 in the minuend (e.g. 10 − 6, 10 − 3) might form another cluster. Or facts *one more than* a small set of easier, known facts might form a cluster.

3. **Model it.** If possible, use manipulatives to dramatize answers for facts within a cluster.

   • *Example 1* (sums of 10): Use chips (two colors) and a 10-frame made by stapling half-pint milk cartons together (see Figure 4-14). Have the children: (1) Count the cartons in the frame (10).

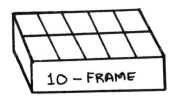

Figure 4-14

(2) Place a chip (all one color) in each of eight cartons. "How many chips are needed to FILL the 10-frame?" (two). (3) Place two chips (second color) in the 10-frame to "fill it up." (4) Pick out the flash card that describes this situation and tape it to the board or chart (Figure 4-15a). Picture the 10-frame as a visual cue with the chart. Repeat, using different combinations for ten.

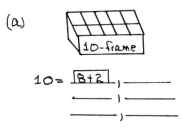

Figure 4-15a

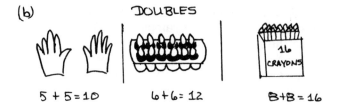

Figure 4-15b

- *Example 2* (addition doubles): Use the suggestions of Section 3 below. Picture the cues with the chart (Figure 4-15b).

4. **Circle it.** Provide worksheet tracking pages on which the children find and circle, from among distractors, facts in a given cluster. Children can refer to the board or wall chart, or even use the model(s) if necessary.
5. **See and write.** Plan short sessions during which flash cards for selected facts in a cluster are presented one at a time. As the cards are flashed, the child says the problem, gives the answer, and then writes it on the line of a worksheet such as that of Figure 4-16a or 4-16b. At first, present only a small number of facts, those easiest or already known by the child. Then gradually, one at a time, introduce harder facts in the cluster.

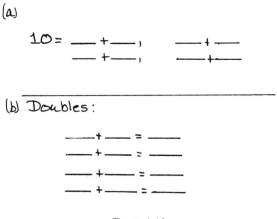

Figure 4-16

6. **Match.** Provide worksheets such as those shown in Figure 4-17. As a form of visual training, the children study the top part of each page before completing the tracking exercise at the bottom.

(a)   10 sums

   8+2   6+4   3+7

Add all 10 sums. "X" all others.

3X6:____   3+7:____

8+2: **10**   2X7: ____

5X6: ____   6+4: ____

(b)   x9

4x9=36   7x9=63
6x9=54   8x9=72

Multiply all 9's. "X" all others.

3x9:____   7x9: **63**

4x9: **36**   8x9: **72**

2x6: ____   3x5:____

Figure 4-17

7. **Find it.** Provide worksheet tracking pages such as that illustrated in Figure 4-18. Have the children find and write answers *only to those facts in a given cluster.* Include about 20 problems from the cluster. Variation: Have the children give answers orally to facts in the given cluster.

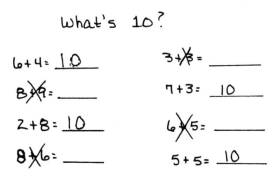

What's 10?

6+4: **10**   3+8 = ____

8x9: ____   7+3: **10**

2+8: **10**   6x5: ____

8x6: ____   5+5: **10**

Figure 4-18

8. **Hear and write.** For each cluster, have the children read facts, problem and answer, into a tape recorder. They can then listen to the playback for extra reinforcement.
9. **Trace and write.** Use the answer side of flash cards. Have the children finger trace facts within a cluster, problem and answer, as they read it aloud. Then have them close their eyes as they say the

problem and answer quietly to themselves. Finally, have the children turn the flash card over, read the problem, and give the answer. If they forget, finger tracing the problem sometimes triggers the response. Some teachers have found it helpful to trace over flash card answers with Elmer's glue. When dried, the raised surface gives an extra stimulus to the finger tracing.

10. **Quiz.** Regular quizzes to test both short- and long-term retention of facts are necessary. Short quizzes of six or eight facts can serve to spotcheck mastery of facts within one or more clusters. Longer quizzes can also be used from time to time. Keeping simple (personal) bar graphs of the number right on each quiz is usually very motivating to students. Oral timed quizzes would not be required of students with auditory discrimination problems. Auditorially, they cannot process rapidly enough to succeed. For similar reasons, timed written tests would not be used with children having visual memory difficulties. Students with expressive language disabilities will also have difficulty with traditional timed tests. One option for these students is to place answers randomly in front of them. The children can then find and point to answers for given fact problems. One way of tracking progress is to make note of the time it takes to find answers to a given number of problems and then compare the timing of several days.

11. **Review.** Systematically review facts from a cluster as other new facts are studied. Games and traditional drill and practice activities and worksheets are appropriate at this stage.

ADDITION FACTS: MODELS AND STRATEGIES

Section 3

Problem area: Difficulty mastering the basic addition facts.

Typical disabilities affecting progress: Difficulties with visual, auditory, or long-term memory; visual or auditory discrimination; expressive language.

Background: The activities of this section focus on strategies and models for learning the basic addition facts. Children good at memorizing do not need to rely on such approaches. The story is quite different for learning disabled students who have the memory or other difficulties identified above. Experience suggests, however, that they can profit from ideas like those outlined below. The basic approach is to help students master easy facts first. Models are used at this point to help the children ''picture'' the facts in their minds. Then harder facts are mastered by relating them to the easier, known facts. Typically, this involves deviating from traditional textbook treatments of the facts.

"Different strokes for different folks." And so it is with learning disabled students who are studying the facts. What helps one child may not prove effective with another. The teacher's role becomes one of suggesting relationships, models, or strategies while remaining open to the children's ideas and sensitive to individual learning styles.

One word of caution: Many learning disabled children need to keep it *very simple*. If presented too many "tricks" for remembering facts, they cannot sort out one from another. Others, however, can handle a "reasonable" variety of strategies during fact learning. The following suggestions are offered for teachers to draw on as needed to plan a tracking sequence for individuals or small groups of students. Ideas for adapting the basic sequence to meet remedial needs are included.

Suggested Sequences of Activities and Exercises

Basic Sequence

Easy Facts First

1. **Count ons.** Review, if necessary, the activities of Sections 3 and 4 of Chapter 2. For sums less than 10 and for other facts having 1, 2, or 3 as an addend, encourage the children to count on from the greater addend rather than count from 1 each time.

   - *Example:* $6 + 3 = $ ____. "That's 6—7, 8, 9." Experience shows that learning disabled children, even the "trainable" mentally handicapped, *can* do this. Children should never resort to counting from one for addition facts.

   - *Note 1:* The relationship of a fact to its commutative should be stressed from the beginning. Refer, if necessary, to the "turnaround" activities in Section 1 above. The children should recognize that, for any given fact, its "turn around" (commutative) has the same answer. "When you know one, you know the other, too."

   - *Note 2:* Teachers may want to take time out at this point to help children note the "+ 0" pattern. $0 + 3 = 3$, $7 + 0 = 7$, and so on. Add 0, and the answer is what you start with.

2. **Ten sums.** Refer to Example 1 in the "model-it" portion of Section 2 above. Use chips and the 10-frame as a model to help the children learn sums of 10. Have the children themselves write the number sentences to describe each situation dramatized.

- *Alternate model:* Some children would rather use their 10 fingers as a model. If this approach is used, check for instant sight recognition of any number of fingers displayed. In Figure 4-19a, for example, the children should be able to say "six" immediately without counting. The important follow-up question for this example is: "How many more fingers make 10?"

Note: Although the 10-frame and hands activities outlined above are related to missing addends, *do not* emphasize this as such. The point is rather to force students to focus on identifying two addends that together make 10. Such recognition is necessary for success with the tracking technique described in Section 2 above. These activities also provide a background that will help later with harder teen sums (see Activity 7 below) as well as teen minuends in subtraction (see Section 6 of this chapter).

- *Variation for the hands model:* Place yarn or string between two fingers and have the children write an addition sentence to describe the situation. For Figure 4-19b: $6 + 4 = 10$, or $4 + 6 = 10$.

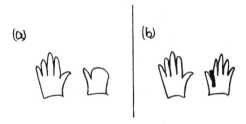

(a)   (b)

Figure 4-19

3. **Doubles.** Use models such as those of Figure 4-20 to help children memorize addition doubles. Among other activities, involve the children in:

- writing number sentences to match cue cards

- reading cue and associated number sentences into a tape recorder and listening to the playback (e.g., $8 + 8$ is the crayon fact. $8 + 8 = 16$)

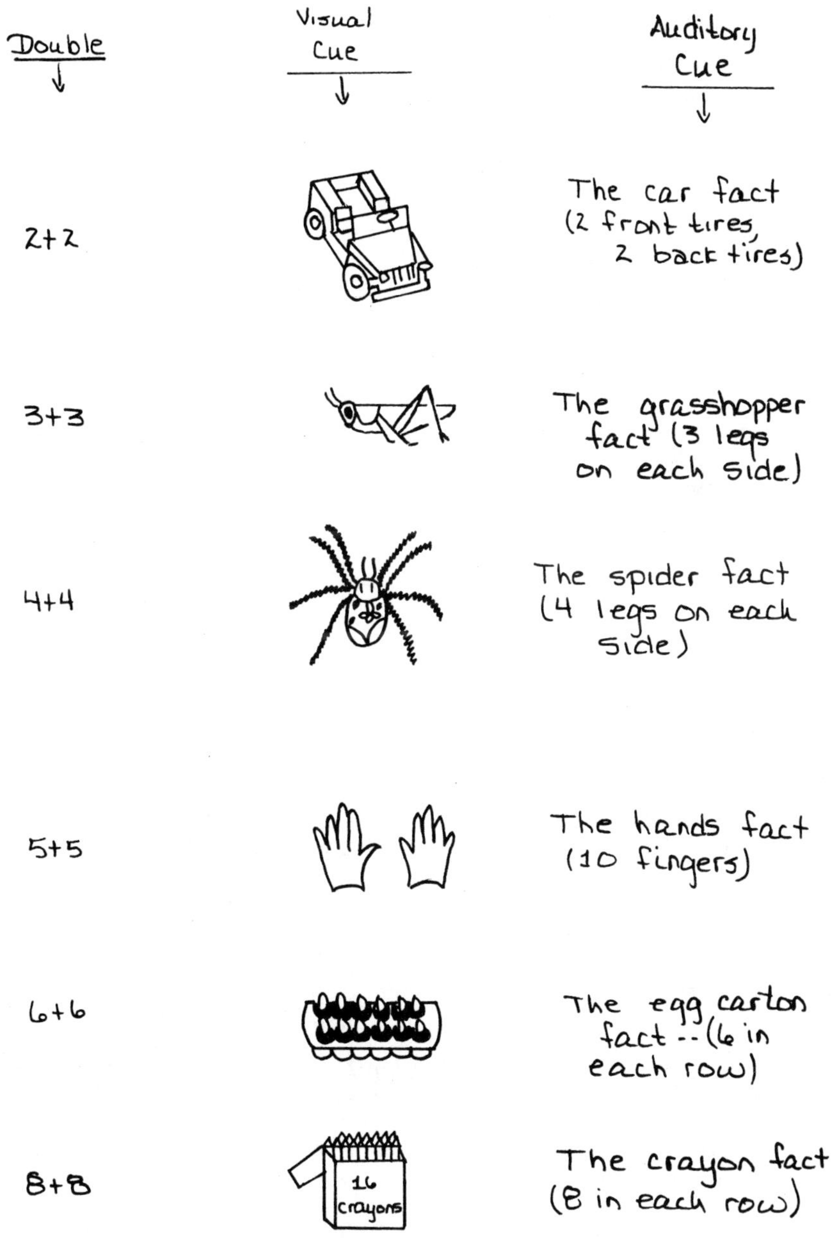

Double	Visual Cue	Auditory Cue
2+2		The car fact (2 front tires, 2 back tires)
3+3		The grasshopper fact (3 legs on each side)
4+4		The spider fact (4 legs on each side)
5+5		The hands fact (10 fingers)
6+6		The egg carton fact -- (6 in each row)
8+8		The crayon fact (8 in each row)

Figure 4-20

- finger tracing over the cue card and then *writing* the double that is illustrated

- practice activities where children match number sentences with associated cue cards; a variation on the card game Old Maid is good for this purpose (see Figure 4-21)

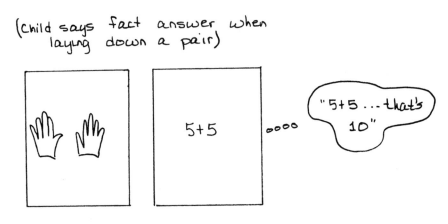

Figure 4-21

Now Harder Facts

4. **One more than.** Help the students master harder facts by relating them to easier, known facts. The "one-more-than" strategy is a powerful help in this regard. Mastering a hard fact is just "one step away." The strategy has a mushroom effect. As facts are mastered, they can be used to help children learn others.

- *Example 1* (based on a double): 5 + 5 = 10, so 5 + 6 is 1 more (11). 5 + 6 = 11, so 5 + 7 is 1 more (12).

- *Example 2* (based on a 10-sum): 7 + 3 = 10, so 7 + 4 is 1 more (11). 7 + 4 = 11, so 7 + 5 is 1 more (12).

- *Aid 1:* When presenting examples like these, orally emphasize the underlined numerals.

- *Aid 2:* It sometimes helps to color code as in Figure 4-22 to emphasize the "one-more-than" relationship. The coding helps children focus on the intended relationship. This approach is particularly helpful for children who are working independently or

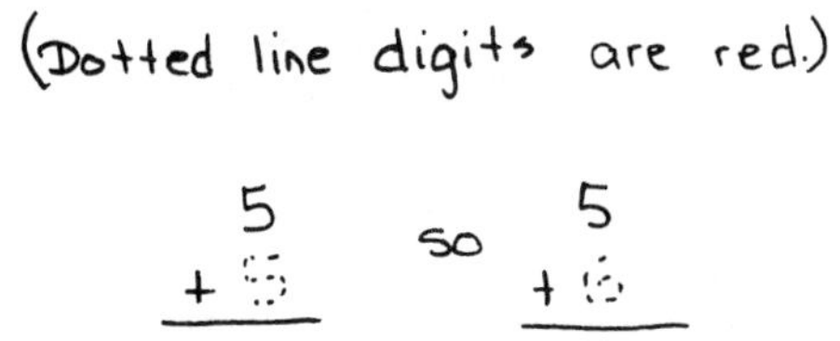

(Dotted line digits are red.)

$$5 \qquad \text{so} \qquad 5$$
$$+ \ \dot{} \dot{} \qquad\qquad + \ \dot{} \dot{}$$

Figure 4-22

who, for auditory reasons, may not hear the oral emphasis placed by the teacher when reading the pair of number sentences. Color coding may be necessary as well for students weak in making associations. The student may not relate the "5" and "6" without cueing.

- *Aid 3:* It is often necessary to dramatize a relationship with children. It is not enough simply to discuss it. For example: (1) Use rocks. Have the children make a picture of 5 + 5 and then write the number sentence to describe the picture (Figure 4-23a). (2) Give a child *one more* rock. "Place the rock with the others. It doesn't matter which side." Have the child write a second number sentence to describe the picture now. (3) Even as the child writes, emphasize the idea that you now have *1 more than 10* (11).

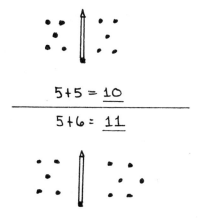

5+5 = 10

5+6 = 11

Figure 4-23

- *Aid 4:* Many children, especially those with expressive language deficits, may have trouble thinking of an easy, known fact to help with a fact they do not know. These same children may be able to use a "helping fact" (the easier, known fact) once it is located. For these students, plan activities like the following with flash cards. (1) Present a fact that is not yet memorized (4 + 7 in the example of Figure 4-24a). (2) Ask the students to select the easy "helping fact" from two other flash cards you place along the chalk tray. (3) Have the children turn over the card that does not help and give answers to the two related facts. ("3 + 7 = 10, so 4 + 7 is 11.") Follow-up worksheets, which direct children to select the helper from two given facts, could also be used. The fact that does not help should be crossed out, as in Figure 4-24b.

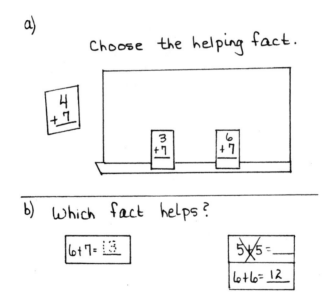

Figure 4-24

- *Aid 5:* Another alternative for helping children use an appropriate helping fact is illustrated in Figure 4-25. Although the exercise is related to missing addends, do not emphasize it as such. The focus should be on building new facts from easy, known facts (e.g., 3 + 7 = 10, so 4 + 7 is one more (11)).

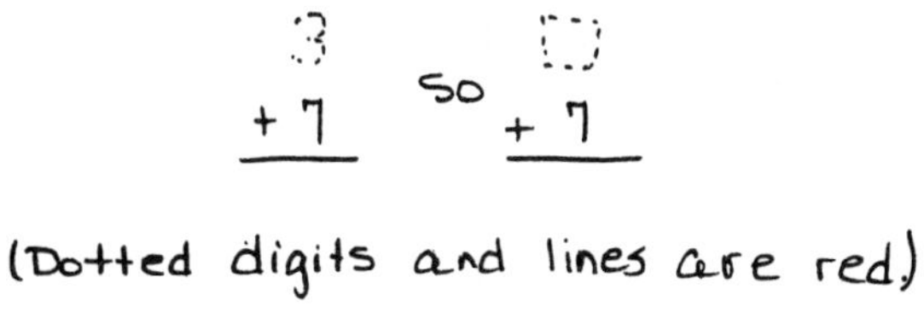

$$3 \qquad \qquad \square$$
$$+\ 7 \qquad so \qquad +\ 7$$

(Dotted digits and lines are red)

Figure 4-25

- *Note:* Children typically find "one more" easier than the following strategies:

    Strategy 1: "One less." 3 + 7 = 10, so 2 + 7 is one less (9)

    Strategy 2: "Two more." 6 + 6 = 12, so 6 + 8 is 2 more (14).

    Strategy 3: "– 1, + 1." 6 + 8 is the same as 7 + 7 or 14.

    (Some children refer to this as the Robin Hood idea of sharing: Take 1 from the "rich" and give it to the "poor.")

Teachers would, of course, allow the children to use any strategy which seems helpful to them, as long as it shows correct thinking. Figure 4-26 illustrates two different approaches for figuring out 5 + 7. Since the addends are large, both illustrate a thinking process that is faster than counting on.

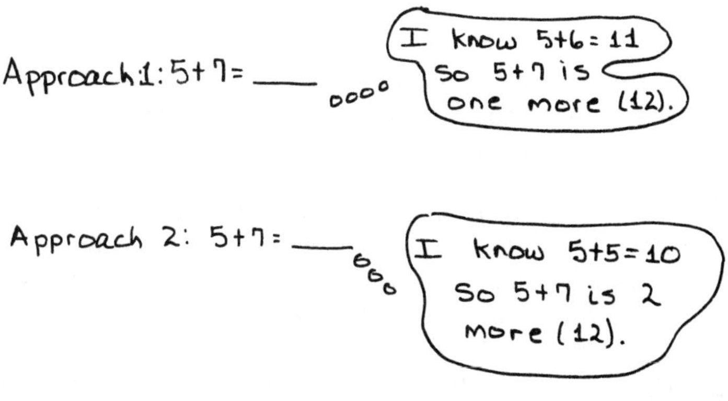

Approach 1: 5 + 7 = _____

I know 5 + 6 = 11
So 5 + 7 is
one more (12).

Approach 2: 5 + 7 = _____

I know 5 + 5 = 10
So 5 + 7 is 2
more (12).

Figure 4-26

5. **Nines.** Children commonly choose from among three strategies for remembering nines.

   - *Strategy 1:* "1 less than adding 10." $10 + 6 = 16$, so $9 + 6 = 15$ (1 less).

   - *Strategy 2:* "Make it a '10' problem." Use the "$- 1, + 1$" idea: "$9 + 6$ is the same as $10 + 5$ or 15."

   - *Strategy 3:* "Note the pattern." The ones digit of the answer is always 1 less than the digit added to 1 (see Figure 4-27).

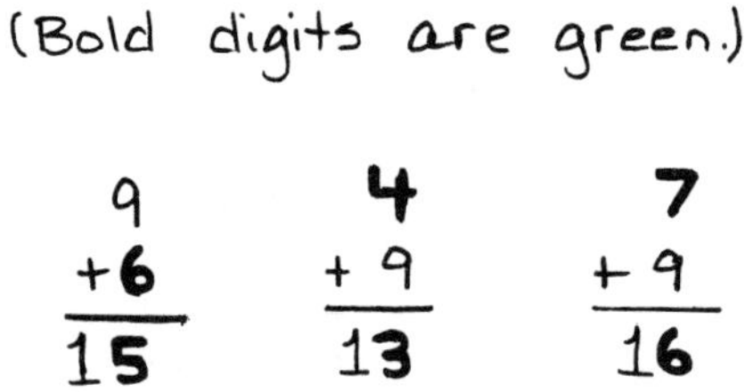

(Bold digits are green.)

$$\begin{array}{r} 9 \\ +\mathbf{6} \\ \hline \mathbf{15} \end{array} \qquad \begin{array}{r} \mathbf{4} \\ + 9 \\ \hline \mathbf{13} \end{array} \qquad \begin{array}{r} \mathbf{7} \\ + 9 \\ \hline \mathbf{16} \end{array}$$

Figure 4-27

While learning disabled students may not independently discover these strategies, many are able to use at least one of them if cued (use suggestions from Activity 4 above). Choose one strategy that you think will be easiest. Even if the child has difficulty, give it a good try before turning to a different approach. Too much change too fast is confusing.

6. **Home free.** Children who know count-ons, $+ 0$ facts, 10 sums, and doubles have already learned a significant number of the 100 basic addition facts (those blackened in Figure 4-28). All facts diagonally below the doubles in the figure have also been shaded, since it is assumed that as the children learn a fact they should automatically study its commutative as well. Nines and other facts one more than 10 or one or two more than a double have also been shaded, since these can be mastered by the "one more," "one less," or other strategies discussed in Activities 4 and 5 above. At this point, it is good to share with children how far they have come toward mastering the 100 basic addition facts.

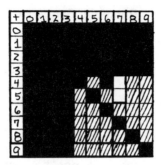

Figure 4-28

7. **To 10 and on.** A final suggestion is helpful for many children in figuring out answers to harder teen sums, including the two unshaded facts of Figure 4-28. Use a 10-frame and chips to help the children "see" that 8 + 5 is the same as 10 and 3 (13). The value of previous work with the 10-frame now pays off, because many children look at "8 + 5" and "see" that 8 and 2 more make 10, so it's a matter of adding in the extra 3. It may be necessary at this time to focus on adding 10 to a number until the children can do so mentally. Visual color cueing, as in Figure 4-29, or auditory cueing through sound emphasis should be used if this seems helpful. The ones digit of the sum and of the digit added to 10 could also be texturized to allow for finger tracing.

(Bold digits are green.)

$$
\begin{array}{r} 10 \\ + 3 \\ \hline 13 \end{array}
\qquad
\begin{array}{r} 10 \\ + 6 \\ \hline 16 \end{array}
\qquad
\begin{array}{r} 10 \\ + 4 \\ \hline 14 \end{array}
$$

Figure 4-29

- *Example:* (Use the answer side of a flash card, with both 4s texturized. One suggestion is to retrace each 4 with Elmer's glue. When the glue dries, it will leave a raised imprint of the digits.) "Read the number sentence." (The child reads 10 + 4 = 14.) "Now close your eyes and trace over the 4s as I read the number sentence. . . . Now put your hands in your lap. . . . Say the answer to this problem: 10 + 4 = ____." Next ask the child, with eyes open, to read the front side of the flash card problem and give its answer.

Remedial Sequence

Many older remedial children know most of the easier addition facts. Their greatest difficulty is often with harder teen sums. One approach for these students is to start with doubles and build *up* from there (see numbers 3, 4, and 5 of the basic sequence above). *Then* review the "count on" idea and "10" sums. And, last of all, introduce or review the idea of using 10 (as in Activity 6 above) to help with any facts not yet mastered. This approach tends to get the students off to a more motivating running start. It avoids spending a lot of time during early sessions on facts they may consider "babyish."

HIDING ACTIVITIES FOR SUBTRACTION

Problem area: Prolonged reliance on counters or fingers for finding answers to subtraction facts.

Typical disabilities affecting progress: Difficulty with visual, auditory, or long-term memory; visual or auditory discrimination; expressive language; abstract reasoning.

Background: In beginning instruction for subtraction, the children are given situations in which they see and count the number of objects in the remaining set (Figure 4-30). After repeated opportunities to remove objects from intact groups, the children good at memorizing will eventually remember this number for solving written or orally presented facts. Children with the learning disabilities identified above, however, can benefit from "hiding" activities like those described below. These activities show objects in the intact group but *hide* the number in the

Figure 4-30

remaining subgroup. Hiding activities challenge the children to think about rather than see or count the number left over each time. For this reason, they are a stepping stone to subtraction work without objects and pave the way to memorizing the facts.

Suggested Sequence of Activities and Exercises

Prerequisite: The basic concept of subtraction, as modeled in take-away situations, must be well established.

Step 1—How many do you see? Use pennies or other small, familiar objects. Let the children see you put five pennies in a box. "How many pennies did I put in the box?" (5. Write this number for all to see.)

Step 2—Cover. Put the lid on the box. "How many pennies are hidden in the box?" (5) If the children are unsure, allow them to open the box and check.

Step 3—Take out. Hold the box high so that children cannot see the pennies as you take the lid off. Take two pennies out. "How many pennies did I take out?" (2. Complete the written expression for all to see: "5 − 2.")

Step 4—How many left? Ask how many pennies are left hidden in the box. Encourage the children to quickly tell, even guess, the number left hidden in the box. They can then empty it or peek to see.

- *Note 1:* Children who can recall addition facts related to given subtraction facts have a ready clue to subtraction answers. For example: "13 − 6 = 7. I know this because 7 + 6 = 13." Most learning disabled children need help in recognizing and using this relationship. (Refer to the ideas of Section 8 below.) Informally, teachers can orally cue children in this regard by the type of feedback they give at this point in the hiding activity sequence. Example: "See—you are right. 5 − 2—that's 3, because these three pennies in the box and two more make the five we started with."

- *Optional follow-up:* Have the children select flash cards for 5 − 2 = 3 and 3 + 2 = 5 and place them side by side on the chalk tray or table near the box. Discuss how the cards help describe the story of the pennies.

- *Note 2:* Repeat to illustrate other subtraction combinations. As the childrem become more familiar with the activity, *they* should be required to write the subtraction sentence that describes each situation.

TEEN MINUENDS

Problem area: Difficulty remembering harder subtraction facts, particularly those with teen minuends. Heavy reliance on counting.

Typical disabilities affecting progress: Difficulty with visual, auditory, or long-term memory; visual or auditory discrimination; expressive language.

Background: Of the 100 basic subtraction facts, those with teen minuends are typically the hardest to master. Some learning disabled children can learn to think of and use related addition facts as a help (see Section 8 below). Example: $13 - 6 = 7$ because $7 + 6 = 13$. Others find it easier to build on facts they already know. Examples based on subtraction doubles: $12 - 6 = 6$, so $13 - 6$ is one more (7); $12 - 6 = 6$, so $11 - 6$ is one less (5). Examples based on 10 in the minuend: $10 - 7 = 3$, so $11 - 7$ is one more (4); $10 - 7 = 3$, so $9 - 7$ is one less (2).

Teachers are aware of the large number of learning disabled students who rely on inefficient counting methods for finding answers to subtraction facts. These are the students who (among other things) do the following:

- Count up: "13 − 6—that's 6—*7, 8, 9, 10, 11, 12, 13.*" (The children finger count as they say the numbers in italics.) "That's 7."

- Count back: "13 − 6—that's 13—*12, 11, 10, 9, 8, 7, 6.*"

- Finger count everything: The children raise fingers to represent the minuend, they lower (take away) fingers to represent the subtrahend, and then count and tell the number left. These students are in real trouble with teen minuends.

Counting of any variation is basically inefficient for larger minuends.

The approach to teen minuends outlined below is not a cure-all. It has, however, helped many of our learning disabled students, though some find it more difficult than the strategies cited in the examples above. This approach is offered as one idea for helping students who otherwise might use more inappropriate methods to find answers to teen minuends facts.

Suggested Sequence of Activities and Exercises

1. **"10" minuends first.** Be sure the children can give answers to facts with 10 in the minuend (e.g., $10 - 6$, $10 - 4$, $10 - 3$, $10 - 7$, and so on). If the children have not yet mastered these facts, they may find it helpful to think of filling the 10-frame (see Example 1 in Section 2 above).

- *Example:* 10 − 6. "4 more will fill the frame. So 10 − 6 = 4." Others may find it easier to use their fingers as a model.

- *Example:* 10 − 6. "10 fingers up. 4 down. That leaves 6." *Sight* recognition of the number of fingers or 10-frame slots, not counting, is desirable at this point. Children should be required to write number sentences that describe the situations dramatized. Tracking pages on "10" minuends and other additional practice activities should also be provided until mastery is reached. Care should be taken to introduce only one or two new facts at a time.

2. **How do they differ?** Write number fact pairs, such as those in Figure 4-31. If necessary, color code as illustrated. Ask the children to tell how a given pair of problems differ. For the first example, children should note that 13 is *3* more than 10. Comment that the answer to 13 − 6, then, is just *three* more than that of 10 − 6. Repeat for other number pairs. For the moment, do not focus on answers at all. Continue until children are aware of the pattern. Then tell the children that you will show them how to find answers to hard problems like this (point to 13 − 6) by first thinking of the easy "10" problem (point to 10 − 6).

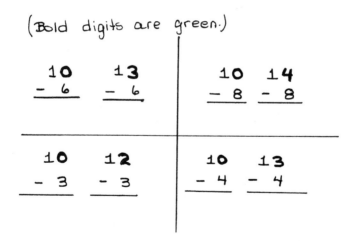

Figure 4-31

3. **The zero finger:** "You'll need a zero finger to help you think of the easy '10' fact." Have the children examine the index fingers of their right hands. Get them to note how the fingernail resembles a "0." "This is your zero finger."

4. **Look alikes.** Refer to the sheet of Figure 4-30 again. Have the children use their zero finger to cover the ones digit of a problem like 13 − 6 (the second of a pair). "See how this problem now 'looks like' the easy '10' problem? With your finger in place it reads '10 − 6.' "

5. **To 10 and on.** (Refer to Figure 4-32.)

   - Write a teen minuend problem like 13 − 6 on a sheet of paper.

   - Have the children cover the ones digit of the minuend with their zero finger and give the answer to the easy "10" problem.

   - The children should then remove the zero finger and add in the extra ones.

   - Repeat for other teen minuend facts.

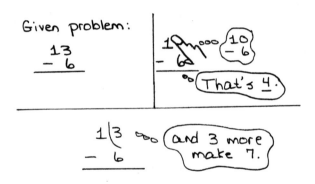

Figure 4-32

COMPARISON SUBTRACTION

Problem area: Adding instead of subtracting for word problems like: "Dick has 7 marbles. Jack has 4. How many more does Dick have than Jack?"

Typical disabilities affecting progress: Difficulty with abstract reasoning, visual discrimination, and receptive or expressive language.

Background: Most young children, including the learning disabled, typically have difficulty with comparison word problems such as that given above. The situation of Dick and Jack represents one general type of comparison problem that can be solved by subtracting. It's a situation in which one determines *how much more one has than another*. A second type of comparison situation is that which asks *how much more is needed*. For example: "Jan has 7¢. An apple costs 12¢. How much more money is needed?" The comparison is between what Jan has and what she needs. Given a comparison situation, children are typically miscued by the word "more" and tend to add rather than subtract.

One root of the difficulty may well be that a higher level of reasoning is required of children to handle problems like these successfully. A second stems from teachers not giving adequate attention to problems of this type. Most children need help in setting up comparison situations as subtraction problems.

When children have developed confidence with the basic subtraction idea that is modeled by "take away" situations, then comparison subtraction problems should be posed. Too often children are left to their own resources to discover independently techniques for solving subtraction problems of this type. A worthy goal is to prepare students in advance for handling comparison subtraction situations. If their first acquaintance with reading problems like these is in a level-two math book, they are quite likely to fail. Suggestions for developing the idea of comparison subtraction with learning disabled children having the disabilities identified above are outlined below. Note that the step size of the instruction is kept very small.

Suggested Sequence of Activities and Exercises

1. **Picture it.** Orally pose a situation such as: "Dick has 7 marbles. Jack has 4." or "Jan has 7¢. An apple she wants to buy costs 12¢." Tape a large sheet to the board and have the children help draw a picture to illustrate each situation posed (e.g. Figure 4-33). Repeat until the children are comfortable with this task. Save the sheets for use in Activities 2 and 3 below.

   - *Follow-up:* Have the children read situations from cards you have prepared. Then help them picture each situation, as above. For children with limited vocabulary, use pictograms on the cards as necessary (substitute pictures for words).

2. **Match.** Use the sheets from Activity 1 above. Review the sheets, one at a time. For each, pose the problem to be solved: "How many more does one have than the other?" or "How much more is needed?" Help the children match one to one to compare the two groups pictured.

   - If this is the first session with the pages, allow the children to count the number left over after the match (Figure 4-34).

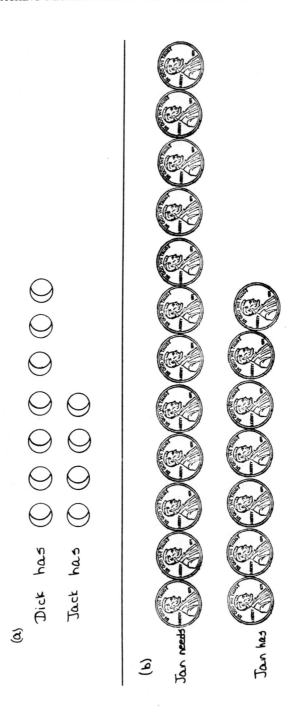

Figure 4-33

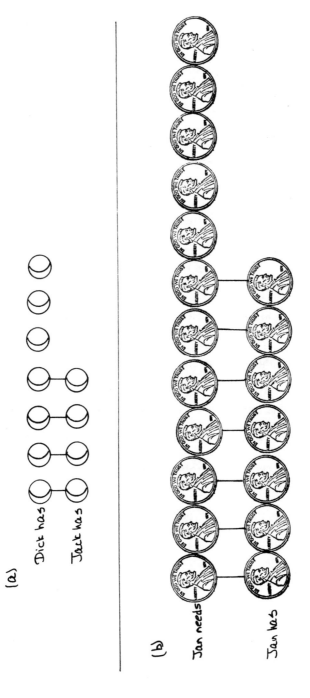

Figure 4-34

- In subsequent sessions, help the children see that they can simply subtract to find this number. Get them to complete the subtraction sentence you have written on the sheet (Figure 4-35). They should then compare their answer with the number left over in the picture after the comparison is made.

- Eventually, the children themselves should write the subtraction sentences that solve situations pictured on the sheets. At this point, one might comment to the children that "It's good to know how to subtract. You can use it to solve so many different kinds of problems."

3. **Sort out.** Review the sheets from Activity 1 again. As a type of tracking exercise, have the children place in a special pile all those sheets that compare *how much more one has than another.* When the sorting is complete, have the children read (even finger trace, if they are strong tactual learners) the subtraction fact that solves each situation. Orally emphasize the relationship between subtraction and this type of problem. "To find how much more one has than another, you subtract. Read the subtraction fact that solves this problem." Underline the question, "How much more does one have than another?" and the subtraction sign of the fact problem written to answer the question with the same color.

    - *Note 1:* At another time, have the students sort out sheets for situations asking *how much more is needed.*

    - *Note 2:* Technically, the "how much more is needed" type of question is a missing addend problem. We *do not* emphasize it as such. Rather, we prefer to focus on the simple subtraction fact that will solve the problem.

4. **Search.** As a follow-up tracking exercise, have the children search for comparison subtraction problems on worksheets or textbook pages that contain a mix of take-away and comparison types (Figure 4-36). For each comparison problem identified, have them draw a picture and write the subtraction sentence that solves the problem.

5. **Make up.** Help the children make up their own word problems for the two types of comparison subtraction. If the children have expressive language difficulties, provide a sheet of sentences that they can draw from while creating their problems. Children could trade, picture, and solve each other's problems.

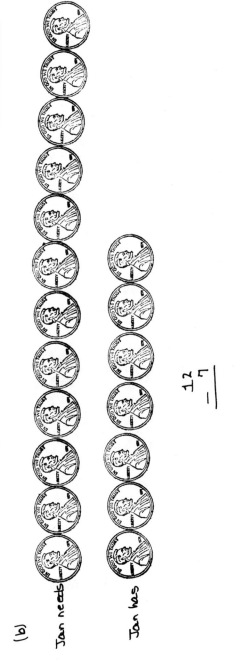

Figure 4-35

> Do those that COMPARE.
> Draw a picture to help.
> "X" all that don't compare.

1. Mary had 15¢ and spent 7¢. How much money does she have now?

2. Ted has 8¢ and Jan has   How much more does Ted have than Jan?

$$\begin{array}{r} 8\cent \\ -\ 6\cent \\ \hline 2\cent \end{array}$$

3) Sharon had 7 cookies. She ate 4 of them. How many cookies does she still have?

Figure 4-36

MULTIPLICATION FACTS: MODELS, PATTERNS, TACTILE CUES

Problem area: Difficulty memorizing the basic multiplication facts. Recourse to wild guessing or inefficient counting techniques.

Typical disabilities affecting progress: Difficulty with visual, auditory, or long-term memory; visual or auditory discrimination; expressive language.

Background: Two things for teachers to consider when planning a program of fact study for learning disabled students are the following:

1. The techniques children use to figure out unknown facts.
2. The sequence in which unknown facts are clustered for study.

Children who have not yet mastered the multiplication facts often use wrong or inefficient techniques for arriving at answers to given facts. Sometimes, particularly when their concept of multiplication is weak, children tend to guess at answers and often miss. Or they may resort to some form of counting. Some, given a problem like 7 × 5, very tediously lay out counters or use tally marks to show seven groups of five, and then count by 5s to determine the total number. Some children do not rely on objects but skip count mentally to find simple products.

Skip counting will enable a child to figure out answers to multiplication fact answers. And it is a relatively easy task to skip count by 2s, 5s, and 10s. But skip counting, while appropriate for early conceptual work with multiplication, has little value for promoting quick recall of multiplication facts. Other techniques and models, such as those outlined below, are more effective for this purpose. If the disability is so severe that children cannot learn to handle the more efficient approaches to memorizing the facts, then serious thought should be given to the use of a hand calculator for multiplication and division needs.

The extent to which children succeed in fact mastery is somewhat tempered by the sequence in which facts are presented for study. Traditional textbook sequences must often be replaced by a program of study that maximizes success and minimizes frustration in early sessions with facts. The sequence given below has proved highly effective in this regard.

The basic plan in the suggested sequence is "easy facts first." Motivated by success at learning "so many facts so fast" (relatively speaking), students are encouraged to study hard the few that remain. First, 2s and 5s, then 9s—since, with the approaches outlined below, these are the easiest to learn. It is assumed that the commutatives of facts would be studied at each step throughout the sequence. Thus, if children also know 0s and 1s, there are only 15 other facts to be studied. Ideas for helping children master these last facts are also included in the activities which follow.

Suggested Sequence of Activities and Exercises

It is intended that the ideas below be used in early sessions with each cluster of facts and that tracking pages and reinforcing practice activities be carried out systematically during later sessions.

1. **2s and addition doubles.** Children who know addition doubles usually have little difficulty with multiplication 2s. Use the models for doubles in Figure 4-20 to help with multiplication 2s.

   - *Example:* $2 \times 6 = 12$ (egg carton model). "Two rows of six, or 2 *times* 6—that's 12." When this fact is established, children should be shown its commutative to study. Use the egg carton model or dots on cards to illustrate that 2 rows of six and 6 rows of two give the same total number: 12. Cueing exercises such as those suggested by Figure 4-37 should be used as necessary. If additional auditory reinforcement is needed, have the children read matching pairs into a tape recorder and listen to the playback.

(a)

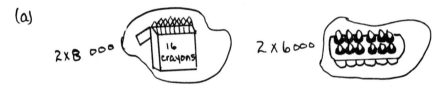

(b) Which has the same answer?

2×6 $\boxed{\begin{array}{c} 6 \times 2 \\ \hline 3 \times 6 \end{array}}$ 2×5 $\boxed{\begin{array}{c} 2 \times 3 \\ \hline 5 \times 2 \end{array}}$

Figure 4-37

   - *Example:* The child reads into a tape recorder: "2 × 8. That's 16, the crayon fact. 2 × 6. That's 12, the egg carton fact. . . ." Matching pairs could also be colored or texturized alike on charts or cards for ready reference.

   - *Note:* Techniques similar to those just presented would be used to reinforce the learning of other multiplication facts as well.

2. **5s and clock times.** If children can tell time on the clock, use this skill to help them memorize multiplication 5s. (For special help in teaching clock times, refer to Chapter 3.) The half hour time should cue the answer to 6 × 5 and 5 × 6 (30). For 9 × 5 and 5 × 9, the children should think of a time like 2:45 (big hand on the 9). For 7 × 5 and 5 × 7, children can think of the big hand on the 7 (2:35). If they cannot recall the minute time right away, cue them to think of the minute hand moving from the 6 to the 7: 5 × 6 = 30 (the half hour fact), so 5 × 7 is 5 more (35). Similarly, if 3 × 5 and 9 × 5, facts associated with the quarter hour times are learned first, then other harder facts can be related to them.

- *Example:* 3 × 5 = 15, so 4 × 5 = 20 (5 more). 9 × 5 = 45, so 8 × 5 = 40 (5 less). It usually helps to use a geared clock during instruction to illustrate answers to flash card problems. Visual, auditory, and kinesthetic cueing should also be used as needed to *teach to* the strengths of individual students. Ideas suggested in Activity 1 above or by Figure 4-38 can be used for this purpose.

Figure 4-38

- *Money as a model for 5s:* If children are strong in money concepts and skills for nickels through 50¢, then money can be used to help them master multiplication 5s. The fact that five nickels are worth 25¢ can be used to cue "5 × 5 = 25." Show five nickels and have students find the flash card (answer side up) that tells the value of the coins. Add another nickel to the pile of five: "5 × 5¢ = 25¢, so 6 × 5¢ is 5¢ more (30¢). Similarly, 5 × 5¢ = 25¢, so 4 × 5¢ is 5¢ less (20¢)." Money is particularly useful for learning 5s facts through 5 × 6 and 6 × 5.

3. **9s and patterns or finger cues.** There are many patterns in the 9s tables (refer to Figure 4-39). For example, the sum of the answer digits is always 9; the first digit of the product is always one less than the factor being multiplied by 9. A few learning disabled students can learn to recognize and use these patterns as a help in fact recall. But most cannot. There are just too many separate patterns to be integrated and remembered to be useful. But students can also use their hands for multiplication 9s. To do so, children first "number" their fingers, left to right, from 1 to 10 as in Figure 4-40a. Then, to multiply 9 × 3 (or 3 × 9), they fold their 3rd finger down (Figure 4-40b) and read the product from their fingers: 2 fingers to the left and 7 to the right of the folded finger: 27. For 7 × 9 or 9 × 7, they fold their 7th finger down (Figure 4-40b) and read the product from their fingers: 6 fingers to the left and 3 to the right of the folded finger: 63. Whether 9s are approached through patterns or finger cues, reinforcement, as noted elsewhere in this chapter, should be provided, along with tracking pages.

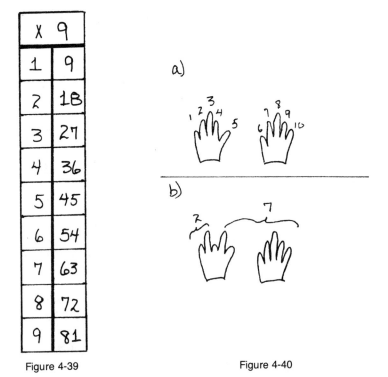

X	9
1	9
2	18
3	27
4	36
5	45
6	54
7	63
8	72
9	81

Figure 4-39   Figure 4-40

4. **Take stock.** If the students do not already know multiplication 0s and 1s, they could be introduced at this point (see Section 9 of this chapter for ideas on "× 0.") It is assumed that the commutatives of facts would be studied throughout the sequence. So when students have mastered 0s, 1s, 2s, 5s, and 9s—the "easy" facts—there are only 15 facts (and their commutatives) left for study: 3 × (3, 4, 6, 7, 8); 4 × (4, 6, 7, 8); 6 × (6, 7, 8); 7 × (7, 8); and 8 × 8. Because the sequence to this point has emphasized the "easy" facts, it helps children learn many facts in a relatively short time. It is important now to "take stock" with the students regarding facts learned and the number still to be studied. Charts like those of Figure 4-41 or 4-42 can be used for this purpose.

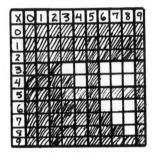

Figure 4-41

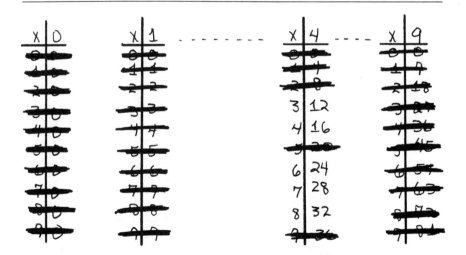

Figure 4-42

- *Note:* While they are not technically "basic" facts, some students may enjoy studying 10s and 11s at this point before turning to harder facts. The children probably can already skip count by 10s, so the multiplication pattern for 10s will be easy to learn. Permit students to use a hand calculator to discover the patterning for 11s.

5. **15 to go.** Some learning disabled students will need to rely solely on tracking pages and other practice activities for mastering the 15 remaining facts. Others can handle cues or strategies like the following in the early stages of learning the facts. Several of the strategies, such as "twice as much" and "add on" below, require a higher level of reasoning. If used, cueing techniques similar to those presented in Activity 1 above, would be employed.

   - **Twice as much.** The distributive property can be applied to "slicing down" harder facts for easier study. The basic idea is to use two easier facts to figure out a harder one. *Example:* 7×8. The child can add as in Figure 4-43. Note that parentheses have purposely been avoided. Still, writing out everything is visually confusing to many children. Keep the presentation oral, perhaps writing just the "$16 + 40 = 56$." The easiest use of this idea is:

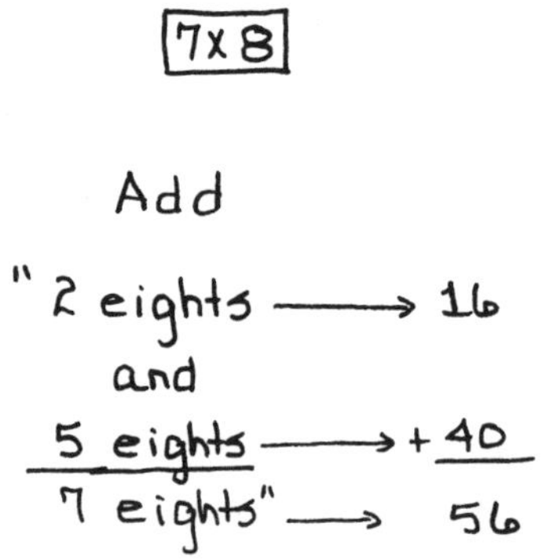

$$\boxed{7 \times 8}$$

$$\text{Add}$$

" 2 eights $\longrightarrow$ 16
    and
   5 eights $\longrightarrow$ +40
   7 eights" $\longrightarrow$ 56

Figure 4-43

"Figure out half, then double it." Approximately half the remaining 15 facts can be learned using this approach. *Example:* "4×6. Think of half $\longrightarrow 2 \times 6 = 12$. Now double it $\longrightarrow 4 \times 6 = 24$." "Twice as many cards," pictured in Figure 4-44, can be used to illustrate the point.

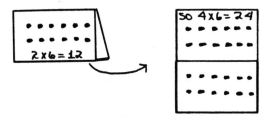

Figure 4-44

- **Add on.** An example of this familiar notion will serve to emphasize the idea: $5 \times 8 = 40$, so $6 \times 8 = 48$ (8 more). Children build from known facts. Encourage them to think: "5 eights. Now we have 6 eights. What do we add?" (8) *Variation:* subtract from (a known fact): $5 \times 4 = 20$, so $4 \times 4 = 16$ (4 less). "5 fours. Now 4 fours. So 4 less."

- **It's a square.** Five of the remaining facts are perfect squares and can be shown as in Figure 4-45. Children with strong visual memories might be cued by thinking of the squares.

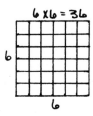

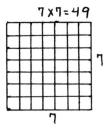

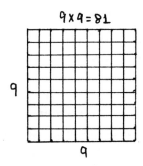

Figure 4-45

- **Other cues.** Children themselves have suggested the following as cues. Sharing ideas like these sometimes helps children to create their own. (1) 6s rhyme: 6 × 4, 24; 6 × 6, 36; 6 × 8, 48. (2) 12 = 3 × 4: "Before you go to the 3rd and 4th grades, you go to the 1st and 2nd." 56 = 7 × 8: "Before you go to the 7th and 8th grades, you go to the 5th and 6th."

FAMILIES TO HELP WITH SUBTRACTION AND DIVISION

Problem area: Difficulty memorizing subtraction or division facts.

Typical disabilities affecting progress: Difficulty with visual, auditory, or long-term memory; visual or auditory discrimination; expressive language.

Background: $6 + 7 = 13, 7 + 6 = 13, 13 - 6 = 7$, and $13 - 7 = 6$. These four facts form a special "family" of related addition and subtraction facts. Similar families can be formed of related multiplication and division facts. Many learning disabled students can learn to recognize facts that are related in this way and use that relationship to figure out quickly unknown subtraction or division answers. Example: $13 - 6 = 7$ because $7 + 6 = 13$.

Relying on the relationship of facts within a "family" is even more critical for division than for subtraction. There is a pattern that some children discover to help with division by 9s: $54 \div 9 = 6; 72 \div 9 = 8$. The answer is always one more than the first quotient digit. Beyond this, however, the very size of dividend figures makes the task very difficult unless the children can recall the multiplication fact. Example: $56 \div 7 = 8$ because $8 \times 7 = 56$.

Since the approach of related facts is a powerful and sometimes necessary one for helping students quickly figure out answers to subtraction or division facts, it should be encouraged. The following ideas should prove helpful in this regard. A general suggestion is to be sure students have mastered a set of addition (multiplication) facts before introducing related subtraction (division) facts.

Suggested Activities and Exercises

1. **Write to tell.** Use materials and pictures in early stages of subtraction and division fact work (Figure 4-46). Have the children write the related addition and subtraction (multiplication and division) facts that describe the grouping pictured.

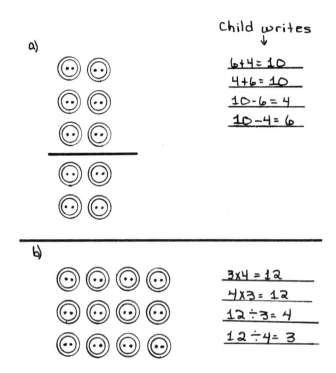

Figure 4-46

2. **Verbal feedback.** No matter how the subtraction or division answer is obtained, follow through when possible with feedback like the following: "Yes, you're right. $13 - 6$ is 7, because $7 + 6 = 13$;" or "Yes, $48 \div 6$ is 8 because $8 \times 6 = 48$." If necessary, use materials to illustrate the relationship between a pair of facts.

   • *Variation:* Have the children write answers to a small set of subtraction or division facts, then listen to a tape recorder for grading. The taped message should give not only the answer but the related fact each time as well.

3. **Find it.** Provide exercises like that of Figure 4-47 in which children cross out the wrong fact and answer the related fact along with that given.

4. **Look to see.** Provide flash card or other activities in which children answer a given subtraction (division) fact, then turn to check. Sometimes the related fact could be given as a hint (Figure 4-48). Use the color cueing as suggested if this seems helpful.

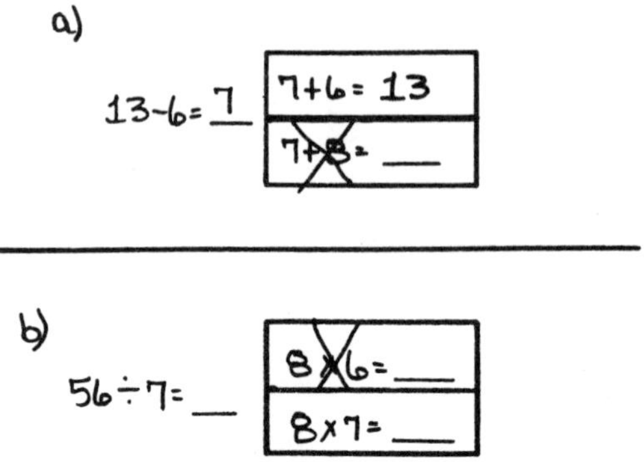

a)

$13-6=\underline{7}$ | $7+6=13$
$7+8=\underline{\quad}$ (crossed out)

b)

$56\div7=\underline{\quad}$ | $8\times6=\underline{\quad}$ (crossed out)
$8\times7=\underline{\quad}$

Figure 4-47

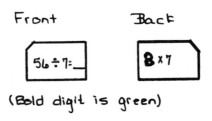

Front   Back

$56\div7=\underline{\quad}$ 8×7

(Bold digit is green)

Figure 4-48

5. **Sort.** Provide an opportunity for the children to sort flash cards into families. Related facts could be color coded alike for early sessions. Alternatively, the backs of cards containing related facts could be keyed alike (e.g. all carry a red dot).

• *Variation:* Provide puzzles of familiar objects with related facts written on the pieces of each puzzle (Figure 4-49). Force thinking by using the same color for pairs of puzzles that the children are asked to piece together.

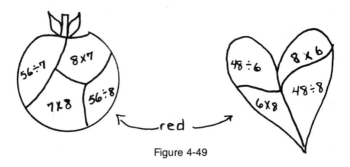

Figure 4-49

6. **Helpers.** Place addition (multiplication) facts that the children *know* at the top of a worksheet. Suggest that the children use them to help answer subtraction (division) fact problems on the page. One could even have students write the helper fact beside that given.

7. **Throughout.** Encourage finger tracing (of textured number sentences) or use color coding throughout the activities above as necessary. Such cues would, of course, be systematically withdrawn until the children can *independently* recall related addition (multiplication) facts to help.

ZERO

Section 9

Problem area: Confusion over answers for facts like $0 + 3$, 0×3, $3 - 0$, and $0 \div 3$. "Is the answer 0 or 3?"

Typical disabilities affecting progress: Difficulty with visual, auditory, or long-term memory; visual or auditory discrimination; expressive language.

Background: It is quite common for students to be confused over fact answers for problems containing 0. Learning disabled students are no exception. Often the problem does not show itself right away in addition and subtraction. After students have been introduced to multiplication, however, it quickly emerges. When *multiplying,* the product for facts containing 0 as a factor is always 0. When *adding* 0 to any other addend, the nonzero digit is the sum. Children now begin to be confused about when to write 0 for a fact answer. The following ideas may help when these difficulties appear.

Suggested Activities and Exercises

1. **Act it out.** Introduce "0" facts dramatically. Have the students "act out" number facts containing 0.

   - *Example:* "3×0." Use a bag filled with candy. Dramatize reaching into the bag *three times* and, each time, bringing out *no* candy. "How much candy did I pull out of the bag?" (None)

2. **Auditory cueing.** In the above activity and on other occasions when a "$\times$ 0" fact appears, use an auditory cue to reinforce (prompt) the correct answer.

   - *Example:* "$\times$ 0 is a wipeout. You get nothing at all."

3. **On the card.** Use number sentence cards for addition and multiplication "0" facts. Color all "+" signs green; all "×" signs brown. Mix the cards. In turn, have the students draw a card, give the answer, and use counters to prove they are right. The students should place counters for addition sentences on a green card and counters for multiplication sentences on a brown card. Get the students to note how the operation sign and card color match. Form two lines with the cards: one line for addition, one for multiplication. Make an issue of the fact that the brown cards have nothing on them. "× 0 is a wipeout—you get nothing at all."

   • *Note:* Though this example focuses on addition and multiplication, a similar approach could be used for zero facts involving subtraction or division.

4. **Sort.** Have the students sort cards containing "0" facts into two piles: "a zero answer" and "not-a-zero answer" pile.

5. **Move.** Create games in which the children draw an "0" fact card to determine the number of moves made along a path. Carry through the color coding on the cards as above, if this seems helpful. The children drawing a "× 0" number fact would stay where they are. "× 0 is a wipeout. You get nothing at all."

USING A HAND CALCULATOR

Here are several suggestions for using a calculator to build concepts for the four operations or basic fact skills.

• *Punch the sign.* Give the students sheets like that of Figure 4-50. The children fill in the correct operation sign, then punch out the problem on their calculators to see if they are correct.

$$
\begin{array}{ccc}
3 & 10 & 6 \\
\underline{5} & \underline{3} & \underline{4} \\
8 & 7 & 10
\end{array}
$$

Figure 4-50

• *Turn arounds*. To review or reinforce the idea of commutatives, give the children sheets like that of Figure 4-51. The children can use the calculator to check that both facts of a pair have the same answer.

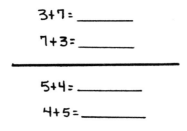

Figure 4-51

• *Beat the calculator*. Have the students compare times for completing a practice sheet of facts—with and without a calculator. They should find that they can work faster without a calculator.

• *Pick the helper* (for subtraction or division facts). Give the students a sheet like that of Figure 4-52. Have the children circle the helper fact, then punch it into the calculator. If they get the green minuend (quotient) number as their answer, they will know they are correct.

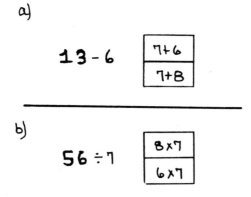

Figure 4-52

Chapter 5

Whole Number Computation

In the previous chapter, whole number operations were discussed. Various methods were highlighted for helping learning disabled students understand and differentiate among the four operations. Ideas were also presented for helping the students master the basic facts for each operation.

This chapter has a dual purpose: (1) to help children extend and apply concepts and skills they know to the longer, more complicated whole number computations; and (2) to point out some of the common difficulties learning disabled students encounter as they now proceed to multistep computations at the abstract level.

Computation involves using symbols and operation signs to arrive at numerical answers. Some children, because of abstract reasoning or integrative or auditory processing deficits, may lack important conceptual understandings necessary for success at the symbolic level. Other learning disabled students may in fact understand the concepts involved but still be unable to succeed with a computation.

Children may lack the memory and association skills that normally allow one to incorporate previously learned skills and to arrive at correct answers. For example, associating the correct operation with a sign or symbol actually involves two skills:

1. the ability to differentiate among all the different symbols; and
2. the ability to associate the correct symbol with the correct process—add, subtract, multiply, and divide.

For many children, these steps are extremely hard. These are the students who often say, ''Tell me what to do; then I can solve the problem.'' That statement does not mean that they do not understand the isolated operations conceptually. They may be perfectly capable of showing what to do for each of the operations. However, at this stage they are not being asked to show what they know. They are being asked to determine the correct process based on a symbol. Once they identify that process, they are on their way.

Children with visual perception problems may have trouble with this type of association because they incorrectly discriminate among the signs. Children with receptive language deficits may be able to associate the sign with the correct *word*—add, subtract, multiply, or divide; but the word may carry no meaning for them. Children with expressive language deficits may not be able to elicit, either verbally or to themselves, the correct process without being cued visually or auditorily.

Once children have associated the correct symbol with the correct process, it is necessary to determine the sequence that applies. Since the computational procedures now involve more than one step, confusion arises. This is complicated by the fact that most computations now involve two or more operations, even though only one sign is used. Consider for example the process of subtraction, as shown in Figure 5-1. In sequence, it is necessary to subtract, add, subtract, and subtract; yet the entire process is called subtraction.

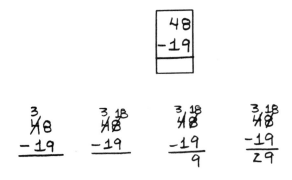

Figure 5-1

Correctly sequencing the steps is an especially difficult task for many students. Those children with additional impairments to learning have an even harder time. The child with a memory-sequencing deficit, whether visual or auditory, is required to use this deficit area in order to learn a skill. Retaining each isolated step is hard enough. To retain steps in the correct order is often impossible.

The child with a discrimination difficulty, who confuses the + and × sign, may perceive the operation differently each time it is seen. Figure 5-2 illustrates how this disability can affect computation. At first glance, it would appear that this student needs more work, conceptually, on the process of multiplying a 2-digit

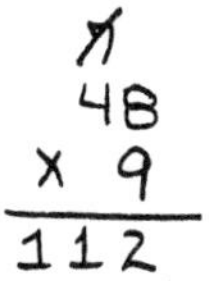

$$\begin{array}{r} \not{7} \\ 48 \\ \times\ 9 \\ \hline 112 \end{array}$$

Figure 5-2

number by a 1-digit number. In this case, listening to the student verbalize the procedure made it apparent that after carrying the 7, the sign was misperceived and the computation was completed as addition.

Alignment is another difficulty. Consider multiplication of two 2-digit factors. Even with a good understanding of place value, basic facts, and multiplication by ones and tens, the ability to align numbers accurately can be very tedious for some children. Figure 5-3 shows a step-by-step breakdown of the mental process involved.

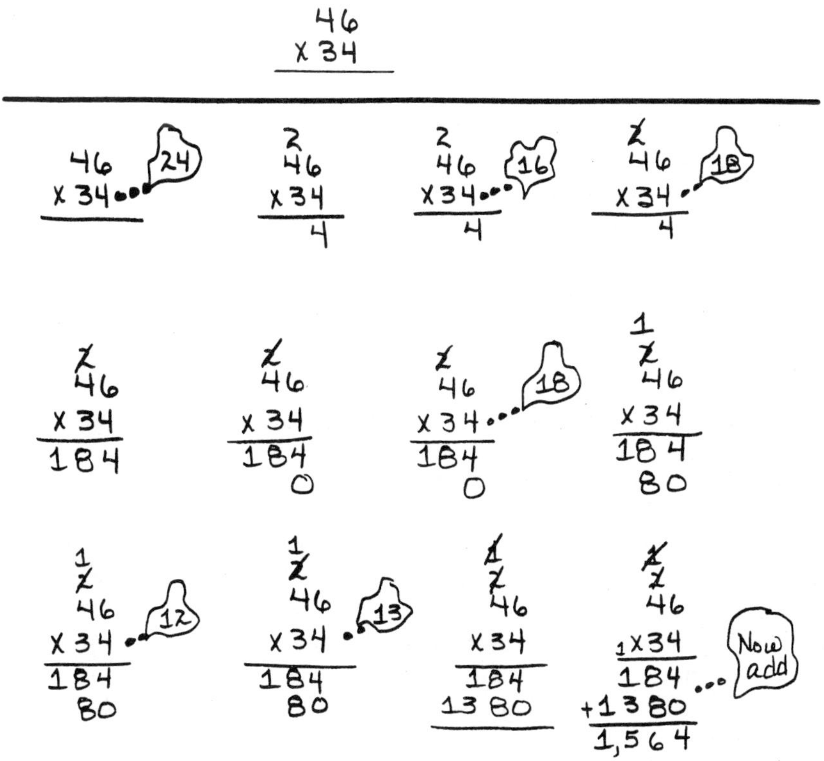

$$\begin{array}{r} 46 \\ \times\ 34 \end{array}$$

Figure 5-3

For the child with poor motor coordination or impaired spatial organization, the actual process of solving the problem becomes twice as long. Every time it is necessary to write a digit, this student must stop and look at the problem. The digits already there must be sorted out, and it is necessary to coordinate what is seen with what the hand does. For this child, although there may be a solid understanding of place value and the steps involved, the sequence is interrupted, considerably and consistently, whenever it is necessary to write a number.

Visual figure-ground deficits and reversal tendencies also impede accuracy with computation. Consider Figure 5-4 in which a child is asked to perform a common subtraction problem. It appeared that the difficulty might be inadequate mastery of facts (and in many instances it may well be). However, upon questioning the child, it became apparent that the difficulty was visually aligning the numbers in order to compute accurately. The first step was correct; the student thought ''6 take away 5'' and wrote 1. Next, the numbers were correctly regrouped. But then the student lost the place and saw 6 subtract 4. The last step, 8 subtract 2, is accurate.

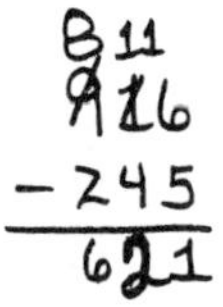

$$
\begin{array}{r}
\cancel{8}\,\overset{11}{\cancel{9}}\overset{1}{1}6 \\
-\ 2\,4\,5 \\
\hline
6\,2\,1
\end{array}
$$

Figure 5-4

For students with reversal and visual memory deficits, regrouping causes special problems. So does long division. Figure 5-5a shows how a child who tends to reverse might solve a division problem. In the first example, the 6 was perceived as a 2, but otherwise the computation and procedure are correct. Obviously, this student understands the steps for long division and at least knows the required facts for the problem. Figure 5-5b shows the same division problem, but this time the difficulties are reversal and discrimination. In this example, the student initially perceived the ''6'' as a 6 and wrote 1 in the quotient. However, at the multiplication step, the divisor was seen as a 2, thus the product 2. In the subtraction step, the 2 was perceived as a 6, resulting in a difference of 2. At first glance, this student appears to be careless and unsure of the basic facts involved. In examples like this, questioning or looking at a computation in light of previous work may reveal instead that the child does know the needed facts and is familiar with the correct process. Specific learning disabilities may be at the root of the problem.

Computational accuracy often involves estimating to check whether an answer is reasonable. This is a difficult task for most students and an especially difficult one for many children with learning disabilities. Although an essential part of the

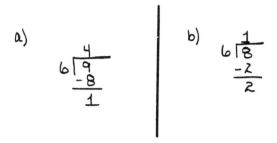

Figure 5-5

process of learning how to estimate involves concrete presentations, the actual application of the skill is abstract and requires a considerable amount of reasoning. For those children who have any kind of integrative processing deficit, it is essential that they learn to estimate through a highly structured approach. Many will not intuitively recognize when an answer is incorrect. Others may sense that something is wrong but be unable to figure out or express exactly what it is.

The following pages suggest sequences and techniques for helping students who have difficulties like those described above. Suggestions are clustered under five major headings. The first, general difficulties with whole number computation, examines special problems that children may experience with basic facts in computation or in associating operation sign and process. Thereafter, ideas are presented for handling computational difficulties for whole-number addition, subtraction, multiplication, and division. Ideas for using the hand calculator to help learning disabled students master whole-number computation are interwoven throughout the chapter.

GENERAL DIFFICULTIES

Controlling for Unknown Facts

Problem area: Failure to succeed in computation because of inadequate fact mastery.

Typical disabilities affecting progress: Difficulty with visual, auditory, or long-term memory; visual or auditory discrimination; expressive language.

Background: Computing involves using the basic facts. Learning disabled students, like their peers, become frustrated and often fail with computation involving facts they have not yet mastered. Many students are ready, developmentally, to learn the more complicated computational procedures but have not yet committed the basic facts to memory. To require them to learn the facts first may hold them back unnecessarily. With these students, it is important to keep in mind, as noted in Chapter 1, the goal of the particular assignment. If the goal is learning and using the various computational procedures, then memorizing the facts is a secondary and separate topic. Below are two approaches for dealing with this issue.

Suggested Activities and Exercises

1. **Controlled fact program.** One approach is to control the entire math program around known facts. This is a very specialized approach, one which involves considerable preparation and care to implement. It requires that one select or create computational exercises so that only *known facts* are required for deriving answers. This approach is obviously not a practical one for mainstreamed or other situations where teachers deal with larger groups of students. It may be necessary in special cases.

   - *Note:* Most children know at least some of the easier facts, such as doubles in addition or twos and fives in multiplication. Easy facts like these can be used to present or review computational procedures in class. In this way, learning disabled children can still be a successful part of the class even though, on the side, they are still working on isolated facts.

2. **Only known facts.** Many children benefit from controlled fact pages as shown in Figure 5-6. Place two basic facts that are being worked on at the top of the page. The computation on the page involves only these facts and any other known facts, in this case twos and fives.

Figure 5-6

3. **Black out.** Give each child a sheet of Ts such as that shown in Figure 5-7. Help the students black out all facts they have already mastered, and allow them to refer to the sheet whenever they need to do so. In the meantime, challenge the students to memorize three or four unknown facts each week. Choose the facts carefully.

Figure 5-7

- *Example:* Select facts that are *one more than* some fact a child already knows. If a child knows $12 - 6 = 6$, select $13 - 6$.

Make sure the children are aware of any relationships between new and known facts; suggest that they use those relationships to help figure out answers if they get stuck. Each day during the week, provide tracking pages on the three or four facts being studied. Then, at the end of the week, test the new facts in a mixed review quiz including other known facts. These facts should be blackened as they are mastered.

Basic Facts: Transfer to Larger Problems

General Section 2

Problem area: Failure to answer correctly known facts embedded within larger computational problems.

Typical disabilities affecting progress: Difficulty with visual discrimination or visual association, abstract reasoning, expressive language.

Background: Many learning disabled students are unable, independently, to use basic facts within a computation until they have learned the procedure and feel comfortable with it. These are students who do reasonably well on fact tests. But they are unable to incorporate the facts into the computation until overlearning has occurred in this area. It requires too much retention and sequencing for them to learn a new skill while trying to recall other isolated pieces of information. Hence they fail to transfer fact learning to its application in computational situations. The suggestions that follow will help to deal with this problem.

Suggested Activities and Exercises

1. **Write it out.** If the children get "stuck" within a larger computation because they cannot recall a known fact, suggest that they write the problem fact to one side. Seeing the fact in isolation often triggers recognition and allows the children to proceed.
2. **Finger trace.** If the students are strong tactual learners, suggest that they finger trace over the problem fact, quietly saying it to themselves. If they are strong auditory learners, simply saying the fact to themselves may do.
3. **Circle.** Another approach is to circle the problem fact within a problem or to write over it as a means of better focusing on it.
4. **Side by side.** Help train for the desired transfer by providing practice sheets that place a basic fact beside a larger computational problem using this fact (Figure 5-8).

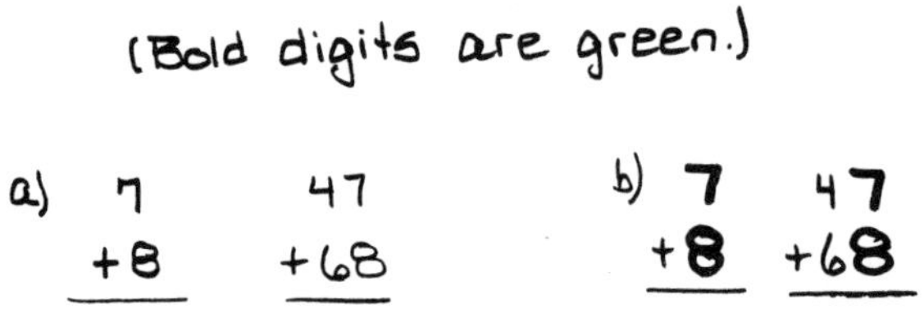

(Bold digits are green.)

a)   7   47   b) **7**   4**7**
      +8   +68   +**8**   +**68**

Figure 5-8

5. **Color code.** Provide extra visual reinforcement, if this is helpful on the Activity 4 sheets above, by color cueing as suggesed by Figure 5-8b.
6. **Track.** Provide tracking pages containing larger computational problems. Have the students look for and circle a given fact any time it appears on the page.

7. **Look to the chart.** Allow the children to use a multiplication chart, Ts, or a fact box. Experience has shown that as children feel comfortable with the computational procedure, the need for these aids will disappear.

Interpreting the Printed Word or Sign for an Operation

Problem area: Failure to associate the correct process with the operation sign or with the written direction to add, subtract, multiply or divide.

Typical disabilities affecting progress: Difficulty with closure, expressive or receptive language, visual discrimination.

Background: This section deals with two related difficulties. The first, discussed in the introduction to this chapter, involves the printed symbol for each operation. Some learning disabled students, despite solid conceptual understandings, either misperceive or misinterpret the written operation signs. A second difficulty involves not knowing what to do when presented with written directions to add, subtract, multiply, or divide. Without the sign as a guide, some children are at a loss to know how to proceed. Many mathematics textbooks, for example, present skill pages of the type shown in Figure 5-9. Within a structured program, this type of page can be very useful for building skills due to language deficits. Initially, however, children with receptive language difficulties may be unable to succeed independently with exercises of this nature. A chart, such as that of Figure 1-19, can be especially helpful to these students.

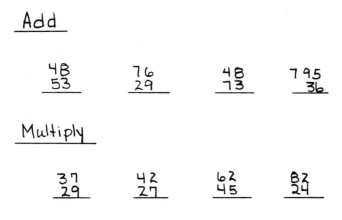

Figure 5-9

The following activities and exercises suggest techniques for dealing with each of the difficulties summarized above. The suggestions assume that conceptual understanding for each operation is well established. If this is not the case, it would be necessary to return to work with physical materials, as outlined in Chapter 4, before proceeding.

Suggested Activities and Exercises

Interpreting the Operation Sign

1. **Circle.** Visual discrimination deficits may cause a child to have difficulty associating properly. Keep textbooks in which the operation signs have been circled, or have the child circle each sign on the page before solving. In this way, attention is drawn more directly to the operation sign.
2. **What is the sign?** Use texture cues or color coding, or allow the students to finger trace before solving, as suggested in Activities 5 and 6 of Section 1 in Chapter 4. Finger tracing the sign before solving may be particularly useful on pages of mixed problem types (e.g. pages of addition *and* subtraction problems). Sometimes, a verbal reminder or visual cue to "Stop! Look at the sign" (see Figure 5-10) is helpful on pages of this type. In severe cases, one might require a student to circle all addition problems and to work these *before* turning to the subtraction examples on a page.

Figure 5-10

Interpreting the Sign or Word for Each Operation

1. Chart it

- Figure 5-11 shows one type of supplemental page that can be prepared at the beginning of the school year and kept on file. Each symbol on the page should be the same color as the word denoting that operation. If the chart shown in Figure 1-19 is hanging, the colors on these pages should match those of the chart. The teacher writes problems in the left column. The child recopies and solves in the appropriate box as shown. For some, this might be a two-day assignment. On the first day, students might merely copy each problem into the appropriate spaces. After the paper has been checked, the problems would be solved.

	Add	Subtract	Multiply	Divide
48 x 6			48 x 6	
54 -19		54 -19		
36 + 8				

Figure 5-11

- If a child's difficulty is in interpreting the operation sign, the focus is on internalizing the meaning of that sign. Eventually these students would learn to copy problems from their textbook into the proper space of the supplemental page.

- If a child's difficulty is in interpreting the written direction ("add," "subtract," "multiply," "divide"), the focus is on building vocabulary by association with numeric examples that use the operation sign. Similar sheets can be used to help the children build associations for "sum," "difference," "product," or "quotient."

Note: For many students, an operation sign is readily associated with the correct word and process when the numbers used are basic facts. However, when multidigit numbers are used in computation, these same children may have difficulty with the association. For this reason, it is important that 2- or higher-digit numbers be used in the problems of the left-hand column.

2. **Page assignment sheets.** Many children tend to perseverate and need continued help in associating the correct process with given words or symbols. Assign textbook pages or problems on a given page in random order as described in Chapter 1. Figure 5-12a shows an example of a page that can be kept in the files and used as an assignment sheet for such children. The child writes the symbol beside the word and then writes the appropriate problem numbers in the right-hand column of the sheet (Figure 5-12b). If necessary, the operation word can be underlined to match the color used for that word on the wall chart.

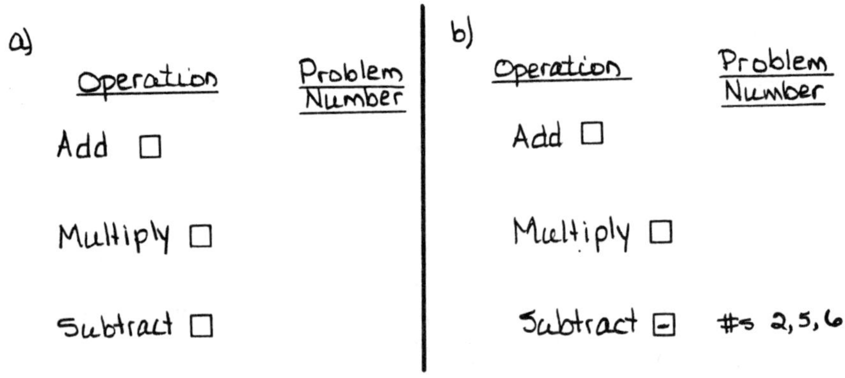

a)

Operation	Problem Number
Add ☐	
Multiply ☐	
Subtract ☐	

b)

Operation	Problem Number
Add ☐	
Multiply ☐	
Subtract ⊟	#s 2,5,6

Figure 5-12

Interpreting Vocabulary for Each Operation

3. **Circle to match.** At the beginning of the year, go through the text and find pages such as those illustrated in Figure 5-9. Circle direction words in the appropriate color to match the wall chart. Instruct the student to place the correct sign beside the word before solving the problems.

4. **Look to the chart.** When the words "sum," "product," "quotient," and "difference" are introduced, use a chart such as that shown in Figure 5-13. Color the chart to match the coding scheme of Figure 1-19. A small copy of the chart can be pasted to the top of a child's worksheet. If more specific practice is needed, use pages like that of Figure 5-14. The children can "X" inappropriate problems, then work the correct one. The color scheme adopted for the charts of Figures 1-19 and 5-13 should be carried through on pages of this type. In the example of Figure 5-14, if "sum" and "+" are green, then "−" could be black, "×" red, and "⌐" blue.

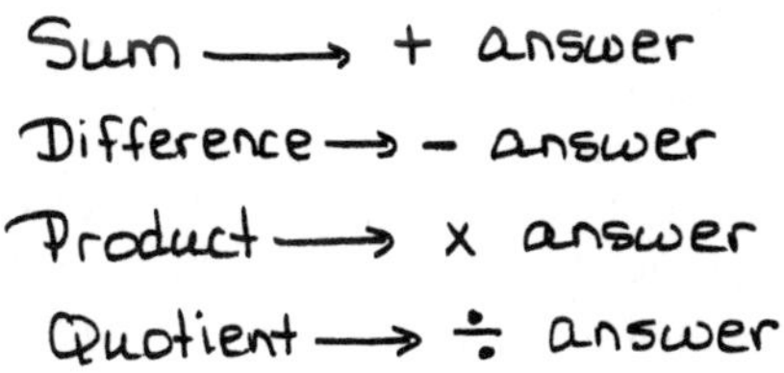

Sum ⟶ + answer

Difference ⟶ − answer

Product ⟶ × answer

Quotient ⟶ ÷ answer

Figure 5-13

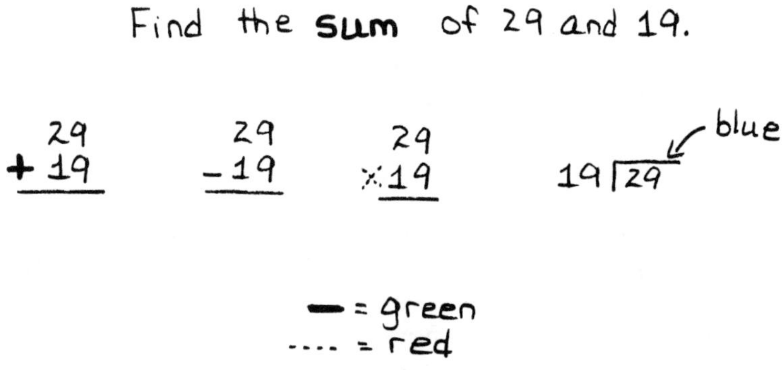

Find the **sum** of 29 and 19.

$$\begin{array}{r} 29 \\ +\ 19 \\ \hline \end{array} \qquad \begin{array}{r} 29 \\ -\ 19 \\ \hline \end{array} \qquad \begin{array}{r} 29 \\ \times\ 19 \\ \hline \end{array} \qquad 19\overline{)29} \quad \text{blue}$$

━ = green

···· = red

Figure 5-14

ADDITION OF WHOLE NUMBERS

Multiples of Ten

Problem area: Difficulty adding 10 or a multiple of 10 to other 1- or 2-digit numbers.

Typical disabilities affecting progress: Difficulty with auditory association, auditory memory, auditory figure-ground, and visual figure-ground.

Background: The ability to add multiples of 10 to other numbers is especially helpful when children regroup in subtraction or perform other mental calculations. Many children who have trouble recognizing relationships or patterns have trouble with these additions. For example, they may not recognize, visually or auditorily, the relationship between "30 + 40" and "3 + 4." They often begin at 30 and count on by 10s. Some students even have difficulty with the simpler additions, such as that involved in adding 10 to a single-digit number. For these students, it is essential to work on the underlying pattern of "adding 10" before introducing regrouping. Once regrouping has been started, frequent review may still be necessary so that the children incorporate the skill.

The suggestions that follow have proved helpful in our work with learning disabled students who have difficulty "adding tens." The suggestions assume that the children have already worked extensively with materials—tens and ones—as the basis for understanding the computational procedure for addition of 2-digit numbers: Add like units; and if there are 10 or more singles, trade for 1 ten. Now, as the children turn to work at the symbolic level, activities and exercises such as those described below are frequently necessary.

Suggested Activities and Exercises
Adding 10 to a single-digit number

(helpful for regrouping in subtraction)

1. **A bundle plus.** Provide numeral cards (one each for 1, 2, 3, . . . 9), a bundle of 10 popsicle sticks, and 9 extra single sticks. Lay out the 10-bundle, making sure the children realize that there are 10 sticks banded together in the bundle. Mix the cards and place them face down in a pile. The children, in turn, draw a card and place that many single sticks beside the 10-bundle (Figure

5-15a). They then tell the number of sticks in all (16 in this example). If a child does not know, ask for a guess before a count is made to check. Encourage the students to count on from 10 rather than count from 1 each time (see Section 4, Chapter 2). Make a chart showing the result of each draw (Figure 5-15b). Color emphasize the like digits.

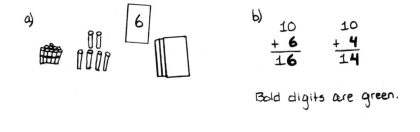

Bold digits are green.

$$\begin{array}{r} 10 \\ +\ 5 \\ \hline \end{array} \qquad \begin{array}{r} 10 \\ +\ 7 \\ \hline \end{array}$$

Bold print is green.
Dotted lines are red

Figure 5-15

- *Follow-up 1:* Assign exercises like that of Figure 5-15c. Allow the students to use a 10-bundle and extra sticks if they are needed.

- *Follow-up 2:* To encourage mental calculation, use a mask like that of Figure 5-16 on the chart of Figure 5-15b. Ask the children to give answers orally. Allow them to use a 10-bundle and extra sticks if they get stuck.

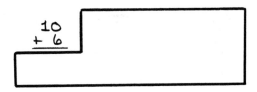

Figure 5-16

2. **Slide and see.** Use a ruler and a "+ 10" card like that shown in Figure 5-17a. The laminated worksheet of Figure 5-17b should also be provided. The teacher writes a single-digit number on a green line of the worksheet to indicate where the child should place the green circle on the ruler (in this example, on the "6"). The child slides a finger along the arrow to get the "feel" of "adding 10." Then the ruler number sentence is read aloud: "6 + 10 is 16." The child writes the result of the addition on the red worksheet line. The children could use a 10-bundle and extra sticks to verify the result. Repeat with the other numbers, until four or five examples are written on the sheet. Help the children analyze the written work. Model the auditory emphasis of the two like digits in each example: "*Six* plus ten is *six*teen." If the children profit from kinesthetic involvement, have them finger trace the like digits in each example they read.

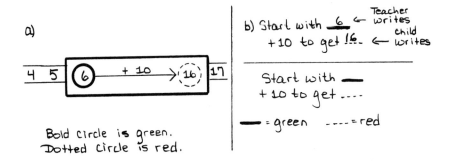

Figure 5-17

3. **Slide and check.** Tape a flap over the red hole of the "+ 10" card (Figure 5-18). Repeat the above activity, but this time have the child tell the sum, then lift the flap to check.

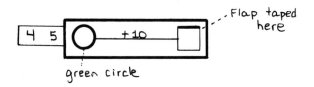

Figure 5-18

4. **On their backs.** Copy incomplete "+ 10" problems like those of Figure 5-19 on the board, and provide the numeral card deck of Activity 1 above. Mix the cards and place them face down in a pile. In turn, the children draw a card, look at it and show it to the teacher, then place it upside down on the table or desk. After the teacher traces this numeral on each child's back, the child walks to the chalkboard and completes one of the "+ 10" problems. (The walk provides the medium for forcing the child to think about the numeral that recurs twice in the completed problem.) When the "+ 10" problem is complete, ask the student to read it aloud. Encourage auditory emphasis of the repeated digit. Then hold up the card the child left behind. Check that the numeral on the card does appear twice in the completed problem. If necessary, the child can use the "+ 10" card and ruler of Activity 1 to correct any error.

10+	10+
10+	10+
10+	10+

Figure 5-19

Adding 10 to 2-digit numbers

5. **Calculator help.** If children have the necessary skills, allow them to use a hand calculator to complete exercises such as that shown in Figure 5-20a. When a page is complete, have the student read across each row as follows: "26 plus 10 is 36, 48 plus 10 is 58." It often helps to give the child a card to uncover the numerals while reading (Figure 5-20b). Toward the end of the page, cover up the answer and have the child say the sentences, giving answers without the visual reinforcement.

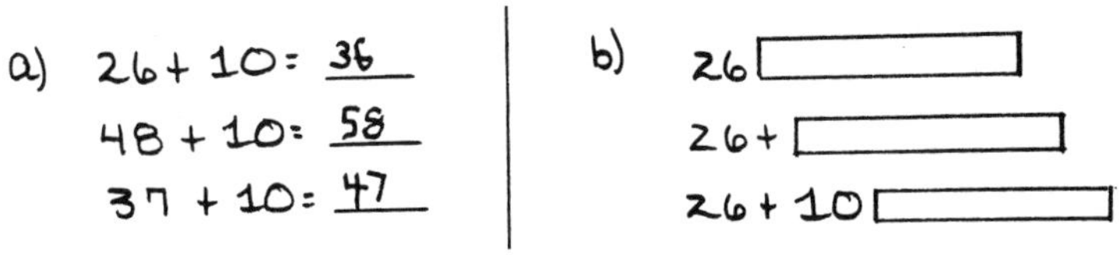

a) 26 + 10 = 36
    48 + 10 = 58
    37 + 10 = 47

b) 26 [＿＿＿]
    26 + [＿＿＿]
    26 + 10 [＿＿＿]

Figure 5-20

6. **Highlight the pattern.** Some children are helped in exercises of this type when a vertical format and colors are used as in Figure 5-21. Highlighting the digits helps to emphasize the pattern of change in the tens digits. The children could be instructed to complete the first part of a page containing problems like those shown, leaving the last six or seven problems unsolved. When the first part has been completed, have the children analyze their work. Help them notice the pattern by pointing first to the green tens digit in the problem and then to the tens digit in the sum. While pointing, say each numeral: "two . . . three," "four . . . five," "six . . . seven." Continue this verbal patterning as the children fill in the green blanks of the unsolved problems. A similar procedure is used with the ones digits. When the page is complete, have them read the problems as in Activity 1 above. Model the auditory emphasis of the tens digit pattern. For example, "*Twenty*-six plus ten is *thirty*-six."

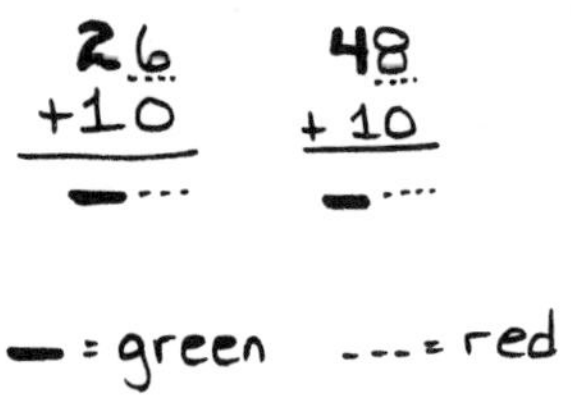

$$\begin{array}{r} 2\,6 \\ +1\,0 \\ \hline \end{array} \qquad \begin{array}{r} 4\,8 \\ +\,1\,0 \\ \hline \end{array}$$

— = green   - - - = red

Figure 5-21

- *Follow up:* To encourage mental calculation, follow up with similar worksheets in which children give answers orally (or dictate them into a tape) before writing.

7. **Practice.** To build up the automatic nature of adding tens, present pages with color-coded horizontal problems, as in Figure 5-22. The colors are used for focusing and visual association with the vertical problems previously completed. The students read the problems as in Activity 1 above and fill in the blanks.

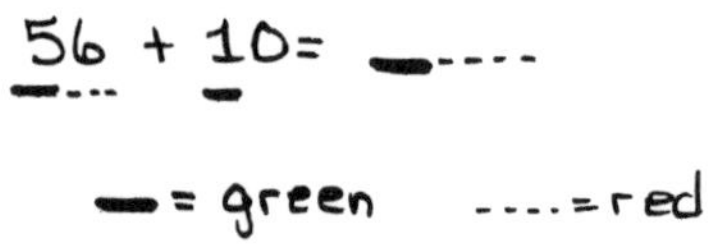

$$56 + 10 = \underline{\quad}$$

— = green   - - - = red

Figure 5-22

8. **Toss up** (a practice activity for two to play). Prepare a gameboard as in Figure 5-23 and laminate the center strip. Using a grease pencil, write 15 two-digit numbers in the center strip. Provide about ten markers for each player and two dice:

> Die 1: Marked 4, 5, 6, 7, 8, 9.
> Die 2: Marked 1, 2, 3, 4, 5, 6.

In turn, the players roll the dice and place them in the squares to the left of the center strip to form a two-digit numeral. This number is added to 10. If the sum is on the board, a marker is placed beside it as shown. If players give an incorrect answer, they must remove one marker from their side of the board. If the sum is correctly stated but not on the board, the dice go to the next player. The winner is the first player to place five markers in a row.

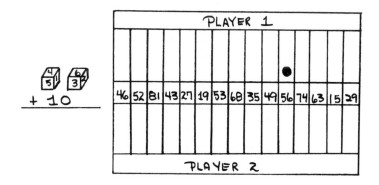

Figure 5-23

• *Variation:* To encourage mental calculation, give each player markers of two different colors (e.g. orange, worth one point; blue, worth two points). The play proceeds as above, but use an orange marker if answers are given after mental calculation; blue otherwise. The winner is the first to accumulate six points.

Adding other multiples of 10 to a 2-digit number

9. **Calculator help.** As in Activity 5 above, but introduce multiples of 10 (20, 30, . . . 90) as the second addend.

10. **Relate to the basic fact.** To help develop the visual/auditory pattern and relate the addition to basic facts, exercises such as that shown in Figure 5-24 are helpful. One could use colors or bold print and underline to focus attention on the related basic facts. In Figure 5-24a, the child begins on the left and reads across the line, filling in the answer on the line. Encourage auditory emphasis to highlight the relationship: "*Six* plus *two* is *eight,* so *six*ty plus *twen*ty is *eighty.*" Examples of this type could later be extended to include adding a multiple of 10 to any 2-digit number, as in Figure 5-24b. The vertical format of this second set of problems is more effective with some students. Whatever the format, finger tracing like parts of related problems might be encouraged for a student who requires a high degree of kinesthetic involvement.

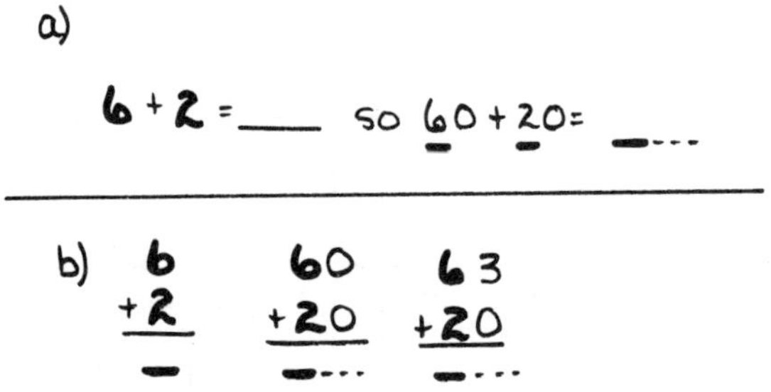

a)

$$6 + 2 = \underline{\hspace{1cm}} \quad \text{so} \quad \underline{60} + \underline{20} = \underline{\hspace{1cm}} \text{---}$$

b)

$$
\begin{array}{ccc}
6 & 60 & 63 \\
+2 & +20 & +20 \\
\hline
\underline{\hspace{0.5cm}} & \underline{\hspace{0.5cm}}\text{---} & \underline{\hspace{0.5cm}}\text{---}
\end{array}
$$

Figure 5-24

- *Follow up:* Encourage mental calculation. Use the exercises described above, but ask the students to give the answers orally before writing. Provide answer keys so that the students working independently can check their own work.

11. **Pick up** (for two or three to play). This game reviews adding 10 or other multiples of 10 to a 2-digit number. Provide a laminated gameboard such as that illustrated in Figure 5-25, 25 chips, and two dice:

Die 1: green numerals, 1 - 6.
Die 2: red numerals, 1 - 6.

The numerals in the left column of the gameboard are green; those in the top row are red. To begin, the students cover the entire board with chips. In turn, the children roll the dice to see

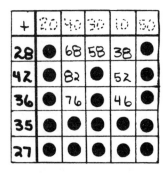

Figure 5-25

which numbers should be added. In the example of Figure 5-25, the green "3" refers to the 3rd green number (left column); the red "4" refers to the 4th red number (top row). These two numbers, 36 and 10, are to be added. The student locates the numbers and says, "36 plus 10 is 46." The player then removes the chip corresponding to the addends to check. If the answer is correct, the child keeps the chip. Otherwise it is replaced. The player with the most chips when the board is uncovered (or at the end of a given number of rounds) wins.

One- and Two-Digit Addends

Problem area: Difficulty adding a single-digit and a two-digit number.

Typical disabilities affecting progress: Difficulty with visual memory, visual discrimination, auditory figure-ground or sequencing, abstract reasoning, and closure.

Background: Study the problems of Figure 5-26. In early developmental work, as background to paper and pencil computations like these, children typically use ten stacks and ones or other physical materials to dramatize the combining of two 2-digits or a 1- and a 2-digit addend. At this early stage, children learn to combine like units—all the ones, all the tens—and to trade 10 singles for 1 "ten" whenever

$$\begin{array}{r} 17 \\ +\ 6 \\ \hline \end{array} \qquad \begin{array}{r} 32 \\ +\ 5 \\ \hline \end{array}$$

Figure 5-26

possible (Figure 5-27a). The result of combining ones and tens is written (Figure 5-27b), so that the children have a record of what was done. Gradually, because the children "see" what the computational procedure is all about, the materials are dropped, and the students learn to compute independently of manipulative aids. The children now enter a practice phase that emphasizes obtaining the correct answers more rapidly.

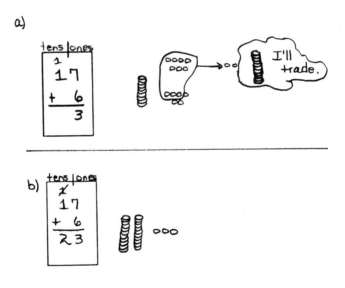

Figure 5-27

At the skill level, addition involving a 1- and a 2-digit addend can be approached in two ways:

1. as a paper and pencil computation, with or without regrouping; or
2. as a mental computation, an extension of the basic facts.

By the time a child is doing fourth- or fifth-grade-level work, problems such as those of Figure 5-26 can be treated as an extension of the basic facts. Strictly speaking, since the problems can be computed mentally, the need to use regrouping marks is unnecessary.

There are payoffs to handling problems of this type mentally.

• The mental calculation approach may help the children "add by endings" in column addition (Figure 5-28a).

• The mental calculation approach prepares the children for multiplication with regrouping (Figure 5-28b).

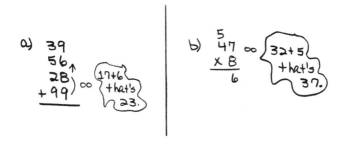

Figure 5-28

Many children who *do* know their basic facts are unable to recognize them in the context of a bigger problem (e.g. *32* + 5, not just 2 + 5). The single-digit addend causes confusion that may be linked to a visual perception or memory difficulty. It may also be associated with an inability to reason abstractly. Or it may be that, auditorily, the children do not hear the basic fact within the problem. Although they say the problem to themselves (silently or aloud), they may not recognize the fact. This latter difficulty may be due to auditory figure-ground or closure deficits. (See Chapter 1 for the definitions of these terms.) If the problem is presented visually, the empty space in the tens place can be extremely confusing, even if there is solid place-value comprehension. For many, adding a "concrete" symbol to an empty space is more difficult than adding two 2-digit numerals.

The following exercises are written to build or reinforce skill in adding a 1- and a 2-digit number. The emphasis is on building confidence with mental calculation. A suggestion for paper and pencil computation of these problem types is inserted at the end of the section. It is assumed that extensive work with materials, such as that outlined above, has already been carried out. This is a necessary prerequisite if the children are to have an intuitive basis for work at the symbolic level like that described.

Suggested Exercises

1. **How does it end?** Figure 5-29 shows an exercise that has proved helpful for relating problems involving a 1- and a 2-digit addend to basic facts. At first, only problems that require no regrouping would be presented. Blank file pages, using the format of Figure 5-29b, can be kept on hand and filled in as needed by the teacher. The colors will

   • focus attention on the basic fact,

   • develop reasoning skills,

   • give visual reinforcement to those with auditory deficits, and

   • give auditory reinforcement to those with poor visual memory.

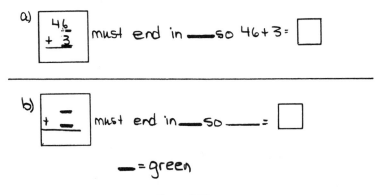

Figure 5-29

As has been pointed out, it is necessary to check for intact color vision for the colors used. In serious cases of color blindness, bold print and underscoring can be substituted to highlight and cue response. In the example of Figure 5-29a, the student begins on the left, reading silently or aloud, depending on the learning style. The horizontal part of the exercise follows the left-right reading sequence. It reflects what a child should *think* while computing a problem of this type. The blanks are filled in as the student approaches them verbally. Figure 5-30 suggests a sequence that may be used to help build the needed skill. By the time a child is working exercises like that in Figure 5-30c, colors may no longer be needed. If they are still necessary, the student could simply underline with a green pen before solving.

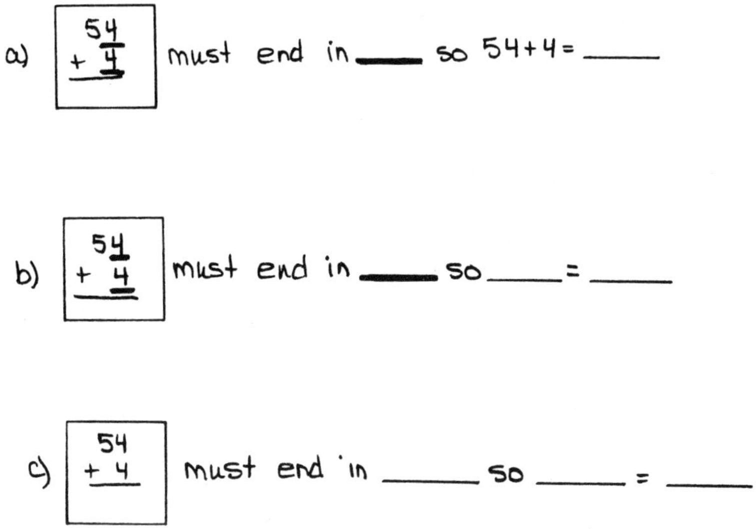

a) $\boxed{\begin{array}{r} 54 \\ + 4 \end{array}}$ must end in ____ so 54+4= ____

b) $\boxed{\begin{array}{r} 54 \\ + 4 \end{array}}$ must end in ____ so ____ = ____

c) $\boxed{\begin{array}{r} 54 \\ + 4 \end{array}}$ must end in ____ so ____ = ____

Figure 5-30

2. **Help for book problems.** These same pages can be used, if necessary, for textbook problems. Have the student copy out the problem, place it in the left-hand box, and then compute.
3. **Listen and read.** For those students who need the verbalization illustrated in Figure 5-29 and 5-30 but cannot read or express themselves well, prepare cassette tapes that match pages you keep on file. Have the child read along with the tape, problem by problem, until the process is internalized and the student feels comfortable. Experience has shown that students can eliminate use of the tape or other external verbalization within a relatively short time.
4. **Flash! How does it end?** Once the thought process is internalized, flash a color-coded card like that of Figure 5-31. Using the card as a cue, the child states the problem and then completes the sentence, as in the exercises of Figure 5-29 and 5-30.

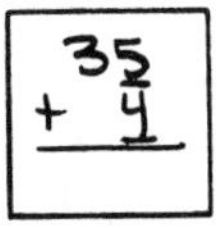

Figure 5-31

5. **Side by side.** For children who have either internalized the above pattern or who can readily see visual patterns, present practice pages containing exercises like that of Figure 5-32. Notice that the exercise, though similar to many now presented in texts, uses a discontinuous pattern. The child is forced to focus on the pattern in each problem, thus eliminating the tendency to perseverate. The approach encourages children to recognize and use a pattern and thus fosters reasoning skills.

Figure 5-32

- *Note:* If color coding is necessary, the original basic fact—in this case 4 + 5—should be written or outlined in green. In the remaining problems, the fact would be underlined in green by the teacher or the student before the problem is solved. Figure 5-33 shows a sample format for sheets that can be prepared in advance and kept on file. These pages can also be used with the controlled fact program described in Activity 1 of General Section 1 above. The specific facts being worked on are then immediately incorporated into actual problem situations.

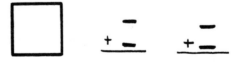

Figure 5-33

6. **Regroup.** Similar pages can be used when regrouping is required.
7. **Three by three.** Keep blank gameboards like that shown in Figure 5-34. Put the boards in plastic holders and give one to each child. Use a grease pencil to fill the boxes along the left side and top with numbers appropriate to the child's level. Figure 5-34 uses numbers that require regrouping only sometimes. A standard deck of cards is needed, with picture cards and 10s removed. Each child is given a

+	3	4	5	6	7
42					
23					
36					
54					
85					

Figure 5-34

set of chips. The child draws two cards (e.g. 5 and 3) and tells the sum. The fact is related, if possible, to the numbers on the gameboard, and the child finishes by saying, "So 85 + 3 must be 88." If the answer is correct, a chip is placed in the appropriate square. Answers can be checked on a calculator or against an answer sheet. The first person to cover a three-by-three square wins.

8. **Paper and pencil work.** When paper-and-pencil computation is to be carried out, allow the children who need the help to place a zero in the empty 10s space before computing.

- *Note:* Do not place the zero in the space for the child. Force the children themselves to deal with the problem. Experience has shown that most children place the zero in the space when it is time to add the 10s digits.

Regrouping for Addition

Problem area: Difficulty regrouping when adding two-digit numbers.

Typical disabilities affecting progress: Difficulty with abstract reasoning, perseveration, figure ground, and reversals.

Background: Many students are unable to retain a lot of information at one time. The many discrete steps involved in adding two 2-digit numbers are difficult enough for them and they may not readily recognize when nor know how to regroup. Automatic recognition becomes even harder as regrouping is extended to the 100s place. The student must continually make decisions while still trying to recall correctly the sequence for carrying out the computation. In many cases, difficulty with regrouping is truly a result of poor conceptual understanding of place value. All too often for the learning disabled child, however, it is simply due to an inability to think without obvious, visual cues.

The following suggestions will be helpful for children who have difficulty knowing when or how to regroup when adding two 2-digit numbers. The suggestions assume that the children

- have adequate numeration understandings for 2- and 3-digit numbers (see Chapter 2), and
- understand, at least informally, that when adding two 2-digit numbers you add like units and trade 10 ones for 1 ten whenever there are 10 or more ones.

The latter prerequisite assumes that the students have used grouping aids such as popsicle sticks (10-bundles and extra sticks), chips (10-stacks and extra chips), or graph paper 10s and 1s to dramatize these ideas. Once this foundation is established and the child is ready to begin to regroup with symbols only, perceptual or other deficits may make it necessary to use activities like those below to aid in the transition. These same activities can, of course, be used in remedial situations as well.

Suggested Sequence of Activities and Exercises

Chips, 10-stacks, and ones are used in this sample sequence. In implementing the sequence, use any grouping aid with which the children are familiar.

1. **Picture it: 10 ones for 1 ten.** Review the idea of exchanging 10 ones for 1 ten, using color-coded tens-ones frames as in Figure 5-35a. The child fills in the spaces to describe the picture on the left and is then reminded that "something is not right." There are two digits in one of the spaces. The student crosses out 10 red chips and replaces them with a green 10-stack on the right-hand frame, again filling in the blanks (Figure 5-35b). Auditorily reinforce what is being done: "Yes, if there are 10 or more ones, trade 10 ones for a 10-stack."

   - *Note:* For those needing concrete aids to review, use 10-stacks and extra single chips together with laminated tens-ones frames as illustrated in Figure 5-36. Make the frame so that no more than nine chips can be placed in the ones column. The inside of a file folder can be used to draw the frames. Simply use a felt-tipped pen to outline the slots in which you wish children to place their 10-stacks and single chips. Problems can be set up as in Activity 1 above, but the children can actually trade 10 single chips for one 10-stack. Using grease pencils or wipe-off markers, they can fill the spaces to describe the pictures both before and after the trade. The limited frame-space idea can also be carried out in follow-up paper and pencil work.

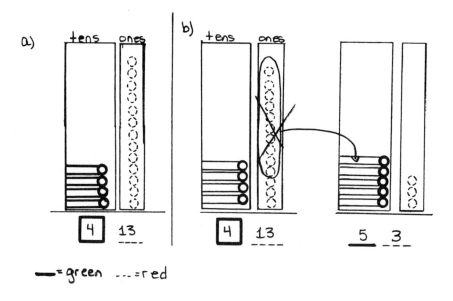

Figure 5-35

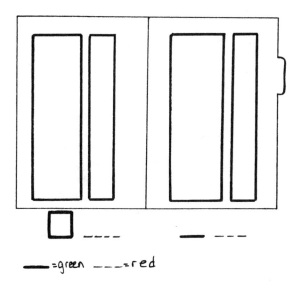

Figure 5-36

2. **Think of the picture.** Once the student masters the work presented in Activity 1 above, introduce exercises like that illustrated in Figure 5-37. Fill in the left-hand boxes with numbers previously used with the tens-ones frames. The basic teaching sequence is illustrated in the following narration:

Teacher (pointing to the left-hand box of Figure 5-37a): "Something is not right. There are two digits in one of the spaces. What did we do with the chips whenever there were 10 or more ones?"

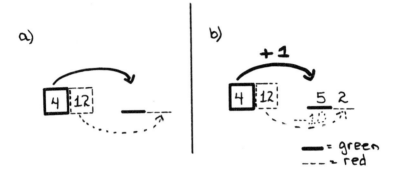

Figure 5-37

Student: "Traded 10 loose chips for a 10-stack."

Teacher: "Yes, and what did we do every time we put another 10-stack in the frame?"

Student: "We wrote a different number on the green line, because now there's one more." (At this point, the teacher writes + 1 on the green arrow and instructs the children to do the same on their sheets.)

Teacher: "That's right, and 4 + 1 is 5" (writing "5" on the right hand green line). "Whenever we put another 10-stack in the frame, what did we do with the red chips?"

Student: "Took off 10." (At this point, the teacher writes − 10 on the red arrow, instructing the children to do the same.)

Teacher: "That's right, and 12 − 10 is 2" (writing "2" on the right hand red line).

Note: For the first few examples, particularly for students with visual memory or sequencing deficits, it may be necessary to use 10-stacks and single chips with the tens-ones frames to dramatize each step.

3. **Need to trade?** One important question should now be asked in conjunction with exercises like those illustrated in Figure 5-38: Are there two digits in one space? Children could be asked to examine the right-hand boxes to answer this question for each example. They could then be instructed to circle those boxes that "are not right"—those in which the ones place is overloaded.

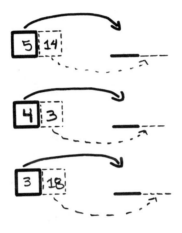

Figure 5-38

4. **If yes, then trade.** Children who have mastered the previous step have an edge in recognizing *when* to regroup. The issue now is knowing *how* to regroup at the symbolic level. The answer to the question of Activity 3 above is now given direct attention (Figure 5-39). A procedure similar to that outlined in Activity 2 above is carried out with the students. At this stage, however, most students do not need to relate vocally each step of a problem to the movement of chips. The children have internalized the concept and need to practice to build skill in regrouping whenever there are two digits in the ones column. Previous work is now extended as the children

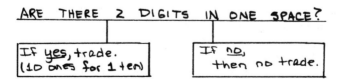

Figure 5-39

fill in the right-hand box in exercises (see Figure 5-40). Note that some of the problems do not require regrouping (Figure 5-40b) in order to force the child to think about when regrouping is necessary. A wall chart similar to Figure 5-39 or a mini-paste-up on the child's page is helpful to many during early stages of independent work with exercises of this type.

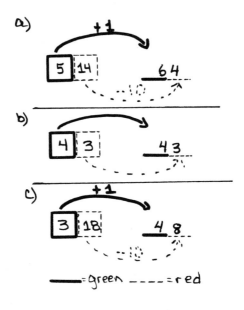

Figure 5-40

5. **Now add.** The previous exercises required the students, working with numerals alone, to recognize when the ones place is overloaded. When this skill is mastered, it is time to apply it to two-digit addition problems. Figure 5-41 shows one type of page that can be used. *The fact that part of the page is visually similar to previous work takes some of the pressure off the student.* Each problem is first solved without regrouping. The answer is then examined, and the student decides whether or not to regroup. If necessary, to point up the similarity to previous work, provide the child with a card to cover up the actual problem. The extra step of seeing two digits in the ones place often provides the reinforcement needed to remember to think about regrouping.

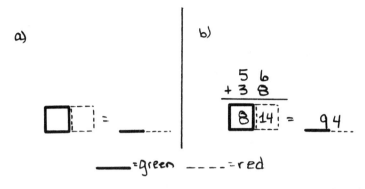

Figure 5-41

- *Note:* The many discrete steps of the preceding sequence are essential for many learning disabled students, particularly for the overlearner or for those with sequencing or abstract reasoning difficulties. Using colors (or other visual highlighting techniques) and repeated drills helps the child more readily learn *when* and *how* to regroup.

6. **A box cue.** Color-coded reminder boxes, such as that pictured in Figure 5-42a, serve two needs; they provide

   1. help in the transition to the standard computational format for addition with regrouping, and
   2. help for students with reversal tendencies.

   In the example of Figure 5-42a, the children first add to obtain 13 ones. The normal pattern for writing 13 is "1" first then "3," so urge the children to follow this sequence when recording their answer. The color scheme of Figure 5-42 encourages this: *1* first (in the *green* box), then *3* on the *red* "stop" line. Figure 5-42b gives an idea for formating pages in advance. These can be then filed and pulled as needed. When preparing the pages, include the boxes on all problems, even when regrouping is not needed. This will force the students to think about whether regrouping really is needed.

7. **Doctor the text.** When using a text or workbook page, allow the students to draw dashes under each problem to match the columns (e.g. two columns, two dashes). This often reminds them that only one digit is allowed per space. If the textbook problems are too small for the students to mark, elicit adult volunteer help to prepare texts in advance.

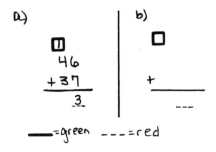

Figure 5-42

Column Addition

Problem area: Inability to complete the sequence in column addition.

Typical disabilities affecting progress: Difficulty with short term or sequential memory and visual figure ground.

Background: Conceptually, a student may understand column addition. Perceptually, however, this can be extremely difficult, especially when "ragged columns" or regrouping are involved as in Figure 5-43. Children with figure-ground difficulties find it especially hard to "keep the place" while copying or computing problems of this type. To complicate matters in this case, the three-addend problem is really a four-addend one because of the regrouping. The child who worked the example of Figure 5-43 handled the ones column addition correctly, even the regrouping, but forgot the "1" while adding the tens column.

Figure 5-43

For some students, the hand calculator for column addition is a viable alternative to paper-and-pencil computation. Indeed, occasions arise in which calculator use or estimation should take precedence over hand calculations. On the other hand, most learning disabled students *can* learn to add a sequence of three or four numbers. Compensatory techniques such as the following have proved effective in helping students acquire this skill.

Suggested Exercises

1. **Step at a time.** Approach column addition a step at a time. Prepare practice pages containing problems like that shown in Figure 5-44a. Use green for the first two addends and the answer line. The arrow and the last addend should be red. Before writing the final sum, the student fills in the blank line with the sum of the first two addends.

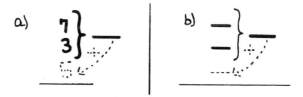

Figure 5-44

- *Note:* Pages using the problem format of Figure 5-44b can be kept on file and used as needed. The teacher can fill in specific numbers if a controlled-fact program is being used. Students can also copy problems from the text onto these pages. Alternatively, if textbook space is not too confining, the students can color-code text problems before solving. If difficulty with column addition is anticipated, the textbooks could be coded in advance, even at the beginning of the school year, by adult volunteers.

2. **Cross out means 10.** For those children with good visual but poor sequential memory, the approach of Figure 5-45 has proved helpful. The child adds down the column until a 2-digit answer ($8 + 9 = 17$) is reached. The last digit added, in this case 9, is crossed out to represent the one 10 in the sum. The student retains the 7 mentally and combines it with the 6. The 6 is crossed out to indicate the one

10 in 13 and the child writes down the 3. The number carried is the same as the number of digits crossed out, in this case 2. This same approach is used for remaining columns.

3. **Write the ones.** If visual memory or reversal deficits require that a child write subsums, the procedure of Figure 5-46 can be used. The student adds the first two addends. Since the sum (16) is a 2-digit number, the second 8 is crossed out and the 6 is written down, in that order. 6 + 9 is 15, so the 9 is crossed out and the 5 is written below the line. As before, the number of crossed digits represents what should be carried.

Figure 5-45   Figure 5-46

4. **Visual helps.** If visual figure-ground or other perceptual deficits are a problem, any one of the following techniques might be used.

   - Teach the children to color highlight a column before adding it (Figure 5-47a).

   - Provide square centimeter paper and instruct the students to write one digit to a square (Figure 5-47b).

   - Provide vertically lined paper and instruct the students to write every digit on a line (Figure 5-47c).

   - Provide a tachistoscopic card for covering columns not being added. The card should only cover the problem, allowing room to write the carried number at the top and the answer in the proper place. As the student works, the card is moved along so that only the numbers being added show through the slot. Figure 5-47d shows a step-by-step approach for using the card to solve an

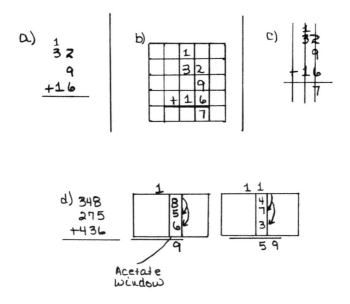

Figure 5-47

addition problem with three 3-digit addends. *Note:* One could cover the entire card with acetate and allow the children to use a grease pencil to write the ones digit of subsums directly on the acetate (the approach of Activity 3 above). The acetate would be wiped clean before adding another column.

SUBTRACTION OF WHOLE NUMBERS

Difficulties similar to those encountered in whole-number addition are also present when children turn to subtraction. It is common for students to have problems subtracting a single-digit from a 2-digit number; some find it hard to subtract multiples of 10. Knowing *when* and *how* to regroup are major stumbling blocks in subtraction, as in addition, especially for children with learning difficulties. Many of the activities described in the previous sections can be adjusted and used to aid in handling parallel difficulties in subtraction. Since some problems with regrouping require slightly different techniques than previously discussed, the following two sections will give additional suggestions for this topic.

Two- and Three-Digit Subtraction With Regrouping

Problem area: Difficulty knowing when and how to regroup in subtraction of two- and three-digit numbers.

Typical disabilities affecting progress: Difficulty with abstract reasoning, perseveration, visual figure ground, reversals, and sequencing.

Background: As with addition, knowing when to regroup in subtraction is hard for many students. A common tendency is to subtract the smaller from the larger number, regardless of position within the problem. Figure 5-48 illustrates this error, typical even of children who do not exhibit specific disabilities. Often this error stems from poor conceptual understanding of the process of subtracting with regrouping. Some learning disabled children, though, have strong concepts but just visually reverse the numbers.

$$\begin{array}{r} 64 \\ -35 \\ \hline 31 \end{array}$$

Figure 5-48

Other factors contribute to the difficulty children experience. Figure 5-1 illustrated, step by step, how subtraction with regrouping is really a combination of subtraction and addition. There is a tremendous amount of mental computation involved and a constant switching from one operation to the next and then back again. Children are continually involved in decision making. They must not only know when to regroup, but also how—and that involves realizing what operation to use and then applying it at each discrete step.

There are several approaches to developing the procedure for 2-digit and 3-digit subtraction with regrouping. It is generally most helpful to use the simplest model, that of "take away," as the basis for subtraction computation. In the problem 68 − 49 for example, the children can be cued to think: "8 take away 9. Since there are not enough ones, a trade must be made (1 ten for 10 ones)." The "take away" approach aptly dramatizes the "big ideas" underlying subtraction computation: subtract like units; if there are not enough, make a trade. This approach underlies the suggestions that follow.

Suggested Activities and Exercises

1. **Fair trade** (to prepare for a natural, meaningful transition into 2-digit subtraction with regrouping). Provide a deck of laminated cards like that pictured in Figure 5-49a and a "band" of 10-stacks and loose chips. In turn, the children draw a card and use the chips to picture the problem on the card. The teacher leads the following discussion:
   "The bank needs another 10-stack. Will you trade one of yours for loose chips? . . . How many loose chips would make a fair trade? (10 loose chips for the 10-stack.) Write what you have now." (See Figure 5-49b.)
   Repeat with other cards, making a record each time of the trade.

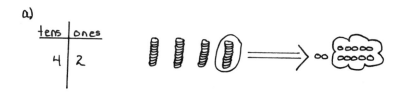

Figure 5-49

2. **Take away.** Relate the trade idea of Activity 1 above to 2-digit subtraction with regrouping. In the example of Figure 5-50a, the children use 10-stacks and loose chips to show what you start with (42). Now subtract: "2 take away 8." There are not enough loose chips to take 8, so trade a 10-stack for ten chips and write to tell the number of 10s and 1s now (Figure 5-50b). Now the children *can* "take away" 8 loose chips and one 10-stack, leaving two 10-stacks and four loose chips (Figure 5-50c).

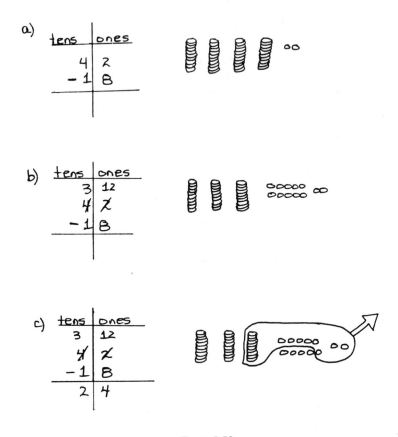

Figure 5-50

3. **Are there enough?** Some children—particularly the careless, impulsive, and those who perseverate—may fall into the pattern: regroup, subtract, regroup, subtract. They then continue the pattern whether regrouping is required or not. Force children to decide about regrouping. One suggestion is to present mixed problem types like those of Figure 5-51. Note that the ones digit of the minuend has been visually highlighted to focus attention on it. The children start with this digit each time and decide whether there are enough, so that they can "take away" the number represented by the digit directly beneath it. (Use chips as in Activity 2 above, if necessary, to dramatize the first few problems.) Ask the children merely to circle the problem if there are not enough. Do not require the students to complete the problems at this time.

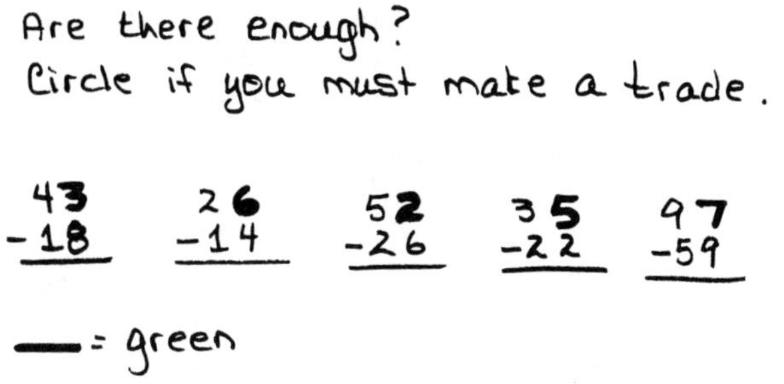

Are there enough?
Circle if you must make a trade.

$$
\begin{array}{ccccc}
43 & 26 & 52 & 35 & 97 \\
-18 & -14 & -26 & -22 & -59 \\
\end{array}
$$

____ = green

Figure 5-51

4. **Help them decide.** Some students need more structured help before they can succeed with the task presented in Activity 3 above. Figure 5-52 shows one type of exercise that can be used to provide the needed assistance. The underlining helps the children focus on the correct starting point in each problem. To force the children to think more clearly about the relationship of the numbers, ask them to read across the line and fill in while doing so. Eventually the sentence becomes internalized and the children are more likely to think about the way the exercise has prompted them as they do other problems.

- *Note:* The phrase "make a trade," used during work with 10-stacks and loose chips in previous activities, is used throughout the rest of this sequence. Some teachers may prefer to use "regroup." The term best understood by the students should be adopted.

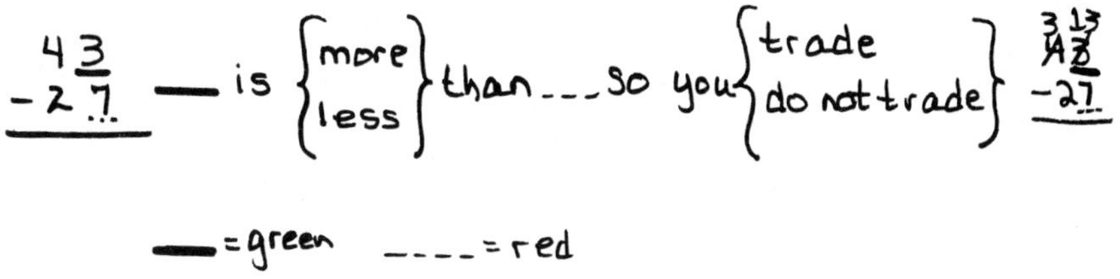

$$
\begin{array}{c}
43 \\
-2\,\underline{7}
\end{array}
\;\underline{}\; \text{is} \left\{\begin{array}{c} \text{more} \\ \text{less} \end{array}\right\} \text{than} \text{---so you} \left\{\begin{array}{c} \text{trade} \\ \text{do not trade} \end{array}\right\} \begin{array}{c} 3\;13 \\ \cancel{4}\,\cancel{3} \\ -2\underline{7} \end{array}
$$

____ = green   _ _ _ _ = red

Figure 5-52

5. **Cue box.** For those children who have trouble sequencing or who do not automatically associate written words with numbers, Figure 5-53 shows a cueing technique that has proved helpful. Problems of this type can be used to reinforce the last step of the sequence discussed in Activity 4 above. Even with the cueing, the students must still decide whether it is necessary to make a trade. If necessary, the teacher can help the student by discussing the number available and the number to be "taken away;" 10-stacks and chips could then be used to verify thinking. If a trade must be made, then there are "1 less ten, 10 more ones."

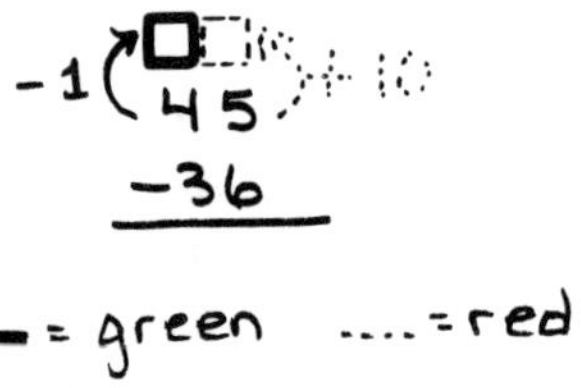

Figure 5-53

6. **Block out.** As regrouping is extended to the tens and hundreds places, it is often necessary to remind students to continue thinking in the correct way. One device that is helpful in this regard is the "block out" card shown in Figure 5-54. The child uses the card as a marker while solving subtraction problems. It serves to block out extraneous numbers, allowing the child to focus on the pertinent ones.

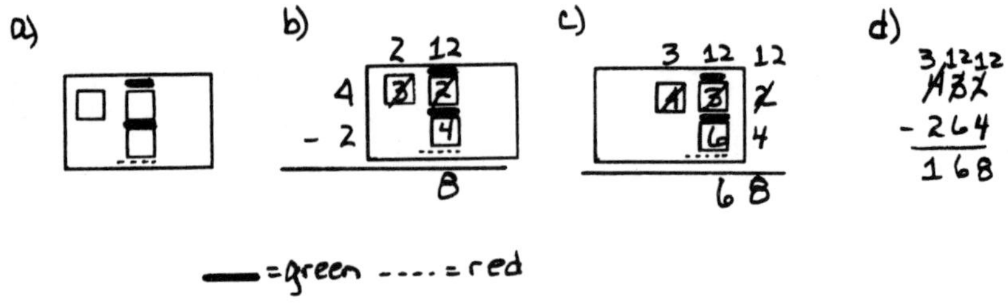

Figure 5-54

7. **Different strokes.** Subtract like units; if there are not enough, make a trade. These are the "big ideas" of subtraction. Some students apply these ideas, step by step, when computing: first ones, then tens, and so on. Others benefit by first going through the entire problem, noting all places where regrouping is necessary. Once this is done, they can backtrack and perform the computation. Children who benefit most from this latter method are those who have trouble sequencing, making many switches in their thought process, and those who have difficulty with number alignment. It is important to note which method is easiest for an individual rather than to force one procedural pattern on all.

8. **Do it backwards!** Children with severe reversal problems often benefit from working problems left to right (see the note below). The approach is similar to the equal-additions methods illustrated in Figure 5-55, but it is easier for children with reversal tendencies to understand and follow. In the example shown in Figure 5-56, the child begins with 9 − 2 = 7. Next, the student thinks, "5 take away 9." Recognizing the need to make a trade, the child crosses out the 7 and writes 6 beneath it. The 5 is crossed out and 15 written above. The explanation is that, after the first subtraction, we still have 7 hundreds left, enough to trade when you need to for the 5. A similar procedure is used to complete the problem. For those who need help with number alignment, use graph paper or pages containing examples like that of Figure 5-57.

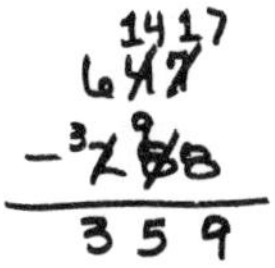

Figure 5-55

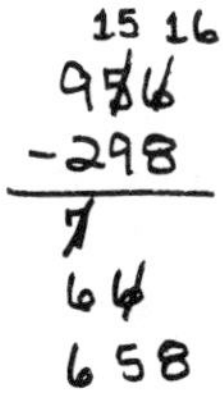

Figure 5-56

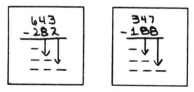

Figure 5-57

- *Note:* This method looks longer and more cumbersome to many of us, but we are not the ones who need this approach. For the learning disabled child with visual perceptual problems, one obstacle to learning, the tendency to reverse, is eliminated.

9. **Into the maze** (for two or three to play). To reinforce the correct sequence, the need to regroup, and the skill of adding 10 to a number, prepare a gameboard as in Figure 5-58a. Also provide a grease pencil and wipe-off rag, a deck of laminated cards with subtraction problems like those of Figure 5-58b, an envelope for the cards, and a game marker for each player. To begin, cards are mixed and placed in the envelope. In turn, the players draw a card, state the problem, and decide whether or not it is necessary to make a trade. If so, a grease pencil is used to show the trade. After the players add 10 to the green number, they move that many spaces. If no trade is needed, the players simply subtract the two numbers. The result is the number of spaces they may move. Answers can be checked by flipping to the back sides of cards. The first to reach the garden in the heart of the maze wins. *Note:* If the deck is used up before a winner is found, the cards are wiped and reused.

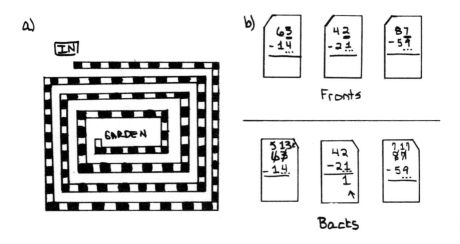

Figure 5-58

Zero in Subtraction

Problem area: Difficulty regrouping when zero appears in the minuend.

Typical disabilities affecting progress: Difficulty with sequencing, spatial organization, and memory.

Background: Zero difficulties are more prominent in subtraction than in addition. In subtraction of two-digit numbers with zero minuend digits, for example, the tendency to reverse is more dominant than when only nonzero digits appear in problems (see Figure 5-59). Some children simply ignore the zero when it occurs (Figure 5-60). Because of these and other erratic errors children make, it is generally more beneficial to the students to teach the concept and process of subtraction with regrouping before introducing zero anywhere into the problem. Then specific lessons, incorporating ideas such as those presented below, could be carried out to help the children deal with zero in subtraction computations.

$$\begin{array}{r} 50 \\ -36 \\ \hline 26 \end{array}$$

$$\begin{array}{r} {\scriptstyle 4 \;\; 15} \\ 505 \\ -196 \\ \hline 4\;9 \end{array}$$

Figure 5-59   Figure 5-60

Suggested Activities and Exercises

1. **Act it out.** Use the "fair trade" and "take away" activities of the previous section to provide a physical frame of reference for 2-digit subtraction having 0 in the minuend. Use multiples of 10 (20, 30, . . . 90) for the "fair trade" activity. Then use these same numbers in the minuend for the "take away" activity. A sample problem for this latter activity is 60 − 13.
2. **Think about it.** Prepare pages using the format of Figure 5-52, placing zero on the green line. If the child does not respond to the verbal association, adapt the "cue box" activity of the previous section to work with zero.
3. **Circle.** Follow up with pages that mix zero and nonzero digits in the minuend for two-digit subtractions. Include both regrouping and

nonregrouping types. At first, just have the students circle those problems where a trade must be made. Then, even at a later time, they can complete the subtractions.

4. **One step.** Show the children how to make a trade (regroup) in one step, as in Figure 5-61. Initially, underline the 60 to focus attention. "We can think of this as 6 one-hundreds and no tens. We can also think of it as 60 tens. That's easier. When we borrow 1 ten we have 59 tens left. Now we give that 1 ten to the 2."

5. **Hidden zero.** The method of Activity 4 above can also be used with a hidden 0, as shown in Figure 5-62. The student still views 71 as 71 tens, thus eliminating one regrouping step.

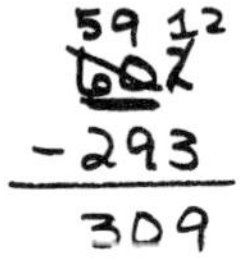

Figure 5-61 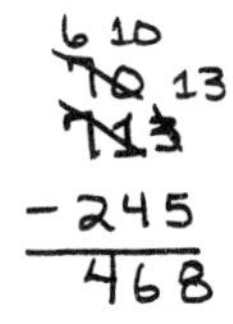   Figure 5-62

6. **Do it backwards.** An alternative to the "one step" is the method of subtraction explained in Activity 8 of the previous section. This has proved helpful to some students when a zero is in the tens place, as in Figure 5-63. Often, children become confused when they reach the step shown in Figure 5-64. Continuity has been broken, and many, particularly those with short-term memory deficits, will forget why they were doing what they did. The "backwards" left-right approach eliminates this problem.

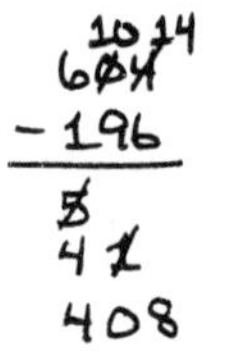

Figure 5-63    Figure 5-64

MULTIPLICATION OF WHOLE NUMBERS

Multiples of Ten

Problem areas: Difficulty knowing how many to record when one or both of the factors is a multiple of ten; inability to "get started" when faced with factors that are multiples of ten.

Typical disabilities affecting progress: Difficulty with abstract reasoning.

Background: An essential part of multiplication involving a 2-digit multiplier is the ability to multiply by a multiple of 10. Often, however, unless it is specifically taught, children do not see the relationship between the number of 0s in the factors and product. For this reason, it is important that, in introducing 2-digit multipliers, the children work on the patterning involving 0s. The ideas that follow may be used for this purpose. As a prerequisite, it is assumed that the children's numeration understandings are strong enough that they can relate 8 tens to 80, 14 tens to 140, and so on.

Suggested Activities and Exercises

1. **Side by side.** Present multiplication problems like those shown in Figure 5-65. Children solve the first problem in each pair of problems. Then, using a calculator, they find the product for the second problem of the pair. If there are not enough calculators for each student, have the children take turns. When the product is read to the class, it can be written on the board or an overhead. Use the colors as indicated to help the students notice the pattern. Gradually extend the process to higher multiples of 10 and color code similarly.

$$\begin{array}{r} 48 \\ \times\ 2 \\ \hline \end{array} \qquad \begin{array}{r} 48 \\ \times\ 20 \\ \hline \end{array}$$

$$\begin{array}{r} 63 \\ \times\ 3 \\ \hline \end{array} \qquad \begin{array}{r} 63 \\ \times\ 30 \\ \hline \end{array}$$

Figure 5-65

2. **Relate.** A problem sequence like that of Figure 5-66 can be used effectively with students who, perceptually, cannot handle the calculator. Remind the students of the relationship between multiplication and addition by initially setting up the problems as in Figure 5-66a. Most children who know their facts and are strong conceptually will use multiplication to solve the problem, even in this form. Even those children who do not know their facts but understand the relationship between addition and multiplication can use a multiplication chart to solve the problems. The colors help the students find answers to individual problems and cue them to the general pattern. The following narration, based on the problem of Figure 5-66a, suggests the type of discussion that might take place.

   Teacher: "Did you add the zeroes each time?"
   Student: "No, they sort of tagged along all the time."
   Teacher: "Right. What about the 4s? Did you add them?"
   Student: "No. 6 × 4 is 24, and that's easier."

By the time the students are working problems like those of Figure 5-66d, they generally note how "it's like multiplying by 2; since 90 ends in 0, though, so does the answer." A similar rationale can be used to support the multiplication of Figure 5-65. For 48 × 20, you write a 0 in the product to show you are multiplying by a multiple of ten. Otherwise it is just like multiplying by 2. Placing related pairs side by side on worksheets, as shown, emphasizes this idea.

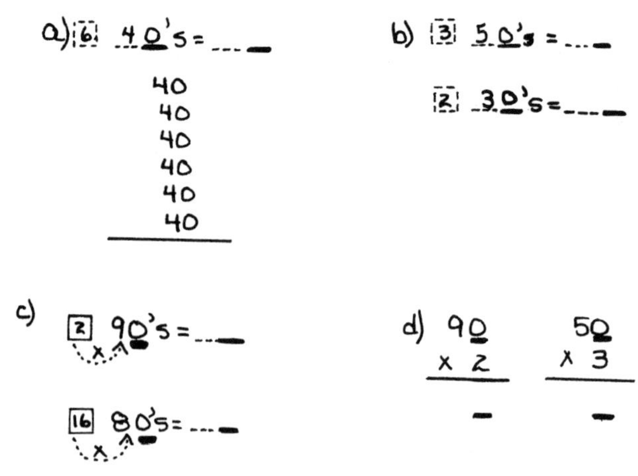

Figure 5-66

3. **Call it** (a practice activity for two to play). Prepare a laminated gameboard like that of Figure 5-67. Write the numerals 1 to 6 (in green) along the bottom row and 1 to 6 (in red) down the left-hand column. Every other gameboard space should show a product, one of whose factors is a multiple of 10. For those just beginning, it is probably best to make one of the factors 10. Later, this can be changed as the students gain experience in the game and confidence in themselves. Provide an answer sheet of possible factors for each product and two dice:

         Die 1 (green):   marked 1, 2, 3, 4, 5, 6;
         Die 2 (red):   marked 1, 2, 3, 4, 5, 6.

Also provide three sets of markers, each a different color: one set for each player, and one set to cover the entire board at the beginning of play. In turn, the players throw the dice and read them as points on a graph. For example, a green 2 and a red 5 correspond to (2, 5) or 720 on the gameboard of Figure 5-67. If the player can correctly name two factors forming the product (one must be a multiple of 10), the black chip is replaced with the child's colored one. If necessary, the student can consult the answer sheet to check. The winning pattern should be determined before the start of the game.

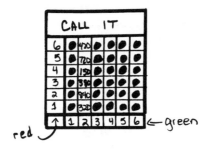

Figure 5-67

Beyond One-Digit Multipliers

Problem area: Difficulty multiplying two multidigit numbers.

Typical disabilities affecting progress: Difficulty with spatial organization, integrative processing, sequencing, abstract reasoning, visual memory, and reversals.

Background: Many children have trouble multiplying two numbers when both factors have two or more digits. The sequence is long and continually broken up by addition. A considerable amount of spatial organization is required, not only to place the numbers on the correct line but also to align the digits properly. Visual memory is needed to retrieve the basic fact and to regroup the correct number.

For many students, although place-value comprehension is strong and the use of the distributive idea for multiplication computation has been established, it is necessary to provide visual or auditory cues in early work involving 2- or higher-digit multipliers. The following activities suggest ways this can be done once the children are ready to begin this work at the symbolic level. It is assumed that the students can multiply two-digit numbers by one-digit factors and by multiples of 10.

Suggested Exercises

1. **Color cue.** Color-coded grid boxes, as in Figure 1-16, have been most effective in helping students organize the multiplication process, both spatially and sequentially. Figure 5-68 shows a sample problem completed by a child using the grid boxes. The student first multiplied by the green number (3). The digit to be carried was recorded in the green circle, and the units digit was placed in the appropriate green box. Next, the child multiplied 3 × 4, and added the 2 in the green circle. After crossing out the 2, the answer (4) was recorded in the next two green boxes. The student proceeded similarly with the multiplication by 20, this time using the red carrying circle and the red boxes.

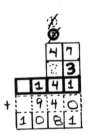

Figure 5-68

Note: It is important that students be taught to write the carried digit first at all times. This will avoid any tendency to reverse. Crossing out the carried digit should be a carryover of work with one-digit multipliers. When the colored circles are no longer used, the crossing-out technique will eliminate confusion over which digit to add whenever two or more carry digits appear.

2. **Fade out.** As the students begin to feel comfortable with the process, the colors can gradually be eliminated. The method of elimination will vary depending on the student. Two suggestions follow.

   1. Those children whose major difficulty appears to be spatial organization may be able to eliminate all the colors almost immediately. It will continue to be necessary to use grid paper for a while, however, until they have overlearned the kinesthetic feeling and sequence. Gradually, the grid paper sheets can be replaced with pages using the format illustrated in Figure 5-69.
   2. Students having primarily sequencing difficulties eventually should be able to eliminate the colors from the boxes, but they may need to retain the color cue for the factor digits and carrying circles for quite some time.

Figure 5-69

Figure 5-70

3. **A special case.** Using the same color-coded grids as described previously, the presentation can be varied for children with more severe reversal difficulties. For these students, the 10s digit of the multiplier is green and the 1s digit is red. The child "goes on green" (Figure 5-70) and multiplies 2(0) × 7. As the product is said, the student writes 1 in the green circle and 40 in the appropriate green boxes. The procedure continues in a similar manner for the remaining digits.

4. **A zero card.** Children with figure-ground or abstract reasoning deficits often benefit by being allowed to use a "zero" card or factor slide. Figure 5-71 shows, step by step, how a child uses a zero card. The student first uses the blank side of the card and covers the 5 (to block out extraneous numbers). After completing this multiplication, the card is flipped over and the 0 is placed over the 7. The idea being reinforced is that, to multiply by 64, you multiply first by 4 then by 60. Finally, you add the result. Figure 5-72 shows how a factor slide can be used in a similar way.

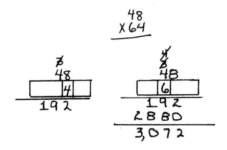

Figure 5-71

Figure 5-72

Regrouping in Multiplication

Problem area: Difficulty adding the carried digit.

Typical disabilities affecting progress: Short-term memory, visual memory, reversals, and sequential memory.

Background: Many students have trouble adding the carried digit because they cannot perform the mental computation. They may know their basic facts, but, if they cannot retrieve an accurate image of the two-digit number, they are bound to have trouble computing with it. Consider Figure 5-73. This student had no trouble with the process of multiplication: numbers were carried properly and aligned properly, and the operations were sequenced correctly. What happened then? Notice the 85 in the product. After correctly recording first the 10s and then the 1s digit of 48, the digits for 18 (6 × 3) were mentally reversed. The child thought "81," and for that number the sum 85 (81 + 4) is correct. The digits of the product 48 were probably not reversed because they were recorded as said. There was no need to sort out a confused visual image.

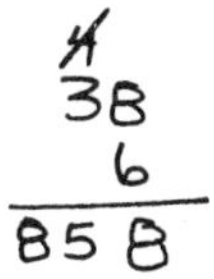

$$\begin{array}{r} \cancel{4} \\ 3\text{B} \\ \underline{6} \\ \text{B5 B} \end{array}$$

Figure 5-73

It has been noted how, as computational skills are expanded, the number of steps increases and accurate sequencing becomes essential. Unless children have a clear conceptual understanding of the process and have overlearned *each discrete* procedure involved, it is often difficult for them to maintain the correct sequence and compute successfully at the symbolic level.

The activities that follow address one small step of the computational process for multiplication: adding the carried digit. They have proved effective in dealing with the problem highlighted in the example of Figure 5-73 and with other related difficulties.

Suggested Exercises

1. **Relate.** If students have difficulty regrouping in multiplication, exercises like those of Figure 5-74 often prove helpful. These are an extension of the work begun in Section 2 of the addition part of this chapter, that illustrated in Figures 5-29 and 5-30. Now an effort is made to relate the addition to its role in multiplication computation. Note that, in Figure 5-74, a multiplication problem using the addition is written to the right of each example. In example 1, students first find the sum of 24 and 4, filling in the spaces as they approach them verbally. The related multiplication is then carried out. Then, when the addition part of the problem is reached, the children can look back at the answer. The need to retain a reversed digit mentally is thus eliminated. In the second example, the students complete the first addition and multiply 68 by 9. They then do the second addition before finishing the multiplication. The speed with which the children can independently incorporate the addition procedure into multiplication will depend on how comfortable they are with the entire multiplication process. In the meantime, allow them to use pages of this type so that they can multiply with a minimum of interference from their learning deficits.

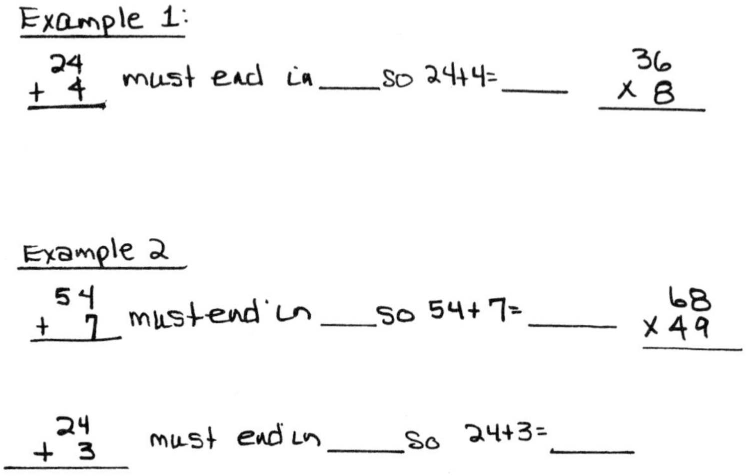

Example 1:

$$\begin{array}{r} 24 \\ + \ 4 \\ \hline \end{array}$$ must end in ____ So 24+4=____ $$\begin{array}{r} 36 \\ \times \ 8 \\ \hline \end{array}$$

Example 2

$$\begin{array}{r} 54 \\ + \ 7 \\ \hline \end{array}$$ must end in ____ So 54+7=____ $$\begin{array}{r} 68 \\ \times \ 49 \\ \hline \end{array}$$

$$\begin{array}{r} 24 \\ + \ 3 \\ \hline \end{array}$$ must end in ____ So 24+3=____

Figure 5-74

2. **Color cue.** If visual discrimination presents little difficulty but the students have trouble sequencing, then Figure 5-75 shows how to use color coding to help the students with the process. The children are reminded to use the colors as a stoplight, thus multiplying first and then adding.

3. **Different strokes.** The previous example can be adjusted as in Figure 5-76 for those who have trouble with revisualizing the product in order to combine it with the carried number. After multiplying the 10s digit, the product (45 in this example) is written on the line and then added to the number carried.

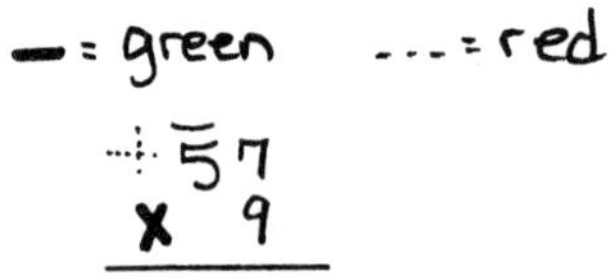

— = green   ... = red

$$\begin{array}{r} 57 \\ \times \ 9 \\ \hline \end{array}$$

Figure 5-75

— = green   ... = red

$$45 \quad \begin{array}{r} 6 \\ 57 \\ \times \ 9 \\ \hline 3 \end{array}$$

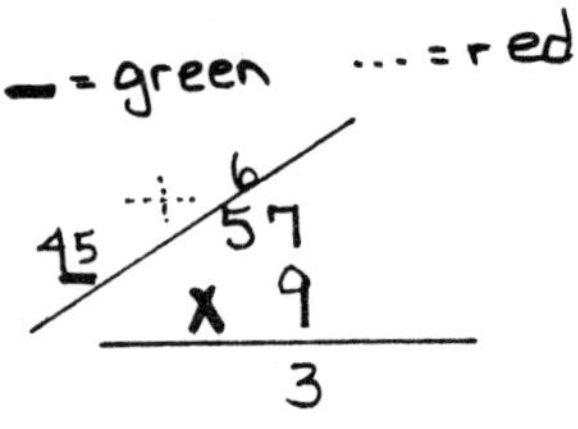

Figure 5-76

4. **Another alternative.** For those whose major difficulty is digit reversal when the number is retained mentally, encourage them to write this number down. Providing a box to the side of the problem, as in Figure 5-77, often is all that is needed to avoid digit reversal. For left-handed students, place the box to the left of the problem.

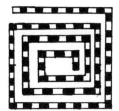

Figure 5-77

5. **In and out.** A board game that provides practice in adding the carried number is shown in Figure 5-78. Each child needs a marker and, if necessary, an answer key. Provide a maze board and a set of cards with partially completed multiplication problems. Each child, in turn, draws a card and states the remaining partial product. In this case, it would be 44. If correct, the child advances a marker as many steps into the maze as the carry box indicates. If the wrong answer is given, the marker is moved back that number of spaces. The winner is the first to get out of the maze.

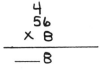

Figure 5-78

DIVISION OF WHOLE NUMBERS

The increased availability and lower cost of hand calculators, together with the infrequent need to use long division in day-to-day situations, has caused mathematics educators to question whether we should continue to teach the long-division algorithm. Until there is a resolution of this issue, however, we must continue to find effective ways of presenting long division. The purpose of this part of the chapter is to provide approaches and alternatives to help classroom and special-education teachers of learning disabled students to accomplish this goal.

Beginning Long Division

Problem area: Difficulty transferring from the concrete to the symbolic level for long division; inability to interpret meaningfully the written long division problem.

Typical disabilities affecting progress: Difficulty with visual memory, sequencing, abstract reasoning, and retrieval.

Background: For many children, the concept of division—using blocks, chips, money, and other concrete aids—is relatively easy to grasp. They soon learn to divide (separate) things into groups with the same number in each group. The difficulty arises when symbols alone are used in the written problem. The functional division sign ($\overline{\smash{)}}$) tends to confuse those with reversal tendencies, whether visual or auditory. Yet the other division sign ($\div$) is not particularly useful at this point. Generally, rather than confront children with both symbols simultaneously, it is better to have them learn to use the more functional one first, relating it as much as possible to concrete aids.

Because of the inherent reversal tendencies and involved sequencing in division, the process lends itself nicely to color coding. The colors provide the student with a starting point as well as a way of determining and maintaining the sequence. Suggestions along this line are outlined below.

Suggested Sequence of Activities and Exercises

1. **Say it with chips.** As children make the transition to symbolic work for long division, it is often helpful to relate the work with materials directly to the written computational problems. Keep puzzles like those shown in Figure 5-79. Have the children cut the puzzles apart before beginning, then place the two pieces of each together, upside down, at the side of the desk. Using an overhead projector or felt board, the teacher uses chips under $\overline{\smash{)}}$ and goes through the sequence described below. The chips being used should be colored green, black, and red to match the colors on the child's puzzles. For each puzzle, the presentation would be similar to that indicated below. The children work with real chips and the *left* side of each puzzle.

   Teacher: "Start with seven green chips." After the seven green chips are taken, the teacher tells the students to find the left piece of puzzle A. "Write 7 on the green line to stand for the seven chips."

Fronts

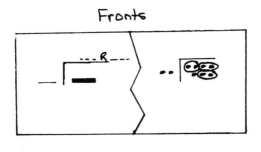

Backs

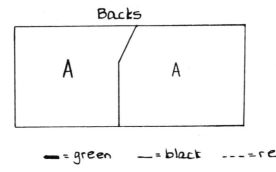

Figure 5-79

Teacher: "Use your chips again. Let's put two chips in each group." In conjunction with this activity, the children write a 2 on the black line of the puzzle piece.

Teacher: (Using the chips under the ⌐, forms groups of two.) "How many groups did I make? Right. I made three and had one chip left over."

The children are instructed to put numbers in the appropriate places of their puzzle pieces to indicate this.

This procedure continues until all left-hand puzzle pieces have been filled in. The children then put the puzzles back together to check their work.

2. **Puzzles alone.** Once the previous work is understood at the concrete level, show the picture part of the puzzles to the students and ask them to rewrite each problem on their own paper, using *numbers* rather than dots. To check, the children again match the puzzle pieces.

- *Note:* This method of presentation and reinforcement is effective even with upper primary children. There is the concrete aspect so essential to comprehension. In addition, the direct teaching of the transition and the overlearning help provide a stronger base than is usually present. Visual memory, sequencing, auditory memory, and abstract reasoning are all reinforced.

3. **Follow up.** After work with chips and puzzles, exercises like those of Figure 5-80 can be used by students with adequate reading skills. These pages are especially good for children who need to verbalize while learning but have trouble retrieving the words. Before solving the problem using numbers, the left-hand section is completed. The teacher fills in divisor dots at the presentation. Then the children fill in the numbers at the right and solve the problem.

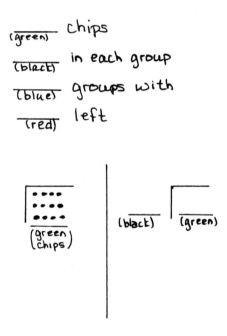

Figure 5-80

4. **Transition.** Figures 5-81 and 5-82 show transitional pages that can be used as the children develop better conceptual understandings and are able to sequence with symbols only.

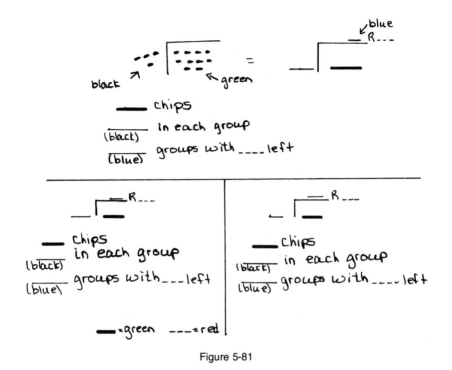

_____ chips

_____ in each group
(black)

_____ groups with ____ left
(blue)

_____ chips
(black) in each group

_____ groups with ___ left
(blue)

_____ chips
(black) in each group

_____ groups with ____ left
(blue)

____ =green ___ =red

Figure 5-81

_____ chips
(black) in each group

_____ groups with ___ left
(blue)

___ chips
___ in each group
___ groups with ___ left

___ chips
___ in each group
___ groups with ___ left

___ =green ___ =red

Figure 5-82

Beginning Long Division: Special Help

Problem area: Using only symbols to solve division problems.

Typical disabilities affecting progress: Difficulty with auditory processing, perseveration, sequencing, visual memory, and closure.

Background: Even when the concept of division is established and the students can interpret the written long division problem as the result of activities and exercises like those of the previous section, many children are still unable to proceed independently. For many, it is an inability to retrieve the needed fact. For others, the sequencing and constant operation switch make it very difficult to complete a problem accurately. Memory deficits may have precluded their learning the basic facts, and perseveration makes skip counting or the use of most charts too difficult.

The following activities provide some suggestions for helping children deal with these problems. The assumption is that the concept base is strong and that the difficulty is primarily due to individual learning difficulties.

Suggested Sequence of Activities and Exercises

1. **In the squares.** Many children need to see and feel what they are saying. To provide this reinforcement, Figure 5-83a illustrates a format idea for pages, that can be kept in the file and used as needed. The children place dots, lines, or chips (if necessary) in each square as they skip count (Figure 5-83b). For those who need

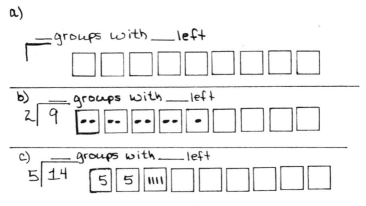

Figure 5-83

assistance with stopping, provide a stoplight above the last box needed. Alternatively, outline this box red. Encourage the students to keep one finger on the dividend number and to compare it with the number of chips placed.

- *Note:* As overlearning occurs, the children independently place numbers rather than pictures or objects in the squares to show the skip count (Figure 5-83c).

2. **Transition.** As a transition to the long division procedure, Figure 5-84 illustrates the format for pages that can be filed and used as needed. The teacher fills in dividend and divisor numbers at the time of presentation (Figure 5-85a). The child fills in the squares and determines the number of groups that have been made. Then a count is made to see how many things in all have been "used up" (15 in this example). The child next subtracts to find the number left over. *Note:* For left-handed children, place the boxes to the left of the problem.

Figure 5-84

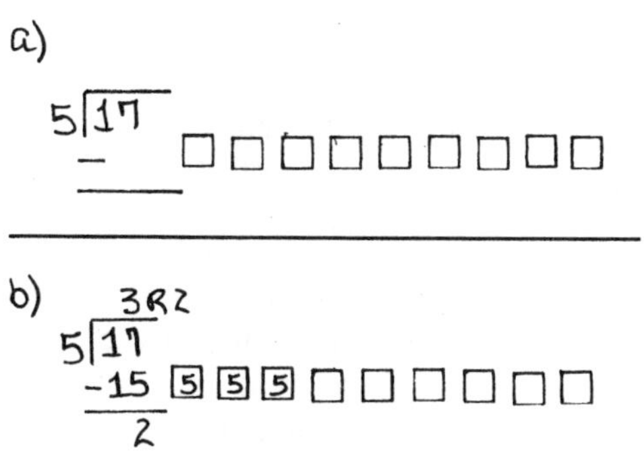

Figure 5-85

3. **Help for sequencing.** As the need to use the squares becomes less but visual cues for sequencing are still needed, use pages containing problems like that of Figure 5-86. After filling in the quotient, the student is reminded to multiply by the box at the left. Figure 5-87 shows an alternative format to help with sequencing. Pages of this type are especially useful for those who have receptive language deficits. The pages can be color coded if necessary. Assuming there is no perceptual or spatial organizational difficulty to bar copying, the students can fill in the blanks with problems from the text. Ideally, the problems should be copied as one assignment and solved as a second.

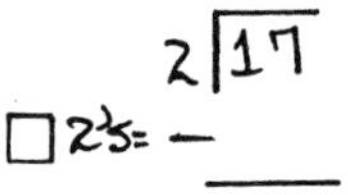

Figure 5-86

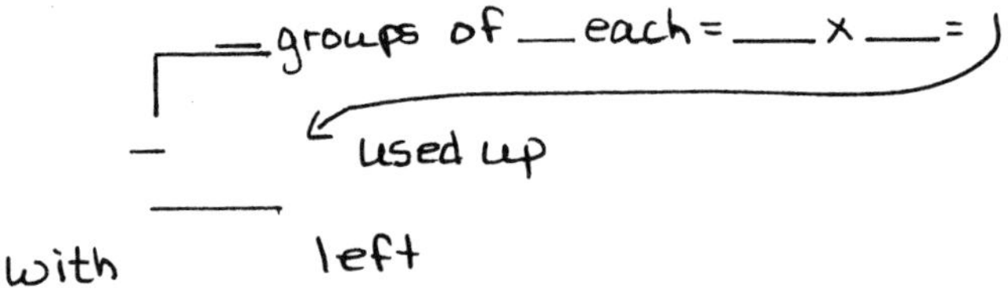

Figure 5-87

4. **Relate.** The sequence suggested by Figure 5-88 can be used to help students more readily determine the correct quotient digit. An effort is made to relate division with remainders directly to basic facts. In the first set of problems, the basic fact answer is given. The child is cued to use this to help solve the given division with remainder. In Figure 5-88b, the children must answer the basic fact problem themselves before computing the long division example. The last problem set requires students to write in the dividend closest to but less than that of the given long division problem. The idea of a left-hand basic fact problem can also be used in conjunction with the exercises suggested by Figures 5-86 and 5-87.

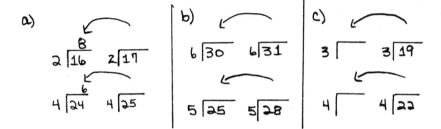

Figure 5-88

Note: Throughout these explanations, the divisor has been used to describe the number of objects in each group. This interpretation has proved successful, given our approach, with the learning disabled students with whom we have worked. Obviously, the divisor can also mean the number of needed groups with the quotient describing the number of objects in each group. This latter interpretation describes situations in which the children divide or "share" a given number of objects (see Figure 5-89). Because of the research support documenting the ease with which regular class children relate to the idea of sharing, it is becoming an increasingly popular approach in mathematics textbooks that present long division. Whatever the approach, it is important to be consistent until the process is learned. Once understanding and retention occur, it is then essential to introduce also the other interpretation. A suggestion for introducing the "sharing" idea is outlined in the storyline that follows.

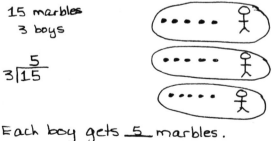

Figure 5-89

5. **Storyline for sharing money.** A money storyline can be used to provide auditory reinforcement for and give meaning to the procedure for long division. The problem of Figure 5-90a can be related to four students who find a bag of money with 2 one-hundred dollar bills, 3 ten-dollar bills and 5 one-dollar bills. They can't locate the owner. After turning it in to the police, they are allowed to keep the money and split it among themselves. How do they go about sharing the money? They are most excited about splitting the one-hundred dollar bills first. (This fact reinforces the left-to-right procedure for computing long division problems.) With only 2 one-hundred dollar bills and four people, what should they do? Tear the bills? No! They trade the 2 one-hundred dollar bills in for 20 ten-dollar bills. Now, with 23 ten-dollar bills, what's the *greatest number* of ten-dollar bills each can receive? (Refer to Figure 5-90b.) The storyline continues along these lines as the children divide what's left. As the story progresses, the long division problem is computed. With 1-digit divisors, play money can be used to dramatize the storyline. Eventually, the students should be asked to analyze the sequence suggested by the storyline and note that there are *five basic steps* (Figure 5-91). Further ideas for focusing on the five basic steps of the long division process are contained in the following section.

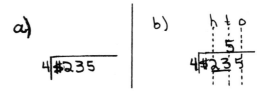

Figure 5-90

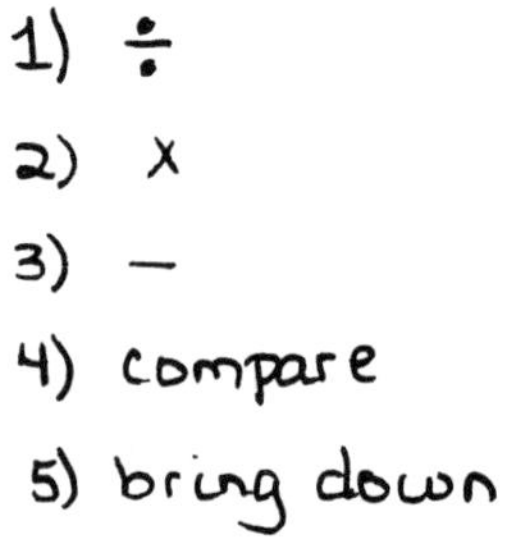

1) ÷

2) X

3) —

4) compare

5) bring down

Figure 5-91

Five Basic Steps

Problem area: Difficulty retaining and sequencing steps in long division.

Typical disabilities affecting progress: Difficulty with memory, sequencing, figure-ground, integrative processing, and spatial organization.

Background: The long division process is cumbersome. It is even more so for those children with the learning deficits noted above. These children's conceptual understanding may be adequate, but they still may not be able to sequence the steps and place the numbers correctly to arrive at an answer. Often visual aids and repeated drill, with the goal of overlearning the sequence, are essential. The following activities and exercises offer suggestions along these lines.

Suggested Activities and Exercises

1. **Fill in.** Figure 5-92 shows a way of helping students organize their thoughts and build up a mental image of the sequence for long division. Before computing, the student fills in the blanks of the rectangle as a reminder of what the numbers represent. The student then continues through the process, reading the words as they are approached to help with the sequencing and to give meaning to the numbers. If necessary, real chips may be used to dramatize problems. Eventually, the procedure should be related to the basic steps of Figure 5-91. It is often helpful to display these steps on a wall chart or to write them on cards that the children can keep at their desks for ready reference. *Note:* If color coding is necessary during early work with exercises of this type, the colors should match those of Figure 5-80.

$$\begin{array}{l} \underline{} \text{ chips} \\ \underline{} \text{ chips in each group} \end{array}$$

$$9\overline{\smash)58} \underline{} \text{groups}$$
$$-\underline{} \text{ used up}$$
$$ \text{left}$$

Figure 5-92

2. **Longer problems.** As problems become longer and more involved, there is typically even greater difficulty in correctly placing digits in computing long division problems. Figure 5-93 suggests one way of handling this difficulty. The words in the center column aid sequencing and eventually lead to overlearning. Encourage the students to memorize them. The color coding within the problem helps the student organize the sequence and properly place the numbers while computing. When dividing by the green three, for example, the quotient is written on the green line. When multiplying by the green numbers, the product is recorded on the green line.

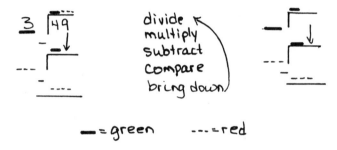

Figure 5-93

- *Note:* Examples of pages similar to that of Figure 5-93 are shown in Figures 1-14 and 1-15. These can be prepared in advance, filed, and used as needed. Problems from the book can be copied directly into the boxes by the students. If help with spatial organization is needed, draw lines on some of the pages. This will help those who have difficulty copying.

3. **Card slide.** For those children who tend to reverse or for those with figure-ground deficits, provide a sliding card as in Figure 5-94. Instruct the children to cover up the digits not being used, as in the sequence shown.

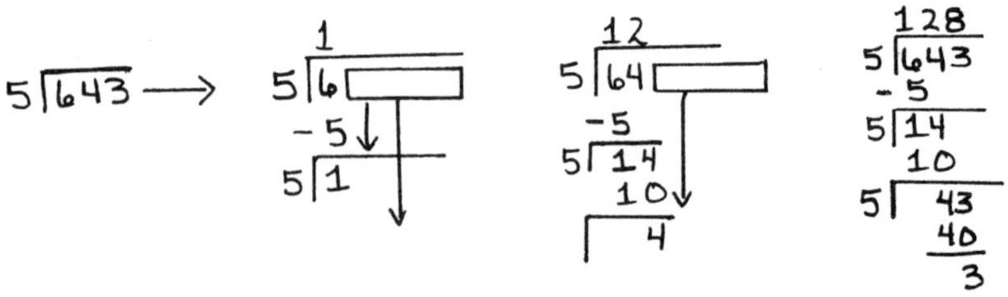

Figure 5-94

4. **"Problem" problems.** In early work with both one- and two-digit divisors, avoid giving the students problem types for which you anticipate a high percentage of errors. One such class of problems is that which has a middle zero in the quotient (Figure 5-95a). Another is that which involves expected rounding errors, as in Figure 5-95b. Give the students the chance to feel comfortable with the computational process for long division before introducing the more difficult problems.

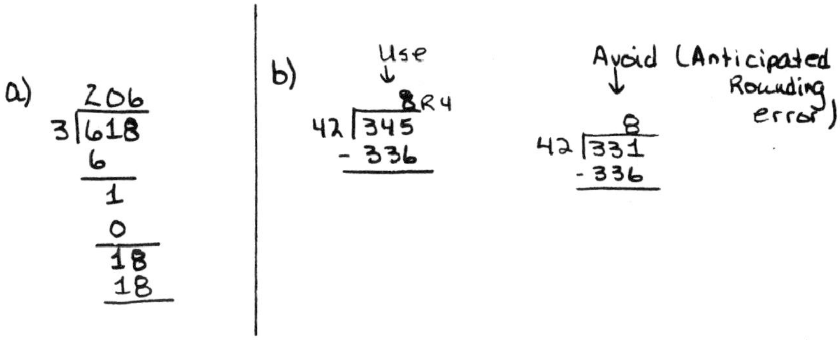

Figure 5-95

5. **Two-digit divisors.** Many of the previous suggestions can be modified for work with two-digit divisors. Even the money storyline in Activity 5 of the previous section can be adapted. The problem of Figure 5-96, for example, might be viewed as sharing $2,176 with 31 people. Using the card slide of Figure 5-94, we can see that there are not enough thousand-dollar or one-hundred-dollar bills to share among so many people. However, bank trades would give us enough ten-dollar bills: 217 of them. The rest of the storyline is adapted similarly.

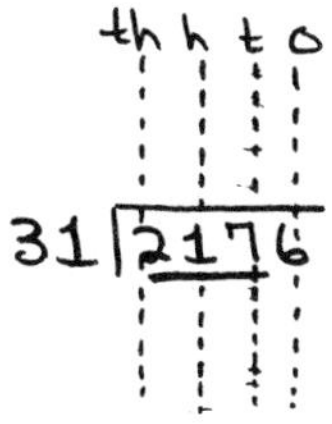

Figure 5-96

6. **Minimize frustrations.** Figure 5-97 illustrates an idea for maximizing drill while minimizing student frustration. Note that the dividend in each example is the same and that the divisors are similar. Only the first problem, then, is "hard." The other two problems provide the necessary practice but should be relatively easy for students.

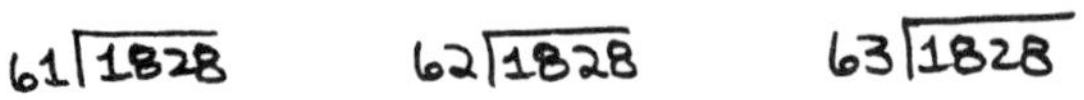

$$6\,1\,\overline{)1828} \qquad 6\,2\,\overline{)1828} \qquad 6\,3\,\overline{)1828}$$

Figure 5-97

7. **Round down.** A mixture of rounding-up *and* rounding-down procedures can be a very efficient means for arriving at correct quotient digits. Some learning disabled students, however, become confused by the many decisions required of them by this approach. It may be simpler to require them *only* to round down (never up) for all examples. Then, if the correct quotient digit is not found right away, as in Figure 5-98a, the direction of the error will always be the same: "Too big, so I'll need to make it one less (Figure 5-98b)."

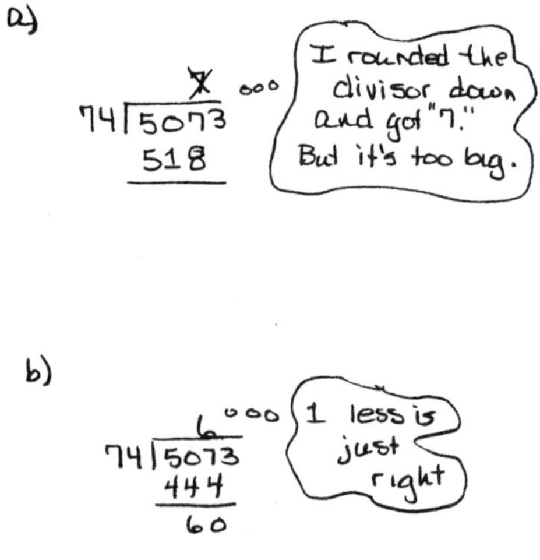

a)

$$74\,\overline{)5073}$$
$$518$$

I rounded the divisor down and got "7." But it's too big.

b)

$$74\,\overline{)5073}$$
$$444$$
$$60$$

1 less is just right

Figure 5-98

Longer Computations: Special Help

Problem area: Difficulty aligning digits or otherwise placing them correctly within the problem.

Typical disabilities affecting progress: Difficulty with visual perception, spatial organization, eye-hand coordination, reasoning, and figure ground.

Background: The division algorithm, aside from being sequentially difficult, also requires good visual perception. Even with strong place-value comprehension, many students have difficulty aligning the digits in the quotient. Others, like the child who worked the problem in Figure 5-99a, are miscued perceptually by the problem itself. In this case, the child understood the long division process. He knew the remainder was too large but was confused because he saw nothing more to bring down! When questioned regarding digit placement in the quotient, he could only correct his error when a card was placed over the 26 (Figure 5-99b) to make the placement more obvious. This technique and others described below make it possible for learning disabled students to succeed with long division.

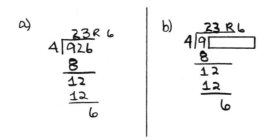

Figure 5-99

Suggested Exercises

1. **Think ahead.** The formated pages of Figures 1-14, 1-15, and 5-93 can be prepared in advance, filed, and used to help students as needed with digit placement in long division.
2. **Show where.** Many children find it necessary to determine the number of digits in the quotient before solving. To do so the students can use a finger or a card and uncover the digits in the dividend one

at a time, as in Figure 5-100. As the student determines where quotient digits should be placed, short lines are drawn to indicate this placement over the appropriate dividend figures.

Figure 5-100

3. **Practice.** Some children have trouble reasoning and therefore do not automatically notice that an answer does not make sense. They will only notice if there is not enough room or too much room for the digits. It often helps with these or other difficulties merely to practice determining where quotient digits should be placed. Have the students place lines above the dividend numbers to show the correct placement, as in Figure 5-100. Do not have them complete problems at this time. Gradually, through discussion and repetition, the student should begin to notice that when the divisor is larger than the first digit of the dividend that space must be empty.

4. **Graph paper.** As with multiplication, graph paper is often helpful for aligning digits for long division. Keep some pages set up as in Figure 5-101. Many children, especially those with severe figure-ground problems, cannot copy numbers onto the graph paper unless it is spatially organized as shown. However, once the initial organization is provided, the graph paper boxes help with alignment. Gradually, as the child feels more comfortable determining the number of digits in a quotient, it also becomes easier to set up and compute the problem independently.

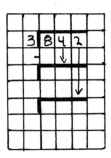

Figure 5-101

Problems Within Problems

Problem area: Difficulty recognizing and solving the subtraction part of a long division problem.

Typical disabilities affecting progress: Difficulty with figure ground, closure, and integrative processing.

Background: Once the sequence of steps for long division has been established, it is still necessary for students to sort out the subtraction problem within the division. Figure 1-2 illustrated how the difficulty can affect computation. Locating and accurately solving the subtraction part of the problem seems to be the hardest at the first subtraction. At that point, there are many numbers to deal with and, especially if regrouping is involved, it becomes difficult to sort out properly. The suggestions that follow help deal with this difficulty.

Suggested Exercises

1. **Block out.** Keep tachistoscopes, as in Figure 5-102, that can be used to block all but the relevant part of a long division problem.

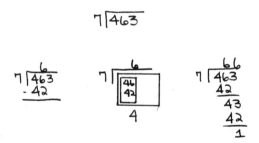

Figure 5-102

2. **Transition.** As a transition to working the problems independently, have the child use the tachistoscope before solving the problem. Figure 5-103a shows the original problem. The student decides where the first digit of the quotient will be, in this case over the six, and places a line to mark that position. The tachistoscope is then placed as shown and the student traces around the rectangle before removing the stencil (Figure 5-103b). The problem of Figure 5-103c is now "ready" for the child to compute.

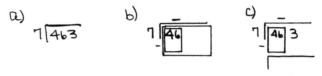

Figure 5-103

3. **Outline the sign.** Sometimes it is helpful to outline the division sign in a bright color. This will help the student more readily distinguish the isolated parts of the problem.
4. **Circle.** Provide practice pages of *completed* problems, as in Figure 5-104. Have the student circle each subtraction (or just the first) within the division. This could be part of a two-day assignment. The first day, the student circles the subtraction problems. The next day, after the page is checked, the student is given a second sheet containing the same problems (*not* worked) to solve independently.

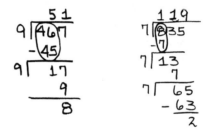

Figure 5-104

Chapter 6

Decimals

Modern school mathematics programs now introduce decimals much earlier than previously was the case. Several reasons account for this emerging trend:

- Computation with decimals is generally easier than fraction computation; there is a great similarity to whole number computation with which students are familiar.

- Most calculators and microcomputers use decimal notation.

- It is appropriate to use decimals to express metric measurements.

Previously, the development of decimal meanings and decimal computational procedures depended on fraction prerequisites. At the present time, there is a gradual shift to a numeration emphasis similar to that used in introducing whole numbers. The following pages will point out, however, that for some learning disabled students and some topics, the use of fractions in basic developmental work is more effective than other techniques. The fractional approach, and other approaches for handling decimal problem areas that are typically troublesome for learning disabled students, are discussed in the six sections of this chapter:

1. naming and writing decimals
2. comparing decimals
3. rounding decimals
4. adding and subtracting decimals
5. multiplying decimals
6. dividing decimals

Before turning to these sections, one final note relative to decimal computation is in order. The authors agree with the view taken by the National Council of Teachers of Mathematics in its *Agenda for Action: Recommendations for School Mathematics of the 1980s* (National Council, 1980, p. 6):

> Insisting that students become highly facile in paper and pencil computation such as . . . or 72 509 ÷ 29.3 is time consuming and costly. . . . For most complex problems, using the calculator for rapid and accurate computation makes a far greater contribution to functional competence in daily life.

Certainly it is important that students' *concepts* for decimals be strong. Certainly it is reasonable to require that they be able to order decimals and carry out simple computations involving decimals. In some cases, because of state or regional minimal-competency examination requirements for receipt of graduation diplomas, more complicated computational skills must also be mastered. Individual situations and needs differ. The general perspective taken in the following sections is that, when it is appropriate to teach a skill, care should be taken to develop it in a way that minimizes frustrations and maximizes success experiences. In this way, learning disabled students will have a greater chance of meeting the potential that is theirs in mastering it.

NAMING AND WRITING DECIMALS

Problem areas: Difficulty interpreting the written symbols in a meaningful way; difficulty attaching "tenth," "hundredth," and other decimal names appropriately to decimals.

Typical disabilities affecting progress: Difficulty with abstract reasoning, auditory or visual memory, auditory discrimination, and expressive language.

Background: Decimals are typically introduced using models like that of Figure 6-1a. As long as the models are present, students may be able to write and read decimals associated with them, as in Figure 6-1b. However, these same students, particularly those with the deficits identified above, may be unable to read written decimals independently of visual aids. A meaningful and effective way of helping students to be functionally independent with written decimals is to relate them to the familiar fractional notation. Even in the symbolic form, fractions are more "concrete" than decimals. The 10 in the denominator of $\frac{1}{10}$, for example, cues a child to say "one tenth." No similar cue for saying "tenth" is given by ".1." Students must simply *remember* what to say, and this can be hard.

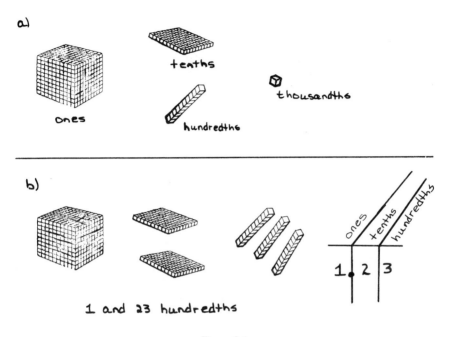

Figure 6-1

The following sequence outlines steps that can be carried out in helping learning disabled students learn to read and write decimals by relating them to fractions. It is assumed that the students have a firm understanding of the fraction concept as equal parts of a whole. It is also necessary that they have worked with the blocks (or graph-paper substitutes) to illustrate decimal numbers.

Suggested Sequence of Activities and Exercises

1. **Review.** Present the four blocks shown in Figure 6-2 and help the children write the fraction for each. Discuss the name of each, orally emphasizing the *th. Note:* Sometimes it is necessary to color emphasize the "th" in words for those with auditory deficits. Doing so focuses attention on the endings, which differ from those used for whole numbers.

2. **Tell it to me.** Present pages like that of Figure 6-3. At first, cover the bottom of the page and have the children match real blocks to those appearing in the top row. Discuss the fraction that is written beneath each. Have the students read the fraction and note the color cueing. "$\frac{1}{10}$ has *one* zero, .1 has *one* decimal place," and so on.

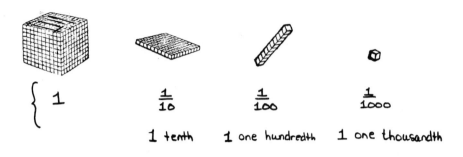

Figure 6-2

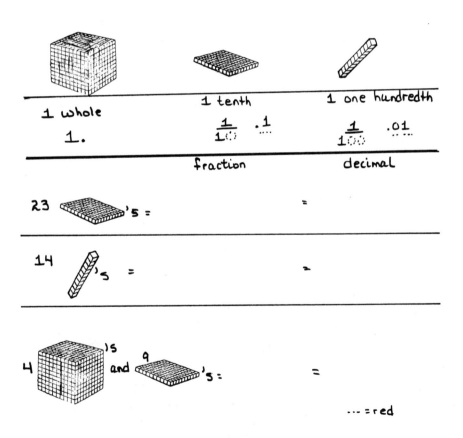

Figure 6-3

3. **Write it out.** Now help the students complete the bottom part of the page. Here an effort is made to relate the visual model (the blocks) *and* the familiar fraction notation to the decimal form. Cue students to look at the number of zeroes in the fraction, which tells the number of decimal places needed. "One zero (one decimal place) for tenths, two for hundredths." *Note:* Initially omit decimal examples like .03, which require a zero in the tenths place, until the children are more at ease writing other numbers with two decimal places.
4. **Reinforce with money.** Once the ideas of decimal place value and writing decimals are established to hundredths, decimals can be related to money as in Figure 6-4. Review writing money (Figure 6-4a), but *focus on the decimal part.* Eventually eliminate the dollars and just use pennies (Figure 6-4b). This is a good time to introduce zeroes in the tenths place: "$ .06—that's 6 out of 100 possible pennies." Color coding can continue to be used if needed. *Note:* In those cases in which money concepts and skills are strong, students with expressive language or visual memory deficits may benefit from introducing decimals by using money as a base.

 = 100

 and 14 = _____

6 s and 9 = _____

8 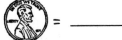s and 7 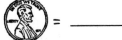 = _____

Figure 6-4a

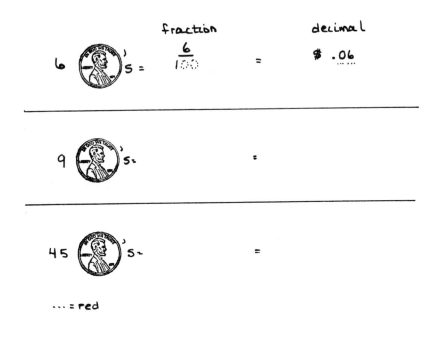

Figure 6-4b

5. **Relate.** To make use of the strong visual association, pages like that of Figure 6-5 can be provided as follow up to the work of Activity 4 above. Pages with mixed fraction and decimal problems can also be presented.

6. **Phase out.** Eliminate picture cues except at the top of the page, and require the students to complete exercises like that shown in Figure 6-6.

7. **Decimal number words.** If the students have auditory weaknesses *but can read,* have them complete exercises like that of Figure 6-7. Initially, be sure they write the fraction form first and *then* the decimal. Doing so helps them internalize the association between the decimal number names and the numerals themselves. Throughout, if the students "get stuck" when reading or writing a decimal, encourage them to think of or write the related fraction. The denominator of the fraction will cue them to say "tenths" or "hundredths" and also indicate the appropriate number of decimal digits.

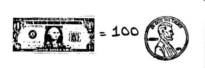 = 100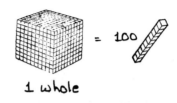

1 whole

Write the fraction and decimal for each.

fraction   decimal

6 's =   =

____

63 🪙's =   =

____

14 's =   =

____

8 's =   =

____

17 🪙's =   =

Figure 6-5

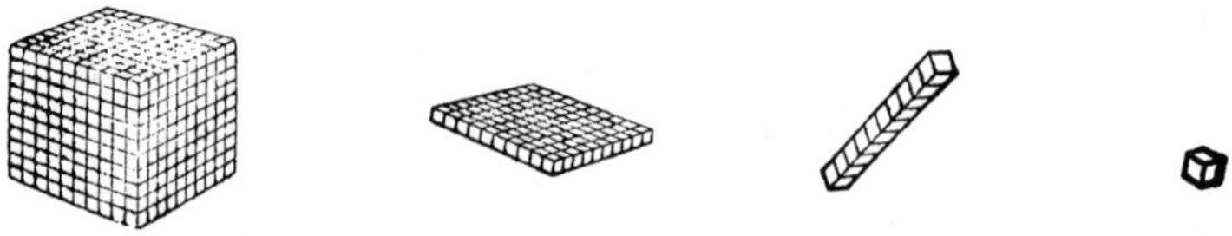

1 whole = 1. $\frac{1}{10}$ = .1 $\frac{1}{100}$ = .01 $\frac{1}{1000}$ = .001

Write the decimal form for each fraction.

$\frac{4}{10}$ = _____ $\frac{7}{100}$ = _____

$\frac{32}{100}$ = _____ $\frac{3}{10}$ = _____

Write the fraction form for each decimal.

.9 =   .47 =

.06 =   .2 =

Figure 6-6

$\frac{6}{100}$ = six one hundredths = .06

$\frac{9}{10}$ = nine tenths = .9

Write the fraction and decimal for each.

	fraction	decimal
four tenths =	=	
eighteen one hundredths =	=	
seven one hundredths =	=	

Write the decimal for each.

	decimal
nine one hundredths	=
sixteen one hundredths	=
five tenths	=

... = red

Figure 6-7

8. **Punch it in** (a practice activity for two to play). As followup to Activity 7 above, provide a hand calculator for each student and a deck of cards, such as those in Figure 6-8a. The children mix the cards and spread them, face up, between the players. Then, in turn, each draws a card. After both players punch the number into their calculator, they compare the visual displays. Children then turn the card over to check. Players earn one tally point for each correct entry.

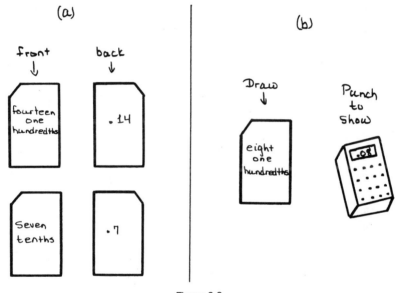

Figure 6-8

- *Variation* (as an independent activity): The child draws cards, one at a time, and punches each number into the calculator. The child then turns over the problem card to check and gets a tally point for each correct answer. Encourage the child to keep a log of the number correct for a given time period and to work to improve that record at another time.

- *Variation* (to build auditory memory and association skills): Ahead of time, "read" (or have the child read) the cards into a cassette tape recorder. Then, at playback, the child listens, punches the number heard, and then uses the card deck (arranged in order) to check. If the tape does not allow sufficient pause between entries, instruct the child to push the stop button after each number is given.

9. **On to thousandths.** As the children become more confident, similar techniques can be used to build up concepts and related decimals skills through thousandths. The children would be cued to associate three zeroes with three decimal places. Figure 6-9 presents an exercise that might be used at this point. As a transition to fading out color prompts, zeroes could be underlined rather than actually written in a different color.

				Fraction	Decimal
1 whole = 1.	$\frac{1}{10}$ = .1	$\frac{1}{100}$ = .01	$\frac{1}{1000}$ = .001		
				$1\frac{11}{1000}$	1.011
3				$3\frac{12}{100}$	3.12

Figure 6-9

COMPARING DECIMALS

Section 2

Problem area: Tendency to focus on the numerals rather than on the place value represented; that is, in examples like .48 and .6, calling .48 the greater. (Here there is a basic confusion between whole and decimal number meanings.)

Typical disabilities affecting progress: Difficulty with abstract reasoning, spatial organization, and auditory memory.

Background: Even students with no disabilities tend to have trouble comparing decimals. For those students with abstract reasoning deficits, the difficulty is compounded. It often is necessary to teach these students a *procedure* for comparing, then, when they feel comfortable with that procedure, to use visuals to demonstrate that it is a reasonable one. For students with spatial organization difficulties, the standard sequence of objects/pictures first in developmental work is appropriate, given that care is taken to avoid numberlines or other aids that rely on accurate size perception.

A sample sequence that has been used effectively with the first group of students is one based on Activities 4 (saving the ''prove'' step till later), 5, 6, and then 1 below, *in that order*. The activities that follow, with the exception of Activity 3, can be carried out with students having spatial organization deficits. Other children with learning disabilities, including those with visual-perception and visual- or auditory-memory difficulties, have been helped as well by these suggestions.

Suggested Activities and Exercises

1. **Shade in.** Given a pair of decimals, have the students shade hundreds squares as in Figure 6-10 to see which is greater.

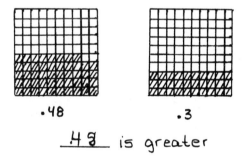

Figure 6-10

2. **Use money** (if money concepts and skills are strong). Figure 6-11 suggests how dimes and pennies can be used as a way of comparing decimals to hundredths.
3. **On the line.** Many school textbooks suggest that students position decimals on a numberline as an aid to comparing and ordering them (Figure 6-12). As has been pointed out, this approach is inappropriate for students with spatial organization or abstract reasoning deficits. The use of "walk-on" numberline segments on which students walk from the lesser to the greater number helps those who profit from kinesthetic/motor involvement.

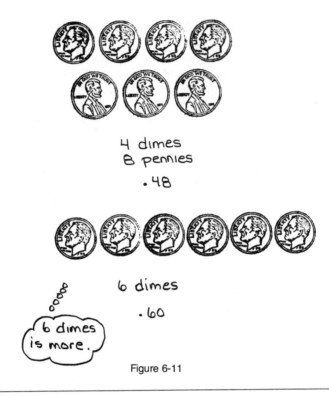

4 dimes
8 pennies
.48

6 dimes
.60

6 dimes
is more.

Figure 6-11

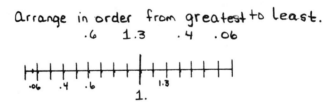

Arrange in order from greatest to least.
.6   1.3   .4   .06

Figure 6-12

4. **Line them up.** It often helps to have students align decimal points
to compare decimals, as in Figure 6-13. Then, digit by digit, they
can "read" left to right to compare the numbers. The procedure is
similar to placing words in alphabetical order. As soon as a difference is found in a column, the number with the greater digit has the
greater value. If students require kinesthetic involvement, have
them finger trace digit pairs, stopping when a difference is found.
Help the students "prove," using ideas from Activities 1, 2, or 3
above, that this procedure always "works."

.486
.468
°°°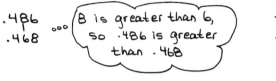

.036
.36 °°°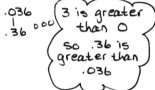

Figure 6-13

5. **Color cue.** Figure 6-14 illustrates how color coding can be used to draw attention to digits critical to the comparison. Students with figure-ground or other perceptual deficits are especially helped by this technique during early developmental work. Eventually, the students themselves can learn to color highlight critical digits as a way of internalizing the comparison.

6. **Add zeroes.** Whenever the number of decimal places in two given numbers differs, many students find it easier to compare when extra zeroes are added, as in Figure 6-15. "Evening out" the number of decimal digits as shown makes the comparison more obvious, particularly when decimal points are aligned as previously suggested. In this case, 360 thousandths, which is greater than 36 thousandths, is illustrated.

.486   .036
.468   .36

■ = green

Figure 6-14

.036
.360

Figure 6-15

ROUNDING DECIMALS

Problem areas: Difficulty remembering what to do in order to round; difficulty sorting out one number from another in the rounding process.

Typical disabilities affecting progress: Difficulty with abstract reasoning, visual figure-ground, closure, and memory sequencing.

Background: By the time students work with decimals, they should have also studied rounding of whole numbers. Applying rounding skills to decimals is not difficult for most students who have mastered the skill for whole numbers. Some learning disabled students, however, particularly those with abstract reasoning deficits, can be misled by the decimal point. "Something is different," and they do not intuitively make the transfer from whole number to decimal use of the rounding rule.

Other students, such as those with figure-ground difficulties or other perceptual deficits, become confused when three or more digits appear in the problem. It is likely that these students also have had difficulty rounding multidigit whole numbers. The decimal point, however, now often causes particular difficulties. The students may automatically "round" by leaving only one or even no digits to the right of the decimal point, regardless of directions given.

Students with memory deficits may have had difficulty rounding whole numbers. This difficulty is carried with them into decimals. A mistake typically made by these students, and also by those with abstract reasoning deficits, is shown in Figure 6-16. In the example, the students rounded by dropping all digits beyond tenths. If the students had been instructed to round to the nearest hundredth, all digits beyond hundredths would have been dropped automatically.

Several suggestions for helping students with these kinds of difficulties are presented below. The section concludes with ideas for adapting the rounding of decimals to a common use in decimal division.

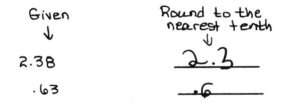

Figure 6-16

Suggested Activities and Exercises

1. **Review.** Be sure the students know and can apply the convention for rounding used in mathematics: To round, examine the digit *after.* If less than 5, round *down;* if 5 or greater, round *up* (see Figure 6-17). *Note:* Here a numberline is helpful so that the students can visualize the counting sequence.

(a) Round .53 to nearest tenth.

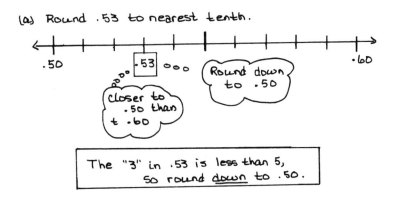

The "3" in .53 is less than 5, so round *down* to .50.

(b) Round .57 to the nearest tenth.

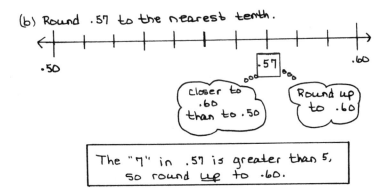

The "7" in .57 is greater than 5, so round *up* to .60.

Figure 6-17

2. **Feel the line.** Have the students position the number to be rounded on the numberline. In the Figure 6-17a example, .53 would be placed on the numberline as shown. Have the students visually inspect the distances from the number to either end and then slide a finger along the line to each end. The finger tracing helps students internalize the concept of "closeness to," basic to rounding. Initially avoid decimals for which "5" is the digit after. When students become more confident of the rounding procedure, the convention used by mathematicians for "5" can be introduced: If the digit after is 5, always round up. *Note:* If the students are strong tactual learners, texturize the line. Then have them close their eyes as they finger slide to either end from the given number.

3. **A fast dime** (rounding to the nearest tenth, informal introduction: a small-group, teacher-led activity appropriate for students who cannot effectively use a numberline). Provide two decks of cards: a "banker's deck" and a "fast dime" deck (see Figure 6-18). Place the banker's deck in a bank box along with extra dimes and pennies. This deck contains one card for each multiple of $.10 (to $.90). The fast dime deck contains cards that list amounts between $.11 and $.89 (no multiples of $.10 included). Until the students understand the activity, remove all multiples of $.05 from the fast dime deck. Shuffle the rest of the deck and place it face down between the players. In turn, the students draw the top card from the deck and place it face up in the playing area. They then use

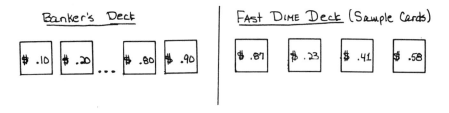

Figure 6-18

dimes (as many as possible) and extra pennies to show the amount on the card. The banker selects the two cards from the banker's deck that are closest in value to that displayed (see Figure 6-19). The child in this example must decide how a "fast dime" can be made. Is $.34 closer to $.30 or to $.40? The child must either add extra pennies to the $.34 pile or take some away to indicate the choice made. Thus, either six pennies would be added (to make $.40) or four pennies would be taken away (leaving $.30). The latter decision earns the child one point, since it involves the least number of coin moves. When the students are comfortable with the activity, add the $.05 multiples to the deck. Introduce the "banker's rule" that for these cards the "fast dime" is always the greater $.10 value.

- *Follow-up 1:* Lay out cards from the fast dime deck, one at a time, and get the students to verbalize the fact that, for example, $.34 is closer to $.40 than to $.30. Allow the students to use dimes and pennies to verify this if necessary.

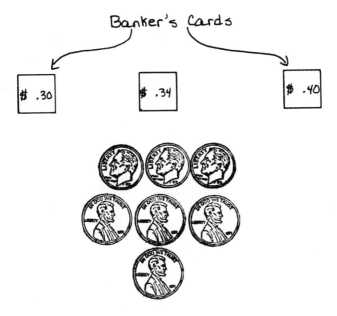

Figure 6-19

- *Follow-up 2:* As above, but use a new deck, one in which *all dollar signs have been eliminated.* If the students hesitate, have them find the matching fast dime card. Seeing the card usually triggers the correct idea. If necessary, allow the students to use dimes and pennies to determine "closeness to." "Yes, 34 hundredths is closer to 30 hundredths than to 40 hundredths."

- *Follow-up 3:* Use worksheets like that of Figure 6-20. Allow students to use fast dime cards as well as dimes and pennies, if these help. When checking the worksheet, relate to the conventional rules for rounding. Post these rules or provide individual index card copies that can be kept in a file box at each student's desk. Be sure the students understand, procedurally, what rounding up (down) means. When rounding to the nearest tenth, for example, all digits beyond tenths will be zeroes (and can be dropped). One uses the *number after* to determine whether the tenths digit itself will be changed to a digit one higher (rounding up) or kept the same (rounding down).

Round to the nearest tenth, then match.
(Some may not have a match.)

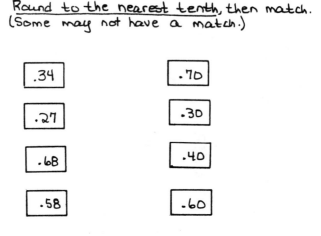

.34	.70
.27	.30
.68	.40
.58	.60

Figure 6-20

4. **Color cue.** Help the students focus attention on the digit to use (the *number after)* by color-highlighting that digit as in Figure 6-21a.

   • *Extension:* If the students are strong in money concepts and skills, Figure 6-21b suggests one way to use money to build or reinforce rounding skills for decimals. Note how, in the example illustrated, green indicates the number of digits in the final answer, while red shows which number to use in rounding.

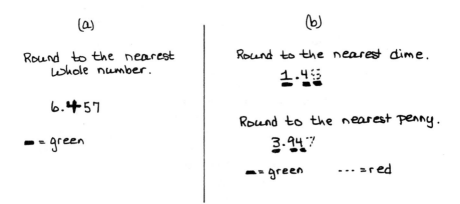

(a)

Round to the nearest
whole number.

6.**4**57

■ = green

(b)

Round to the nearest dime.
1.4⣸

Round to the nearest penny.
3.94⣶

■ = green   ··· = red

Figure 6-21

- *Follow-up practice game:* Rounding war (for two to play): The students mix and deal out all cards of a two-digit decimal deck. Each child turns over the top card and rounds it to the nearest tenth. The player with the greatest tenth captures both cards. Ties are resolved in traditional "war" fashion. The winner is the first to capture all cards.

5. **In decimal division.** Children frequently must round in conjunction with decimal division. To help students with this skill, follow the sequence suggested by Figure 6-22. At first, give problems for which the division is complete, but underscore or box (as in Figure 6-22a) the *digit after.* This technique helps students focus on the digit they should use in the rounding. Gradually introduce exercises like that of Figure 6-22b. The division is not given, but the cue box remains to remind students which digit they should use when rounding. Eventually the cue box as well would be eliminated.

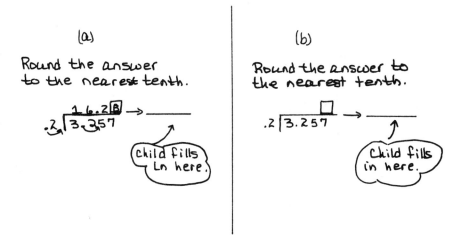

Figure 6-22

Note: At first, avoid presenting division problems like 24 ÷ .3, where zeroes must be introduced in the dividend to carry the rounding out as far as is requested. Techniques similar to those illustrated above can be used to help students whenever the need for extra zeroes is introduced.

- *Follow-up practice game:* Take one (an independent or small-group activity). Provide a deck of cards showing decimal division problems, already computed, with at least two decimal digits in each quotient. Also provide a second deck of arrow cards (see Figure 6-23). Note the green top stripe and the bottom red stripe on the arrow cards. The stripes help the children determine whether the card is a "round up" or a "round down" arrow card. To begin, the arrow deck is shuffled and placed face down between the students. Cards from the problem deck are spread face up in the playing area. In turn, the students draw an arrow card. If it is a round-up arrow, they select one problem card for which it is necessary to round up to obtain the nearest tenth. Similarly, if a round-down arrow card is drawn, the student must select one problem card for which one rounds down to arrive at the nearest tenth. Students keep any matches they make. The player with the most pairs when all cards are used up wins the round. Note: It is helpful to provide an answer key for students to use when they are in doubt.

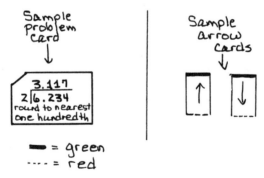

Figure 6-23

ADDING AND SUBTRACTING DECIMALS

Section 4

Problem areas: Difficulty visually aligning digits within a column in order to compute; a tendency to be generally misled by the decimal point or by decimal problems that are not right justified.

Typical disabilities affecting progress: Difficulty with visual figure-ground, spatial organization, abstract reasoning, auditory memory.

Background: It is common for learning disabled students to make mistakes like those illustrated in Figure 6-24. In Joey's work, digits rather than decimal points were aligned. Ann mistakenly added the 4 to the 5 as the first step of her computation. In the last step, she also skipped columns and added the whole number 8 to .2 before completing the addition.

In Figure 6-24b the child started by bringing down the 3, then continued the subtraction. In Figure 6-24c, the decimal part, then the whole number part was added. Both subsums were recorded independently. While sometimes mistakes like these are careless ones, they can stem from specific disabilities, particularly those identified at the beginning of this chapter. Children forget what to do, find it difficult to relate meaningfully to numbers (and then make all kinds of errors), or have problems sorting out all the numbers within the computation. Ideas for dealing with problems, such as these for decimal addition and subtraction, are outlined below.

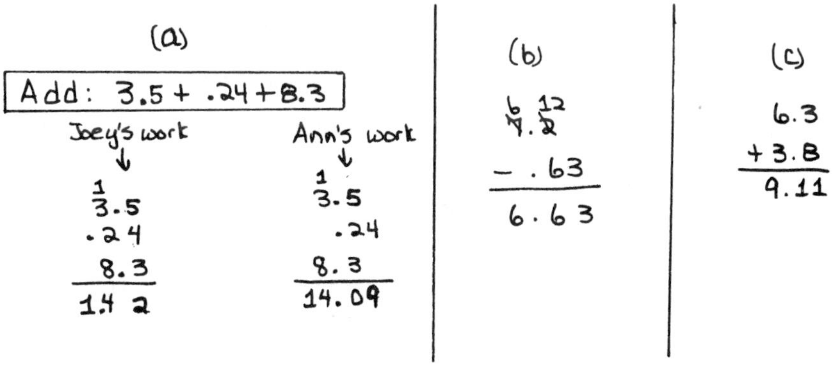

Figure 6-24

Suggested Activities and Exercises

1. **Use blocks** (or graph paper pieces) as a prerequisite to help children understand which decimals need to be aligned. Working with the students, have them use blocks to picture written problems, then physically move the materials to carry out the indicated operation. As with whole numbers, they will move things together for addition and separate into two groups for subtraction. At each step, have the students record what is done in the problem itself.

2. **Use auditory cueing.** Get the students themselves to verbalize what they are doing. If necessary, review the first "big idea" of addition (subtraction) of decimals: add (subtract) like units (Figure 6-25). Help the students see that doing so helps to align decimal points.

Add (Subtract) Like Units

$$\frac{1}{10} = \frac{10}{100}$$
$$+\frac{4}{100} = \frac{4}{100}$$
$$\frac{14}{100}$$

$$.1 + .04$$
$$.1$$
$$+.04$$
$$= .14$$

Figure 6-25

- *Note:* If the students have abstract reasoning difficulties, use the idea of auditory cueing *first* until they feel comfortable with a procedure they can follow. Then help them see that the procedure makes sense by using the idea of Activity 1 above.

3. **Line them up.** If the students have visual perception difficulties, encourage them to do the following:

- Add extra zeroes to right justify problems like that of Figure 6-24a (Ann's) and Figure 6-24b.

- Use a highlighter, pen, or pencil to mark vertically all digits in a column before adding or subtracting.

- Use square cm paper and write one digit to a space. Show the students how to place decimal points on a line.

- Turn lined paper 90° and use the lines as a vertical guide to column alignment.

- Make the decimal point a bright color, as in Figure 6-26a. This helps the students notice it when they recopy the problems to compute. *For special cases, color highlight the decimal point for* the students and, during early work, also align the points in vertical form as shown in Figure 6-26b. Those with spatial or figure-ground deficits may require this additional assistance until they have learned to deal with the decimal point. *Note:* If the children are strong tactual learners, it helps them to finger trace all numbers in a column (all like units) before adding or subtracting.

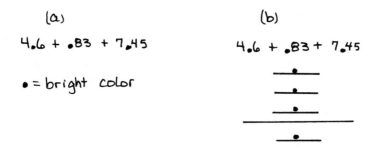

(a)

4.6 + .83 + 7.45

• = bright color

(b)

4.6 + .83 + 7.45

Figure 6-26

MULTIPLYING DECIMALS

Section 5

Problem area: Misplacing the decimal point in decimal products.

Typical disabilities affecting progress: Difficulty with abstract reasoning, sequencing, auditory memory, visual figure-ground, and spatial organization.

Background: Students who have mastered whole number multiplication have a good start toward learning to multiply with decimals. The goal now is primarily learning to place the decimal point in the product. For learning disabled students this can be a very difficult task. One of the most common errors made by students, including those with specific disabilities, is illustrated in Figure 6-27. The problem may stem from confusion with the familiar procedure for addition and subtraction. Other reasons, stemming from the disabilities identified above, may also contribute to the mistakes made. Given that skills for multiplying whole numbers are strong, the suggestions below have proved effective in helping students to avoid falling into errors with decimal multiplication. They also have been useful for correcting erroneous practices that have been adopted.

$$
\begin{array}{r}
1.2 \\
\times\ .4 \\
\hline
4.8 \\
\end{array}
$$

Figure 6-27

Suggested Sequence of Activities and Exercises

1. **Prerequisites.** The most critical prerequisite for decimal multiplication is student ability to handle whole number multiplication. But another (and often overlooked) prerequisite is the ability to count correctly the digits of a number. This skill is used in placing the decimal point in products. If students have difficulty interpreting a teacher request or other written instruction to "count the number of digits," provide exercises like that illustrated in Figure 6-28. Keep pages on file that use one of the two suggested formats. At first, for exercises like that in Figure 6-28a, write a number in each circle and then have the students copy each digit of that number in the space provided. The colors help focus attention properly so that the students can differentiate between the meaning of *number* and *digit.* Later, when the students recognize the distinction, they can independently copy given numbers into the circles before rewriting the digits. In exercises patterned after Figure 6-28b, numbers are given for which students indicate the number of digits involved before writing them in the spaces provided.

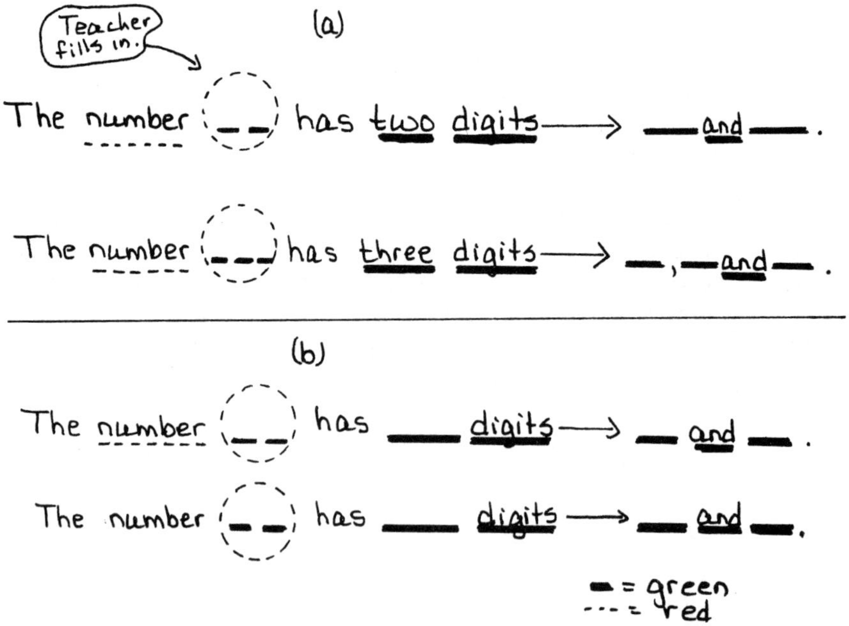

Figure 6-28

2. **Find and chart.** Have the students find products for decimal multi-plication problems using one of the approaches described below. Make a chart of all completed problems.

- *Use fractions.* If the students can multiply fractions well and have no difficulty changing from decimal to fraction form (and vice versa), have them solve decimal multiplications as illustrated in Figure 6-29. Color coding as shown helps those with sequencing and memory difficulties. Choose multiplication problems that can readily be calculated mentally (though the student is required to change to fractions, compute, and rewrite as directed).

1) Change each decimal to a fraction.
2) Multiply.
3) Write the answer as a decimal.

Steps 1 and 2	Step 3
a) $.4 \times .03 = \frac{4}{10} \times \frac{3}{100} = \frac{12}{1000}$	.012

Steps 1 and 2	Step 3
b) $.8 \times .6$	

Figure 6-29

- *Use area.* If students have studied area, this topic can be used to help with decimal products. Figure 6-30 illustrates, for example, how $.1 \times .1 = .01$ (1 of the 100 squares) and $.6 \times .2 = .12$ (12 of the 100 squares).

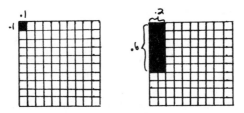

Figure 6-30

- *Estimate.* Present problems like those of Figure 6-31a, where .5 (one-half) and .9 (almost 1) are used as factors. Notice that the product is complete except for placing the decimal point. Help the students estimate to place the point correctly in the product. Suggestions for doing so are illustrated in Figure 6-31b.

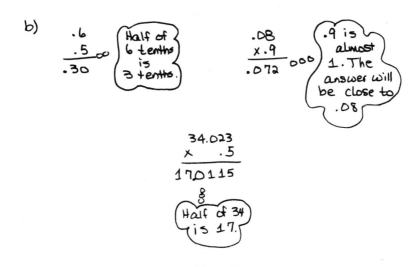

a)
```
   .6          .08        34.023
   .5        x .9        x    .5
  ──────     ──────      ────────
   30          72         170115
```

b)

Figure 6-31

- *Use a calculator.* A final approach for those who can read a calculator effectively is to allow students to use one to obtain decimal products for given problems.

3. **Study the chart.** When decimal products are determined and charted using one of the approaches outlined in Activity 2 above, help the students study the chart and note the recurring pattern (see Figure 6-32a). Color coding as in Figure 6-32b (same colors as in Activity 1a above) helps the students with self-discovery, something which frequently is difficult. Leading questions also help: "Hm-m, three decimal digits in the problem (circle the problem part). How many are in the product?"

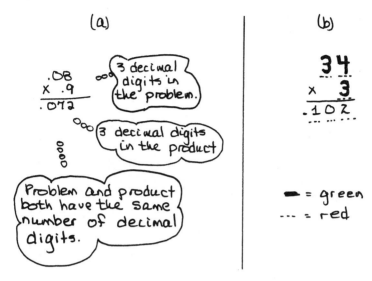

Figure 6-32

4. **Carry through.** Now assign problems like that of Figure 6-33, using either a horizontal or vertical format. The color scheme, the same as that used earlier, outlines the sequence to be followed. The green box and digits cue the first step: "Multiply given digits." Red indicates the last step: "Count digits and place the decimal point."

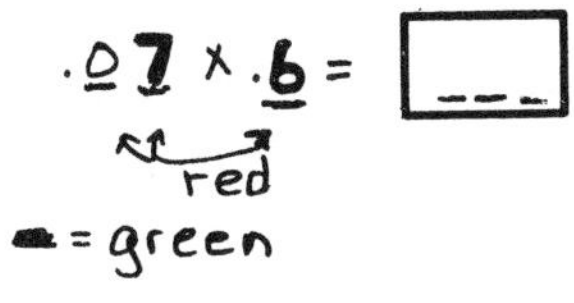

$$.0\,\underline{7} \times .\underline{6} = \boxed{}$$

red

■ = green

Figure 6-33

- *Note 1:* The red digits are purposely placed in the center of the green box to force thinking in placing extra zeroes.

- *Note 2:* At this point, keep the products simple so that they can be computed mentally.

5. **The one step.** To reinforce the pattern for decimal point placement in products, gradually eliminate colors and present problems like those of Figure 6-34. The students complete just the one last step of each problem: that of placing the decimal point in the product.

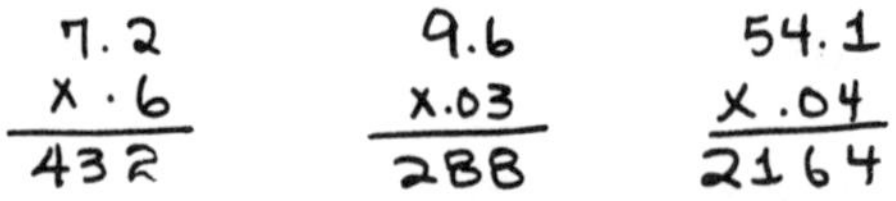

$$
\begin{array}{r} 7.2 \\ \times\ .6 \\ \hline 432 \end{array}
\qquad
\begin{array}{r} 9.6 \\ \times .03 \\ \hline 288 \end{array}
\qquad
\begin{array}{r} 54.1 \\ \times .04 \\ \hline 2164 \end{array}
$$

Figure 6-34

6. **Different from +, −:** To reinforce further the decimal multiplication procedure, present exercises like that of Figure 6-35. Pages like that shown can be prepared in advance and kept on file. The teacher (and later the students themselves) fills in addition, subtraction, and multiplication problems involving decimals down the

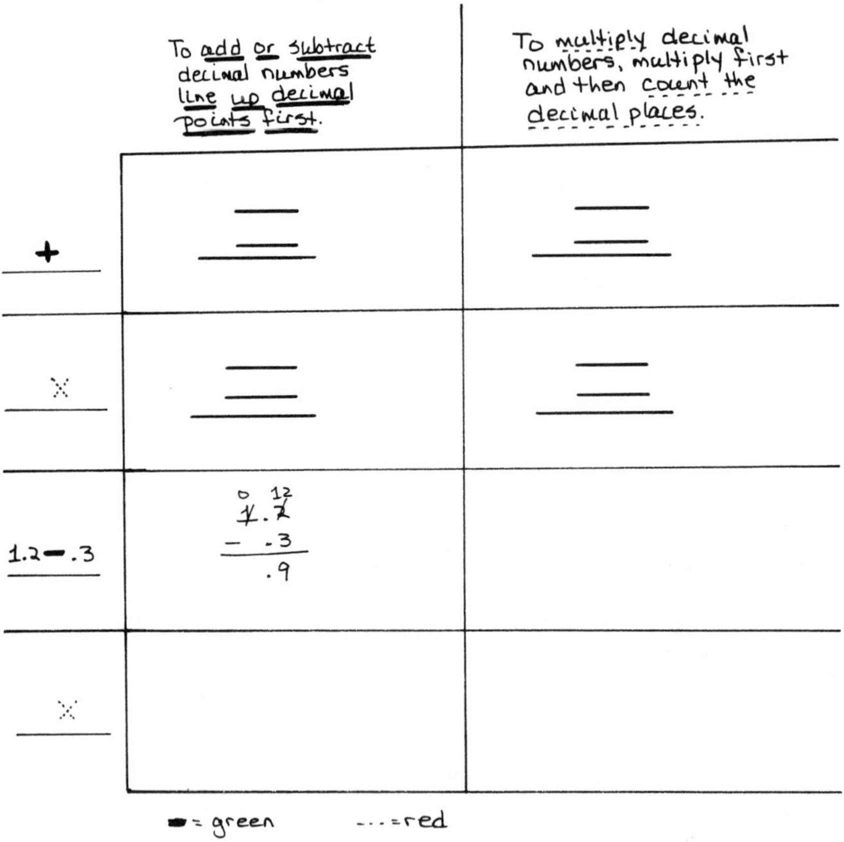

	To add or subtract decimal numbers line up decimal points first.	To multiply decimal numbers, multiply first and then count the decimal places.
+		
×		
1.2 ← .3	$\begin{array}{r} \overset{0}{\cancel{1}}.\overset{12}{\cancel{2}} \\ -\ .3 \\ \hline .9 \end{array}$	
×		

●= green   ---=red

Figure 6-35

left edge of the sheet. The children then recopy in the appropriate column. The two-column arrangement highlights, procedurally, the basic distinction between addition/subtraction and multiplication. The column headings serve as backup in case the students forget or confuse the sequence for adding, subtracting, and multiplying. When the work is checked, it is important to get the students themselves to read or verbalize independently the procedures summarized in the column headings.

- *Note:* Problems along the left edge of the paper are purposely written in horizontal form. This forces the students to think, when recopying into vertical form, whether it is necessary to align decimal points to carry out the computation. For students who have visual-motor or other perceptual deficits that make the transfer from horizontal to vertical form difficult, provide lines as in the first two problems to help with alignment.

DIVIDING DECIMALS

Problem area: Difficulty knowing where to place the decimal point in decimal quotients.

Typical disabilities affecting progress: Difficulty with abstract reasoning, sequencing, auditory memory, visual figure-ground, and spatial organization.

Background: Even learning disabled students who are confident with the long division process may have special problems with division involving decimals. Figure 6-36 illustrates a typical error. The students automatically place the decimal point in the quotient just above that in the dividend, just as they do when dividing money amounts by whole number divisors. When decimal division is included as a mathematics learning goal for a learning disabled child, the suggestions that follow may be helpful.

$$\overset{5.3}{.3\,\overline{\smash{)}15.9}} \qquad \overset{1.21}{.04\,\overline{\smash{)}4.84}}$$

Figure 6-36

Suggested Sequence of Activities and Exercises

1. **Color highlight.** School textbooks typically begin decimal division with easy problems first: those with counting numbers as divisors. Since dividing money amounts is a common occurrence in daily life, problems like that illustrated in Figure 6-37 are often posed. Some textbooks may include problems like that of Figure 6-38. In either case, color cueing can be used as illustrated in Figure 6-39 to help students focus on the decimal placement in the quotient of an "easy problem": *right above* that of the dividend.

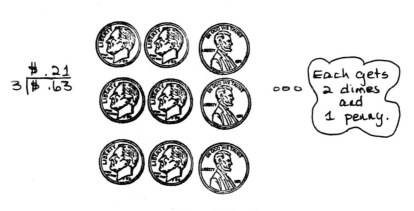

Figure 6-37

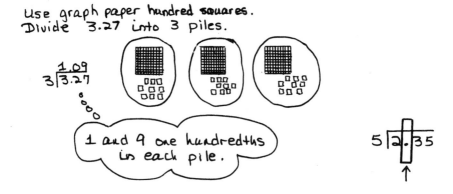

Figure 6-38   Figure 6-39

2. **"Hard" problems now:** decimal divisors. A child's interests and learning strengths will dictate which of the following approaches should be used for introducing problems with decimal divisors.

- *Use fractions.* If the students are skillful with fractions, they can find answers to given decimal division problems by (1) rewriting as a fraction and dividing; (2) writing the answer as a mixed number; and (3) rewriting, finally, as a decimal. Figure 6-40 illustrates the format of a color-coded worksheet that can be used to help students with memory, sequencing, and perceptual or spatial organization deficits.

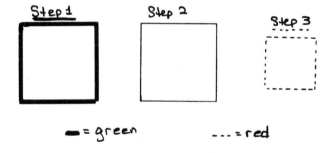

1) Rewrite as a fraction and divide.

2) Write the answer as a mixed number.

3) Rewrite as a decimal.

Step 1   Step 2   Step 3

━ = green   ⋯ = red

Figure 6-40

- *Use a calculator.* (Prerequisites: The students can carry out decimal divisions for problems having whole number divisors, and they can efficiently handle a hand calculator.) Allow the students to use a calculator to find answers to problem sets like that of Figure 6-41. The students will find that each pair of problems has the same answer. "To divide hard problems with decimal divisors, change them to easy problems like those shown."

a) $.3\overline{)21.9}$ $3\overline{)219}$

b) $.05\overline{)15.845}$ $5\overline{)15845}$

c) $2.6\overline{)31.46}$ $26\overline{)3146}$

Figure 6-41

Follow-up 1: Should I move it? To change a "hard" problem into an "easy" one, the students must move the decimal point in the divisor to make it a counting number. Of course, the decimal point in the dividend will be moved similarly, as illustrated in Figure 6-42. As a first step, present a mixture of problems—some with decimal divisors and others with counting numbers as divisors. Have the students simply circle any problem for which the decimal point *should be moved* to turn it into an "easy" problem. Save their papers for use in the following activity, to be carried out during a subsequent session.

$$\overset{2\,0.\,2}{.4\overline{)8.08}} \qquad \overset{12.3}{.24\overline{)2.952}}$$

Figure 6-42

Follow-up 2: Then do it. (Use papers from the preceding activity.) Reexamine the above problem set. Many students can be helped to see that, in moving the decimal point to get a counting number as divisor, one really multiplies *both* divisor and dividend by 10 or by 100 or . . . (by some power of 10). Procedurally, one must orally emphasize:

> "What you do to the divisor,
> you do to the dividend, too."

Color-coded exercises using the format of Figure 6-43a or 6-43b can be used to emphasize the movement of the decimal point within given problems. In Figure 6-43a, the green coding emphasizes the need to move the decimal point *first.* Last of all, the students divide. In Figure 6-43b, color highlighting is used to help the students focus on the number of digits involved in the decimal point shift. *Note:* Decimal division problems like 24 ÷ .3, where extra zeroes must be added in the dividend, should be omitted until students are comfortable with other decimal divisions.

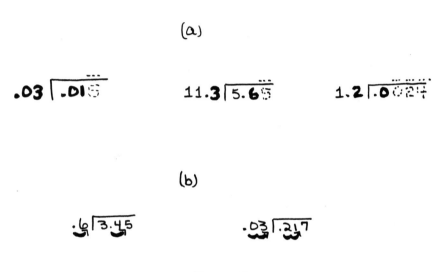

Figure 6-43

REFERENCE

National Council of Teachers of Mathematics. *An Agenda for Action: Recommendations for School Mathematics of the 1980s.* Reston, Va.: The National Council of Teachers of Mathematics, Inc., 1906 Association Drive, Reston, Va. 22091, 1980.

Chapter 7

Fractions

There is ongoing discussion within the mathematics education community concerning the emphasis to be placed on fraction topics in the elementary school mathematics curriculum. Many educators feel that with metrication and the widespread use and availability of the calculator, the need for involved computations and work with any but the more commonly used fractions is obsolete. On the other hand, fractions will continue to be part of our daily lives. People still will think in terms of halves, fourths, and other more common fractions. Although some calculators can handle fractions without converting them to decimals, most do not. Students need to understand the relationship between decimals and fractions in order to use calculators efficiently. In addition, as pointed out in the last chapter, the only way to a clear understanding of decimals for many is through the more concrete path of fractions.

Perceptually, fractions can be a very difficult topic. The mere act of writing a fraction correctly requires spatial organization that many children lack. It is not unusual to see children writing fractions or mixed numbers as in Figure 7-1. This type of copying may appear careless when, in fact, children may be perceiving the positions exactly as written.

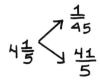

Figure 7-1

Figure-ground deficits can make it hard for some children to sort out the relevant parts of a picture. Textbook illustrations like that shown in Figure 7-2 can be visually confusing, making it impossible for students to use them effectively. These same children may have trouble computing because all the isolated digits of the fraction run together.

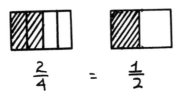

Figure 7-2

Students with language deficits often have difficulty with the terms used to describe or name fractions. Suppose a teacher writes "$\frac{3}{4}$" on the board and instructs the children to shade three-fourths of a rectangle. The numbers used sound familiar, but because they are positioned vertically when written, it is hard for some students to associate them with the words. When the language of fractions is used to describe a group of things, such as a third of a class, the relationship becomes even more abstract. The child hears the fraction, but it is meaningless in this context. How much is a "third of a class"? There may not be a number that is readily associated with the words "of a class."

As concrete as the idea of fractions can be, much of what we teach children about them relies on a high degree of abstract reasoning. We show them, with objects and pictures, that $\frac{1}{3}$ means one out of three equal parts. The idea is fairly simple; and, after repeated presentations with whatever aids are needed, most children learn to label fractional parts of geometric regions and, eventually, of groups of objects. However, consider Figure 7-3 in which both pictures represent the fraction for $\frac{2}{5}$. For children who have trouble with multiple meanings, this type of understanding is extremely complex. The concept "two out of five equal parts" may be clear. The difficulty arises because the equal parts of the two shapes are different sizes. The unit, the "one whole" in each case, is different.

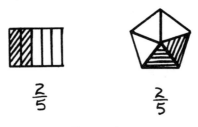

Figure 7-3

The use of concrete aids is essential during early developmental work with fractions. Manipulative experiences help give meaning to the written work. Eventually, however, the use of physical objects becomes cumbersome, and it is necessary to rely on pictures. For most children, the use of pictures is not a problem; they make the transition from objects to pictures easily. However, some children have real trouble with textbook illustrations. As pointed out earlier, they may be unable, visually, to interpret the pictures as intended. Suppose the task is adding fractions with unlike denominators, such as $\frac{3}{4} + \frac{1}{3}$. The children may understand and enjoy representing each fraction with its fraction strip, then trading the $\frac{3}{4}$ for a $\frac{9}{12}$ strip, the $\frac{1}{3}$ for a $\frac{4}{12}$ strip, and adding the twelfths. These same children may have difficulty sorting out the steps from textbook pictures that accompany the explanation of finding denominators. They may even have difficulty interpreting pictures for simpler problems, such as the addition of Figure 7-4a. Sometimes, for textbook illustrations like this, it is necessary to provide children with pictures, like those of the textbook, which are unshaded, as in Figure 7-4b. Placing a card over all but the first addend in the equation, as in Figure 7-4c, the student colors $\frac{1}{7}$ of the figure. Moving the card so that the next addend is exposed (Figure 7-4d), the child next colors in an additional $\frac{2}{7}$ of the rectangle. The card is then removed and the answer written down. Finally, a comparison is made of the worksheet and textbook page.

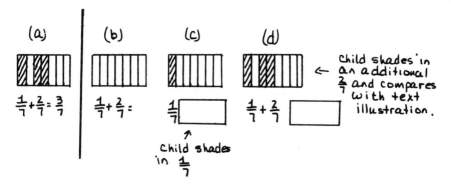

Figure 7-4

At about the fourth or fifth grade level, a high degree of abstraction is required as explanations begin to deal more with numbers than with either concrete aids or pictures. As the children begin to use symbols, their ability to recognize patterns is important. Patterns are often used in the development of rules for fraction computation. Patterning requires that the students be able to draw conclusions, a skill specifically taught in reading but not always in elementary school mathematics.

Students also need to be able to retrieve and apply basic facts spontaneously if they are to succeed with fraction computation. As pointed out in Chapter 5, some children may know their basic facts quite well but have trouble incorporating them while learning a new skill. Until they feel comfortable with the procedures being learned, it may be necessary to adapt ideas from the first sections of Chapter 5 to help children with fraction work.

The previous discussion is meant to point out some of the areas that can prevent learning disabled children from succeeding with fractions. The following pages present specific ideas for dealing with these and other areas that tend to present difficulties for such children. Ideas are clustered into the following 11 sections:

1. general areas of difficulty
2. writing fractions
3. using a ruler
4. fraction numberlines
5. quotients, improper fractions, and mixed numbers
6. equivalent fractions
7. reducing fractions
8. finding common denominators: comparing, adding, and subtracting fractions
9. regrouping in subtraction
10. multiplying fractions
11. dividing fractions

It clearly is not possible to deal with every type of problem that learning disabled students experience. It is hoped, however, that the ideas presented will suggest ways of dealing with other topics so that learning disabled children learn, retain, and use fractions in an efficient, productive manner.

GENERAL AREAS OF DIFFICULTY

Spatial Organization

A major hindrance to computing successfully with fractions is the inability to write the numbers accurately. Generally, we write letters or numbers in one direction, horizontally, and left to right. With fractions, however, the spatial organization is different. Students are now required to write both horizontally *and* vertically. Many students cannot clearly discriminate these differences. The task is particularly difficult for younger students. As children mature, they develop an ability to handle these distinctions unless specific learning disabilities interfere. Many learning disabled students, for example, need visual cues to guide correct writing and placement of the fractions as they learn the various computational processes. Figure 7-5 presents ideas for types of preformated pages that can be kept on file and used for this purpose. Example 1 in the figure is useful when teaching children to add or subtract mixed numbers. With the boxes already there, the children need not be as concerned about number placement. Attention can rather be focused on the major goal: that of deciding whether to find a common denominator. The page is set up in two columns to help children in the decision-making process. The child writes in the first column when it is necessary to find a common denominator, and in the second when this is not necessary. Examples 2 and 3 of Figure 7-5 illustrate similar page ideas for multiplication and division.

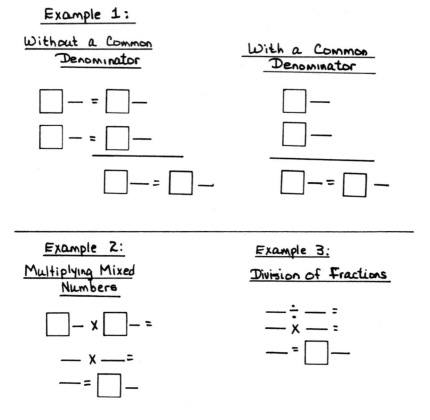

Figure 7-5

These pages reinforce reasoning as well, since the *maximum* number of spaces is presented. The student must decide whether it is necessary to use all the spaces. Figure 7-6, for example, shows a sample problem that does *not* require the student to use all the spaces provided.

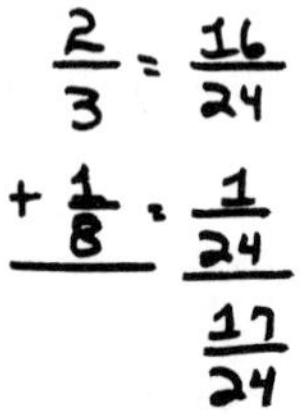

$$\frac{2}{3} = \frac{16}{24}$$

$$+\frac{1}{8} = \frac{1}{24}$$

$$\frac{17}{24}$$

Figure 7-6

Another simple yet important practice that helps spatially to organize the writing of fractions deals with the fraction bar separating numerator and denominator. Encourage children to draw this line *horizontally* ($\frac{3}{5}$), not diagonally (3/5). With the horizontal bar, there is less tendency to read a fraction as a whole number (35 or 315 for $\frac{3}{5}$) or to confuse mixed numbers ($\frac{42}{7}$ for $4\frac{2}{7}$).

A final suggestion, helpful to children who must copy fraction problems from a textbook, is to provide a stencil as in Figure 7-7. The stencil should be made of clear plastic so that the entire problem can be viewed. The framing helps the students focus on just one fraction at a time. As a result the children tend to make fewer errors in copying.

Sequencing

Aside from spatial organization, sequencing is probably the next greatest problem in computing successfully with fractions. As computational processes become more involved, what appears to be a single step may actually be two or

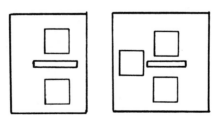

Figure 7-7

three. Consider the problem of Figure 7-6, where the student is required to add two proper fractions with unlike denominators. What generally is considered the first step, that of finding the common denominator, is actually three steps:

1. deciding whether or not a common denominator is required,
2. deciding what the common denominator should be, and
3. deciding what each numerator should be.

Those children who have trouble retaining the isolated steps of a sequence often benefit from performing *one step at a time* until the sequence becomes automatic. For example, if the children fail to check whether a common denominator is needed, have them focus on this one step before introducing additional steps. The practice page ideas presented in Figure 7-8a may help. Instruct the students to copy problems from the book onto the pages, as in Figure 7-8b. The green circles in the denominators will help draw their attention to what the first step should be: check for *common* denominators. For those who have difficulty copying problems from a text, keep workbooks or textbooks in which the denominators have already been circled green. This could be done in advance, even at the beginning of the year.

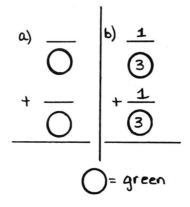

Figure 7-8

When children have mastered individual steps and must now put them all together, pages with the format of Figure 7-9 are helpful. This example is set up to show the maximum number of steps needed for adding or subtracting fractions. Encourage decision making. Remind the students that not all problems require all steps.

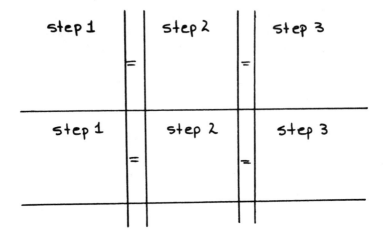

Figure 7-9

Vocabulary

The language of fractions involves many familiar words used in a new context. Most children have heard the words third, fourth, fifth, and so on. By about the second grade, most children readily associate these words with ordinal counting. Now, as they work with fractions, they are required to associate an old symbol (3, 4, 5) with an old word (third, fourth, fifth) in an *unfamiliar* way. To complicate matters, they must now be able to relate words and meanings fairly routinely. Most children do this with little or no difficulty. Some learning disabled students, however, are slowed down in their work because they do not automatically transfer to new ideas and uses.

These same children frequently experience difficulty when other fraction terms are introduced: equivalent, common, simplest, reduced, improper. The children are asked to relate fractions to each other using any of these or other words. The task overwhelms many children. The words are used over and over again in slightly different contexts, and many find it hard to retrieve and associate the proper meanings at the proper time. For example, although we give different names to each fraction in Figure 7-10, they are all equivalent. Many students do not readily recognize the relationship.

$$\frac{8}{6} = 1\frac{2}{6} = 1\frac{1}{3}$$

Figure 7-10

Since most fraction terms can easily be associated with numbers or concrete objects, it helps to make a "dictionary" available to students (see Figure 7-11). Store it in a place to which children have easy access. Keep it at the teacher's desk or on a nearby shelf. Alternatively, make it into a wall chart that can be readily referred to by students when they are faced with a troublesome word during class or independent study.

$$\text{Improper Fraction} \rightarrow \frac{4}{3}, \frac{7}{2}$$

$$\text{Mixed Number} \rightarrow 1\frac{1}{3}, 2\frac{3}{4}$$

$$\text{Proper Fraction} \rightarrow \frac{2}{5}, \frac{5}{8}$$

$$\text{Equivalent Fractions} \rightarrow \frac{4}{6} = \frac{2}{3} = \frac{10}{15}$$

$$1\frac{7}{8} = 1\frac{28}{32} = 1\frac{14}{16}$$

Figure 7-11

Patterning

Making the transition from concrete aids to symbolic understanding requires a strong ability to recognize number patterns. The fractions in Figure 7-12 can be used to illustrate how children use patterning to learn and retain various steps in fraction computation. Although the goal in each instance is to understand, conceptually, how the fractions within a pair are related, it also helps to be able to see the patterns of the numbers themselves. Even though children dealing with the problems of Example 1 in Figure 7-12 may be able to explain the reasoning behind what happens, ultimately they remember because they know they must "multiply the 4 and the 3 and then add 2." It helps students to see what the numbers do as they conceptualize what is actually happening as in Example 2 of Figure 7-12. Often it helps to *hear* the pattern as well, as in Example 3: "Eight-ninths becomes nine-eighths; three-sevenths becomes seven-thirds." Retention is stronger when both understanding and visual patterning are established.

Example 1: Mixed numbers to improper fractions

$$4\frac{2}{3} = \frac{14}{3}$$

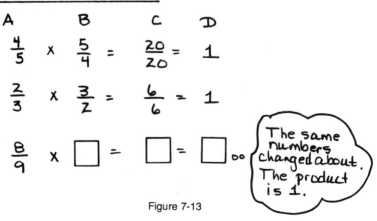

Example 2: Like Denominators

$$\frac{4}{7} + \frac{1}{7} = \frac{4+1}{7} = \frac{5}{7}$$

$$\frac{4}{10} + \frac{3}{10} = \frac{4+3}{10} = \frac{7}{10}$$

ooo *Add the top numbers. The denominator stays the same.*

Example 3: Reciprocals

$$\frac{8}{9} \rightarrow \frac{9}{8}; \quad \frac{3}{7} \rightarrow \frac{7}{3}$$

ooo *The same numbers, changed about.*

Figure 7-12

Specific exercises in recognizing visual patterns as they occur in work with fractions are very helpful. Students with figure-ground deficits will be helped by such exercises which force them to sort out digits. Children with reasoning deficits will be helped to build reasoning skills by the focus on relationships. Completing charts, as suggested by Figure 7-13, is one popular method of focusing on visual patterning. Getting children then to describe patterns they see is the next important step.

Complete the chart.

A	B	C	D
$\frac{4}{5}$	$\times \;\; \frac{5}{4}$ =	$\frac{20}{20}$ =	1
$\frac{2}{3}$	$\times \;\; \frac{3}{2}$ =	$\frac{6}{6}$ =	1
$\frac{8}{9}$	$\times \;\; \square$ =	$\square$ =	$\square$

oo *The same numbers changed about. The product is 1.*

Figure 7-13

WRITING FRACTIONS

Problem area: Difficulty writing fractions and mixed numbers.

Typical disabilities affecting progress: Difficulty with spatial organization, eye-hand coordination, and receptive language.

Background: Once fraction concepts have been established, it generally is assumed that children will have little difficulty actually writing the numbers. This is not always the case. Sequentially, students may know the order in which fraction digits should be written. Spatially, they may be unable to place the digits properly (see Figure 7-14). Auditorially, they may hear the correct sounds and associate them with the symbols. Retrieving and writing the symbols properly may be an entirely different matter.

$$34 \text{ instead of } \frac{3}{4}$$

Figure 7-14

For younger students or for those with learning difficulties, it often is necessary to provide specific practice in writing fractions, much like the way it is done with handwriting. As these students are making the transition from concrete or pictorial representations to symbolic representations, it may be especially necessary for the teacher to recognize the goal of individual lessons. Is the goal to *associate* the correct fraction with its concrete or pictorial representation? Is it to *write* the correct fraction? All too often we think of these steps as one and the same, but for many learning disabled children they are not. Students with the learning deficits noted above must internalize what it *feels like* to write the digits of a fraction in the proper spaces. Only then will they be able to concentrate on what the numbers mean. Until they begin to feel more comfortable with the spatial orientation needed to write fractions, most of their energy will be expended on number placement rather than on understanding.

The following activities suggest ways to help children write fractions correctly. The major assumption is that the children's difficulties are not due to conceptual misunderstanding.

Suggested Sequence of Activities and Exercises

1. **Trace.** Felt numbers or a sand or salt tray often help those who need kinesthetic involvement and gross motor activity while learning to write fractions. Children trace over a given fraction and then

immediately write it again, perhaps with chalk or a large crayon. The gross motor activity helps build the harder, fine motor control needed for standard paper-and-pencil writing of fraction digits.

2. **Color cue.** When the students are ready for paper-and-pencil work, start by using exercises such as those in Figure 7-15. The goal is to help the students develop the spatial organization, *visually* and *kinesthetically,* to write fractions correctly. As previously, colors are used to help with sequence and number placement: "When you write, green goes first, on top." Coat the green shading and box outline of several examples with Elmer's glue. When the glue is dry, the children can finger trace over the raised surfaces. Eventually they will write the number independently (at the end of the line following the equals sign).

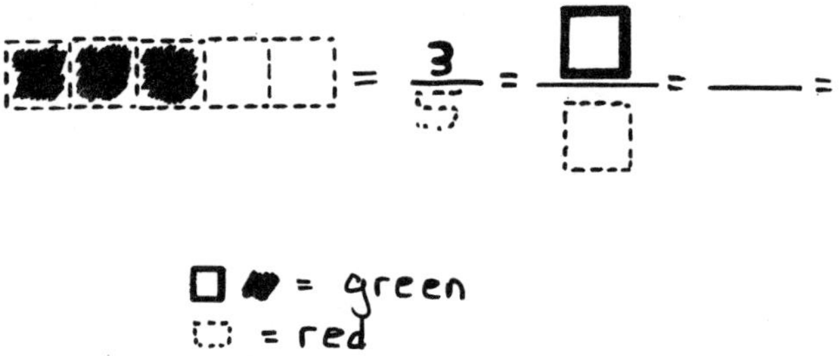

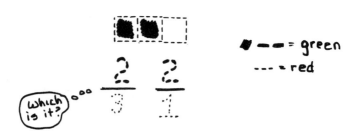

Figure 7-15

3. **Choose.** When the goal of the assignment is to write fractions to describe a shaded region, Figure 7-16 shows a way to avoid difficulties due to spatial deficits. The children cross out the wrong answer and write over the correct one. The fraction is then written independently, immediately after tracing.

Figure 7-16

4. **Mixed numbers.** Writing mixed numbers presents even greater problems for those with spatial difficulties. Now a sense of midpoint is added, in addition to up and down. Figure 7-17 shows one type of exercise that can be prepared in advance and kept on file. The colors are used to help the students

- develop the correct sequence for writing numbers,

- locate the correct position for each digit, and

- associate the parts of the number with the related parts of the picture.

The goal of the assignment is to help the students spatially organize their writing of mixed numbers.

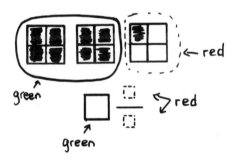

Figure 7-17

5. **Stencil first.** For those students with more severe deficits, keep stencils as in Figure 7-18a. Instruct the students first to use a stencil to write a fraction, and then to write the fraction again without the stencil. The two fractions, the stencil and the nonstencil copy, should be written side by side. In this way, the first serves as a pattern for writing the second.

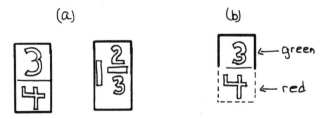

Figure 7-18

6. **Tape it.** The stencils shown in Figure 7-18a can also be used for students who have trouble writing fractions without a visual cue. Provide boxed paper as described in Chapter 1. Have the students listen to a tape recorder and write the fractions dictated. If color coding is needed, put tape around the sides of the stencil as in Figure 7-18b. Students "go" on green and write the *first* digit of each proper fraction dictated on top (in the numerator).

7. **Words to numerals.** Many students have trouble associating number words with the correct position of the digits in a fraction. Color-coded exercises, as in Figure 7-19, often help both with spatial organization and language association. Note that the students rewrite the fraction independently as a last step to the exercise.

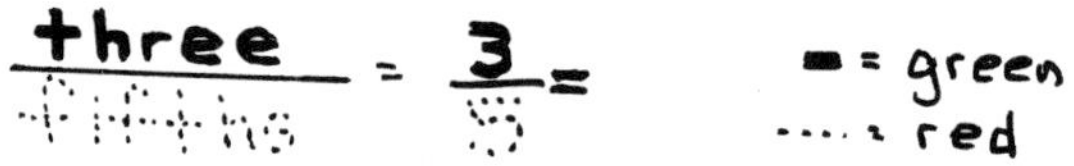

$$\frac{\textbf{three}}{\text{fifths}} = \frac{\textbf{3}}{5} = \qquad \blacksquare = \text{green} \\ \cdots = \text{red}$$

Figure 7-19

- *Extension:* To develop the idea further, the colors can be used as in Figure 7-20. In the first two examples, children read the words, fill in the blanks, then write the fraction independently. The variation in the last example requires the students to describe the picture verbally before proceeding.

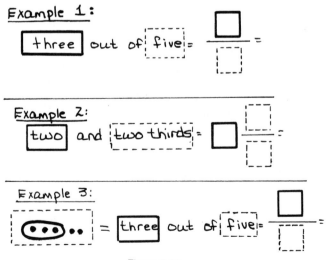

Figure 7-20

- *Note:* Throughout these exercises, bold, dotted, or regular line drawings can be used instead of color cueing for color-blind students.

8. **Fringo.** A variation of Bingo can be used to reinforce basic fraction concepts and provide practice in writing fractions. Make a set of calling cards representing fractions, as in Figure 7-21a. Also make a set of gameboards with fractions in each square (Figure 7-21b). Instead of chips, provide the players with plastic overlays and grease pencils. Each player in turn pulls a card and states the fraction name. If the symbol is on the gameboard, the student writes over it with the pencil. The winning pattern should be determined before the game. *Note:* If necessary, for those with auditory sequencing or memory problems, the calling cards can be color-coded. Use the suggestions from the exercises of this section for the coloring scheme.

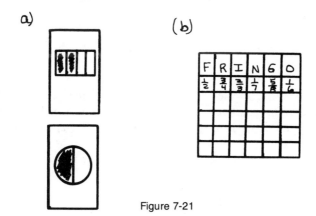

Figure 7-21

USING A RULER

Problem area: Difficulty reading fractional parts of an inch on a ruler.

Typical disabilities affecting progress: Difficulty with abstract reasoning, visual perception, and eye-hand coordination.

Background: Centimeter rulers are considerably easier for children to use than inch rulers, which are based on fractions. Visually, centimeter rulers are less confusing, with fewer lines. Each line on the ruler is associated with a specific numeral (see Figure 7-22). Even if students have difficulty retrieving the correct decimal number name, there is still the readily available "one point three centimeters." Language and retrieval deficits do not interfere the way they do when children try to read inch rulers.

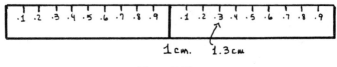

Figure 7-22

Visually, the inch ruler causes problems for the following reasons. Rather than just being able to associate a specific number with a specific line, the student must also

- differentiate visually among four different lengths;

- associate the length of the line segment with an abstract spatial idea;

- with no cueing, pair a visually difficult symbol with the above idea; and

- read or write a symbol that is visually, spatially, and auditorially difficult to sequence.

When actually using an inch ruler to draw a line, the added difficulty of eye-hand coordination interferes. This section will not deal with this problem except to say that, if the goal is accurate measuring, give the students guide lines to follow, as in Figure 7-23, or allow them to use lined paper. The latter alternative, for children with figure-ground deficits, can, however, be more difficult than the use of guide lines.

Figure 7-23

To date, the United States has not made giant strides toward "going metric." This fact underscores the need for the students to use both centimeter and inch rulers. The basic approach to teaching ruler use involves children in *measuring* many objects. Along with this, some children may require more specialized instruction, such as that outlined below.

Suggested Sequence of Activities and Exercises

1. **Simplified rulers.** Younger children and children with learning disabilities usually begin working with simplified rulers, which show only quarter, half, and whole inches. Even then, they may have trouble perceiving size differences for the various parts of an inch. Colors often help to deal with this difficulty. Properly used, the colors can focus student attention and make size differences more obvious. Figure 7-24a shows an example of a homemade ruler that can be run on ditto paper and kept in the files. As children are ready, the paper can be cut and glued to cardboard and marked as in Figure 7-24b. Covering rulers with contact paper makes them more durable.

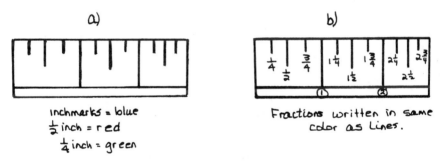

Figure 7-24

- *Variation 1:* For color-blind students, use bold, dotted, and regular line markings.

- *Variation 2:* For very young or developmentally immature children, prepare rulers with only inch markings or with only inch and half-inch markings.

2. **Measure.** To help children use the ruler of Activity 1 above, provide opportunities for them to measure many objects. Structure these experiences as follows: Attach masking tape strips to several items, as shown in Figure 7-25a. At first, mark the items so that the measurement is an exact number of inches. Later, the actual tape mark can be slightly longer or slightly shorter, so that the children can be instructed to measure to the *nearest* inch. Half and quarter-inch lengths are gradually introduced. If the measurement is to be made to the nearest inch, the colored line segment on the tape

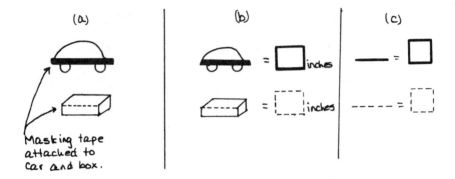

Throughout, line and box for answer match colors on ruler.

Figure 7-25

should be blue to match the inch marks on the ruler. Similarly, the tape marks are red (green) when half-inch (quarter-inch) measurements are to be made. This color-cueing technique draws the child's attention to the appropriate ruler mark needed for a given measurement. The fact that the numbers are already on the ruler is especially important for those who require overlearning or have difficulty with retrieval. After an object is measured, the measurement is recorded on the worksheets that picture the object (see Figure 7-25b).

- *Extension:* As a followup to work with objects, have the children find and record the measurements of line segments drawn on paper. Figure 7-25c shows one sample exercise. Figure 7-26 shows another type of page that is helpful for students who have spatial deficits, making it hard to write proper fractions and mixed numbers, or who have retrieval or expressive language deficits and need visual cues. The color-coding scheme, introduced earlier, would be used as long as it seems helpful.

Figure 7-26

3. **Draw a line.** The color coding of Activity 2 above, can also be used to help students draw a line that is a specific length. A sample exercise is presented in Figure 7-27a. The children use their rulers to *draw over* the given line, then draw another line of the same length under it. Gradually, still using color to specify the length (Figure 7-27b), instruct the students to draw the segment indicated. There is still some guidance in this latter exercise, because the color used for the written direction draws attention to the appropriate marks on the ruler. Even nonreaders quickly pick up on the cueing and learn to do the measurements accurately. *Note:* Some students may require the additional guidance of "start" and "stop" marks, as in Figure 7-27c, as a transition between exercises like those shown in Figures 7-27a and 7-27b.

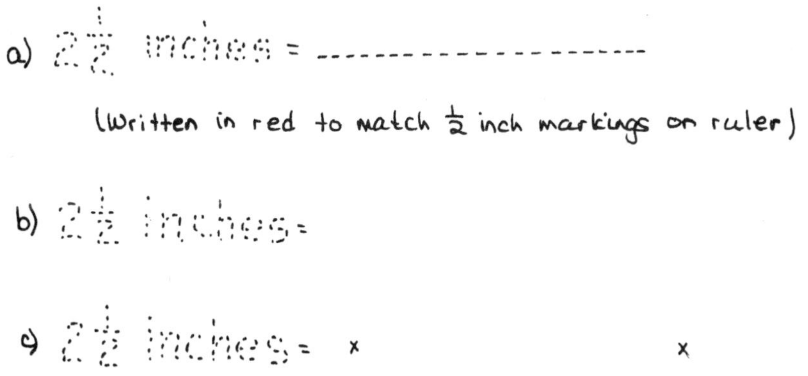

a) $2\frac{1}{2}$ inches = _____

(Written in red to match $\frac{1}{2}$ inch markings on ruler)

b) $2\frac{1}{2}$ inches =

c) $2\frac{1}{2}$ inches = x   x

Figure 7-27

FRACTION NUMBERLINE

Section 4

Problem area: Difficulty finding numbers on a fraction numberline.

Typical disabilities affecting progress: Difficulty with abstract reasoning, visual figure-ground, spatial organization, and size discrimination.

Background: Much work done with whole numbers and fractions involves the use of a numberline. The numberline is a convenient reference for number sequence and is helpful for comparing, ordering, or rounding numbers. It often is useful for visualizing equivalent fractions (Figure 7-28). The numberline even helps students develop a feel for the infinitude of numbers. There is always one

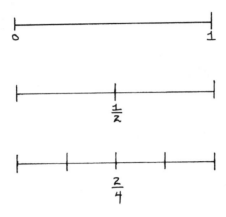

Figure 7-28

more space to be labeled on a line; we can always extend that line to add another number.

Many students, however, particularly those with the disabilities identified above, have difficulty dealing meaningfully with the numberline. The typical numberline used for introducing fractions looks like that in Figure 7-29. For the

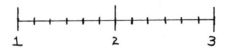

Figure 7-29

learning disabled students we are focusing on in this section, this type of picture does not readily lend itself to recognizing fractions and mixed numbers. These children may be able to label correctly the shaded part of a geometric region. But there is so much more to sorting out numbers on a numberline. Visually, there are a lot of lines to distinguish, and students often have a hard time making the necessary differentiations. If the students have severe visual-perception (figure-ground, size discrimination) difficulties, the numberline may be entirely inappropriate as a teaching/learning tool. For other students, a carefully structured program that provides a transition between the more concrete geometric region models and numberline use is needed. Suggestions along these lines are outlined below.

Suggested Sequence of Activities and Exercises

1. **Fraction strips on the numberline.** Allow the children to use fraction strips, like those pictured in Figure 7-30, during early developmental work with fractions. Later, when fraction numberlines

Sample Fraction Strips

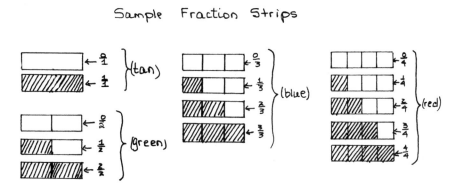

Figure 7-30

are introduced, allow the children to place the fraction strips under the numberline. The example of Figure 7-31, for instance, shows $\frac{3}{2}$. The numberline segmented into halves is green; the denominator digits are also green.

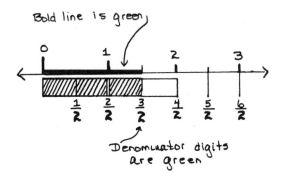

Figure 7-31

2. **Colored overlays.** Present the numberline of Figure 7-32a. If necessary, place the "unit" fraction strip under it so that the children will more readily understand that the segment represents "1 whole." Now, one at a time, use plastic overlays to "break" the line into halves (Figure 7-32b), then fourths (Figure 7-32c), and so on. The colors on the overlays *should match those of the fraction strips* with which the children have worked. Figure 7-32d shows a completed numberline through fourths. Next, a clear numberline, broken into eighths, would be placed over this drawing and marked

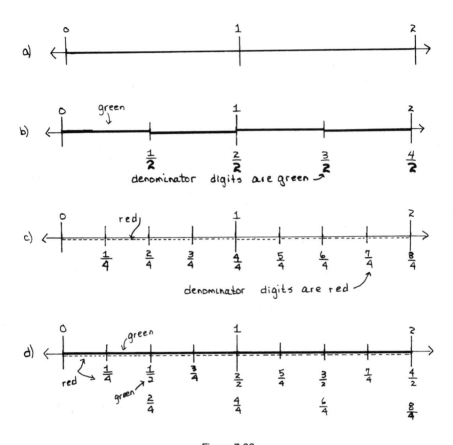

Figure 7-32

from it. To enable the children to follow the presentation more easily, give them a worksheet that parallels, step by step, what is done on the overhead or demonstration chart. Because the colors used match those of the fraction strips, and because a step-by-step approach is used, meaningful transition to the numberline is possible for most learning disabled students we have worked with.

3. **Graph paper numberlines.** Many students find it easier to make the transition to the standard numberline if they first use graph paper as shown in Figure 7-33a. For some students, it may be best to break this diagram into three separate ones, as shown in Figure 7-33b. This way, the students can more easily place a traditional numberline over the colored sections—to count or "read" the related fraction.

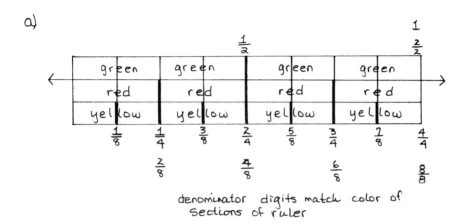

denominator digits match color of
sections of ruler

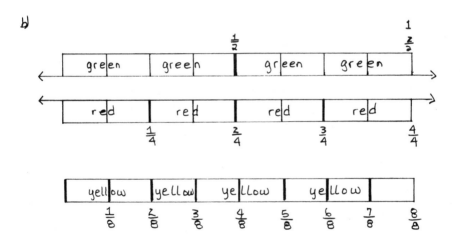

Figure 7-33

4. **Still in transition.** Figure 7-34 shows another type of numberline that can be used in transition. The miniature fraction strips pictured above the numberline provide immediate reference to the concrete. The strips themselves can be made available for children to place above the numberline. Because of the visual cueing, the students tend to proceed more comfortably with work on the numberline shown, as well as with similar numberlines on worksheets or in textbooks.

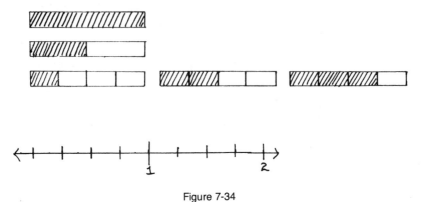

Figure 7-34

5. **Five in a row** (a practice activity for two or three to play). Materials for a game that children enjoy playing are shown in Figure 7-35. Prepare a numberline, colored as in Figure 7-35a, and a set of cards like those of Figure 7-35b. Use the cards to match the points on the numberline. Provide a set of game markers for each player (each set a different color) and a set of chips or construction paper circles on which fractions for each point on the line are written. (See the circles under the numberline of Figure 7-35a.) To begin, the fraction circles are aligned beneath the points they represent (by the teacher, if necessary) and then turned upside down. The

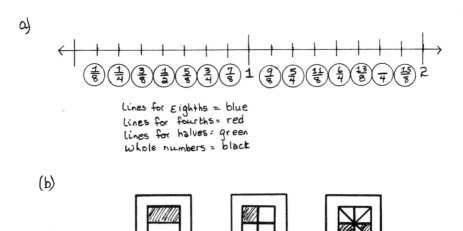

Figure 7-35

players then shuffle the cards and place the deck face down between them. In turn, the players turn over the top card and tell the fraction represented by the picture. They then turn over the circle under the numberline that they think represents that picture. If they are right, they leave the circle face up and claim it by placing one marker above the spot on the numberline. Otherwise, the circle is replaced, face down, and play is continued. The winner is the first person to label five points in a row correctly.

QUOTIENTS, IMPROPER FRACTIONS, AND MIXED NUMBERS

Problem area: Difficulty writing a quotient as a mixed number; difficulty changing an improper fraction to a mixed number.

Typical disabilities affecting progress: Difficulty with spatial organization, visual figure-ground, abstract reasoning, sequencing, and auditory processing.

Background: Many students need specific, structured help if they are to learn how to write a quotient or an improper fraction as a mixed number. Spatially, writing and aligning the numbers is difficult enough. At the symbolic level, because there are often many numbers to sort out, children may forget what the numbers mean. As a consequence, they lose track of the sequence for writing the digits. There are techniques for dealing with these types of problems. The exercises that follow have proved most successful in this regard in our own work with learning disabled students.

Suggested Sequence of Exercises

1. **Color code.** Color-coded pages, as in Figure 7-36, provide the initial practice needed to help students spatially organize their work. The children follow the color cueing and merely copy the numbers in the correct boxes. Then the mixed number is rewritten, independently, to provide extra reinforcement. Note that the completed division example is given at this stage. The focus is specifically to help students learn the correct placement of digits for the mixed-number equivalent of the given quotient. The color scheme controls for extraneous interferences by drawing student attention only to relevant digits and their placement.

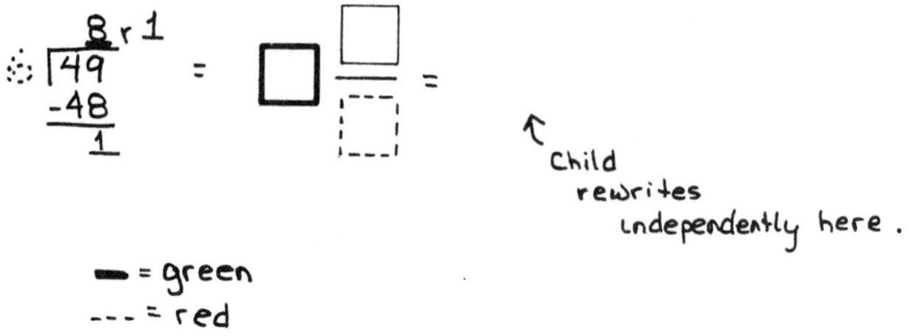

Figure 7-36

2. **Divide, too.** Once the students begin to feel more comfortable in transferring the quotient to a mixed number, have them do the division as well (see Figure 7-37). It is generally a good idea to encourage the children first to write the final answer in the form _____ R _____. This method tends to prevent the remainder from being lost in the mass of other numbers. Then the transfer to the mixed number form can be made. As in previous exercises, the Figure 7-37 example requires that students rewrite the mixed number independently as a final step.

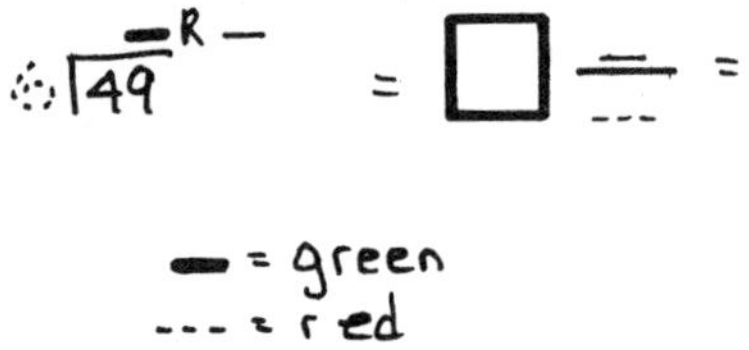

Figure 7-37

3. **Sample problems.** Pages with color-coded examples at the top can be used to help students make the transition from colors to no colors. Colors would not be used for the other problems on the page. If the children get stuck, they can simply refer to the coded example at the top of the sheet. *Variation:* Keep a poster on the wall with the color-coded example or provide a card for the children to keep at their desks as needed.

4. **Relate.** Figure 7-38a shows a way to help students discover the relationship between a fraction and the division process. The exercise also paves the way for changing improper fractions to mixed

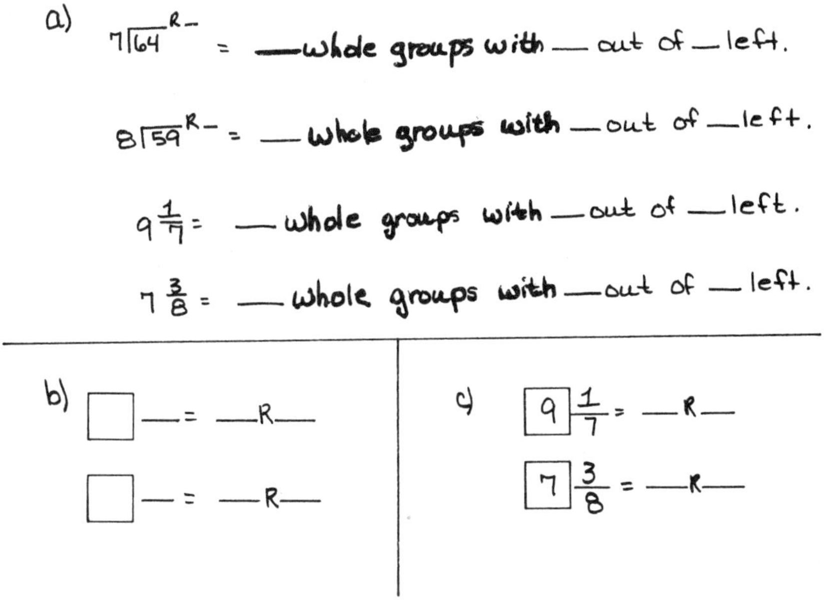

a)

$7\overline{)64}^{R-}$ = —— whole groups with —— out of —— left.

$8\overline{)59}^{R-}$ = —— whole groups with —— out of —— left.

$9\frac{1}{7}$ = —— whole groups with —— out of —— left.

$7\frac{3}{8}$ = —— whole groups with —— out of —— left.

b)
☐ —— = ——R——

☐ —— = ——R——

c)
☐ $9\frac{1}{7}$ = ——R——

☐ $7\frac{3}{8}$ = ——R——

Figure 7-38

numbers (see Activity 5 below). The students solve the division and fill in the blanks. Have the children read aloud and, for selected examples, partition the objects into groups to dramatize what is said. As a followup, present exercises like those of Figure 7-38b. The children could copy mixed numbers from previously worked division problems into the boxes and then rewrite each in the form _____ R _____ (Figure 7-38c). Have the children verbalize how the quotient (_____ R _____) and the mixed number expressions really mean the same thing. Tie this in with the work of Figure 7-38a by allowing them to place small objects in groups to prove the equivalence.

5. **Improper fractions to mixed numbers.** Figure 7-39a shows an idea for a preformated page that can be kept in the files and used with teacher-made problems or with those problems the students copy from the text. Colors, as suggested by the example, are often essential at this point. They lessen difficulties due to deficits in visual perception and spatial organization. They help emphasize associations that lead to understanding the process for changing from an improper fraction to a mixed number. As before, the objects can actually be divided into groups to dramatize what is said. A completed example is presented in Figure 7-39b.

a)

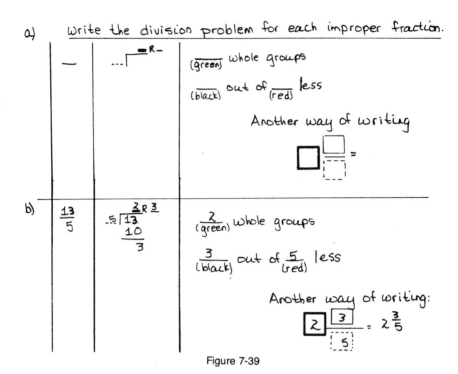

Figure 7-39

6. **Tic tac toe.** Make a set of cards with division problems, like those shown in Figure 7-40a. Until the children are more advanced, do not include problems whose quotients require reducing when written as a mixed number. Have the children fill in tic tac toe boards with the mixed number for each quotient (see Figure 7-40b). After checking the boards, laminate them or cover them with contact paper. For practice, the students play tic tac toe, alone or with a partner, by drawing a card and circling the correct mixed number if it is on the board. The first person to circle three in a row wins.

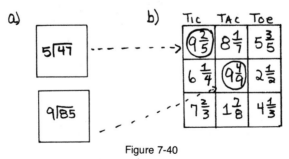

Figure 7-40

EQUIVALENT FRACTIONS

Problem area: Difficulty finding equivalent fractions.

Typical disabilities affecting progress: Difficulty with closure, visual memory, integrative processing, abstract reasoning, retrieval, and visual figure-ground.

Background: Equivalence, an essential part of computation with fractions, is also one of the most difficult areas for many children to understand. The concept itself, although readily illustrated with physical models, requires a considerable amount of abstract reasoning. In addition, work with equivalent fractions requires several discrete subskills:

- knowing *when* to find an equivalent fraction is appropriate

- knowing *how* to find an equivalent fraction; this can vary depending on the circumstance

- knowing how to determine the greatest common factor or the lowest common multiple

- recognizing when a fraction is in simple form (lowest terms)

Problems associated with the last two skill areas will be discussed in Sections 7 and 8 of this chapter. The present section will focus principally on developing the concept of equivalence and the skill in finding equivalent fractions.

During early developmental work with equivalent fractions, when the emphasis is on *understanding the concept,* it is necessary that physical and pictorial models be used to dramatize the concept of equivalence. Typically, the children will be asked to compare shaded parts of regions, as in Figure 7-41. For children with figure-ground or spatial deficits, it may not be readily apparent that an equal amount of space is colored in both drawings. The added lines in Figure 7-41b can be very confusing and prevent children from making the comparison visually.

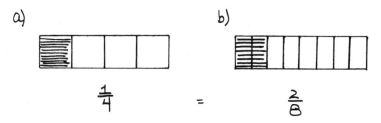

Figure 7-41

Children with this problem need more careful instruction if they are to form correct mental images for equations like $\frac{1}{4} = \frac{2}{8}$.

Though specialized techniques like those described below can help children establish a conceptual basis for equivalence, other difficulties related to finding equivalent fractions must still be resolved. Some children can write a "family" of equivalent fractions by multiplying a given fraction first by $\frac{2}{2}$, then by $\frac{3}{3}, \frac{4}{4}$, and so on (see Figure 7-42). But these same children may have difficulty finding the numerator for a given denominator, as in Figure 7-43. Consider what is involved in finding a fraction equivalent to $\frac{3}{4}$ with a denominator of 24. The student must

- find the missing factor for the equation $4 \times \underline{\hspace{1cm}} = 24$,

- switch the thought process to a more standard form of an equation,

- find the product of 3×6, and

- fill in the numerator.

$$\frac{1}{3} = \frac{2}{6} = \frac{3}{9} = \frac{4}{12} = \frac{5}{15} = \cdots \qquad\qquad \frac{3}{4} = \frac{\square}{24}$$

Figure 7-42   Figure 7-43

Children with memory, sequencing, or closure difficulties often find this procedure especially difficult.

One *can* learn to deal with the problems highlighted above. Their resolution requires that we actively involve the children in a learning program that is carefully tailored to meet their special learning needs. Suggestions for planning such a program for early work with equivalence are outlined below. Emphasis is on developing strong visual images with language and kinesthetic reinforcement. The intent is to keep the step size small and, equally important, to make provision for overlearning.

Suggested Sequence of Activities and Exercises

1. **Match ups.** Give the students a construction paper rectangle like that of Figure 7-44a. In the example, two-thirds of the region is shaded. Have the children themselves verbally name the fractional part that is colored. If the children are strong tactual learners, texturize the shaded part. Glue felt, or spread glue and sprinkle salt or sand, over the region; then glue string or straws

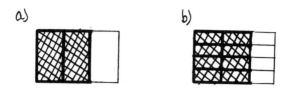

Figure 7-44

over the lines that partition the shape. Have the students close their eyes, feel, and then name the fraction represented by the texturized area. Repeat the procedure with the rectangle of Figure 7-44b. Prompt the students to note that the second rectangle is the same shape and size as the first. If necessary, the children can place the two shapes on top of each other to check. As a final step, have the students cut out the shaded part of the second shape and place it on top of the shaded part of the first. Have students themselves verbalize how the two shaded regions match up: "$\frac{2}{3}$ of the first rectangle is 'just as much' as $\frac{4}{9}$ of the second." Repeat with other examples.

- *Note:* Visually, some students cannot "see" equivalence. They need to *feel* it by finger tracing. They need to manipulate it by seeing that one shape, although divided differently, actually fits over another. The above activity provides for these needs.

2. **Write it out.** As above, but this time have the students write the fractions they name. In the final step, the children would write $\frac{2}{3} = \frac{4}{9}$. Tell them that we use the equals sign to describe the fact that the shaded parts *match up.*

3. **Pictures now.** Because many children cannot readily see equivalence when comparing two pictures they cannot move (see Figure 7-41), it often helps for them to use only one picture. In Figure 7-45, the students are presented first with the rectangle divided into thirds. Have them tell you, then *write,* that two-thirds of it is colored. Next, direct them to connect the hatchmarks with a ruler and write the fraction that describes the colored part. Several problems of this sort, in which the student actually uses the same space, help build up the equivalence idea without totally relying on visual perception.

Figure 7-45

4. **Plastic overlays.** Using permanent marker and clear plastic overlays, draw rectangular shapes as shown in Figure 7-46a. Provide predrawn worksheets (Figure 7-46b) that picture shapes congruent to those on the overlays, as shown. In the first part of the assignment, the children color in a designated fractional part of each shape on the worksheet (see Figure 7-46c). To determine equivalence, the students then match the plastic overlays with the rectangles they colored. When they think they have a matching shape, a grease pencil is used to outline the shaded area as a means of checking. The fractions represented by the colored regions of the two rectangles are then written below the worksheet shape, as in Figure 7-46d.

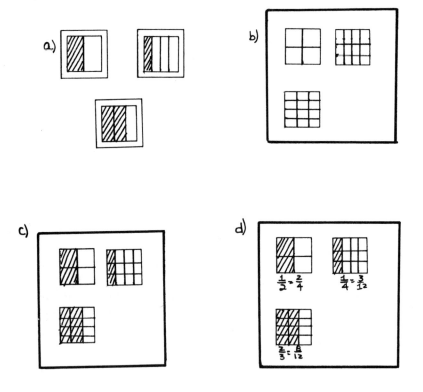

Figure 7-46

5. **Dot it.** Figure 7-47 illustrates another technique to help eliminate visual confusion and focus attention correctly. Matching shapes are aligned one above the other on worksheets, and a dotted line is used to help the students recognize the equivalence being demonstrated. It also helps to have the children draw around the colored (uncolored) area of both figures to get a better "feel" for the congruence in size.

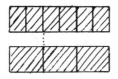

Figure 7-47

6. **Help in transition.** To help the students make the transition to symbolic representation only, have them write equations (e.g. $\frac{2}{6} = \frac{1}{3}$), or find equation cards that describe the shaded (unshaded) parts of pictures like those of Figure 7-47.

7. **Talk about it.** Set aside time to analyze the equivalence demonstrated by picture pairs. The following dialogue, based on the example of Figure 7-48, suggests how the discussion might proceed:

> *Teacher:* "You said that $\frac{2}{5}$ of this figure (7-48a) is colored. Into how many equal parts is the rectangle divided?"
>
> *Student:* "5."
>
> *Teacher:* "Correct. This second rectangle (Figure 7-48b) has the same amount of space colored, but we divided it up differently. This time we used ten equal-sized parts. We could also say Rectangle B has two times as many pieces as Rectangle A. Therefore, how many times as many colored pieces are in Rectangle B?"
>
> *Student:* "Two times as many."
>
> *Teacher:* "That's right, and did you notice, we colored in four parts of that rectangle, which is two times as many as were colored on the first one."

Figure 7-48

- *Note 1:* If the children have trouble with the above presentation, make sure they understand the words, "Two times as many as." It may be necessary to review this idea even though the notion of multiplication is clear. Some children may not readily make the transfer to the multiplication idea in the new context.

- *Note 2:* Tenths were used in the example for this activity. Tenths *should be used* along with halves, thirds, fourths, and other commonly used fractions during early developmental work. This paves the way for an earlier introduction and use of decimals.

8. **The general idea: multiply.** When the children are comfortable with discussions like that in Activity 7 above, introduce the idea of forming equivalence "families" by multiplying. Have the children use fraction strips for $\frac{1}{3}$ and $\frac{2}{6}$. If necessary, lay them on paper and draw in the dotted line, as in Figure 7-47. Have the children verbalize that, compared to the strip for $\frac{1}{3}$, $\frac{2}{6}$ has 2 *times* as many colored parts; 2 *times* as many parts in all. "Yes, and $\frac{2 \times 1}{2 \times 3} = \frac{2}{6}$." We can multiply and get the same result. Repeat for other fractions equivalent to $\frac{1}{3}$. Lead the children to see how a whole family of equivalent fractions can be formed by multiplying both numerator and denominator times 2, or times 3, and so on. In early work, the children should use the fraction strips to verify the multiplication. Three or four strips can be placed under each other (on paper, using dotted lines, if necessary) to picture families that have been formed.

9. **You multiply by "1."** Gradually, strips or pictures are eliminated, and the children use the multiplication technique to find fractions equivalent to a given fraction. One final point should be made before pictures are entirely laid aside. Use the technique of Figure 7-49 to color-emphasize that you really multiply by $\frac{2}{2}, \frac{3}{3}, \frac{4}{4}, \ldots$ when you find equivalent fractions. That is the *same as multiplying by 1.* All you actually change are the size and number of pieces on the strip. The colored space stays the same size.

$$\frac{1 \times 2}{3 \times 2} = \frac{2}{6}; \qquad \frac{1 \times 3}{3 \times 3} = \frac{3}{9}$$

— = green

Figure 7-49

10. **Find the numerator.** Difficulty in finding a new numerator for a given denominator is often the result of an inability to retrieve the missing factor. Many students need specific training on retrieving the factor and also a controlled fact program like that described in Section 1 of Chapter 5. Initially, the equivalent fractions used on workpages would involve only basic facts the children have worked on, as in the examples of Figure 7-50. In Example 1, the children use the given multiplication sentences to help them identify the missing factor in the denominator and in the numerator. After they fill in the number, they can use the fraction-strip picture cue to check their work. Example 2 of Figure 7-50 is similar, but here the picture cue is withdrawn. If necessary, the children can use a set of fraction strips to check. In Example 3, the extra space reminds students of the multiplication to be done. Allow them to extend the fraction line and write "×2" in the numerator and in the denominator if this is helpful. This practice can be continued even when the space to the left of the equals sign is less obvious. Gradually, the multiplication helps at the top of workpages should be eliminated. Children can refer to a chart or use basic fact T's, as suggested in Section 1 of Chapter 5.

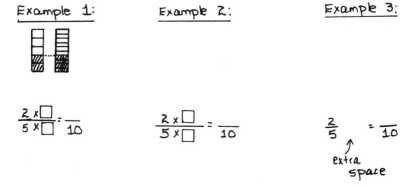

Figure 7-50

- *Note:* Experience has shown that it is generally preferable *not* to encourage dividing the new denominator by the old one in order to determine the missing factor. This practice just adds an extra step to the already complicated thought process. Although the student may obtain the correct missing factor, the division step often interferes with what should be done in the numerator. The visual cueing of Figure 7-50 prompts children to "think multiplication" instead.

11. **Turn over** (a practice activity for two to play). Make a gameboard and an answer sheet for missing numerators as shown in Figure 7-51. Also make two sets of 50 circles, each set a different color. Place the numbers 1 through 20 on the circles and give each child a set. To begin, all circles are placed upside down. In turn, the children flip one of their circles, exposing a number. The circle is placed on the board so that *an equivalent pair of fractions is formed.* A player can be challenged if it is thought an error has been made. If the person challenged cannot prove, by correctly stating what to multiply the numerator and denominator by, the circle must be removed. The answer sheet can be used to resolve any differences. The winner is the first to form five pairs of equivalent fractions.

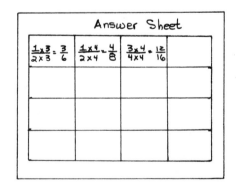

Figure 7-51

- *Note 1:* Forming equivalent fractions by *dividing* the numerator and denominator by the same number should now be introduced. Adapt activities of this section to accomplish this goal. Also refer to the suggestions of Section 8 above.

- *Note 2:* A topic related to that of this section, finding decimal equivalents of given fractions, is an important one. It generally is necessary to convert fractions to decimals in order to compute with a calculator. Some fractions, like those of Figure 7-52 are equivalent to fractions with 10, 100, or 1000 in the denominator. The exercises of this section can be extended to help students deal with these fractions. Then the changeover to decimals is relatively simple for students who can read and write decimals. Examples: $\frac{5}{10} = .5$; $\frac{75}{100} = .75$; $\frac{375}{1000} = .375$.

$$\frac{1 \times \boxed{5}}{2 \times \boxed{5}} = \frac{5}{10} \qquad\qquad \frac{7 \times \boxed{5}}{20 \times \boxed{5}} = \frac{35}{100}$$

$$\frac{3 \times \boxed{2}}{5 \times \boxed{2}} = \frac{6}{10} \qquad\qquad \frac{9 \times \boxed{25}}{40 \times \boxed{25}} = \frac{325}{1000}$$

Figure 7-52

- *Note 3:* Sometimes children find it easier to divide, as in Figure 7-53, to find the decimal equivalent of a fraction. The "divide numerator by denominator" rule is simple enough, and a calculator can be used to carry out the division. Some children can understand why the division "works." The focus, of course, is on

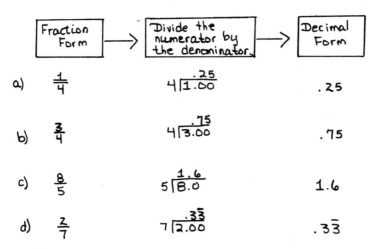

Figure 7-53

the denominator, which tells the number of parts into which the one whole is divided. For the fraction of Figure 7-53a, the one whole is divided into fourths (.25), and we have *1* of those parts, .25 of the whole. In Figure 7-53b, the one whole is also divided into fourths (.25), but we have *3* of them, or .75 of the whole. Instead of dividing into fourths and then multiplying by 3, we really combine steps when we divide 3 by 4, numerator by denominator.

REDUCING FRACTIONS

Problem area: Difficulty writing fractions in simple form.

Typical disabilities affecting progress: Difficulty with visual memory, sequencing, and abstract reasoning.

Background: When children compute, we generally ask that all answers be expressed in simple form. This is standard practice, since it makes for greater ease in constructing answer keys and grading student work. The ability to simplify fractions, however, involves more than understanding what to do. Actually, the easiest part is dividing the numerator and the denominator by the same number. The difficulty arises because children either

- do not know what divisor to use for numerator and denominator in order to simplify a fraction, or

- fail to recognize the need to simplify further.

These problems arise because, in day-to-day work, there really are no immediate clues to help the student. It is often best to eliminate as much reduction as possible. For example, when teaching students to add or subtract fractions, encourage them to choose the *least* common multiple rather than *any* common multiple. It is also important, in early work with equivalent fractions, to examine equivalences like: $\frac{4}{6} = \frac{2}{3}$ or $\frac{6}{8} = \frac{3}{4}$. Then the children will have a background for *dividing* numerator and denominator by the same number. All too often this emphasis is slighted, since most examples are those in which one *multiplies* to find an equivalent fraction.

It is also possible to deal directly with the problems children encounter when reducing fractions to simple form. The ideas outlined below have proved helpful in our own work with learning disabled students. The focus is on:

- knowing when to reduce

- recognizing the correct divisor for numerator and denominator

Suggested Activities and Exercises

1. **Prime strip.** Post a strip listing prime numbers less than 30. Tape the strip along the chalkboard or have each student glue it to an index card that can be kept for personal reference. As the children begin reducing, the strip can be used to recognize when a fraction has only prime factors.

2. **Factor tree the fraction.** Prime factorization with a factor tree provides a structured approach to reducing fractions. Too often children are expected to factor fractions into primes immediately (see Figure 7-54). For many students, this requirement involves too

$$\frac{6}{8} = \frac{2 \times 3}{2 \times 2 \times 2}$$

Figure 7-54

much mental calculation. Allow the children to use factor trees for fractions as shown in Figure 7-55. The format shown helps students organize their thinking by breaking the factorization into very small steps. The children can refer to the prime strip of Activity 1 above if they need help in recognizing primes. Once the numerator and denominator numbers have been factored into primes, the student can then cancel out common factors, as in Figure 7-55b. *Note:* Some children will benefit from using a card to block out all but the prime factors while cancelling.

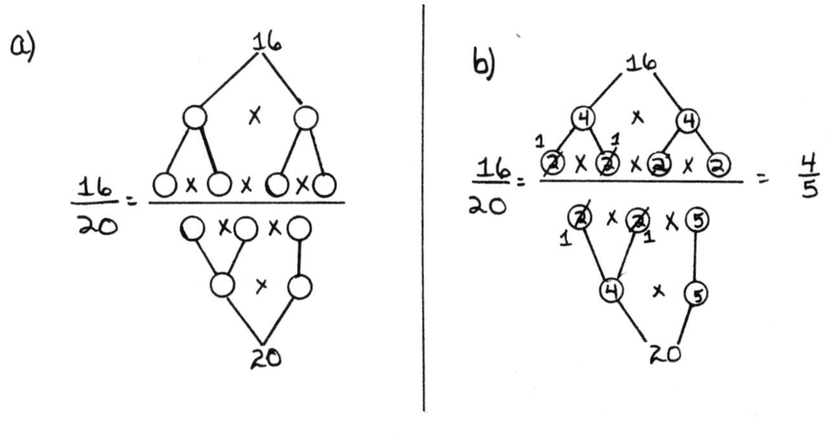

Figure 7-55

3. **Factor tree cards.** An alternative to the above is to make a set of partially factored cards, as in Figure 7-56. As an initial assignment, the students factor the number on each card as far as the card allows. The cards are then used in the last step, when it is time to reduce. The appropriate card is chosen for the numerator and placed above the circles as shown. The student then continues the prime factorization. The cards are removed, and the final steps (cancelling and multiplying) take place. This is a less visually confusing approach for many students and also allows steps to be broken down into small, manageable increments.

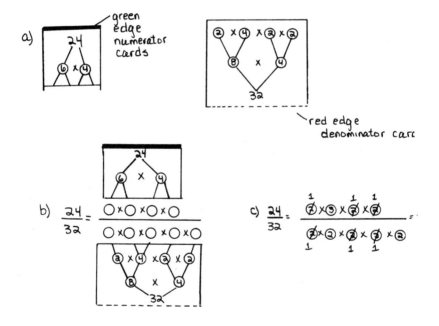

Figure 7-56

4. **Divisibility rules.** Even with a list of primes, many children still have trouble factoring because they do not know what number to divide by. Divisibility rules are often very helpful for these students and stimulate interest in number patterns. In our experience, children who know the rules find it easier to recognize what to divide by initially.

FINDING COMMON DENOMINATORS

Problem area: Difficulty finding the least common denominator of two fractions in order to compare and to add or subtract them.

Typical disabilities affecting progress: Difficulty with closure, sequential and long term memory, and visual memory.

Background: Children use the idea of finding common denominators both to compare *and* to add or subtract fractions. This section discusses ways to help learning disabled students master the technique of finding common denominators so that it may be applied to comparing or computing fraction sums and differences.

Comparing Fractions

Learning disabled students generally have little difficulty at the concrete level in using physical models of fractional regions to compare fractions. For a given circular unit, for example, they might lay a "$\frac{1}{2}$" piece on top of a "$\frac{2}{3}$" piece and see that $\frac{2}{3}$ is more. Or they might compare shaded parts of fraction strips, as in Figure 7-57a. Students with perceptual deficits might experience some difficulty when asked to compare fractions *pictured* on worksheets or textbook pages. (Ideas from the "plastic overlay" and "dot it" activities of Section 6 above can be adapted to help these children.) However, the real difficulty arises when students are asked to compare fractions using either the common denominator or the cross-products method illustrated in Figures 7-57b and 7-57c.

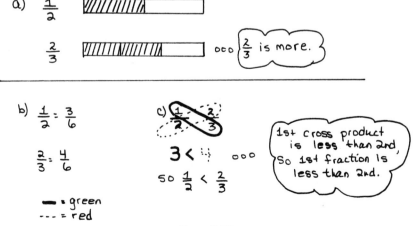

Figure 7-57

Of these two approaches, the more popular for early work involves changing each fraction *to an equivalent fraction with a common denominator*. Suggestions for supplementing and reinforcing traditional textbook treatment of this technique are presented below. If teachers are interested in developing the cross-products approach with students, the use of fraction strips as in Figure 7-58 may be helpful. Students can cross multiply and chart several examples of *each type* of comparison shown to develop or verify the general pattern. The color cueing illustrated in this figure is helpful to many students: green first, then red when finding cross products.

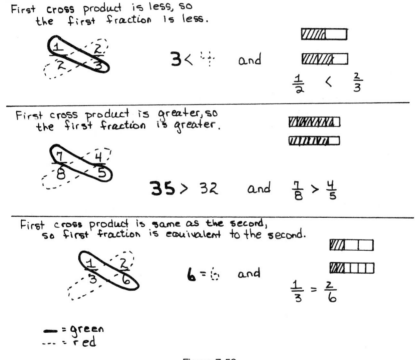

Figure 7-58

Adding or Subtracting Fractions

The most difficult aspect of adding and subtracting fractions is finding like denominators. This is the first step in carrying out the computation for fractions with different denominators. Finding equivalent fractions when the new denominator is already given and determining the common denominator for two given fractions are two completely different skills. The former requires far less abstract thinking because much of the final answer is already in sight. The latter skill requires a great deal of overlearning and quick retrieval. It is necessary that students master this latter skill in order to be successful with addition and subtraction of unlike fractions.

The Lowest Common Denominator

The least common multiple of two denominator numbers, when used as the *new* denominator for the two fractions, becomes the lowest common denominator for the fractions. Generally speaking, it is desirable for students to find the lowest common denominator when comparing or when adding or subtracting fractions. There are two general methods students can use to find the least common multiple of two denominator numbers:

1. List multiples of each denominator and then locate the least of the *common* multiples listed for each number.
2. Find the prime factors of each denominator number and multiply, being careful to use as factors only the minimum number of primes needed to make the product a multiple of each denominator number.

Both of these methods can be cumbersome and difficult for students. With larger numbers, using primes may be more efficient. Often, though, when students are first learning, using primes only adds steps. The primes must still be sorted and multiplied. *In our experience, it is easier to use the first approach in early work.* Listing the multiples also reinforces the basic multiplication facts for those children who still need practice.

When dealing with more frequently used denominators, it is desirable for students to recognize automatically the least common multiple. Though some children may find it difficult, this generally comes with practice for more common pairings. Ideas for helping students in the interim to become familiar with the procedure for determining the lowest common denominator of two fractions are outlined below.

Suggested Sequence of Activities and Exercises

1. **Multiple strips.** Use heavy tagboard to make a personal set of multiple strips for each student (refer to Figure 7-59). If the children are familiar with multiplication charts, have them cut apart the rows, as in Figure 7-60, and glue them onto tagboard. If possible, laminate the strips or cover them with contact paper. Check that the children understand the meaning of "multiples"—answers you get when you multiply.

Multiple Strips

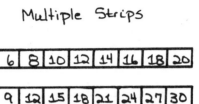

Figure 7-59

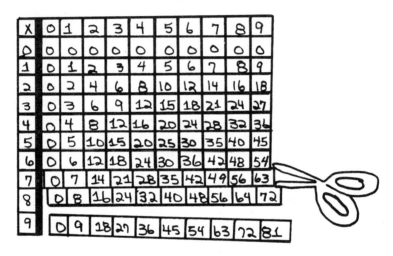

Figure 7-60

2. **Find it** (developmental activity for individuals or small groups). Provide two decks of cards. The first deck should contain a card for each of the more commonly used denominator numbers between 2 and 24. Make the second card deck a different color, and have two cards for each number between 2 and 50. Arrange these cards *sequentially,* to make it easier to locate specific cards. Also make a pocket chart like that of Figure 7-61a, or use masking tape on the floor or desk to partition a space into three columns. The chart should be labeled as shown. The children take turns drawing two cards from the first deck. In the example of Figure 7-61a, the cards 6 and 9 were drawn. After being placed in the chart, the children work together, using multiple strips if needed, to take multiples of 6 and 9 from the second deck. These cards are placed in the appropriate "multiple" column of the chart. The children then examine the

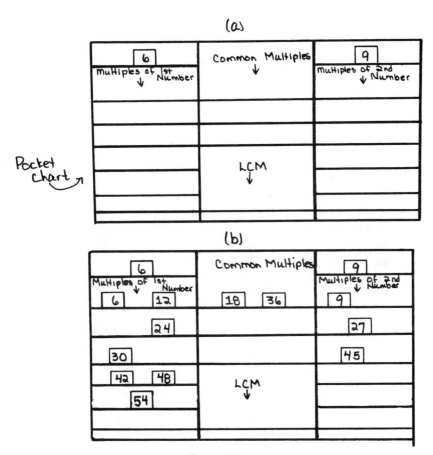

Figure 7-61

chart and remove any numbers that appear in *both* "multiple" columns. One card for each of these numbers is moved to the "common multiple" section of the chart (Figure 7-61b). Finally, the smallest multiple (18) is moved to the "least common multiple" section. Replace the cards in the decks and draw again.

3. **Just the denominator.** Give the students a workpage of about 10 addition or subtraction problems with unlike denominators. Allow them to use their multiple strips (to build visual memory) and find just the *lowest common denominator* of the two fractions. Given the problem of Figure 7-62a, for example, the students may find it helpful to circle common multiples on the laminated strips, match up the strips as in Figure 7-62b, and then write the smallest of the common multiples (18) as the new denominator for the problem

(a) $\frac{5}{6}$

$+\frac{1}{9}$

(b)

(c) $\frac{5}{6} = \frac{}{18}$

$+\frac{1}{9} = \frac{}{18}$

Figure 7-62

(Figure 7-62c). Do not require the children to finish the problems at this time. The sheets can be collected, checked, and at a later date redistributed so that the problems can be completed.

- *Note:* If the multiple strips are not laminated, show the students how to place the strips under a clear plastic sheet in order to circle common multiples (see Figure 7-63a). Alternatively, for children with severe motor, figure-ground, or discrimination problems, glue the multiple strips to longer pieces of paper for use in a homemade tachistoscope. Children pull the strips through the tachistoscope and stop when one number appears on both strips. This is the lowest common multiple (Figure 7-63b).

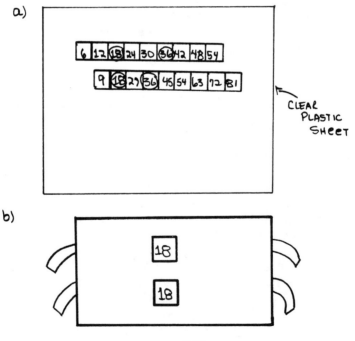

Figure 7-63

4. **Color cue.** Some students need to *write out* the multiples of each denominator in order to identify the least common multiple. To help students organize their workspace when listing the multiples, set up pages as shown in Figure 7-64. Highlighting the space where the common multiple will fall helps children with perseveration or figure-ground deficits know when to stop.

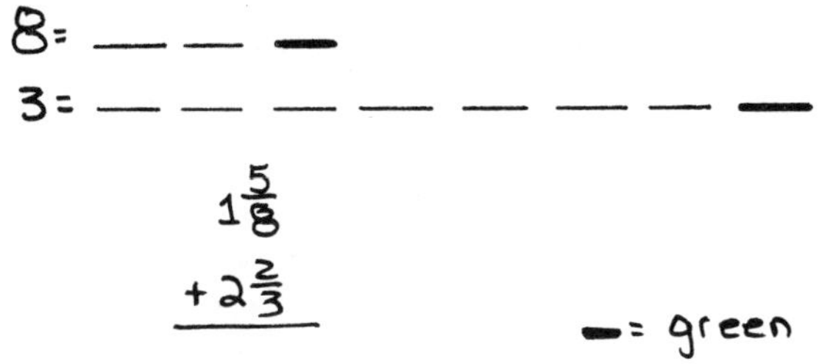

$$8 = \underline{\ \ } \ \underline{\ \ } \ \rule{0.4cm}{0.5mm}$$
$$3 = \underline{\ \ } \ \underline{\ \ } \ \underline{\ \ } \ \underline{\ \ } \ \underline{\ \ } \ \underline{\ \ } \ \underline{\ \ } \ \rule{0.4cm}{0.5mm}$$

$$1\tfrac{5}{8}$$
$$+ 2\tfrac{2}{3}$$

$$\rule{0.4cm}{0.5mm} = green$$

Figure 7-64

5. **Transition.** As the students become more proficient at finding multiples, a simpler cueing system, as suggested by Figure 7-65, can be used. Instead of listing all the multiples, the child skip counts until reaching the circle and then writes the number in that circle. This method has proved particularly helpful for children who need help organizing their work for computation.

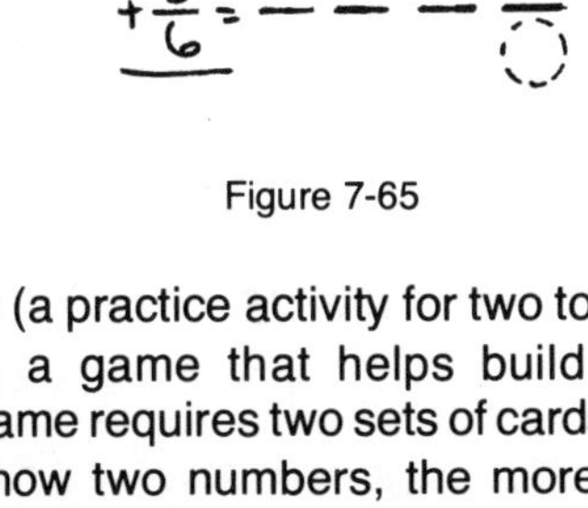

$$\bigcirc = red$$

$$\frac{3}{8} = \underline{\ \ } \ \underline{\ \ } \ \overline{\bigcirc}$$

$$+ \frac{5}{6} = \underline{\ \ } \ \underline{\ \ } \ \underline{\ \ } \ \overline{\bigcirc}$$

Figure 7-65

6. **Concentration** (a practice activity for two to play). Students enjoy Concentration, a game that helps build retrieval and visual memory. The game requires two sets of cards. The cards of one set should each show two numbers, the more commonly used denominator numbers between 2 and 24. The cards of the second set should show the least common multiple for each pair in the first

deck. Shuffle each deck and lay them out in two separate groups, face down. In turn, the players turn over one card from the first deck and try to select its match from the other set of cards. Concentration rules are followed. The winner is the one with the most pairs of cards at the end.

- *Variation:* As an independent activity, have the students time how long it takes them to pair cards from the two sets. Encourage them to keep a log of their time and to try to improve their records.

REGROUPING IN SUBTRACTION

Problem area: Confusion over renaming 1 (the tendency to think of "borrowing" 1 ten rather than of "borrowing" the number indicated by the denominator); difficulty sequencing the series of steps in the regrouping procedure.

Typical disabilities affecting progress: Difficulty with memory sequencing and abstract reasoning.

Background: Students may realize *when* they must regroup and even *why* they need to do so. These same students may not, however, know *how* to regroup. The error in the Figure 7-66 problem is typical. The student confused the regrouping with the familiar whole number procedure: 1 less ten, 10 more ones. Having completed the subtraction, the child reduced to lowest terms, unaware that anything was wrong.

$$\overset{2\ \ \overset{11}{\cancel{1}\cancel{1}}}{\cancel{3}\frac{\cancel{1}}{8}}$$
$$-1\frac{5}{8}$$
$$\overline{1\frac{6}{8}=1\frac{3}{4}}$$

Figure 7-66

Anticipating difficulties like this, many teachers use materials to dramatize the regrouping during early developmental work. Trading activities are often used. In the example of Figure 7-67a, the children use materials to model $3\frac{1}{8}$. They trade 1 whole for 8 eighths and record the total number of eighths (9 eighths). Repeated

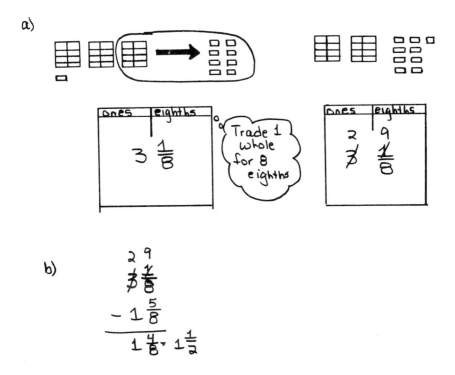

Figure 7-67.

experiences with fair-trade activities of this type for different fractions help most children "see" what is happening. They are then able to apply correctly the regrouping procedure to subtraction problems like that of Figure 7-67b. In this figure, the *similarity* between the recordkeeping format of (a) and the regrouping shown in (b) helps children transfer the regrouping skill to its use in computation with fractions.

Some students, however, do not make the transfer. Despite the care taken in early developmental work, specific learning disabilities cause them to fail at the symbolic level. Abstract reasoning difficulties may inhibit the meaningful transition of the procedure to paper-and-pencil computation. Or memory sequencing deficiencies may make it very hard for students to remember all the isolated steps of the regrouping process. Given subtraction problems requiring regrouping, these children may refuse even to attempt the work, or they may revert to the more familiar procedure of always adding 10 whenever regrouping is necessary. For these students, more specialized cueing techniques, such as those illustrated in the following sequence, are necessary.

Suggested Sequence of Activities and Exercises

1. **Regroup.** Before turning to regrouping within subtraction, the focus should be on just renaming numbers that might appear in the minuend of subtraction problems. Figure 7-68a presents the format for a color-coded page that can be kept on file and used as needed. This type of page has proved helpful to children with visual, sequential, or abstract reasoning difficulties. Figure 7-68b presents a completed example of the problem. If the children recognize the need for regrouping, the colors remind them what to do. They serve to order the steps and increase reasoning. Experience has shown that, because the students notice the different colors, they tend to recall more readily the reason why the various steps are carried out.

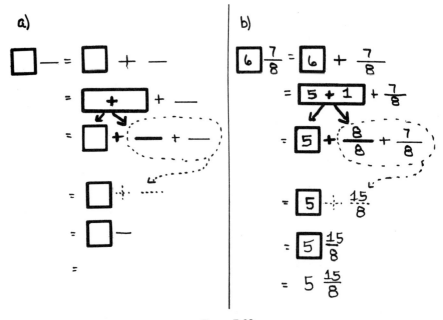

Figure 7-68

2. **Talk about a shorter way.** After practicing the above isolated step, most students will begin to notice the pattern for regrouping. Some, however, will need extra help in eliminating the longer procedure. Make a chart of problems that have previously been solved through the longer procedure (Activity 1 above), but this time write only the original number and the regrouped one as in Figure 7-69. If the

students have figure-ground deficits and cannot readily sort out the numbers, use the colors as shown. The denominator of the second fraction is green to indicate a starting point. Most students will quickly notice that the denominators in both pairs are the same. A discussion can then proceed to the pairs of black numbers and finally to the red ones. The basis of discussion for the sample problem of Figure 7-69 is the idea that *1 whole* or 3 thirds is taken from the 8 and added to the $\frac{1}{3}$. This gives a result of 7 and *4 thirds.* Similar discussions would take place for other number pairs. If helpful, materials could be used at this point to show that the regrouping is correct. After analyzing the chart numbers in this manner, the students should be given other problems for which they independently carry out the regrouping.

3. **A middle step.** To help children retain the sequence while going to the standard format for regrouping, the intermediate step shown in Figure 7-70 is often useful. It is a step that many students will find necessary to use for a while.

4. **Now subtract.** Next, present subtraction problems like that of Figure 7-71. Once the children recognize the need to regroup, allow them to use a card, if necessary, to block out all but the minuend number until the regrouping is complete. *Note:* If the students have difficulty recognizing whether regrouping is needed, adapt suggestions from Chapter 5 on whole-number subtraction to work with fractions, then proceed with the ideas outlined above.

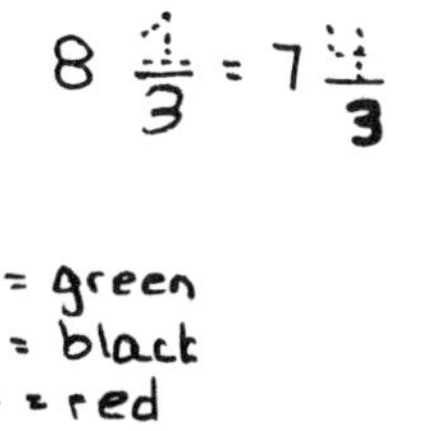

$$8\,\tfrac{1}{3} = 7\,\tfrac{4}{3}$$

■ = green
— = black
··· = red

Figure 7-69

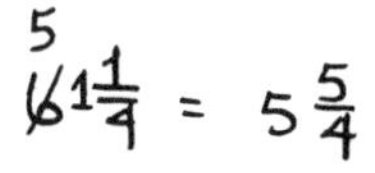

$$\cancel{6}1\tfrac{1}{4} = 5\tfrac{5}{4}$$

Figure 7-70

$$6\tfrac{1}{4}$$
$$-2\tfrac{3}{4}$$

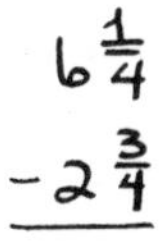

Figure 7-71

MULTIPLYING FRACTIONS

Problem areas: In finding common denominators, confusing the process for multiplying with that for adding or subtracting fractions; difficulty changing mixed numbers to improper fractions for multiplying; difficulty remembering the step-by-step procedure for multiplying.

Typical disabilities affecting progress: Difficulty with figure ground, sequential memory, and abstract reasoning.

Background: In daily situations, we rarely need to carry out paper-and-pencil calculations involving multiplication of fractions. Sometimes the skill is useful when converting recipes. It is often helpful when buying material or deciding on how much carpet is needed to cover a room. If necessary, however, one can convert fractions to decimals and use a hand calculator to derive these answers.

On the other hand, multiplication of fractions is still part of the modern mathematics curriculum. The skill should be taught to those who can learn it. Besides, it is a necessary skill for students who plan to take algebra in high school. The procedures for handling rational algebraic expressions have their basis in the simpler computations with fractions.

Relatively speaking, multiplication of fractions is easy to teach. Some teachers, particularly those planning upper-grade review sessions, prefer to present multiplication as the first area of computation with fractions. Because there are no common denominators to be found, most students find multiplication easier than addition or subtraction. The goal is to capitalize on this fact and build in many success experiences by dealing with multiplication early in the computational sequence.

The suggestions that follow have been used successfully with learning disabled students. The format includes a basic sequence as well as alternative techniques within that sequence that have been helpful in meeting special needs. Whether the multiplication topic is approached first or after addition and subtraction, the ideas should prove useful.

Suggested Sequence of Activities and Exercises

1. **Shaded discs.** Using discs or construction paper circles, shade $\frac{1}{2}$ of 2, $\frac{1}{3}$ of 6, $\frac{2}{5}$ of 10, $\frac{2}{3}$ of 9, and so on. Help the students to write equations to describe the shaded parts. *Example:* $\frac{1}{2}$ of 2 = 1; $\frac{1}{3}$ of 6 = 2.

2. **Picture it on paper.** Provide worksheets that contain geometric regions like that of Figure 7-72. Have the students use pencil or crayons to mark $\frac{1}{2}$ of 2; $\frac{2}{3}$ of 6; $\frac{2}{3}$ of 9, and so on. Then, as above, have the students write equations to describe the shaded parts.

Figure 7-72

3. **Look for patterns.** Have the students note that answers could be found simply by multiplying numerators, multiplying denominators (or, alternately, multiplying numerators, then dividing by the denominators). Rewrite each equation to use the multiplication "times" symbol ($\times$) instead of the word "of." *Examples:* $\frac{1}{2} \times 2 = 1$; $\frac{1}{3} \times 6 = 2$.
4. **Different strokes.** Some students may suggest the pattern of divide first, then multiply. *Example:* $\frac{2}{3}$ of 63. First, divide 63 into 3 equal groups (21 in each group). Then take 2 of the groups, or 42 things.

   - This approach may be the best one at this stage for students who have trouble sequencing. Figure 7-73 illustrates how color coding can be used to support this thinking during early work. Because the vocabulary is low, reading generally causes no difficulty.

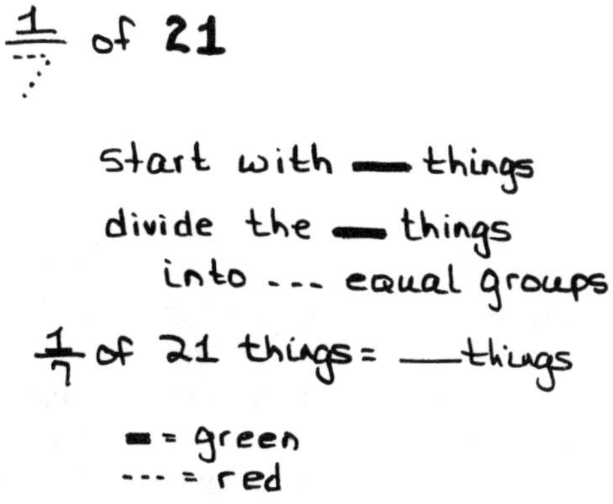

$$\frac{1}{\cdots} \text{ of } \mathbf{21}$$

start with ━ things
divide the ━ things
into ⋯ equal groups
$\frac{1}{7}$ of 21 things = ___things

━ = green
⋯ = red

Figure 7-73

- A variation of color cueing for factors other than unit fractions is presented in Figure 7-74a. In this example, a child's attention is focused first on the number of equal groups into which 16 is divided (8), and then on the number of groups to be used (5). To help the children picture this multiplication, give them a sheet like that of Figure 7-74b and a set of geometric shapes. After the shapes are drawn, the children place chips in the shape to illustrate the problem (Figure 7-74c). For this example, the children take 16 chips and place them, *one by one,* into the shapes until all 16 are distributed. They then note that 10 of the 16, or $\frac{5}{8}$ are inside the red frame. When the students are ready to eliminate visual/manipulative aids like this, color-coding digits as in Figure 7-74a can serve to remind them of what was done previously with shapes and chips. As previously, help the students see that there is a pattern in what the numbers do. *Note:* Placing chips in the shapes requires one-to-one matching. Some students may need specific help with or review of this skill.

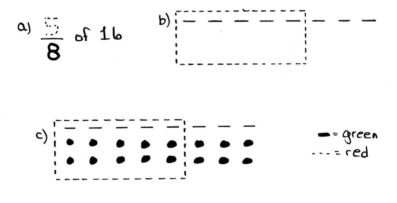

Figure 7-74

5. **Whole number × fraction.** Use construction-paper fraction discs (all the same size). Subdivide some into halves, some into thirds, some into fourths, and so on. Have the students label the pieces and cut them apart on the subdivision lines. Now ask the students to push the pieces together to show 2 of the $\frac{1}{2}$ pieces, 6 of the $\frac{1}{3}$ pieces, 10 of the $\frac{2}{5}$ pieces, and so on. They should write equations to describe the finished picture each time. *Example:* $2 \times \frac{1}{2} = 1$; $6 \times \frac{1}{3} = \frac{6}{3}$ or 2; $10 \times \frac{2}{5} = \frac{20}{5}$ or 4.

6. **Both factors a fraction.** Repeat Activities 1 to 3 above, asking the students to show $\frac{1}{2}$ of $\frac{1}{8}$, $\frac{1}{4}$ of $\frac{1}{3}$, $\frac{1}{3}$ of $\frac{1}{2}$, and so on. Have the students verbalize the pattern for multiplying fractions: multiply numerators, multiply denominators. They could check each equation to see if it follows the pattern.

7. **Alternative approach.** Some students have difficulty changing a mixed number to an improper fraction in order to carry out the computation. Given a problem like $4 \times 2\frac{3}{5}$, they tend to multiply the whole number 2 by both the numerator *and* denominator of $\frac{3}{5}$. In order to eliminate the extra step of changing to an improper fraction, it is helpful at times to teach the students to multiply a whole number by a mixed number using the distributive property. Figure 7-75 presents an example using this approach.

$$4 \times 2\frac{3}{5} = 4 \times \left(2 + \frac{3}{5}\right)$$
$$= (4 \times 2) + \left(4 \times \frac{3}{5}\right)$$
$$= 8 + \frac{12}{5}$$
$$= 8 + 2\frac{2}{5}$$
$$= 10\frac{2}{5}$$

Figure 7-75

DIVIDING FRACTIONS

Problem area: Confusion over which fraction to invert; a tendency to invert the dividend rather than the divisor.

Typical disabilities affecting progress: Difficulty with memory and abstract reasoning.

Background: Many students invert the dividend rather than the divisor when dividing fractions. This is a problem common to all students, not merely the learning disabled. The activities of the following sequence have proved helpful in dealing with this problem.

Suggested Sequence of Activities and Exercises

1. **Color highlight.** To divide fractions, we invert the divisor and multiply. When this idea is developed with students, color-underscore the divisor in each of several problems to emphasize which fraction should be inverted.
2. **Box it.** As a followup, provide a sheet with several fraction division problems. Instruct the students to box or finger trace the divisor—the number to be inverted—for each problem on the sheet.
3. **Do just one step.** Now have the students do just the *one step* of writing the first equation toward solving each problem on the sheet (see Figure 7-76).

$$\text{Given} \longrightarrow \frac{3}{4} \div \frac{2}{3} = \underline{\quad}$$

$$\text{Child writes} \longrightarrow \frac{3}{4} \times \frac{3}{2} = \underline{\quad}$$

Figure 7-76

Chapter 8

"Hard-to-Learn" Upper-Grade Topics

This chapter deals with some of the topics generally developed in the upper elementary and junior high grades. The following areas are emphasized, although other topics are included when relevant:

- ratio
- proportion
- percent
- integers
- exponents

Each of these topics involves the transfer of lower-level concepts and skills to new contexts. Unfortunately, for learning disabled students, the transition may not be easily made. Many students can, for example, master simpler concepts or computational skills related to ratio, proportion, and percent. They may be able to solve a proportion problem by filling in a missing numerator or denominator. However, setting up the correct proportion for a written problem or even recognizing the need to use a proportion in a given situation is a typically more difficult task. Students may be able to describe the shaded part of a 10×10 grid using percents but be unable to determine the percent for a base other than one hundred.

In some instances, students may not have mastered prerequisite concepts and skills. Hence the making of important associations is not possible. At other times, difficulties with sequencing, abstract reasoning, or visual or auditory memory may interfere with the retrieval and application of previously learned material.

357

As integers, exponents, and rules governing the order of operations are introduced, other difficulties emerge. Visual perception problems, for example, are the root of many errors. The exponent is easily misperceived by many; some may even see it as a whole number (see Figure 8-1). Students with abstract reasoning or receptive or expressive language deficits often have difficulty with the new language (Figure 8-2). To be successful with integers, good visual memory and discrimination as well as memory sequencing skills are required. A strong language base also helps. Throughout these topics, students are asked to compute using well-known operations. Difficulties like those identified above, and the fact that the context is new, cause many learning disabled students to be unsuccessful with computations they attempt.

$$5^3 \longrightarrow 53$$

Figure 8-1

$$5^3 \longrightarrow \text{Five to the third power}$$

Figure 8-2

An effort has been made in the following pages to deal with several of the "hard-to-learn," upper-grade topics from the point of view of how learning disabilities affect understanding, retention and application. In some instances, the suggested sequence differs from that commonly used. Generally, however, the emphasis is on directly relating new material, visually and auditorially, to previously learned concepts and skills. The approaches outlined are among those that have proved effective in our own work with learning disabled students.

RATIO

Problem area: Difficulty with the language and symbolism of ratio.

Typical disabilities affecting progress: Difficulty with receptive and expressive language, abstract reasoning, closure and visual perception.

Background: Ratio involves *comparing* the number of one group to that of another. Typically the comparison is that of dissimilar units: balls to bats, or cups to spoons, as in Figure 8-3a. Ratio situations can also involve similar units, like that pictured in Figure 8-3b (balls to balls).

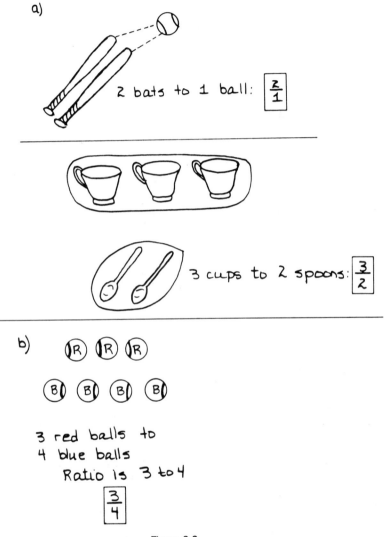

Figure 8-3

While a ratio is not a fraction, the fraction form is often used to represent a ratio (Figure 8-4). Conceptually, this can be very confusing to students who are used to thinking of $\frac{7}{4}$ in the manner illustrated in Figure 8-5. When students are introduced to ratios, they must learn to relate to a familiar symbol in a new context and give that symbol a different interpretation. What used to be thought of as a fraction is now visually the same but means something different. The language of ratio is

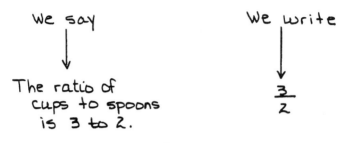

Figure 8-4

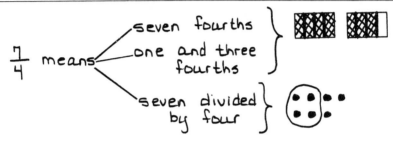

Figure 8-5

abstract and that adds to the difficulty. The ratio $\frac{7}{4}$ is often read "7 to 4." The statement itself is relatively confusing. A much more meaningful but longer statement would be: "Think: for every 7 (cups) of (flour) we need 4 (cups) of (milk)." It is far easier to make the necessary language association with this second type of expression.

Setting up a ratio from a simple one-step problem like that of Figure 8-6 is generally easy for students. The word "ratio" triggers the general idea and the problem presents the numbers in the correct order for writing the ratio. The difficulty arises when the numbers are not presented in the correct order and when the word ratio is not used. Students also have trouble finding equal ratios. This problem will be discussed below in the section on proportion. The suggestions that follow focus on the needs of learning disabled students and on ways of supplementing standard approaches for introducing ratio to meet those needs.

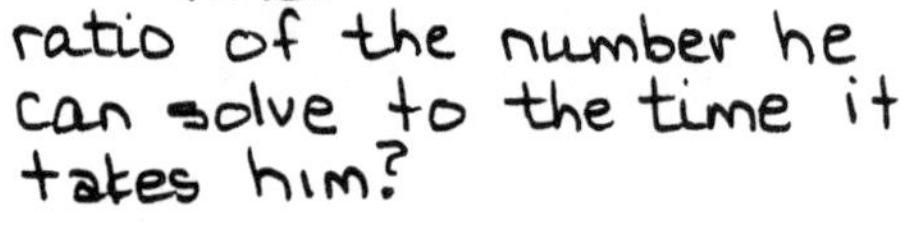

A man solves 8 puzzles in 4 hours. What is the ratio of the number he can solve to the time it takes him?

Figure 8-6

Suggested Activities and Exercises

1. **Focus.** Figure 8-6 presents a typical introductory ratio problem. When asked to find the ratio, students not uncommonly say "2." To help the children focus on the concept of comparing one thing to another, have them underline related parts of the problem with the same color. For example, one might underline everything associated with the first number green and everything dealing with the second number red. Figure 8-7 illustrates this technique. *Note:* Initially, it might be best for the teacher to underline the related parts ahead of time. A discussion should follow to help the students understand the thought process.

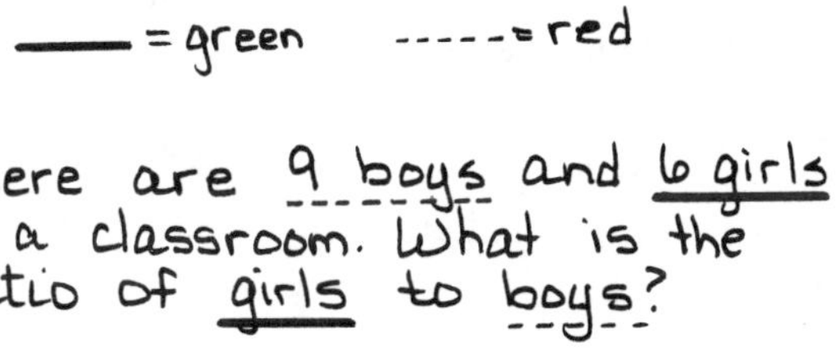

_____ = green   - - - - - = red

There are 9 boys and 6 girls in a classroom. What is the ratio of girls to boys?

Figure 8-7

2. **Match.** It often is necessary to practice determining the proper ratios for given questions. Even if students understand that a ratio is written in the form of a fraction, number placement is often hard. A combination card game and puzzle is fun and helpful at this point. Use large index cards (8 by 12) and make puzzle shapes as in Figure 8-8. On the left side of each puzzle piece, write a problem and on the right fill in the ratio. A set of 50 cards works well for a class. Cut the puzzle pieces apart on the dotted lines. The problem side of the card is placed in a central "draw" pile and each player is dealt five of the ratio cards. The remaining ratio cards are placed face down in a second pile. The first player turns over a problem card. If the correct ratio is held by the player, a match is made (placed on the board). If not, the player calls for the ratio card. If another player has what is requested, it is given to the caller. Otherwise the caller draws one ratio card from the pile. When a match is made, the caller puts the pair of cards down on the board. Should an incorrect ratio be requested (the puzzles act as a check), the caller keeps that ratio card and draws another from the pile. The winner is the first person to run out of cards.

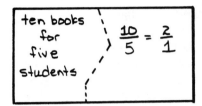

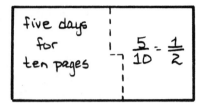

Figure 8-8

3. **Write it out.** Encourage the children to write the words, as well as the numbers, when setting up a ratio. The chance to *see and say* the words helps give the numbers more meaning (see Figure 8-9). *Note:* At this point, it is unnecessary to reduce the ratio. The primary goal is to understand and set up the ratio.

We need 12 pencils for 9 students. What is the ratio of students to pencils?

$$\frac{\text{— students}}{\text{— pencils}} \rightarrow \text{For every — students we need — pencils.}$$

Figure 8-9

4. **Three ways.** To help the children recognize and use the three ways of writing a ratio, post a chart like that shown in Figure 8-10 to which the students can refer. The chart will be especially helpful to those with language or visual memory difficulties.

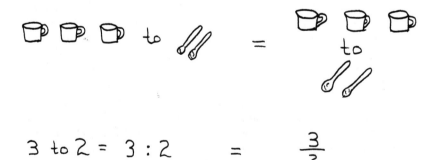

Figure 8-10

5. **Practice.** Make a set of ten cards, numbered 1 to 10. On each card, place groups of common objects that represent ratios like the following: $\frac{2}{3}, \frac{4}{3}, \frac{1}{2}, \frac{1}{4}, \frac{1}{3}, \frac{5}{3}, \frac{5}{6}, \frac{7}{8}, \frac{8}{3}, \frac{2}{7}$. Under each picture also write the ratio to be expressed. Have the students number their papers from 1 to 10. Next to each number, they write the ratio shown on the corresponding card.

   • *Followup:* Write the proper ratio on the *back* of a card deck similar to that described above. Have the students study the pictures and write the ratio to describe each picture, then use the backs of the cards to check.

6. **Color code.** Similarity involves ratio; it is thus often helpful to use colors to help focus attention. Keep a set of pages as in Figure 8-11, with color coding as shown. To aid the transition to noncolor-coded presentations, have the students put in the colors to describe statements about each. In written work, it may help at first to color code statements to match the figures. For children who have trouble processing what they read, this approach helps to break the steps down to manageable size. The focus here, of course, is on recognizing ratios in an application setting, not on setting up or solving proportions.

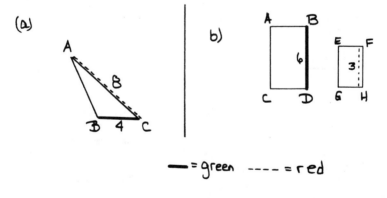

Figure 8-11

   • *Note:* Sometimes letters are used to describe the comparison of sides. With many learning disabled children, this can be confusing as it is far too abstract. When numbers are assigned to the ratio, as in Figure 8-11, the relationship can be more readily internalized by students.

PROPORTIONS

Problem area: Difficulty setting up proportions for given situations.

Typical disabilities affecting progress: Difficulty with receptive language, sequencing, abstract reasoning, and closure.

Background: Most learning disabled students, once they have learned about equivalent fractions and solving equations, have little difficulty solving proportions that *have already been set up*. Figure 8-12 illustrates typical approaches the students might use.

a)

<u>Child is given</u>

2 pencils for 15¢. If I buy 6 pencils, how much will it cost?

$$\frac{2}{15} = \frac{6}{\square}$$

<u>Child uses idea of equivalent fractions and thinks</u>

$$\frac{2}{15} \times 3 = \frac{6}{\square}$$ ooo $\left(\begin{array}{l} 2 \times 3 \text{ is } 6 \\ \text{so multiply} \\ 15 \text{ by } 3, \text{ too} \end{array}\right)$

b)

<u>Child needs</u>

2 cups of flour to make 3 dozen cookies. I only have $1\frac{1}{4}$ cups of flour. How many cookies can I make?

$$\frac{2}{3} = \frac{1\frac{1}{4}}{\square}$$

Recognizing no easy equivalence, child uses "cross multiply" rule and solves the following equation:

$$2 \times \square = 3 \times 1\frac{1}{4}$$

Figure 8-12

Problems arise when students must independently determine the proportion that applies to a given situation. Consider, for example, the example of Figure 8-13. The wording in this problem does not allow for using key words to set it up. The student must fully understand the concepts of ratio and proportion. Many students, particularly those with the disabilities identified above, *are* able to set up simple ratios and solve proportions. They just need help in "getting started," so that they

- recognize the need for a proportion in a given situation, and
- can set up the correct proportion.

A recipe for 3 dozen cookies uses 2 cups of flour. How many cookies can you make if you only have 1¼ cups of flour?

Figure 8-13

The suggestions which follow may prove helpful in this regard.

Suggested Activities and Exercises

1. **Construct a chart.** Help the students learn to set up a chart, like that of Figure 8-14, for proportion problems. Charts like this help them to organize their thinking and to set up the proportion properly. The sample chart is based on the following problem: "On the map 1 cm is equal to 80 km. If the distance from Santa Barbara to Los Angeles is about 144 km, how far away are the two cities on the map?" The chart helps students to recognize and compare like terms of the written problem.

distance in km	=	distance in cm
80 km	=	1 cm
144 km	=	__ cm

Figure 8-14

2. **Map out an alternative.** It often is better to present alternative methods to students to help them solve problems. For example, although proportions can be used to compare prices at a grocery store, it is easier for many to use unit pricing (Figure 8-15).

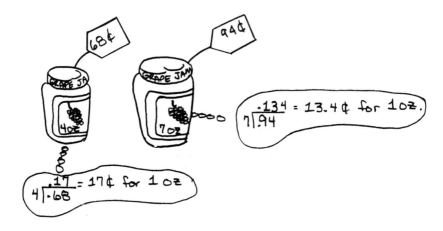

Figure 8-15

PERCENT EQUIVALENTS

Problem area: Changing percents to decimals or fractions.

Typical disabilities affecting progress: Difficulty with sequencing and visual discrimination.

Background: Generally, when students are introduced to percent, they are shown a hundreds square with part of it shaded. Often the explanation is given that percent means "per one hundred" or "out of one hundred." These examples and explanations are rather easily understood by most students. Quite often, in fact, the basic concept of percent is less difficult for learning disabled children than some of the topics presented up to this point. The difficulty arises in applying percent to its use in everyday situations. Aspects of the broader problem are discussed in this and the following two sections of this chapter.

Usually, when solving problems involving percent, it is necessary to express a percent either as a fraction or as a decimal. Changing whole-number percents to fractions is usually not terribly difficult for students. Most readily recognize what to do and remember to put the number itself over 100. Similarly two-digit whole-number percents are fairly easy for students to convert to decimals. Single-digit percents are sometimes more difficult, and it is not uncommon for teachers to see the following: 6% = .6. Even harder is the conversion of percents like that of Figure 8-16 to decimals or fractions. When learning this latter skill, the children must think through each step to the point of overlearning. The ideas that follow should help with this and other aspects of instruction for finding percent equivalents.

Figure 8-16

Suggested Activities and Exercises

1. **Fractions first.** As noted in Chapter 6, decimals are often most meaningfully introduced by relating them to the familiar, *less abstract* fraction notation. Similarly, it is often most meaningful, when converting percents to decimals, first to change the percent to a fraction with the denominator 100. Seeing the two zeroes in the denominator often provides the instant reminder of where to place the decimal point. This approach is particularly effective for helping students avoid the 6% = .6 error cited above. The underscoring technique of Figure 8-17 can be used to emphasize the fact that the correct decimal equivalent of a single-digit percent has *two* decimal places.

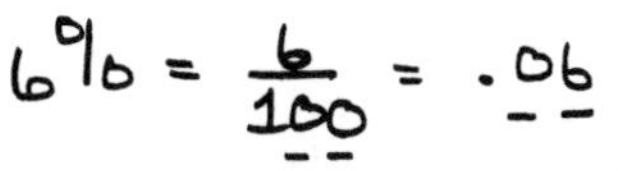

$$6\% = \frac{6}{100} = .06$$

Figure 8-17

2. **Make it easier.** Given a percent like 5½%, students can be instructed to change the ½ to .5 right away. This makes it easier to then change the percent to a fraction. In Figure 8-18, 5.5% is first expressed as a fraction with denominator 100, then changed as necessary to eliminate the decimal.

$$5\tfrac{1}{2}\% = 5.5\% = \frac{5.5}{100} = \frac{55}{1000} = .055$$

Figure 8-18

3. **Chart it.** Using charts as in Figure 8-19 helps those students who have trouble with memory sequencing. Such a chart also provides the necessary structure for those who cannot provide it for themselves. Since many students enter the fifth or sixth grades with an intuitive understanding of the relationship of percents to fractions and decimals, this structure is especially important. It helps them begin to realize how the conversions are derived.

Percent	=	Fraction (Denominator of 100)	=	Decimal	=	Reduced Fraction
50%	=	$\frac{50}{100}$	=	$.50$	=	$\frac{1}{2}$
8%	=	$\frac{8}{100}$	=	$.08$	=	$\frac{2}{25}$
$5\tfrac{1}{2}\% = 5.5\% =$		$\frac{5.5}{100} = \frac{55}{1000}$	=	$.055$	=	$\frac{11}{200}$

Figure 8-19

4. **Make a book** (a practice activity for two or three to play). Provide a deck of 51 cards, 17 showing percents and the remainder giving the fraction or decimal equivalent of each percent. After each player is dealt five cards, the rest of the deck is placed face down between the players. The object of the game is to make books of three cards: the percent and its fraction *and* decimal equivalent. If, at a player's turn, there is no book in hand, then the top card from the discard pile or from the draw pile is taken. The player then discards one card and the next person has a turn. During a player's turn, all exposed books can be played. The winner is the one with the most books when one of the players runs out of cards.

PERCENT FORM OF A FRACTION

Problem area: Difficulty changing fractions to percents.

Typical disabilities affecting progress: Difficulty with memory, abstract reasoning, and closure.

Background: Converting fractions to percents when the denominator is 100 is relatively easy. The difficulty arises when the denominator is not 100. The general technique for handling situations like this is illustrated in Figure 8-20: cross multiply and solve the equation for X. Most textbooks include problems of this type in the section on proportion. For brighter students, those with good memory and abstract reasoning skills, this approach is fine. In fact, for students who have closure difficulties, it is sometimes simpler than alternative methods. The kind of retrieval required is different and easier for the students. For other learning disabled children who have difficulty solving proportions, the following sequence might be considered. Because the sequence involves very small learning increments, relates to the familiar process of finding equivalent fractions, and makes adequate provision for overlearning, it has proved helpful to the students with whom we work.

$$\frac{4}{7} = \frac{X}{100}$$

$$(4)(100) = 7X$$
$$400 = 7X$$
$$57\tfrac{1}{7}\% = X$$

Figure 8-20

Suggested Sequence of Activities and Exercises

1. **Build prerequisites.** Be sure that the children have adequate understandings and skills associated with naming and writing fractions and their equivalents. Then introduce the concept of percent in the usual manner.
2. **Easy things first.** Now help the students write percents as fractions (in unreduced form) and fractions *(having a denominator of 100)* as percents.

3. **Review.** Be sure the children can apply the idea of equivalent fractions to reducing given fractions to lowest terms.
4. **Now reduce.** The students should now be able to write percents as fractions in reduced form.
5. **Use what you know.** Next turn to writing fractions (with the *denominator a factor of 100*) as percents. Help the students use the idea of equivalent fractions, as in Figure 8-21. The children first find an equivalent fraction having a denominator of 100, then rewrite as a percent.

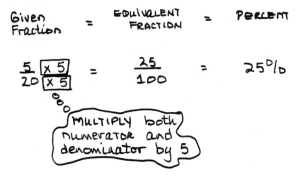

Figure 8-21

6. **One last step.** Finally, have the students write as percents fractions whose denominators are *not* factors of 100. As before, the students first write the percent as a fraction whose denominator is 100. To find this fraction, the students must divide (Figure 8-22a) to determine the factor for multiplying numerator and denominator (Figure 8-22b). Then the fraction can be rewritten as a percent as shown.

a)

$$\frac{4}{7} = \frac{\square}{100}$$

$$7\overline{)100} \quad 14\frac{2}{7}$$

b)

$$\frac{4 \times 14\frac{2}{7}}{7 \times 14\frac{2}{7}} = \frac{57\frac{1}{7}}{100} = 57\frac{1}{7}\%$$

Figure 8-22

- *Note:* Students who have difficulty both with the proportion *and* with the equivalent fraction approach to writing fractions as percents might be permitted to use a calculator. This suggestion is viable only if the students have adequate visual perception skills. Initially, assign fractions that have exact two-digit decimal equivalents. Review the idea of converting a fraction to a decimal, and allow the students to use a calculator to divide the numerator by the denominator. The students can then move the decimal point two places to the right (to show division by 100) and add the % sign in forming the percent equivalent (see Figure 8-23).

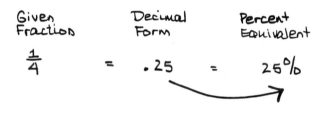

Figure 8-23

PERCENT IN EVERYDAY SITUATIONS

Problem area: Difficulty using percent to solve problems.

Typical disabilities affecting progress: Difficulty with abstract reasoning, sequencing, visual perception, and short term memory.

Background: Many learning disabled students intuitively are able to solve problems using the more common percents, such as 50 percent, 10 percent, and sometimes 25 percent and 75 percent. However, as they begin to deal with other percents, things become more difficult:

- What method should be used to solve the problem?
- Should a fraction or a decimal equivalent be used?
- Now that I've found the answer, does it need to be rounded off?

Decisions like these must be made, and longer, more complex sequences must be employed. In addition, applying meaning to the final answer is often difficult. Too often, a student ends up knowing only that x = 20. The number is not related to the original problem. Ideas for helping students handle difficulties like these are outlined below.

Suggested Activities and Exercises

1. **From problem to equation.** As in other areas, determining the appropriate equation for a given word problem can be the most difficult part. It is often helpful to teach children the vocabulary related to the page and then to use the color-coding technique of Figure 8-24 to help them set up the equation. Structuring problems into "one-liners," so that the equation can be written directly beneath the problem, helps students during early work translate more easily the verbal statement into an equation. Children learn, for example, to associate the word *of* with "x" and *is* with "=."

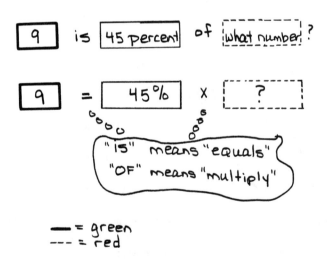

Figure 8-24

2. **Three easy pieces.** If the children have memory, sequencing, or abstract-reasoning difficulties, provide preformated pages using the idea of Figure 8-25. Help the students analyze sample prob-

lems to see that percent situations typically involve *three pieces of information* (refer to the three boxes of Figure 8-25): the part, the whole or base, and the percent figure. A percent problem-solving exercise provides two of these pieces of information and requires you to find the third. The format shown in Figure 8-25 can be used to help solve any of the three possible types of percent problems:

1. percent figure missing
2. the "part" missing
3. the "whole" or base missing

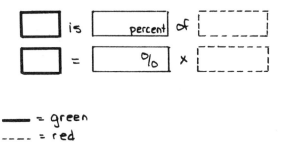

Figure 8-25

It thus becomes a matter of placing information from the verbal statement into the appropriate boxes and then solving for the unknown piece of information. Gradually, the students themselves can be taught to format their own papers when necessary to solve percent problems. When an answer is found, encourage the students to write it above the appropriate box in the problem statement. This step is necessary for some students. Relating the answer to the original problem provides meaning that otherwise would be missed.

3. **Using proportion.** Students with good sequencing, abstract-reasoning, and spatial-organization skills may prefer the proportion method for solving percent problems. The color-coding technique of Figure 8-26a, similar to that discussed earlier, can be used if necessary. Figure 8-26b illustrates how a page can be preformated for this purpose and kept on file. If the proportion method is used, encourage the students, as suggested in Activity 2 above, to relate the answer back to the original problem statement.

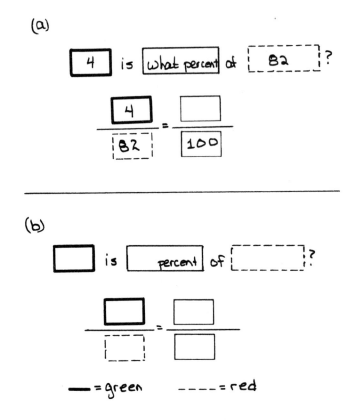

Figure 8-26

INTEGERS: NEW SYMBOLISM

Problem area: Difficulty associating meaning with the abstract representation.

Typical disabilities affecting progress: Difficulty with visual or auditory association, integrative processing, visual perception, and receptive or expressive language.

Background: We use the idea of integers regularly in our everyday lives. We *borrow* money from a friend and then we *pay it back*. Do we still *owe* money? The temperature *drops* eight degrees but then *climbs* nine degrees the next morning. A salary *increase* means we earn more money, but then we might take a *cut* in salary of $10 when we switch jobs. All of these ideas are familiar to children. Even the learning disabled child has little difficulty comprehending their meaning in context. However, when these same ideas are expressed symbolically with positive or negative integers, many children become confused. Most can readily tell you how much a friend owes them if $4 was borrowed, and they may even use the expression, "I'm $4 in the hole." However, the mathematical representation ⁻4 is not as easily explained, although it may have the same meaning.

Poor visual or auditory association skills coupled with poor integrative processing abilities make it difficult for many students to deal meaningfully with the written integer form. Students are now asked to relate an old idea to old signs (+ and −) in a new way and with new language. Doing so requires them to decide what that familiar sign now means: "add" or "positive;" "subtract" or "negative." To complicate matters, children typically are presented with new skills and language simultaneously. Those with expressive or receptive language deficits may understand the difference between the words (add/positive; subtract/negative). But difficulty is experienced because it is hard for them to elicit or associate the word with the correct meaning in context. These students require considerable overlearning, consistent verbal and pictorial association, and small learning increments in early work with integers.

Suggestions for dealing with these difficulties during early concept development for integers are outlined below. The ideas presented can be used to supplement textbook treatments that typically focus on the application of integers to real-life situations. An attempt is made in this and the following four sections to present integers in such a way that learning disabled students can learn and possibly continue on to algebra.

Suggested Activities and Exercises

1. **Color code.** Children with language deficits often benefit from color-coded pages like that of Figure 8-27. The assumption at this point is that the student understands the vocabulary used. The colors help reinforce understanding by allowing the student to focus directly on the ideas of more and less. Related symbolism is highlighted and associated with the related terminology.

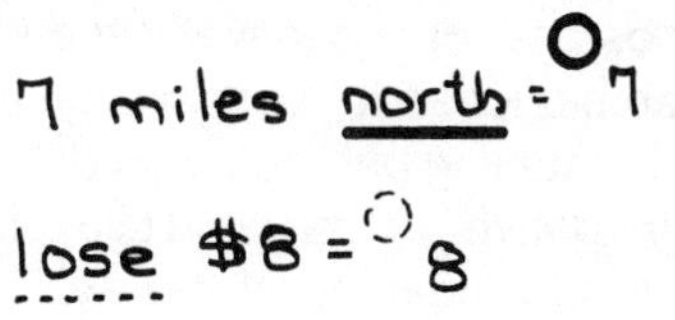

7 miles north = ⁰7

lose $8 = ⁰8

Figure 8-27

2. **Time out.** To help students develop an automatic association of integers with their use in real-life situations, it is helpful to take time out to build up vocabulary. Exercises like those in Figure 8-28 make it easier for students to focus on the necessary language. A sense of usefulness develops, and the children begin to use the numbers more appropriately. The exercise also serves as a transition to eventually eliminating colors.

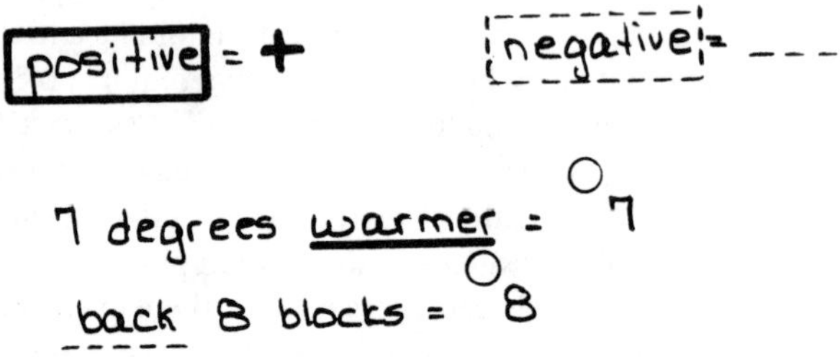

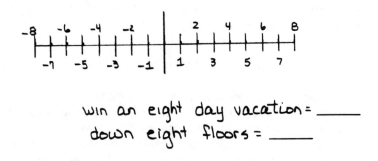

Figure 8-28

3. **Numberline.** As the children begin to use the numberline, have them use examples from everyday situations to describe verbally points on the numberline. Figure 8-29 presents a sample exercise.

win an eight day vacation = _____
down eight floors = _____

Figure 8-29

4. **Picture it.** As a class activity, present pictures with related phrases that describe "positive" or "negative" situations. Figures 8-27 and 8-28 present sample ideas for possible situations. If possible, put the pictures and matching phrases on a ditto with the guide words "positive" and "negative" at the top in two different colors. Discuss with the students the meaning of the two terms and have them underline the key words or phrases to match the color of the guide words.

5. **Point plotting.** As the students begin to plot points in all four quadrants, a color-coded grid, like that of Figure 8-30, often helps with directionality. Ordered pairs are coded according to quadrant, as shown.

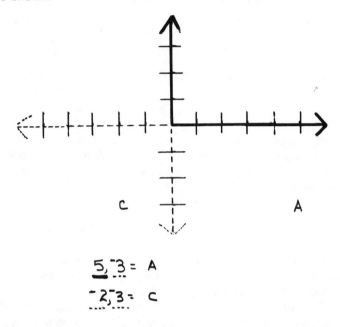

Figure 8-30

INTEGERS: POSITIVE AND NEGATIVE SIGNS

Problem area: Difficulty interpreting signs used with integers.

Typical disabilities affecting progress: Difficulty with visual perception, spatial organization, and closure.

Background: For many students, the greatest difficulty in dealing with integers is misreading or misplacing the sign. Although computation with integers is not especially difficult, it can cause problems when students have trouble interpreting the various signs. For this reason, it is essential that the teacher be consistent in the placement of signs used with integers. When signs are to be interpreted as negative or positive, they should be placed in a *raised* position, as in Figure 8-31. When used to denote an operation, the sign should be centered between the two numbers that are involved. Figure 8-32 shows

⁻7 means "negative seven"

−6 means "subtract six"

Figure 8-31

7−8

Figure 8-32

a typical problem that can be very confusing. Does the sign in front of the 8 mean "subtract" or "negative?" The following ideas have proved useful in dealing with the problem of sign interpretation. In our experience, they have helped to make computation with integers easier for students.

Suggested Activities and Exercises

1. **Circle to focus.** Preview the text being used and circle the raised signs on the first several pages of the chapter on integers. Adult volunteers can be called upon to help with this task.
2. **Label all numerals.** Some students, especially those with memory difficulties, tend to forget that numbers without signs are assumed to be positive. It is not unusual for them to misread the 9 of Figure 8-33 and treat it as a negative integer. For these students, it helps to *label all numerals* until the children become more comfortable with the signs in integer computation.

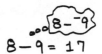

8−9 = 17

Figure 8-33

3. **Do it first.** Until the children become familiar with the raised positive and negative signs, teach them to circle the signs of a text or worksheet page prior to carrying out any computation. This will help focus their attention on the meaning of the signs. When it is time for computation, the bright color or dark circle will serve to remind the students that "this sign means something different."

4. **Use graph paper.** If the students need help in spatially organizing their writing of signed numbers, allow them to use graph paper. Show them how to place the signs and numbers on the lines as in Figure 8-34. Students with severe visual perception deficits will find this activity too difficult. For others, however, the graph-paper technique makes the task of writing integers and computing much simpler. *Note:* Graph paper with six squares to the inch works well.

Figure 8-34

- *Variation:* For those needing even more assistance to organize their writing spatially, use the format of Figure 8-35a to prepare sheets in advance. The students fill in the problem as shown in Figure 8-35b. The adaptation for vertical alignment of numbers is shown in Figure 8-36.

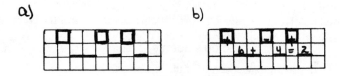

Figure 8-35

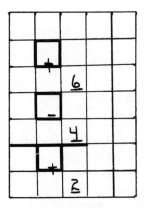

Figure 8-36

5. **Use parentheses.** Often, just inserting parentheses within a problem, as in Figure 8-37, is all that is needed to make signs easier to interpret. Parentheses, instead of circles, could be used to mark raised signs on textbook pages, as suggested in Activity 1 above.

$$9 - (^-3) + (^+4) = 9 + 3 + 4 = 16$$

Figure 8-37

COMPUTATION WITH INTEGERS

Problem area: Difficulty with computation involving integers.

Typical disabilities affecting progress: Difficulty with visual perception, sequencing, abstract reasoning, and memory.

Background: Assuming that visual perception or spatial deficits do not interfere or have been controlled, computing with integers still requires more sequencing and mental regrouping than previous computation involving positive integers. When teaching any of the computational skills, it generally is important to encourage learning disabled students to proceed step by step through *all* the steps, even when they think they can do the work mentally. It may also be necessary for the students to spend more time practicing than others might in order to assure overlearning. Suggestions for supplementing or reinforcing textbook treatment of integer computation for the four operations follow.

Suggested Activities and Exercises

Addition

1. **Informal beginnings.** Most textbooks suggest activities with chips, cards, or walk-on numberlines to introduce informally addition of integers. Generally, it is important to carry out rather than omit these activities for learning disabled students because they help develop the mental imagery necessary for dealing successfully with addition of integers.
2. **Different strokes.** Textbook treatments typically present numberline or other exercises that lead students to verbalize the patterns or "rules" for adding integers. A chart similar to that of Figure 8-38

Addition of Integers

Given problem	What to do	Sign of Sum
positive + positive	Add	+
negative + negative	Add	−
negative + positive or positive + negative	Subtract to find distance between	sign of the greater addend

Figure 8-38

is then provided for reference. Eventually the students memorize the procedures for adding integers. If the students have abstract reasoning difficulties, it generally is more helpful to

- present the chart and discuss it in conjunction with several examples so that, procedurally, the students can use the chart to solve integer addition problems;

- have the students copy the chart onto a file card for ready reference;

- have the students use the rules to work out a number of problems until they become familiar with the general procedures for adding integers; and

- *then* use a walk-on numberline to verify that the sums they have derived in this manner actually do "make sense" before attempting to memorize the procedural rules.

This last step is usually first in the standard sequence. It is an important tie-in to earlier, informal work.

3. **For other folks.** For other students, such as those with memory or perceptual difficulties, the standard sequence would be followed with additional reinforcing measures like the following: (1) color code signs to emphasize them whenever they appear within integer addition problems; (2) use the graph-paper technique of Figure 8-36 when this is helpful; (3) provide kinesthetic/motor involvement in analyzing or verifying the procedural rules for adding integers.

- Allow the students to dramatize simple additions, as in Activity 2 above, on a walk-on numberline.

- Have the students think of their bodies as numberlines. Spreading both arms out, they can let the left arm represent the negative integers and the right arm the positive ones. Their body is the zero. To add a negative 5 to a positive 4, for example, they must pass through 0 and on to negative 1. Doing this for several sample problems helps children *internalize the action* of integer addition. The general technique, when used later for verifying that indeed the "chart (Figure 8-38) always works," strengthens retention of the procedural rules.

- *Variation:* An alternative to arm stretching is to tape a smaller numberline from shoulder to shoulder across a child's back. The body midline, then, is the "zero." As the teacher dramatizes a simple addition problem by finger movement on the child's back, the student can either (1) close eyes and reverbalize the problem as it is enacted, or (2) with eyes open, mimic the teacher's movements by "finger walking" the addition on a personal numberline placed on the desk in front of the child.

Subtraction

Note: Suggestions presented for integer addition have obvious implications for helping learning disabled students with integer subtraction. Informal introductory work is important. The variation of the standard subtraction sequence for students with abstract reasoning difficulty would be similar to that outlined for integer addition. The compensatory techniques outlined in Activity 3 of the addition section should be reviewed and adapted to work with integer subtraction. The following ideas also deserve special emphasis.

1. **Act it out.** There generally is great value to having students use a walk-on or "back" numberline (Activity 3 above)

   - to solve simple integer subtraction problems (this often results in noting the pattern summarized in the Figure 8-39 "rule" statement) and

To subtract two integers:
add the 1st integer to
the opposite of the 2nd.

Figure 8-39

- to verify that given answers, or those obtained by using a calculator, can also be derived by "following the rule."

2. **To the rule.** Assume that one is interested in carrying out the first suggestion under Activity 1 above with students who have no abstract reasoning difficulties.

- **Use the numberline.** A problem like that of Figure 8-40a might be posed and the students cued to think of the related addition problem. "What must be added to $^+4$ to get $^-7$?" Starting at $^+4$ on the numberline, the children find that they must take 11 steps in a negative direction to get to $^-7$. This result should be charted along with others obtained in this manner. Using previously solved problems, help the students notice the pattern by grouping like problems, as in Figure 8-40b. Have them verbalize the pairs $^-7 - ^+4$ and $^-7 + ^-4$. Help them to determine the rule: "To subtract two integers, the first can be added to the *opposite* of the second." Use the numberline to verify the equivalence.

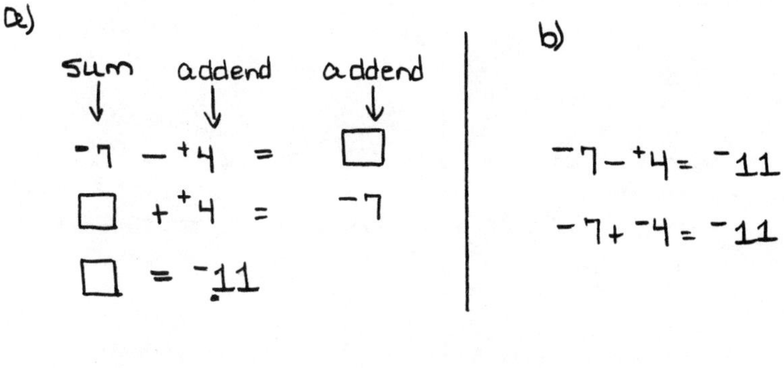

a)

$$\underset{\downarrow}{\text{sum}} \quad \underset{\downarrow}{\text{addend}} \quad \underset{\downarrow}{\text{addend}}$$

$$^-7 - ^+4 = \square$$
$$\square + ^+4 = ^-7$$
$$\square = ^-11$$

b)

$$^-7 - ^+4 = ^-11$$
$$^-7 + ^-4 = ^-11$$

Figure 8-40

- **Match.** Design worksheets or card-sort activities in which the students solve and then match an integer subtraction problem to an equivalent addition problem. For example:

Solve:

$$^-7 - {}^+4 = \underline{\hspace{1cm}} \qquad ^-8 + {}^+5 = \underline{\hspace{1cm}}$$

$$^+3 - {}^-2 = \underline{\hspace{1cm}} \qquad ^-7 + {}^-4 = \underline{\hspace{1cm}}$$

$$^-8 - {}^-5 = \underline{\hspace{1cm}} \qquad ^+3 + {}^+2 = \underline{\hspace{1cm}}$$

Pair them:

a. $^-7 - {}^+4 = \underline{\hspace{1cm}}$ and $^-7 + {}^-4 = \underline{\hspace{1cm}}$

b. $\underline{\hspace{2cm}} = \underline{\hspace{1cm}}$ and $\underline{\hspace{2cm}} = \underline{\hspace{1cm}}$

c. $\underline{\hspace{2cm}} = \underline{\hspace{1cm}}$ and $\underline{\hspace{2cm}} = \underline{\hspace{1cm}}$

When all matches are made, the students would be required to use a numberline to verify the equivalence of each match contained in a circled statement.

- **Just one step.** Next, give the students integer subtraction problems and instruct them to carry out just the *first step* of each. As in Figure 8-41a, have the students just rewrite the problem, without solving. After the papers are checked, the problems can be completed. Note: Most texts present integer computation horizontally, although for many learning disabled students the vertical format is easier. As shown in Figure 8-41b, it may be necessary to help the students rewrite the horizontal form.

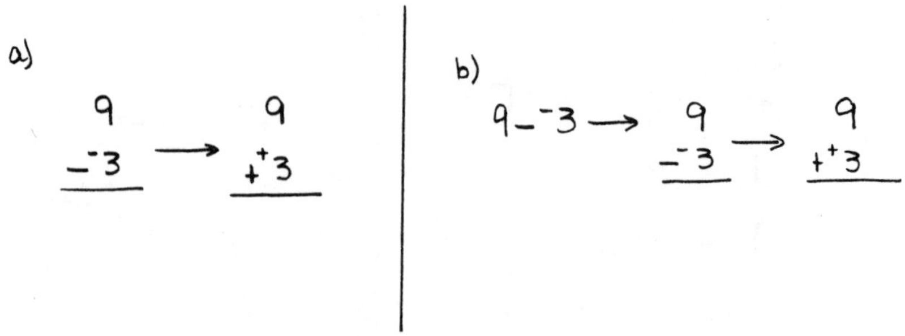

Figure 8-41

3. **Different strokes.** The sequence outlined in Activity 2 above starts intuitively with numberline moves, notes an equivalent method for finding answers (adding the opposite), then drills on that method. Some students may have difficulty with this more sophisticated, standard method of using the additive inverse to solve integer subtraction problems. For these students:

   • **Use numberline moves** as above to introduce integer subtraction intuitively. As before, cue the students to think of the related addition problem. Using the example of Figure 8-42a, ask the students, "What must be added to a positive 4 to get negative 7?" The students *rewrite* the problems, as in the second line of Figure 8-42b, to match the question being asked. Starting at $^+4$, children then *move back* to zero and *on* to negative 7, for a total of 11 spaces in a negative direction. This result ($^-11$) is now recorded (Figure 8-42c). Note: Either the walk-on or the "back" numberline discussed earlier can be used in this activity.

a)

$$-7-^+4 = \square$$

b)

$$^-7-^+4 = \square$$
$$\square + ^+4 = ^-7$$

c)

$$-7-^+4 = \square$$
$$\square + ^+4 = ^-7$$
$$\square = ^-11$$

Figure 8-42

   • **Write it out.** To reinforce the subtraction-addition relation and to help children internalize the procedure for subtracting, use the technique of Figure 8-43. The subtraction sign in the problem is written in a bright color. Verbally write out the procedure for subtracting as shown. The students solve the problem by filling in the blanks. Later, just put an example at the top of the page as a reminder, but continue to highlight the subtraction signs.

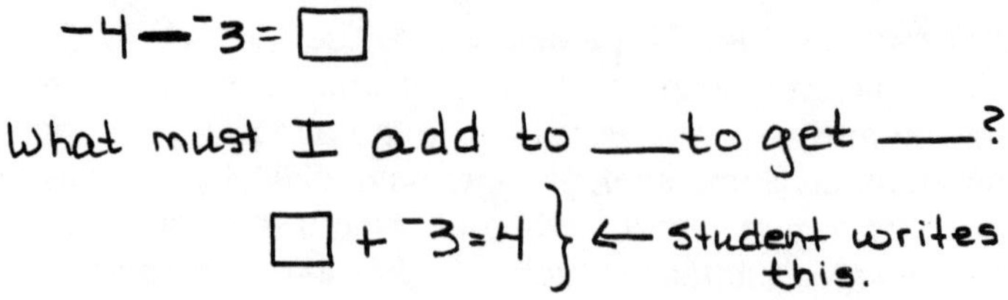

$$-4 - ^-3 = \Box$$

What must I add to ___ to get ___?

$$\Box + ^-3 = 4 \left.\right\} \leftarrow \text{student writes this.}$$

Figure 8-43

- **The whole thing.** As the children now begin to solve integer subtraction problems independently, encourage them to picture the numberline.

Example 1

$$8 - ^-3 = \Box$$

Child rewrites: $\Box + ^-3 = 8$.

Child thinks: "Start at $^-3$, move forward to 0,
then on to 8. A move of $^+11$. $\Box = ^+11$."

Example 2

$$36 - ^-25 = \Box$$

Child rewrites: $\Box + ^-25 = 36$.

Child thinks: "Start at $^-25$. Move forward to 0,
then on to 36." (Child now adds
25 and 36 on scrap paper.) "A move
of $^+61$. $\Box = ^+61$."

- *Note:* The method just discussed does not utilize the traditional rule for subtracting integers—that of adding the opposite (additive inverse). It is based on the addition-subtraction relationship, but it allows children to remain very concrete in their thinking. The children are encouraged to picture (or actually make) numberline moves *first to zero, then on* to a target number. It is a two-step process that can also be used with larger two- and three-digit numbers.

Multiplication and Division

1. **Prerequisites.** For some students, it may be necessary to review briefly the concept of multiplication as repeated addition and remind them that multiplication is commutative.
2. **Products and unlike signs.** With prerequisites in hand, the sign for the product of a positive and a negative number can readily be identified. *Example:*

   > $7 \times {}^-6$. "That's seven negative 6's." One could repeatedly add, if necessary, to obtain the $^-42$. And, since multiplication is commutative, $7 \times {}^-6 = {}^-6 \times 7 = {}^-42$.

3. **Products and like signs.** Many students can recognize and continue the pattern to the answers in Figure 8-44a. Each product is 5 less than that directly above it. Similarly, in Figure 8-44b, each product is 4 less than that directly above it. Further, when the answers are filled in, the students can see how, each time, the product of two negative numbers is always positive. Some students, particularly those with abstract reasoning difficulties, may not follow the logic of this exercise but will merely remember that, as long as the signs are the same, the product is positive.

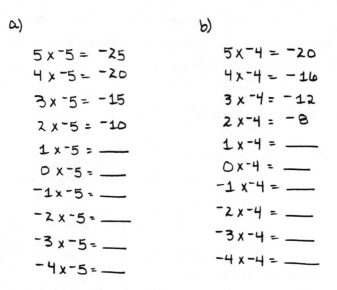

Figure 8-44

4. **Mail time.** A table like that of Figure 8-45 can also be used as a storyline to dramatize the sign patterns for products. Since most students like to get mail, that is positive. No one likes to receive bills, that is negative.

If letters (+) are brought (+) that's positive (+).
If bills (-) are brought (+) that's negative (-).
If letters (+) are taken away (-) that's negative (-).
If bills (-) are taken away (-) that's positive (+).

Figure 8-45

5. **Same as multiplication.** Most students have little difficulty remembering how to handle the signs in division once they are comfortable with multiplication of integers. They are used to relating multiplication and division, so it is easy to remember (and verify) that sign rules for quotient figures are analogous to those for products:

Divisor and Dividend	Quotient
Like signs ⟶	Positive
Unlike signs ⟶	Negative

Example 1: $^-45 \div 5 = {}^-9$. ("Yes, because $^-9 \times 5 = {}^-45$.")

Example 2: $^-63 \div {}^-7 = 9$. ("Yes, because $9 \times {}^-7 = {}^-63$.")

EXPONENTS: BASIC CONCEPT

Problem area: Difficulty understanding, reading, and writing exponents.

Typical disabilities affecting progress: Difficulty with short term memory, visual perception, expressive language, and abstract reasoning.

Background: Most students are introduced to the concept and symbolism of exponents as early as fifth or sixth grade. At that point, the idea is dealt with basically in conjunction with factoring and primes. As students advance in mathematics, computation involving exponents becomes more commonplace. Mathematical problem solving applications in a number of fields—including medicine, science, and computer science—regularly use exponents to express both very large and very small numbers. Students with interests in fields such as these benefit from a firm foundation in exponents.

At the prealgebra level, the development of adequate understanding of and skill with exponents is both important and necessary for students planning to continue mathematics in high school. The following activities suggest ways of making exponents more understandable and usable, especially for those with language deficits. The topic itself is not particularly difficult, except that it introduces a new terminology and new notation that can be visually confusing.

Suggested Activities and Exercises

1. **Factors first.** Color coding can be used to help students remember how to read and write exponents. Generally, since an exponent indicates the number of times a number is used as a factor, it is best to have students first write the exponential form from a list of factors (Figure 8-46). This sequence especially seems to help students with expressive language deficits, as it reinforces the meaning of the numbers used. Figure 8-46 gives an idea for an exercise that can be kept on file and used *prior to* the textbook introduction of exponents.

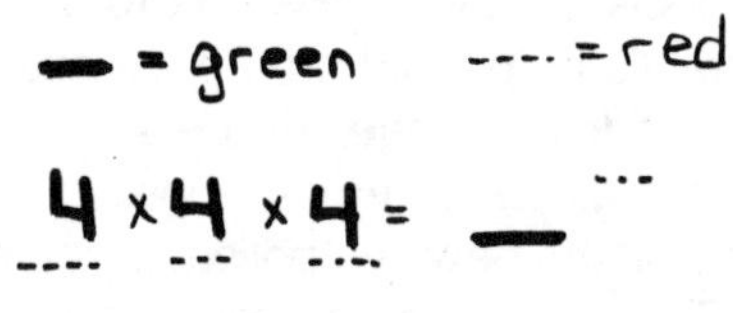

Figure 8-46

2. **Reverse what's given.** Once the students can write the exponential form from the factored form, provide practice translating the exponential form. Color coding again can be used as in Figure 8-47.

Figure 8-47

3. **I call.** Make a deck of 52 cards. 26 cards should show a number in exponential form, 26 in factored form, as in Figure 8-48. After each child is dealt five cards, the rest of the deck is placed face down between the players. The game is played by making pairs of an exponential card and one with matching factors. In turn, the players request one card from the player to the left. If that player has what is requested, the card is given to the caller who can lay a pair down. A turn continues until no more pairs can be made. If the caller does not get what is requested, a card is drawn from the pile and play continues. The first player to run out of cards wins.

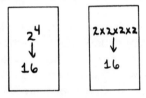

Figure 8-48

4. **New terminology.** For many students, the language involved in exponents is the most difficult. These students have a difficult time meaningfully associating the words "six to the third power" with any visual image. To help build up the necessary language, it is often helpful to provide language drill that is separate from computational drill. Pages such as those shown in Figure 8-49a are useful. They present the new symbolism together with the associated language. Figure 8-49b presents an alternative exercise that visually reinforces the fact that the exponent is raised.

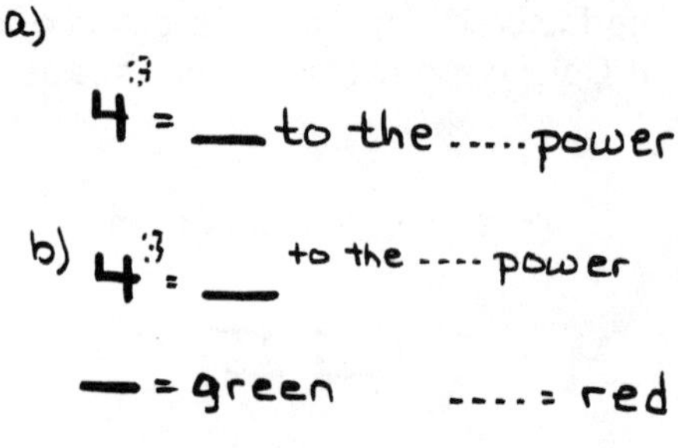

a)

$$4^{:3} = \underline{\quad} \text{ to the } \ldots \text{power}$$

b) $4^{:3} = \underline{\quad} \text{ to the } \ldots \text{power}$

$\underline{\quad} = green \qquad \ldots = red$

Figure 8-49

SCIENTIFIC NOTATION

Problem area: Using exponents for scientific notation.

Typical disabilities affecting progress: Visual perception, figure ground, sequencing, and closure.

Background: Scientific notation is used in many fields to express both very large and very small numbers. The successful conversion of numbers to (or from) scientific notation requires several major prerequisites:

- strong numeration concepts and skills

- the ability to multiply and divide by powers of 10

- a basic understanding of and skill with exponents

- the ability to read decimals.

The application of all these isolated understandings and skills when writing numbers in scientific notation requires good reasoning, recall, and sequencing. These are weak areas for many learning disabled students. In addition, closure or visual perception deficits can lead to confusion when reading the numbers. Too often, these deficits make it seem that the student does not understand what to do when in fact it really may be a matter of losing the place or not being able to recall information. The following suggestions offer ideas for handling some of the more common problems children face as they deal with scientific notation.

Suggested Activities and Exercises

1. **Color highlight.** During early work, for students with figure-ground deficits, it sometimes helps to highlight the digits to be used. Figure 8-50 illustrates two alternatives for color coding the digits. Highlighting in this manner helps minimize the chance of losing the place or misperceiving the numbers read.

a) $6,240,000 = (6.24) \times 10^{6}$

b) $6,240,000 = (6.24) \times 10^{6}$

—— = green   .... = red

Figure 8-50

2. **Use a mask.** Some students need to use a card, as in Figure 8-51, to block out part of the number field while counting digits. The students write the answer, digit by digit, while moving the card.

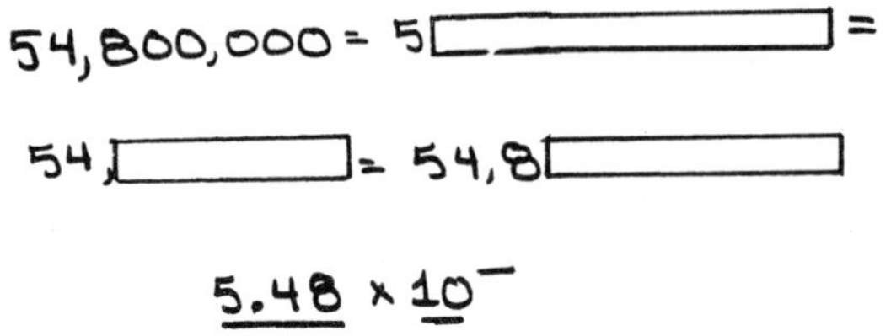

$$54,800,000 = 5\boxed{} =$$

$$54\boxed{} = 54,8\boxed{}$$

$$\underline{5.48} \times \underline{10}^{-}$$

Figure 8-51

3. **Help for computation.** When multiplying with scientific notation, color-highlight, as in Figure 8-52, to help students apply the distributive law. The visual field can otherwise be very confusing. Texts can be highlighted as in Figure 8-52a. Pages, formated as in Figure 8-52c, can be kept on hand for students to use.

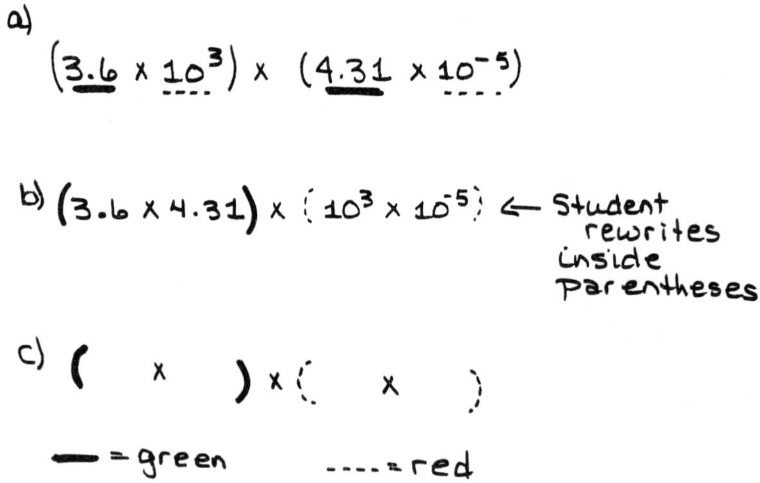

a)
$$\left(\underline{3.6} \times \underline{10}^{3}\right) \times \left(\underline{4.31} \times \underline{10}^{-5}\right)$$

b)
$$\left(3.6 \times 4.31\right) \times \left(10^{3} \times 10^{-5}\right) \leftarrow$$ Student
                                                        rewrites
                                                        inside
                                                        parentheses

c)
$$\left(\quad \times \quad\right) \times \left(\quad \times \quad\right)$$

—— = green   ---- = red

Figure 8-52

Chapter 9

Problem Solving

CURRENT EMPHASIS AND SUGGESTED APPROACHES

The National Council of Teachers of Mathematics, in its *An Agenda for Action* for the 1980s, has set goals calling for more emphasis on problem solving at all levels (National Council, 1980, p. 1). Teachers are encouraged to take a fresh look at approaches for helping students develop problem solving skills. Some of the more effective of these approaches are summarized below.

- Use interesting problems that are within a child's experience. Films, resource personnel, field trips, and firsthand experiences are all helpful in familiarizing children with various situations.

- Pose problem situations *orally*. This is especially appropriate for first grade beginners and for students who have difficulty reading. *Note:* Providing *concrete visual reinforcement* for each problem that is posed orally helps children who have auditory processing difficulties.

- Use concrete objects, drawings, and diagrams to clarify the problem, find the solution, and verify the answer. Have children *act out* the problems.

- Assign problems to children that match their experience, background, reading level, and mathematical understanding.

- For problems with larger numbers, help students substitute smaller, easier numbers if paper-and-pencil computation is required and is difficult. The role of word problems is to encourage thinking and the application of mathematics to real-world situations, not primarily to provide extra practice with computation.

- Have children write the mathematical sentences for the problems *but not compute the answers*. This places importance on the operation used, not on finding the correct answer. *Note:* For children who have expressive language difficulties, allow them to choose the appropriate sentence from several that are provided.

- Arouse the curiosity of pupils in any way possible to make them want to solve the problem.

- Give children just enough help so that frustration does not become critical.

- Give the students immediate reinforcement whenever possible. Compliment them on problems done correctly and point out mistakes in those done incorrectly. Encourage them to rework to correct any errors made.

- Use open-ended problems (problems with more than one possible solution) to foster creative thinking.

- Use large numbers in problems and allow students to use a calculator to solve them.

- Have children restate problems in their own words to make sure they understand them.

- Use problems with too much or too little information and have students tell what is still needed or what information is extra.

- Have students make up problems for solution in class. To offset the tendency to make them too difficult, require that children be able to solve their own problems or tell why they cannot be solved. This technique has proved to be a highly motivating one for students.

- Present students with solved problems, showing the work for each step. Have them explain what is learned at each point.

- Many mathematics textbooks today present, in short form, flow charts based on the following six points:

  1. Read the problem.
  2. Picture what is happening.
  3. Think: What's the question?
  4. What must you do to answer it (add, subtract, . . .)?
  5. Compute the answer.
  6. Check. Is the answer reasonable?

Use the chart to provide structure to a child's approach to solving written problems.

- Encourage the children to solve problems in many different ways. Children gain more problem-solving skill by solving the same problem in several ways than by solving several similar problems the same way.

- Do more than mark problems right or wrong. Assign fewer problems so that more time can be devoted to discussing solutions and how they are obtained.

- Have the children devise word problems for given computational exercises. Their problems should illustrate situations in which the numbers of the problem might be used outside the classroom in a problem situation.

- Present several pieces of numeric information. Use a picture, as well, if it seems helpful. Have the students use the data/picture to create their own word problems.

- Encourage the children to estimate the answer before actually figuring it out. Show them ways of estimating that are reliable and easy.

- Use problems without numbers to check if the students know when to use certain operations. Encourage them to insert low numbers to help determine the operation.

- Use problems without questions. This helps students realize that they cannot tell what to do until they know what to find. Follow through by having the students themselves pose suitable questions for given problems.

- Have the children give each answer in a complete sentence. This helps them check to see if an answer makes sense.

- Make sure you understand the child's thinking before you comment on work done. Praise students for a good attack, even if it fails.

- Reverse the usual procedure. Give the students an answer and ask them to formulate several problems having this answer.

- Supplement textbook problems with your own. These can deal with classroom experiences or include the children's names.

- Post a "problem of the week" on the bulletin board.

- Keep a file with problems on index cards. The students can choose one, copy it, sign it on the back, and return it to the file.

- In class discussions of problem situations, allow the children enough time to think. Do not call on the first child to raise a hand. Follow through by asking for alternative suggestions or methods for solving a problem.

- Present problems orally, on tape, or use "picture stories" to minimize the reading problem if this is the difficulty.

- Try giving just one or two problems a day, not pages at a time.

- Offer challenging problems for the students to solve on their own time. Give recognition and praise for their efforts.

- Be sure the children know the mathematics needed to solve problems that are assigned.

- Pose nonverbal problems: let pictures do the talking. Present "before" and "after" pictures with appropriate sets of numeric data. Have the children write (or simply state) the question that is apparent to them and then answer it.

- Do not always tell the children whether they are right or wrong. Ask questions to help them evaluate their own work.

- Give the students many opportunities for practice.

PROBLEM SOLVING AND THE LEARNING DISABLED STUDENT

Many of the suggestions listed above are helpful for learning disabled students as well. One must carefully reexamine the situation, however, when making specific recommendations for the learning disabled. Exactly what is involved in problem solving? Clearly, there are several components—affective, cognitive, and mathematical—that play a part in successful problem solving.

Problem-solving situations call upon children to apply skills they have previously learned. Knowing basic arithmetic skills and knowing when and how to incorporate these skills in new contexts, however, are two completely different tasks. All too often we assume that students understand how to solve a problem if they understand and can carry out the operations involved.

As difficult as it may be for learning disabled students to learn a particular skill, it generally is considerably more difficult for them to *use* that skill in new contexts, such as that posed by oral or written word problems. The use of skills like multiplication or addition of two-digit numbers requires a high degree of reasoning, expressive language, and visual memory that many children lack. For this reason, most learning disabled students will be helped in the problem-solving process if they are given specific help in

- decision making,

- language use,

- vocabulary,

- sequencing, and

- patterning.

Because of their importance in the problem-solving process, each of these aspects deserves special consideration in a mathematics program for learning disabled students.

Decision Making

All problem solving involves making decisions. Even in the broader context, as students begin working with larger numbers and more complex situations, they are required to make decisions. Very young children make a decision when they tell whether the symbol in front of them is a two or a three. As they progress and learn more skills, decision making continues to enter their daily work in mathematics. Does that sign mean to multiply or divide? Do I carry? How can I add two fractions with different denominators? Should I use a decimal or a fraction to find the percent of that number? What do I do first to solve that problem?

The decision-making process is a complex one. It involves strong abstract reasoning ability. It requires that a student be able both to receive and express words in a meaningful way. It requires the ability to draw on previously learned concepts and skills, to distinguish among them, and to choose the one that is appropriate in a given situation.

Language

In order to solve problems, students must be able to formulate and express the key ideas involved. They must understand what question or questions are being asked. They must also be able to isolate given information within a problem. Sorting out irrelevant information is essential in some problems. In real-life situations, we are not always told in advance that some of the information is not essential. Similarly, on a day-to-day basis, we are not told what we need to know in order to solve a problem. We must be able to determine the missing information. All of these requirements demand language, both receptive and expressive. For many children, problem solving is difficult, not because of the computation, but because they are unable to use language appropriately. They are unable to express their ideas or associate the words with the appropriate meanings involved.

Vocabulary

Like reading, mathematics has a vocabulary. The vocabulary varies depending on the level of the material, but it is still an integral part of the program. For younger children, the relevant vocabulary involves associating a word with a symbol, as in Figure 9-1, and understanding that word when it is spoken or read. For older students, generally fourth grade and above, it involves a rapidly expanding vocabulary, including many words with multiple meanings (e.g. "and," "factor," "times," and so on). When new vocabulary is used, many learning disabled students may not automatically know the meaning just by the context. At best, they may know that a familiar word does not make sense in its current context. Because of the many special problems involved, vocabulary is considered apart from the more general use of language in relation to problem solving.

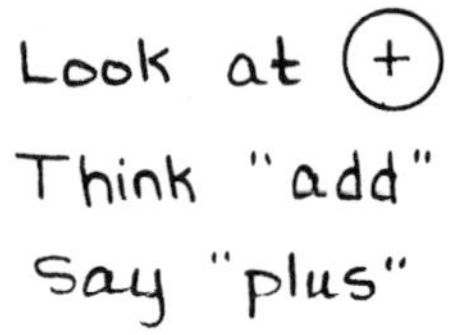

$$\text{Look at } \bigoplus$$
$$\text{Think ``add''}$$
$$\text{Say ``plus''}$$

Figure 9-1

Sequencing

In Chapters 5 and 7 we noted how, as computation becomes more complex, the sequence of steps involved becomes longer. Two-digit multiplication, for example, is really a twelve step process, as shown in Figure 5-3. Problem solving, too, involves sequencing. Problem-solving situations in daily life, for example, require not only using skills that have been learned, but using them in a *properly organized way*. However, unlike computation where the sequence does not vary, the sequences needed to handle real life problems can vary from situation to situation. In one instance, it may be necessary to add first then multiply; in another, the reverse procedure might be required.

Patterning

Generally, when we think of patterning in mathematics, we think of numbers or shapes that follow a specific order, as in Figure 9-2. Patterning is also involved in solving common daily problems. In Chapter 3, we pointed out the complex patterning needed to count money. An extension of this type of patterning underlies a student's ability to decide which of the four basic operations to apply in a given situation. Can the students notice and retrieve the similarities and differences between a given problem and those previously worked using a particular operation? (See Figure 9-3.) Some learning disabled students cannot "see" what is laid out by the words of a problem—that the situation really *fits the pattern* of addition, or division. They do not see the similarity between this and previous work with addition, division, or some other operation. Unfortunately, it is often easier for

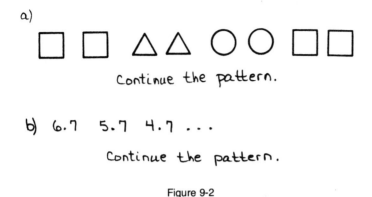

a)

□ □ △ △ ○ ○ □ □

Continue the pattern.

b) 6.7   5.7   4.7 . . .

Continue the pattern.

Figure 9-2

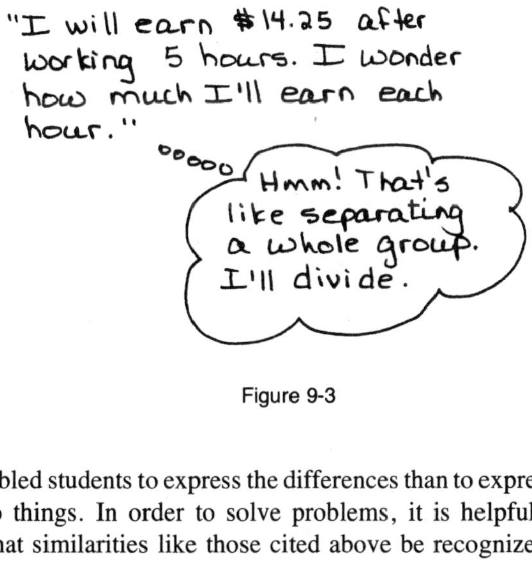

"I will earn \$14.25 after working 5 hours. I wonder how much I'll earn each hour."

Hmm! That's like separating a whole group. I'll divide.

Figure 9-3

learning disabled students to express the differences than to express the similarities between two things. In order to solve problems, it is helpful, and sometimes necessary, that similarities like those cited above be recognized.

Overview

Decision making, language use, vocabulary, sequencing, and patterning—all are key aspects of the problem-solving process. Aware of their importance, teachers of the learning disabled can help students by the attention they give these aspects within the mathematics program. Learning to compute accurately is extremely important, but it is not the most important skill we can teach learning disabled children. Even the use of a checkbook, which primarily involves computation, is impossible if one does not know when to add or subtract. We must present students with situations that require that they apply in meaningful situations the operations they have learned. At the same time, we must help students develop skills in the five areas discussed in this section so that they can successfully handle the problem situations they meet. The ideas that follow give specific suggestions for helping learning disabled students develop these skills throughout the mathematics program.

DETERMINING THE CORRECT OPERATION

Typical disabilities affecting progress: Difficulty with abstract reasoning, visual memory, and receptive or expressive language.

Suggested Activities and Exercises

1. **Prerequisites.** Be sure the children have a strong mental picture of each operation. For young children who are still at the concrete level, use objects and follow-up color-coded pages as in Figure 9-4 to help them associate the ideas of addition with the number sentence using the addition symbol. Review the other operations in a similar manner.

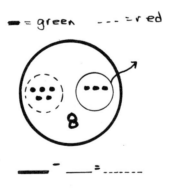

Figure 9-4

2. **You tell.** In early work with simple number combinations, help the students develop reasoning skills by presenting problems with answers, as in Figure 9-5. Have the students supply the correct sign. As a preliminary exercise, discuss with them what the possibilities are. For a page like that illustrated, help the students verbalize that

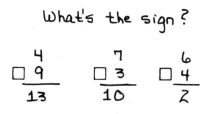

Figure 9-5

the answers to addition problems have to be larger than the addends involved. Similarly, the answers to subtraction problems must be smaller than what you "start with" (the subtrahend).

- *Note:* Similar work would be carried out in early work with multiplication and division. Once facts are learned, answers are given spontaneously, and students tend to ignore the real reason for the sign. Given 5, 6 and 30, for example, they will choose the multiplication problem because "I know that 5 × 6 = 30." Hence, it is essential to incorporate these exercises early, *before* facts are committed to memory.

3. **Do it with big numbers.** As the students begin to use larger numbers, a similar exercise can be used (see Figure 9-6). When using larger numbers, try to keep the pace fairly quick so that the children do not have time to compute. Discuss the numbers involved. Make sure the students can tell whether (and why) the answer will be larger or smaller than what you "start with."

$$\begin{array}{r} 463 \\ \square\ 297 \\ \hline 760 \end{array} \qquad \begin{array}{r} 834 \\ \square\ 129 \\ \hline 705 \end{array}$$

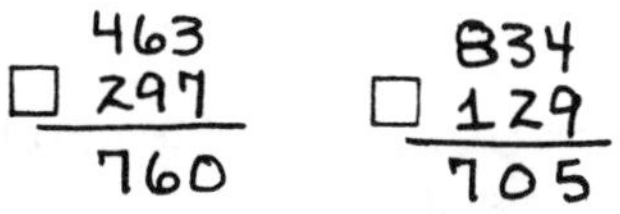

Figure 9-6

4. **Special help.** Students with visual memory or visual discrimination deficits may have trouble retrieving the correct sign without the symbols in front of them. For these children, keep strips as in Figure 9-7 for them to use at their desks. As they solve problems, the strip will serve as a visual reminder of the alternatives.

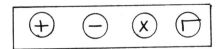

Figure 9-7

5. **Do the easy one first.** Older students who have learned when to use each of the four operations in situations involving whole numbers often have trouble with fractions and decimals in

- recognizing which operation to use, and
- carrying out the appropriate operation.

For these students, it is helpful to parallel two problems that are solved similarly but involve different types of numbers. Figure 9-8b shows an equation that gives many middle school and junior high students trouble. It is made much simpler when paralleled with that in Figure 9-8a.

a) $9A = 73$
$A = 72 \div 9$

$A = 9\overline{)73} \quad = 8\frac{1}{9}$
$\quad\ \underline{-72}$
$\qquad\ 1$

$A = 8\frac{1}{9}$

b) $4\frac{1}{2}A = 64$
$A = 64 \div 4\frac{1}{2}$

$A = 64 \div \frac{9}{2}$

$64 \times \frac{2}{9} = \frac{128}{9} = 14\frac{2}{9}$

$A = 14\frac{2}{9}$

Figure 9-8

6. **Tell what to do, then stop.** Follow through on these ideas in verbal problems by having the students

- read the problem
- picture what is happening
- use objects or draw to picture the problem if this helps (similar to work in Activity 1 above)
- think about what is being asked
- tell what to do (add, subtract, multiply, divide)

At first, do not require the children actually to compute. After the papers are checked, the computation can be carried out and the result checked.

DETERMINING WHETHER AN ANSWER IS REASONABLE

Typical disabilities affecting progress: Difficulty with abstract reasoning and closure.

Suggested Activities and Exercises

1. **Choose.** Present questions and multiple-choice answers as in Figure 9-9. From the answers, have the student select those that are more reasonable. Discuss with them why the other choices "won't work."

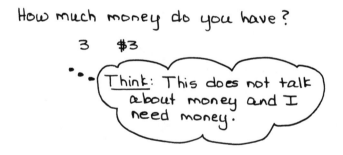

Figure 9-9

2. **Estimate.** For both computational exercises and verbal problems, help the children to estimate answers *before* they compute. Show them how to round off numbers and get a "ball-park" figure (Figure 9-10).

   • *Follow up.* Have the students tell how they arrived at the "ball-park" figure. Hearing how other children derive estimates gives others ideas on how to proceed and makes children generally more confident of "trying it themselves."

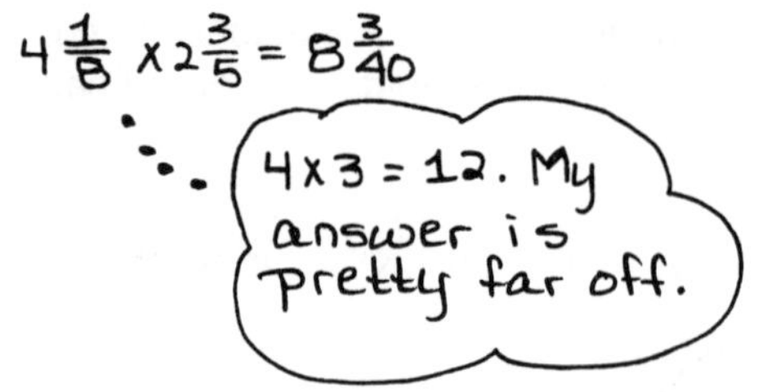

$$4\tfrac{1}{8} \times 2\tfrac{3}{5} = 8\tfrac{3}{40}$$

4×3 = 12. My answer is pretty far off.

Figure 9-10

3. **The whole thing.** Make sure that, when the students arrive at an answer to a written word problem, they fill in the word that the number describes, as in Figure 9-11. Then have them read or say the entire sentence as illustrated to determine whether, in context, the answer appears to make sense.

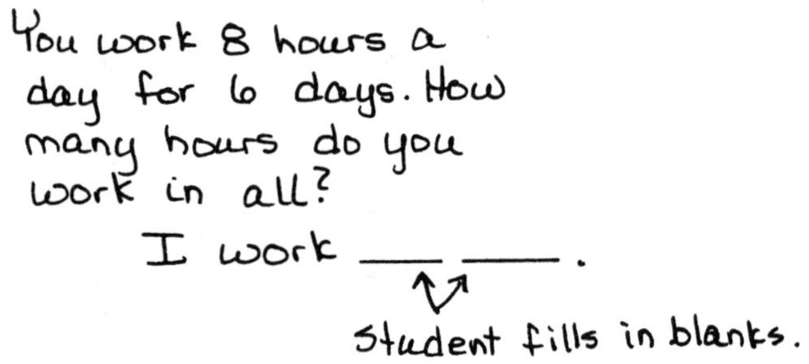

You work 8 hours a day for 6 days. How many hours do you work in all?

I work ___ ___.

Student fills in blanks.

Figure 9-11

KNOW WHAT INFORMATION TO USE

Section 3 Decision making

Typical disabilities affecting progress: Difficulty with closure and abstract reasoning.

Suggested Activities and Exercises

1. **You choose.** Present a list of data, such as the names of the players and the scores made by each. Help the students to select numbers from the given data and to create simple problem situations using those numbers.
2. **"X" what's not needed.** Present problems as in Figure 9-12 and have the students cross out any information that is not needed (in this case, the number of pages). Generally, the assignment is best spread over two days so that it can be checked and discussed before the students actually carry out the computation. For younger students, or for initial presentation, highlight the needed items, as in Figure 9-13. As they become more proficient, have the children themselves highlight the items in the question and then in the statement part of the problem itself.

Figure 9-12

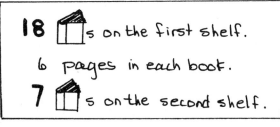

Figure 9-13

3. **Tell what's missing.** A similar procedure can be used to help the students determine missing information. Initially, present problems where the question asks for something that is not learned from the information given. Highlight the word in the question that calls for the missing information.

4. **Two steps.** Problems involving two steps can be color coded as shown in Figure 9-14. The colors help the children associate the necessary information with the correct step. As above, do not require the students to compute answers to the problems until this one step of identifying proper information for each step is checked.

You earn $2.25 each hour. You work for 6 days, 8 hours each day.

1) How long do you work all together?
___ days
___ hours
↗
(Child fills in and circles the correct word.)

2) How much do you earn? ___

■ = green
····· = red

Figure 9-14

DETERMINING WHAT INFORMATION IS GIVEN

Section 4
Language Use

Typical disabilities affecting progress: Difficulty with receptive or expressive language, abstract reasoning, visual memory, and auditory processing.

Suggested Activities and Exercises

1. **Just give the data.** Present short "problems" that do not ask a question but merely supply information. Have the students determine what they know from this small amount of information. Figure 9-15 illustrates the format for an initial presentation that is generally useful, even with students who have retrieval or expressive language deficits. The goal at this point is to identify what information is supplied and useful since that is what will be used.

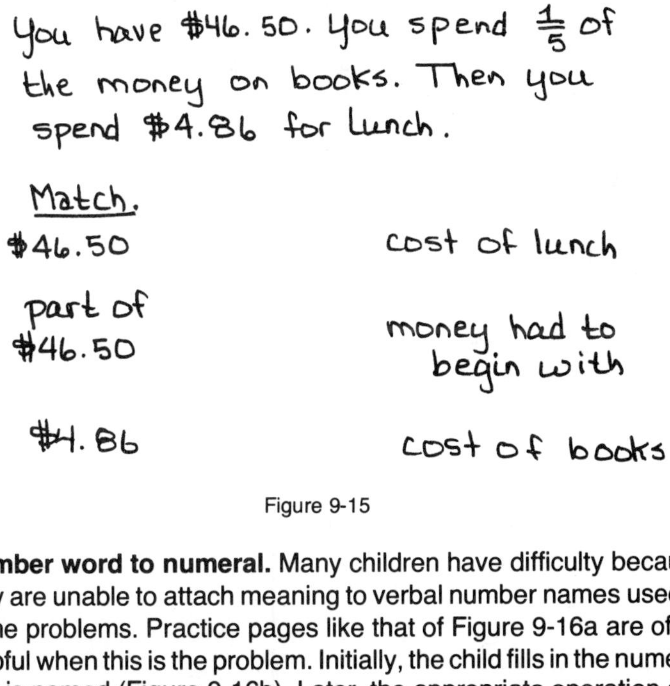

You have $46.50. You spend $\frac{1}{5}$ of the money on books. Then you spend $4.86 for lunch.

Match.

$46.50   cost of lunch

part of
$46.50   money had to
                                begin with

$4.86   cost of books

Figure 9-15

2. **Number word to numeral.** Many children have difficulty because they are unable to attach meaning to verbal number names used in some problems. Practice pages like that of Figure 9-16a are often helpful when this is the problem. Initially, the child fills in the numeral that is named (Figure 9-16b). Later, the appropriate operation can be determined and the computation carried out.

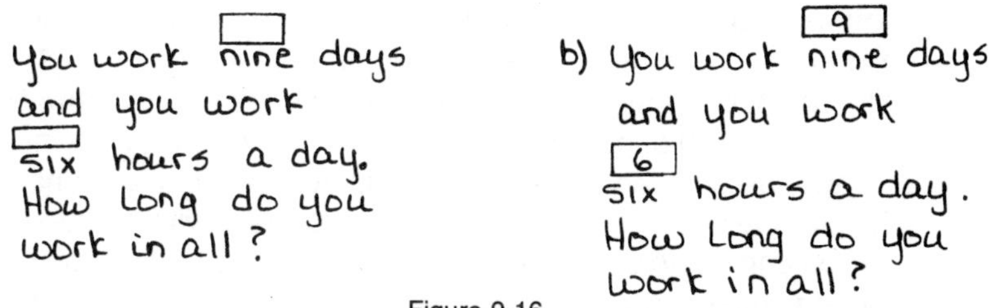

a) You work ☐ nine days and you work ☐ six hours a day. How long do you work in all?

b) You work 9 nine days and you work 6 six hours a day. How long do you work in all?

Figure 9-16

3. **Special help.** Once the children are better able to identify, in context, numerals in written form, they may still have trouble verbalizing, either aloud or to themselves, what needs to be done to solve the problem. To help in this situation, present problems like that of Figure 9-17. Steps for solving the problem are shown in *random order*. Seeing the information usually helps the children verbalize what is to be done. Then, step by step in the spaces provided, they write up the computation in correct order to solve the problem. Gradually, as the children become more proficient with practice, eliminate showing one or more of the completed steps.

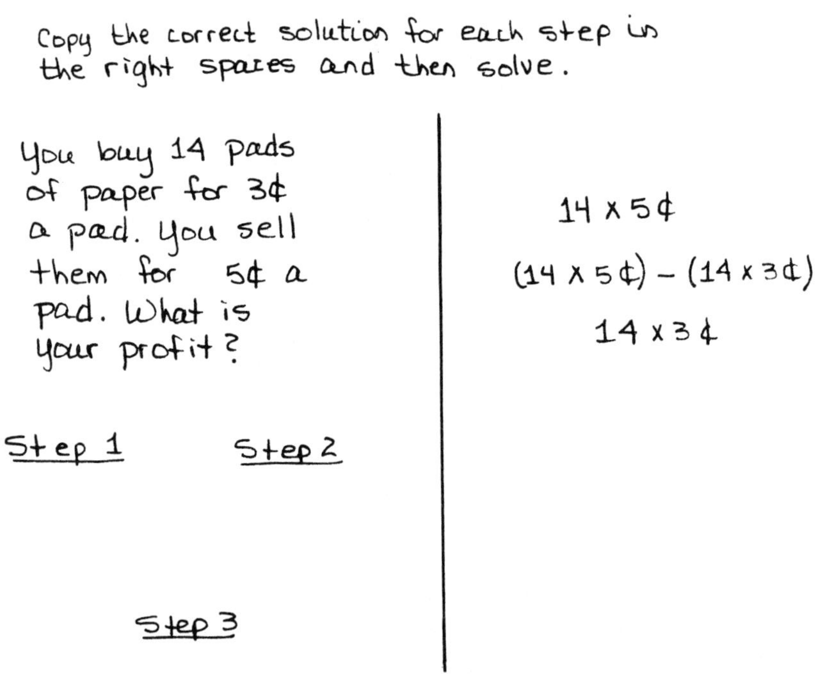

Copy the correct solution for each step in the right spaces and then solve.

You buy 14 pads of paper for 3¢ a pad. You sell them for 5¢ a pad. What is your profit?

$$14 \times 5¢$$
$$(14 \times 5¢) - (14 \times 3¢)$$
$$14 \times 3¢$$

Step 1   Step 2

Step 3

Figure 9-17

4. **Picture choice.** A variation of the above procedure for younger children is to present a choice of pictures as in Figure 9-18. The children choose the picture that best describes the problem, write the number sentence beneath, and then solve the problem. Encourage the children to state the completed number sentence orally. Gradually, as they become more proficient with practice, the children can be helped to draw their own pictures to describe given problem situations.

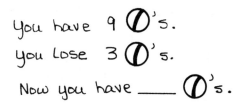

You have 9 ⓪'s.
you Lose 3 ⓪'s.
Now you have ____ ⓪'s.

⓪ ⓪ ⓪
⓪ ⓪ ⓪
⓪ ⓪ ⓪
and
⓪ ⓪ ⓪

⓪ ⓪ ⓪
⓪ ⓪ ⓪
⓪ ⓪ ⓪

_____   _____

Figure 9-18

MATHEMATICAL MEANING OF WORDS AND SYMBOLS

Section
5
Vocabulary

Typical disabilities affecting progress: Difficulties with closure, abstract reasoning, and memory.

Suggested Activities and Exercises

1. **Focus.** Help the students associate words with numbers and symbols by presenting exercises like those shown in Figure 9-19. That in Figure 9-19a would be used in conjunction with word problems

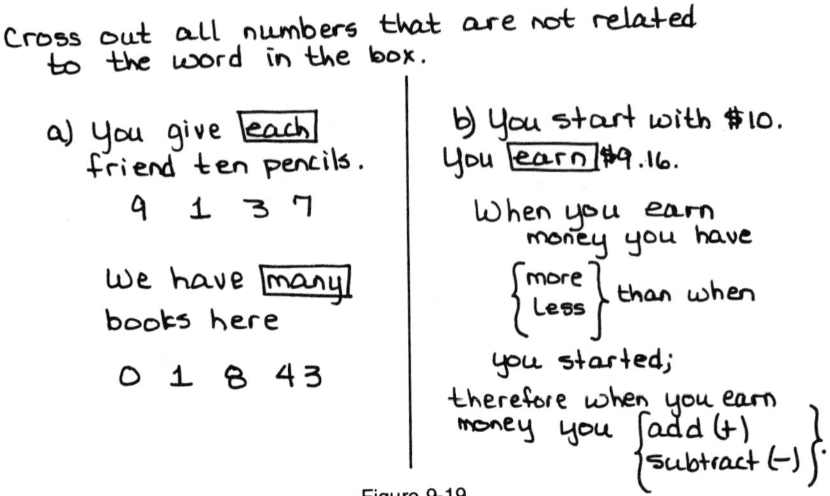

Cross out all numbers that are not related
to the word in the box.

a) You give |each|
friend ten pencils.

   9 1 3 7

We have |many|
books here

  0 1 8 43

b) You start with $10.
You |earn| $9.16.

When you earn
money you have

{ more / Less } than when

you started;
therefore when you earn
money you { add (+) / subtract (−) }.

Figure 9-19

that contain the troublesome terms "each" and "many." The exercise helps students internalize, numerically, the meaning of the terms. In the example, "each'" means 1, not 9, or 3, or 7. "Many" could mean 8 or 43, but never 0 or 1. The exercise of Figure 9-19b focuses on the development of meaning for the term "earn." Similar exercises should be developed for other vocabulary terms that cause students difficulty.

2. **Key words.** Exercises like that of Figure 9-20 help children begin to associate mathematical meaning with words. Key words and their meaning are placed just before each problem and are highlighted within the problem.

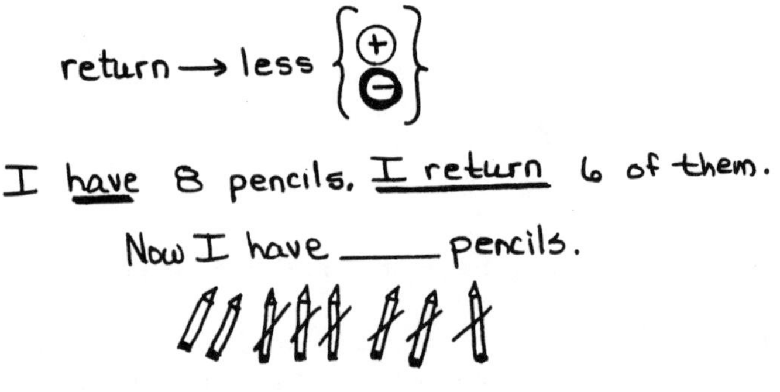

return → less { ⊕ / ⊖ }

I <u>have</u> 8 pencils. <u>I return</u> 6 of them.

Now I have _____ pencils.

Figure 9-20a

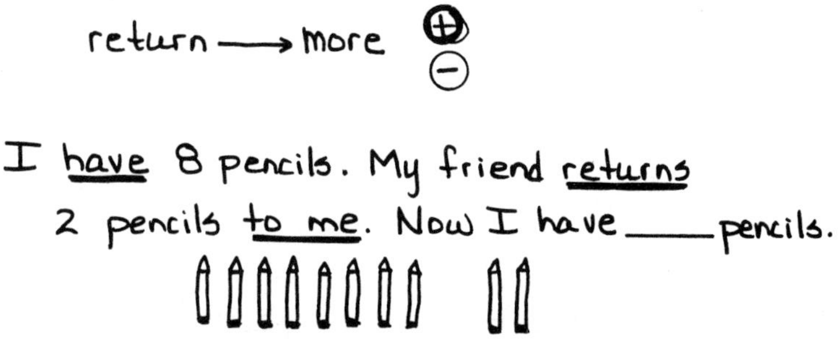

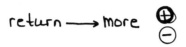

I have 8 pencils. My friend returns
2 pencils to me. Now I have ____ pencils.

Figure 9-20b

3. **Chart it.** Post a chart, or help the students make a personal file, that pairs troublesome terms or symbols with their meaning.

DETERMINING THE CORRECT SEQUENCE

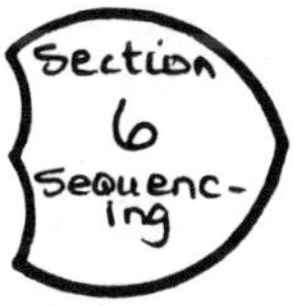

Typical disabilities affecting progress: Difficulty with short term memory, temporal organization, closure, and expressive language.

Suggested Activities and Exercises

1. **Before-after.** Correctly sequencing steps toward problem solution involves the idea of "before" and "after." Many learning disabled students need to be made aware of this relationship since it may not be intuitive. They need to learn a thought process to help them determine the sequence that other children will know automatically. To this end, it often helps to set problems up with the before-after concept clearly presented. This is especially true in a two-step word problem in which only one question is asked (Figure 9-21a). To help with this, provide worksheets as shown in Figure 9-21b. The students should cross out the wrong choice and then solve the problem. *Note:* Prior to the start of the year, have an aide or adult volunteer preview the book and make up pages as shown to go along with the problems in the book. If necessary, color code as illustrated in Figure 9-21c.

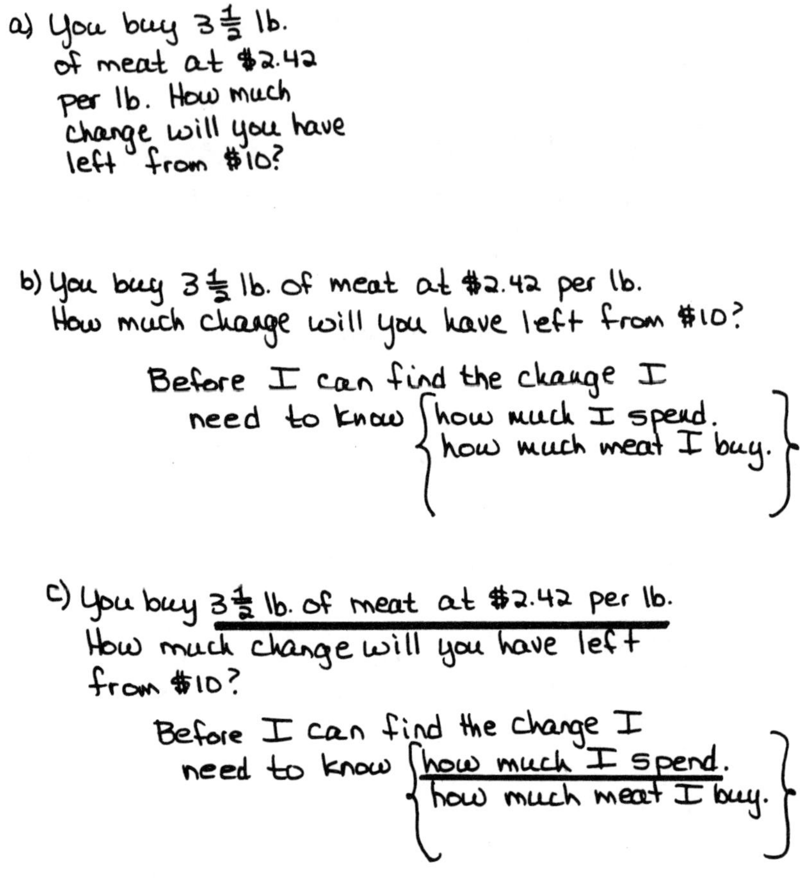

a) You buy $3\frac{1}{2}$ lb. of meat at $2.42 per lb. How much change will you have left from $10?

b) You buy $3\frac{1}{2}$ lb. of meat at $2.42 per lb. How much change will you have left from $10?

Before I can find the change I need to know $\left\{\begin{array}{l}\text{how much I spend.}\\ \text{how much meat I buy.}\end{array}\right\}$

c) You buy $3\frac{1}{2}$ lb. of meat at $2.42 per lb. How much change will you have left from $10?

Before I can find the change I need to know $\left\{\begin{array}{l}\underline{\text{how much I spend.}}\\ \text{how much meat I buy.}\end{array}\right\}$

Figure 9-21

2. **Color cue.** Various activities in the previous pages have highlighted the effectiveness of color coding as an aid in sequencing. Figure 9-22 shows one way of color coding a word problem so that the students can begin to internalize the correct sequence for solving the problem.

3. **Phase out.** As the children begin to develop sequencing skills, randomly list the steps that are necessary and have them number in the correct order. If necessary, color code the word problem, but not the steps, as in Figure 9-23. When checking the numbering, have the students note alternative sequences that their friends chose when this is appropriate. After the sequences have been checked, the students can solve the problems.

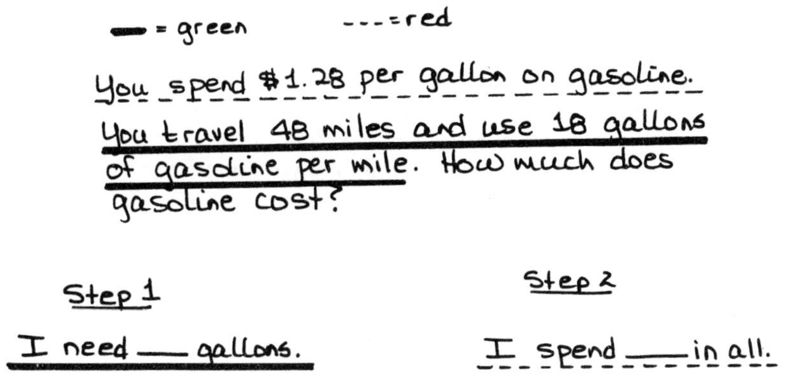

━━ = green   - - - =red

You spend $1.28 per gallon on gasoline.
You travel 48 miles and use 18 gallons
of gasoline per mile. How much does
gasoline cost?

Step 1

I need ___ gallons.

Step 2

I spend ___in all.

Figure 9-22

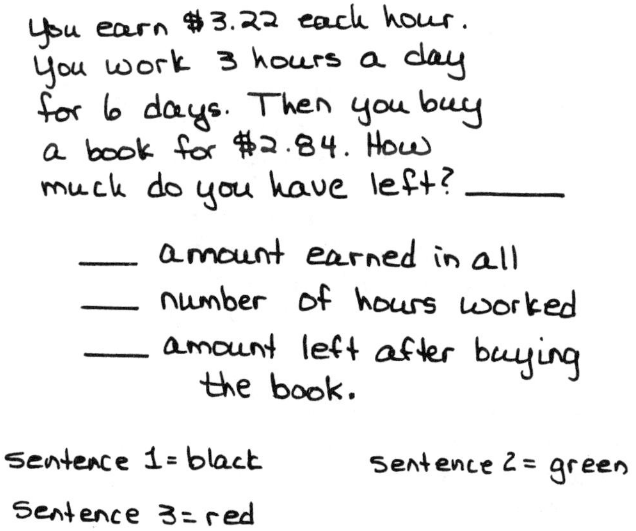

You earn $3.22 each hour.
You work 3 hours a day
for 6 days. Then you buy
a book for $2.84. How
much do you have left? ___

___ amount earned in all
___ number of hours worked
___ amount left after buying
the book.

Sentence 1= black   Sentence 2 = green

Sentence 3 = red

Figure 9-23

RECOGNIZING THE PATTERN OF A PROBLEM

Typical disabilities affecting progress:
Difficulty with abstract reasoning, and
auditory processing.

Suggested Activities and Exercises

1. **See the pattern.** Present simple visual problems and have the students circle the best solution. Help them notice the pattern of their solutions. In the example of Figure 9-24, the numbers 2, 3, and 5 use multiplication because they deal with finding the total when the groups have the same number in each group.

Figure 9-24

2. **Word problems now.** As the children become better able to recognize the pattern for applying a given operation, gradually introduce word problems. At first, present assignments in which they use only one operation. Use different numbers in the problems and help the students use concrete aids or draw a picture of the problem, as in Figure 9-24. Rather quickly get to pages of mixed problem types. Throughout, encourage the students to look for a pattern: separating groups, finding the total of groups equal in size, and so on. Allow the children to use the concrete aids or to draw a picture of the problem as long as this seems helpful.

3. **Easy one first.** Earlier in this chapter, we pointed out how working a parallel problem with whole numbers can help students solve one containing fractions or decimals. A similar technique helps in problem solving. Some students "go blank" when they notice that a word problem contains a fraction or decimal. Giving these students a parallel problem with whole numbers often helps them recognize the general pattern to the solution (add, subtract, multiply, divide), which they then can apply to solving the original problem with fractions or decimals.

Reference

National Council of Teachers of Mathematics. *An Agenda for Action: Recommendations for School Mathematics of the 1980s.* Reston, Va.: The National Council of Teachers of Mathematics, Inc., 1906 Association Drive, Reston, Va. 22091, 1980.

Index

M

ABOUT THE AUTHORS

Nancy S. Bley is director of research and mathematics curriculum development at Park Century School in Santa Monica, California, where she has been a member of the staff for five years. Park Century is a private school specializing in individualized one-to-one programs for the learning disabled child. She has presented workshops in southern California on diagnosing and remediating mathematics difficulties, has spoken to the Research Council for Diagnostic and Prescriptive Mathematics, and has acted as consultant to Science Research Associates on adaptation of materials for the learning disabled child. She is presently working on a research grant from the Foundation for Children with Learning Disabilities on the applicability of Fingermath for the learning disabled. She has taught at the elementary and high school levels over the past 12 years. In addition, she maintains a private practice working with learning disabled children.

Carol A. Thornton is an associate professor in the Department of Mathematics at Illinois State University, Normal, Illinois. She has published numerous articles in both mathematics education and special education journals; has created a special education filmstrip and a videotape on computational skills; has been a speaker and workshop leader at numerous state, regional, and national meetings; is the author of several books for teachers, elementary school students, and special education students; and has had 10 years of experience as an elementary and high school teacher. She has been the recipient of several grants related to the mathematics education of learning disabled and other exceptional children. Since 1977, she has been the director of a clinic for children with severe learning difficulties in mathematics. Primary among her publications have been her articles and instructional materials related to helping children master basic arithmetic facts by emphasizing thinking strategies.